THE OTHER POWERS

THE OTHER POWERS
Studies in the Foreign Policies of Small States

Edited by R. P. Barston

BOOKS
10 East 53d St., New York 10022
(a division of Harper & Row Publishers, Inc.)

Published in the U.S.A. 1973 by
HARPER & ROW PUBLISHERS, INC.
BARNES & NOBLE IMPORT DIVISION

ISBN 06-490319-2

Printed in Great Britain

Acknowledgments

A number of people have directly and indirectly contributed to the preparation of this book. Not all are mentioned here, but my thanks nevertheless go to them. I should like to thank Dr August Schou, Chairman of the Nobel Symposium Committee, and Arne Olav Brundtland for organizing Nobel Symposium 17, which was held in Oslo in 1970. The Symposium provided a valuable opportunity for international discussion of small states. An earlier version of the Introduction, *The External Relations of Small States*, was published in Nobel Symposium 17, *Small States in International Relations* (1971). I wish to thank the publishers, Almqvist and Wiksell, Stockholm, for their permission to draw substantially upon this material. I am indebted to my department for supporting financially my research work and to my colleagues who were generous of their time. In particular my thanks go to Professor P. A. Reynolds, Professor P. Nailor and Dr I. Bellany who read some of the manuscripts and provided valuable comments. In addition, Robert Purnell and I. G. John, Department of International Politics, Aberystwyth, have over a number of years given encouragement. My thanks go also to those ministers and officials in several of the countries dealt with in this book who, although often hard-pressed, were generous of their time through interviews, discussions and the speedy provision of information which was not readily available. I am indebted above all to the contributors who, over a period of some eighteen months, have co-operated with patience and understanding in spite of many other calls on their time. Finally, my thanks go to Miss Jean Carr for her valuable secretarial assistance.

R. P. BARSTON

University of Lancaster
February 1972

327
B280

Notes on Contributors

PETER RENÉ BAEHR is Professor of International Relations at the University of Amsterdam. From 1965 to 1970 he was editor of *Acta Politica*, the Netherlands Journal of Political Science. He has written articles on foreign policy analysis and European politics. He is the author of a number of books, including *De Studie de Buitenlandse Politiek: Toegang tot de Internationale Betrekkingen* (The Study of Foreign Policy: Entry to International Relations) (1970) and *The Role of a National Delegation in the General Assembly* (1970).

RONALD P. BARSTON is Lecturer in Politics at the University of Lancaster. He has written articles on various aspects of foreign policy analysis and on the Cyprus problem. He carried out during 1968–70 a special study on the role and effectiveness of the United Nations Peace-Keeping Force in Cyprus.

MARION BONE is a post-graduate research student at the University of Sussex, where she is completing a D.Phil. thesis on the *Foreign Policy of the Republic of Zambia, 1964–71*. From 1966 to 1970 she worked as an Administrative Assistant at the University of Zambia under the Ministry of Overseas Development 'Study and Serve Overseas' programme.

Professor JACQUES FREYMOND is Director of the Graduate Institute of International Studies in Geneva and Professor of Contemporary International History at the University of Geneva. He was formerly Professor of Diplomatic History at Lausanne. He is a member of the International Committee of the Red Cross and was Vice-President from 1965 to 1970. He has written an extensive number of articles and books on European politics and the theoretical aspects of international relations. His books include *The Saar Conflict, 1944–55* (1959), *Western Europe since the War* (1964) and *Contributions à l'histoire du Comintern* (1965).

Dr REG HARRISON is Senior Lecturer and Director of Graduate Studies in Politics at Lancaster University. He was formerly Senior Lecturer in Politics at Victoria University, Wellington, New Zealand, and is the author of numerous articles on New Zealand's external

9

relations. A study of integration theory on which he is currently engaged will be published by Allen & Unwin in Spring 1973.

Professor FRANK H. H. KING is Director of the Centre of Asian Studies, University of Hong Kong. He was editor of the *Journal of Oriental Studies* (University of Hong Kong) from 1969 to 1971. He has written extensively on Asian politics. Amongst his books are *The New Malayan Nation: A Study in Communalism and Nationalism* (1957) and *A Concise Economic History of Modern China, 1800–1960* (1969).

Professor NILS ØRVIK is Director of International Studies and of the Research Group in International Politics at the University of Oslo, and from 1970 has been Professor in International Relations at Queen's University, Ontario, Canada. He has held civilian posts in the Norwegian Ministry of Defence, and from 1965 to 1969 was Secretary to Halvard Lange in the European Social Democratic Parties Committee for Security and Arms Control. He has written a considerable number of books and articles on the Nordic area and on European security problems. His books include *The Decline of Neutrality* (1953, 1971), *Europe's Northern Cap and the Soviet Union* (1963) and *Departmental Decision Making* (1972).

Dr JACOB REUVENY is Senior Lecturer in the Department of Political Studies, Bar Ilan University, Israel. Prior to this, since 1955, he has held government positions in the field of civil service training and was a Lecturer at the University of Tel-Aviv. During 1968–71 he took part in a comprehensive study of Israeli technical assistance to developing countries in Africa. His publications include a series of articles on ideology, cross-cultural communications and international relations (*International Problems*, Israel 1967–69), and he is the co-author of *The Dynamics of Organisation* (1970).

DAVID STANSFIELD, formerly Lecturer in Politics at the University of Lancaster, is Lecturer in Politics at the Institute of Latin American Studies, University of Glasgow. He held a Ford Fellowship at the University of New Mexico in 1967–68 and was also a Fulbright Travel Fellow. In 1970 he travelled widely in Mexico and the Central Americas. In 1972 he visited Cuba. His forthcoming publications are *Patterns of Elite Politics in Mexico* and *Problems of Political Development in Mexico and the Central Americas.*

Contents

Content

INTRODUCTION

R. P. BARSTON

The study of the foreign policies of small states is a neglected aspect of the discipline of international relations. The focus of academic literature has generally been upon the foreign policies of great powers, or where regional studies have been made, the concern has often been with domestic policies. Annette Baker Fox's *The Power of Small States* (1959) marked an important contribution to understanding the limitations and possibilities of small states during the Second World War. However, academic concern has remained fixed upon the great powers. The literature providing systematic coverage in depth of the foreign policies of small states has been sporadic. This situation was somewhat offset though as the post-1945 decolonization increased and a growing body of literature appeared which dealt with a variety of issues such as economic aid and development, the role of small states in alliances, neutralism and non-alignment and voting behaviour in international organization. More recently, the general study of Professor David Vital, *The Inequality of States* (1967) was published at a time when three small states, Israel, Rhodesia, and North Vietnam, captured attention by their remarkable capacity for survival in conflict situations.[1]

In the following chapters we aim to examine the foreign policies of nine small states. The chapters will include analyses of the factors which shape the framing of foreign policy objectives, the organizational structures used to formulate and implement foreign policy, the range of choice, areas of interest and the methods employed to deal with the issues and problems which make up and stem from external policies.

DEFINING THE SMALL STATE

Before discussing the various approaches to defining the term

13

small state, some comment is required on what is meant here by foreign policy. Put briefly, a government's foreign policy is the range of external actions pursued to achieve certain defined objectives or goals of which these may or may not have internal cognizance or approval. The essential elements of policy are: (1) capability, e.g. internal human and material resources, organization, political will; (2) purpose; (3) means, which will range from statements of position, diplomatic negotiations, foreign visits, economic agreements, cultural-technical exchanges, to the threat and use of military force. A government's policies will be shaped not only by internal factors but by the interplay between these and external restraints such as the dominance of a more powerful neighbour, limitations arising out of membership of an alliance and so on. For action to constitute *policy* it must essentially take the form of concrete measures, other than merely verbal statements, carried out by a government with a view to solving a particular problem (e.g. re-financing an economic development project) or achieving a political objective. Clearly, the range of choice open to a government may in practice be severely limited. In such circumstances foreign policy is being conducted only in a *minimal* sense, when a government professes its support for certain aims or goals in statements of position but lacks the capacity to give effect to them beyond a declaratory level. In other words, for some small states a predominant part of their external relations (apart from a limited number of regional or area issues) will consist of *generalized objectives,* e.g. statements expressing a belief in international peace and security, verbal support for universal human rights and the condemnation of aggression.

The problem of defining what is a small state is complex for several reasons. The most important difficulties relate to the question of size. What is a *small* state? Difficulties arise partly because it is only in the 'polar' cases – the isolated states with minimal populations, resources and geographical areas – that the 'small state' category is perhaps most easily distinguishable. The cut-off point for what is or is not a small state in fact becomes blurred at the upper limit of the postulated category. This occurs because the factors which explain why certain small states at the upper limit of the category are small tend to be political – stemming from the 'external' setting – and are thus difficult to quantify. In these cases resource restraints are not the *critical* variables. Furthermore it is clear that states can have different combinations of capability factors. Some of these factors will change only slowly over a period of time, if at all; others may alter quite rapidly. Thus the restraints stemming from geographical location are likely to remain relatively constant in terms of their perceived significance, whilst the exploitation of previously undiscovered or unworked mineral resources may rapidly alter the small states' economic circumstances and in the process probably generate new political, economic or military problems. A further difficulty is the asymmetry which can occur between the apparent capabilities of a state and the type of international role it plays.

Four possible approaches to defining the term 'small state' are, firstly, arbitrarily delimiting the category by placing an upper limit on, for example, population size; secondly, measuring the 'objective' elements of state capability and placing them on a ranking scale; thirdly, analysing relative influence; and fourthly, identifying characteristics and formulating hypotheses on what differentiates small states from other classes of state. The first approach used with the remaining three will permit comparison and contrast within and between categories. The second and third methods are similar in that they share the common approach of defining the small state in terms of *weakness*. Some writers have therefore concentrated on a particular characteristic common to certain small states. Thus, Professor Rothstein selects the *security dilemma* of some small states, but adds that the 'Small Power is not defined by specific qualities it possesses (or lacks) but rather by a position it occupies in its own and other eyes'.[2] Using a different methodology, Professor Vital, for example, has analysed the small state through the paradigm, selecting the 'isolated, maverick, unaligned power, the small power *alone* – the state which can rely least on outside help and which, by virtue of its situation, is compelled to make its own decisions on the basis of its own understanding of that situation and such resources as are available to it'.[3] However, it seems preferable to regard the four approaches outlined above not as mutually exclusive, but, rather, as being complementary.

For the purposes of this discussion a small state is defined as having a population with an upper limit of between 10 and 15 million.[4] In order to distinguish states within this category from the middle range states (Canada, West Germany, Japan,

India, Italy, France, United Kingdom) and the great powers (United States, Soviet Union, China) relative capabilities and influence must be considered. Great powers are distinguished from small states by criteria such as resources, economic development, military capability and the success of their foreign policies, pursued either alone or in association with others, on a wide range of issues. The middle range states are distinct from small states for similar reasons though the middle range state has a less extensive external involvement than the great power. Although Japan pursues a passive foreign policy, it must also be considered on economic grounds as being a middle range state. Most small states have low levels of economic development and their gross national products (GNP) are normally below, in some cases critically lower than, approximately one billion U.S. dollars per annum. However, a few small states do have comparatively developed economies and pursue active foreign policies on a limited number of issues beyond their own region. Most small states have a low level of international involvement; the interests of the small state are usually regional and economic considerations will be placed higher on a scale of interests than for the great power. The underdeveloped small states are not only economically dependent upon the major industrial states but are less able to withstand external pressures on their economies from, for example, a shortage of international reserves or the terms of an economic assistance agreement. Unlike the great power, the actions of a small state are usually of limited consequence to most other members of the international system. Nor does the small state, when it is involved in a conflict situation, have to adopt a *multilateral* focus (assessing the likely effects of its actions on friends, allies, neutrals and non-aligned and international organization) to the same extent as a great power.

These are some of the characteristics which distinguish the small state category from great powers and middle range states. An upper limit of population has been set in this study at between 10 and 15 million for the small state purely to establish the boundaries of the subject for analytical purposes. It is clear that there are states which fall outside this boundary and yet may be classified as small states. However, Indonesia, West Pakistan, Bangladesh, Thailand and the Philippines, for example, are distinct from the small state category partly because of their very large geographic area and population size. These states might best be conceptualized as *immobile*. They are to be distinguished from small states because as a result of their population size and economic base, internal restraints – such as lack of capital, natural resources, rudimentary administration, high level of illiteracy and recurrent domestic instability – become critical. The immobile states are therefore quantitatively and qualitatively differentiated from small states. It is in fact difficult to conceptualize the immobile state in developmental terms and its essentially static condition is not likely to change greatly in the near future. In a further distinct category are those states (e.g. Spain, Brazil) which, despite their economic resources and potential, are, for different reasons, politically isolated and do not have active foreign policies.

The remainder of the chapter will discuss the utility of ranking methods based upon the 'objective' aspects of state capability and the foreign policies of small states in terms of the limitations they face and the types of role they play. All empirical material has been drawn from the post-1945 period and general statements apply to the contemporary international system and not to any other historical period or type of international system unless specifically stated.

RANKING METHODS

The use of quantification methods, the second approach indicated above, enables various categories of states to be distinguished.[5] Ranking tables can be constructed from the quantifiable elements of state capability – population, gross national product (GNP) and defence expenditure. These may be supplemented by measuring GNP and defence expenditure on a *per capita* basis and by quantifying relational indicators such as diplomatic representation, membership of regional and international organizations and the volume and pattern of foreign trade. The population ranking table shows that of the 147 states considered (see Appendix), twenty-nine possess populations of under one million, whilst a further fifty-two have populations between one and five million, i.e. over 50 per cent of the current members of the international system. On the GNP table (Appendix) the United States and Soviet Union are clearly distinguished with GNPs of 977 billion and 490 billion dollars respectively. In

17

addition, a cluster of seven states – India, Canada, Italy, United Kingdom, France, West Germany and Japan, with GNPs ranging from 49 to 195 billion dollars – form a grouping whose members are commonly titled 'middle range powers'. The GNP of the People's Republic of China falls within this group, but for political and military reasons Communist China must be considered a great power.

The above ranking methods are partly for technical reasons[6] only approximate indicators of status. Whilst population, GNP, defence expenditure, volume and pattern of trade and diplomatic representation are indicators of broad categories of states, it is also often difficult to make meaningful distinctions *between* states within a category. Ranking tables could indicate that a government is a member of several international or regional organizations but would not tell us how important it is within the organizations or the influence of the organizations on its foreign policies.

Ranking techniques are useful then as methods of broadly mapping out categories of states and supplementing or confirming the suppositions and findings of other approaches. Thus, in addition to the categories of great powers and middle range states, ranking methods indicate a class of state, within the category of small states, which have populations of under one million and correspondingly low gross national products. Secondly, the population/GNP tables highlight the different ranking of certain states, e.g. Indonesia, Pakistan, Belgium; or show those states with high *per capita* GNP, e.g. Kuwait. Comparative defence expenditures do show also several states, located in areas of international tension, with very high military budgets, e.g. Czechoslovakia, East Germany, Egypt, Sudan, Israel and Congo (Kinshasa). Thirdly, the diplomatic exchange tables[7] do indicate the area of interest of a state, the extent to which other states consider it necessary to report it, and the correlation between external diplomatic representation and commercial interests. Several small states, including Sweden, Israel, and Taiwan, which, for different reasons, pursue active foreign policies, can be distinguished therefore by their comparatively high external diplomatic representation.

LIMITATIONS ON SMALL STATES

In order to outline the limitations on the policies and influence of small states, it is necessary to modify the elements of capability mentioned above by the inclusion of other factors such as tradition, strategic location, the degree of domestic stability, organization and personality. Two points need to be distinguished here: firstly, the differing combinations of capability factors, and secondly, the impact of capability on policy. A survey of the capabilities of states with populations of 10 to 15 million or below reveals several diverse combinations. Some of these have already been noted, e.g. the high *per capita* GNP of Kuwait. Also there are states with small populations but comparatively developed economies (e.g. Belgium, Holland, Denmark and Sweden), states with large geographic areas and small populations (e.g. Mongolia, Mauritania, Togo, Niger, Paraguay), or states which are limited in size, population and resources, e.g. the former British High Commission Territories.

The above examples suggest some of the possible combinations of capability factors. What then is the relationship between capability and policy? As we suggested earlier, small states do not have an extensive international involvement. For the most part the primary interests of the small state are of a regional nature. The dependence of the Icelandic economy on the fishing industry, for example, has meant that a significant part of the island's foreign policy has been concerned with fisheries disputes and international conventions on the extent of the territorial sea. The small state will normally not have a wide range of means with which to implement external policies and will be vulnerable to external pressure.[8] Having less margin for error than more powerful states, the small state must carefully manage its external relations in order to minimize risks and reduce the impact of policy failures. Thus the cost of continued viability as a national entity is often political quiescence, compromise, or the sacrifice of political principles to economic necessity.

Many small states have only a limited machinery for conducting foreign policy. In the smallest states the volume of foreign policy activity can perhaps be judged by the fact that the post of foreign minister is often held (sometimes with many others) by the premier or head of state, as for instance of Jamaica, Western Samoa and Nepal. The foreign ministries of small states tend to have few personnel, although this limitation is to some extent reduced through the external policy work

19

carried out by the 'domestic' ministries of industry, finance and tourism.[9] The quantity and quality of information available to a state is partly dependent on the type and extent of its diplomatic representation. However, most small states, with the exception of those located mainly in Western Europe, have a limited number of overseas missions because of the problems of costs and lack of adequately trained personnel. To deal with the problem of overseas diplomatic representation a number of small states have joint and/or non-residential accreditation, e.g. Luxembourg is partly represented by the Netherlands; and the West African Conseil de l'Entente has common accreditation in Liberia. Certain small states have, in addition, shown a high degree of adaptiveness in their use of non-diplomatic personnel, e.g. journalists, academics, lawyers and parliamentarians, on short-term contracts, as representatives at international conferences or specialists in the overseas missions.

The type and scope of a state's foreign policy can be limited by historical factors. Thus, for the Finns, traditionally unsettled relations with Russia, combined with the events leading up to the Winter War in 1940–41, were decisive factors in shaping the nature of Finnish neutrality after 1945.[10] The impact of historical factors can also be clearly seen in the continuing links between Britain, France and their former African colonies. In addition to the residual influences of language, culture and in some cases political alignment, the economies of these states remain tied to varying degrees to the former colonial powers through trade, financial loans, technical assistance, advisors and the sterling area/franc zone arrangements.[11]

The freedom of manoeuvre of a small state may be restricted by its strategic location. Thus, the freedom of choice and type of external relations of Botswana, Lesotho and Swaziland is very limited because of economic dependence resulting largely from their land-locked geographical location *vis-à-vis* South Africa and Rhodesia. Similarly, the position of Nepal and the efforts of the former Sihanouk government to maintain the fiction of Cambodian neutrality further illustrate the point. The nature of the terrain of a state, though, does sometimes assist national survival in a military conflict. Thus this factor, together with a flexible politico-military administration, has enabled North Vietnam to withstand the effects of the United States strategic bombing. Certain small states are geographically isolated (e.g.

Mongolia or most of the Latin American states,)[12] but with-drawal from international relations will occur as a result of the dominance of domestic problems such as chronic socio-economic backwardness, continued subversion and political instability, e.g. Rwanda, Burundi, and Haiti.

Even though a number of small states are comparatively economically developed, they face varying degrees of restraints in the conduct of their foreign policies. The problem of limited political influence can be seen in the attitudes of the smaller members of the post-war European economic and security organizations. A common concern (though not always exclusive to them) has been with the dominance of the great and medium powers in the collective decision-making process. Yet, within Eastern Europe, those who have strayed too far and too quickly in their domestic or foreign policies have paid heavy penalties in terms of their political independence. By contrast, French policy towards NATO and the EEC, during the Presidency of Charles de Gaulle, would appear to underline the importance of personality and the essential differences between middle range and small states in terms of the availability of policy options and the degree of political influence. However, it is conceivable that the bargaining power of the smaller members of the EEC will be increased through 'coalition' possibilities and majority voting in the expanded Community.

Finally, some comment is required on the external relations of those states with populations of under one million. Within this category a sub-group must be distinguished which includes the tiny European principalities and republics, Monaco, Andorra, San Marino and Liechtenstein. These states are distinct by virtue of their minute populations and geographic size. The economies of this group (which may be termed the ceremonial states) are similar, based upon tourism, supported by smuggling, concessionary tax laws, foreign company registration and postage stamps. Liechtenstein does not have independent external relations but relies upon Swiss embassies, whilst Andorra is formally under Franco-Spanish suzerainty. Both Monaco and San Marino are nominally fully sovereign but their external relations are of a limited nature and in fact are predominantly bi-lateral with France and Italy respectively. The Vatican is also classified in the category of states with populations of under one million. The Vatican formally possesses the attributes of a sovereign state, despite its minute size, but it must be considered as a distinct unit in the international system because of the unique role of the modern papacy *vis-à-vis* the International Catholic Church and on moral and humanitarian issues.[13]

As a sub-category, those small states with populations of under one million, with some exceptions, would appear to face maximum internal and/or external restraints.[14] For some the problem of viability is less acute through the possession of substantial natural resources (e.g. Luxembourg and the Persian Gulf oil states) or location in a favourable climatic area. But Mauritius provides an extreme illustration of a densely populated island, with a single crop economy, racial tension, and which is subject to a severe cyclonic climate. For the tiny island republic of Nauru, for example, the problem of viability is acute because most of the island is phosphate with little or no arable land. The economy is maintained by the export of phosphates and soil has to be imported. The foreign policies of this sub-category then are of a very limited kind. It is extremely doubtful whether several of these states (Maldive Islands, Western Samoa, Mauritius, Nauru and Tonga) do in fact pursue a foreign policy in any meaningful sense. It would seem preferable to describe the external relations of these states as being of an 'administrative' nature.

THE ROLE OF SMALL STATES

Arnold Wolfer's comment on the 'power of the weak' is not without theoretical and practical significance. In order to explore this further, a number of general propositions will be outlined about the kind of circumstances and systemic conditions in which a small state can exercise disproportionate influence to the ranking suggested by the 'objective' elements of its capability. First, a state may be economically weak, have low military strength and be politically unstable; but its weakness can be a source of bargaining power if a great power perceives the territory of the small state to be of strategic importance and is prepared to commit conventional military forces to its assistance. The influence of the small state will increase if the initial commitment of forces by the great power is of a limited nature and the conflict becomes protracted. Second, the bar-

22

gaining power of small states involved in a military conflict will be increased if there is a clear and overt commitment by *both* great powers to opposite sides. Third, a coalition of small states which is weakly organized, with disputed leadership and whose members have differing political systems and ideologies, will have a high degree of stress within it over the formulation and implementation of common objectives, when involved in a military conflict. Fourth, a small state can sometimes act with impunity against a great power. The response of the great power will be determined primarily by the type of threat, the degree of its active involvement elsewhere, and concern lest any retaliatory action might adversely affect its relations with other states in the region. Fifth, small states can use international organization to mobilize support for their policies by widening the arena of debate and criticism. Sixth, a small state will be able to resist collective non-military sanctions if it receives support from border states and if the collective sanctions are not universally or equally applied by members of the international organization.

Let us now empirically illustrate the propositions. The first can be illustrated by the influence of elements of the South Vietnamese leadership between 1963–69 on the United States conduct of the Indo-China War. The second and third propositions are illustrated by the Middle East conflict. Here the commitment by both great powers to opposite sides meant that they found it almost impossible to resist, prior to and after the June 1967 War, demands for arms and replacement equipment and also difficult to control their 'client' states. The weak political and military co-operation of the Arab states was also one of the factors which enabled the Syrian government to pursue an independent policy and exert considerable pressure on the Egyptian government. The Middle East conflict not only illustrates the potential influence of small states but suggests that this can also be a function of great power weakness.[15]

The fourth proposition can be illustrated by two situations involving the United States. In the first case the United States found it difficult to apply counter measures against North Korea after it had seized the USS *Pueblo*. Two reasons might be tentatively suggested: firstly, because of the intelligence functions of the vessel, and secondly, as military action was the only applicable instrument that the United States could employ against North Korea in the circumstances, the concern that this might provoke even more serious action probably accounts for no counter-measures being taken. The second case involves the conflict between the United States and Chile, Ecuador and Peru on the latter's claim of a 200-mile fisheries jurisdiction. Despite demands by a number of congressmen for naval action and 'showing the flag', the United States took no action, apart from non-recognition of the claim, in order that this issue would not be allowed to affect other aspects of its relations with the Latin American states.[16]

The Rhodesian sanctions case will be used to illustrate the fifth and sixth propositions. The transference of the Rhodesian question to the UN after the unilateral declaration of independence in 1965 and the demands of the African states in particular for military and economic sanctions to be applied against Rhodesia reduced the freedom of action of the British government. The effective area of decision making was widened and the British government's control over the handling of the situation was weakened by the pressure exerted on it within the UN. Rhodesia was able substantially to evade the effects of sanctions because of the support given by South Africa, the restructuring of the Rhodesian economy to reduce the level of imported goods and because sanctions were not universally applied nor were they applied to the same degree by UN member governments.

The foreign policies of many small states are dominated by the question of economic development. The basic problems they face are similar: restructuring the economy, building up reserves and export diversification. Small states have attempted to resolve these problems by negotiating capital and technical assistance agreements with organizations such as the International Bank for Reconstruction and Development and through bilateral government and private loans and investment. But this latter method has led to difficulties over the time and form of repayment, the impact of the agreements on the economies of the receiving state and the problem of economic dependence— classically illustrated in the case of post-Nkrumah Ghana.[17] Therefore small states have shown a preference for multinational or consortium arrangements and have pursued policies aimed at diversifying the sources of assistance and investment, e.g. Tanzania, Tunisia and Guinea. Somalia, for example, receives technical assistance from the Soviet Union, and in 1968 granted concession rights for the exploration of uranium to West German, Italian and American companies. Attempts have also been made to deal intra-regionally with the problem of economic viability through customs and economic agreements. In the long term these approaches would seem preferable to relying largely on external capital and technical assistance, in order to avoid the distorting effect of the latter on the economy of the recipient state. But, outside Europe, most attempts such as the West African Customs Union, the Afro-Malagasy Common Organization and the Caribbean Free Trade Area have been limited in scope and success.

Small states also use economic techniques for political purposes as do great powers. But the objective of the small state is quite different from that of a great power. For a small state the marginal redirection of export trade or securing competing sources of technical or capital assistance are attempts essentially to achieve or emphasize *political independence*. Conversely, these methods can be used if a small state seeks the support of a great power or wishes to indicate ideological sympathy.

Mention too should be made of those small states which perform concession and 'servicing' roles, e.g. Panama and Liberia, a large part of whose revenue is obtained from the registration of merchant shipping. Switzerland, as a banking, organization and conference centre, has considerable international importance. Its primary influence is confined to international financial transactions though as a neutral state it does carry out a number of other roles.

The foreign policy posture of neutralism, or non-alignment as it is usually termed, is probably the best-known device employed by many of the newly independent states, from the early 1950s onwards, to emphasize their new-found sovereignty and maintain freedom of action.[18] The much publicized non-aligned conferences of Bandung, Brioni, Belgrade and Cairo have served to confirm and establish the credentials of the participants. Non-alignment is not a policy in itself but rather a means of establishing a diplomatic identity distinct from the great powers or other small states which have become subsumed in great power alliance networks. The contribution which the personality of the leader of a small state can make to its international prestige can be seen in the cases of Tito, Nkrumah, Nyerere, Nasser and Makarios. What might have been little-known national capitals, appear, like the leaders, regularly in the Press. However, the *collective* political influence of the group is restricted to a small number of issues.

The neutral states, Sweden, Switzerland, Finland and Austria, must be distinguished from the non-aligned. Most of the neutral states pursue active foreign policies beyond their own region on international peace and security issues, as mediators and providers of personnel for the United Nations and UN peace-keeping operations. The extra-regional policies of the Scandinavian neutrals can partly be accounted for by the difficulties incurred in co-operating within the Scandinavian bloc, because of Finnish-Soviet relations, the different economic links of the members, and the membership of two of the Scandinavian states in NATO. The neutral states perform two other important subsidiary roles: as international conference centres and as diplomatic representatives for states which have either no accreditation or which have broken off diplomatic relations.

Finally, the network of United Nations institutions and related agencies provides the small state with an arena for international contact, the opportunity to express its political views and at times exert disproportionate influence.[19] A few small states, through legal expertise, play active roles on the technical and rule-making aspects of international relations.[20] Others become experts in *single* subjects through sub-committee membership, e.g. Malta in the UN Ad Hoc Committee on the Peaceful Uses of the Seabed. In short, whilst some small states prefer alternative political, economic and military arrangements, many see the continued existence of the United Nations and its agencies as a symbol of their identity as national units in modern international relations.

NOTES AND REFERENCES

1. See also the following: R. Butwell (ed.), *Foreign Policy and the Developing Nations* (Lexington, Kentucky, 1969); B. Benedict (ed.), *Problems of Smaller Territories* (Athlone Press, London, 1967); August Schou and Arne Olav Brundtland (eds), *Small States in International Relations* (Almqvist & Wiksell, Stockholm, 1971). The following articles are also useful: R. O. Keohane, 'Lilliputians' dilemmas: small states in international politics', *International Organisation*, vol. 23, no. 2 (1969) pp. 291–310; W. E. Patterson, 'Small States in International Politics', *Co-operation and Conflict*, no. 2 (1969) pp. 119–23; Annette Baker

Fox, 'The Small States in the International System 1916-69', *Inter national Journal* (Canadian Institute of International Affairs), vol. 24, no. 4 (Autumn, 1969) pp. 751–64.

2. R. L. Rothstein, *Alliance and Small Powers* (Columbia University Press, New York, 1968) p. 7.

3. David Vital, *The Inequality of States* (Clarendon Press, Oxford, 1967) p. 4. See also *The Survival of Small States: Studies in Small Power–Great Power Conflict* (Oxford University Press, London, 1971).

4. Cf. Vital, *The Inequality of States*, p. 8; and A. D. Knox, 'Some Economic Problems of Small Countries', in Benedict, op. cit., p. 36.

5. For further discussion see: D. O. Wilkinson, *Comparative Foreign Relations* (University of California, Los Angeles, 1969), especially ch. 3.

6. These include type and frequency of population census, population sampling, differing national accounting systems, undisclosed or 'hidden' budgetary items and trade transactions, and estimating the dollar purchase equivalents for the communist states.

7. Cf. Algar and S. J. Brams, 'Patterns of Representation in National Capitals and Intergovernmental Organisations', *World Politics*, vol. 19, no. 4 (July, 1967) pp. 647–63. For a different approach see J. Macrae, 'World Interest Balances and Non-Residential Diplomatic Accreditation' (mimeo), University of Lancaster, Lancaster (May, 1969).

8. See Vital, *The Inequality of States*, op. cit., ch. 5.

9. On this point see I. W. Zartman, *International Relations in the New Africa* (Prentice Hall, Inc., Englewood Cliffs, N.J., 1966) ch. 2.

10. An excellent discussion of the problems of pursuing a neutral foreign policy in *peace time* is by the Finnish diplomat Max Jakobson, *Finnish Neutrality* (Hugh Evelyn, London, 1968).

11. See, for example, John J. Okumu, 'The Place of African States in International Relations', in Schou and Brundtland, op. cit., pp. 147–55.

12. For a discussion of the role of Latin American states, see C. A. Astiz and Mary F. McCarthy, *Latin American International Politics* (University of Notre Dame, Indiana, 1969).

13. See R. A. Graham, *Vatican Diplomacy* (Princeton University Press, Princeton, N. J., 1959).

14. See A. D. Knox, 'Some Economic Problems of Small Countries' and D. P. J. Wood, 'The Smaller Territories: Some Political Considerations', in Benedict, op. cit., pp. 22–44. The problems of the so-called 'mini-state' are fully dealt with in 'Status and Problems of Very Small States and Territories', UNITAR Series no. 3, 1969. This study has been subsequently revised and published by Arno Press, New York.

15. See Robert J. Pranger, 'American Policy for Peace in the Middle East 1969–1971: Problems of Principle, Maneuver and Time', *Foreign Affairs Study* (American Enterprise Institute for Public Policy Research, Washington), December 1971.

16. For a highly readable account see Wesley Marx, *The Frail Ocean* (Ballantine Books, New York, 1967).

17. For a detailed treatment of the problem of economic dependence see R. H. Green and Ann Seidman, *The Economics of Pan Africanism* (Penguin, Harmondsworth, 1968).

18. See L. W. Martin (ed.), *Neutralism and NonAlignment* (Frederick A. Praeger, New York, 1962); P. Lyon, *Neutralism* (Leicester University Press, Leicester, 1963), and Radovan Vukadinović, 'Small States and the Policy of Non-Alignment', in Schou and Brundtland, op. cit., pp. 99–114.
19. See J. E. S. Fawcett, 'The New States in the United Nations', in W. V. O'Brien (ed.), *The New Nations in International Law and Diplomacy* (Stevens and Sons, London, 1965) pp. 229–52.
20. See M. M. Sibthorp, *Oceanic Pollution: A survey and some suggestions for control* (David Davies Memorial Institute of International Studies, London, 1969). This short study deals partly with the attitudes and technical problems most small states face in this area. See also Johan Kaufmann, *Conference Diplomacy* (A. W. Sijthoff, Leyden, 1968).

Chapter 1

NORWEGIAN FOREIGN POLICY
THE IMPACT OF SPECIAL RELATIONSHIPS

NILS ØRVIK

THE PROBLEM AND THE VARIABLES

In using the small-great perspective we assume that there are three major groups of states: those that are indisputably small, those that are just as definitely large, and thirdly, those in between, the 'intermediaries' that go in one or the other category depending on the criteria one chooses to use.[1]

The questions we would like to raise refer to the external relations of states that without hesitation would be placed in the small nations category. We would like to turn to this group of indisputably small states and ask: What are the variables that determine the development of their external relations?

All of them, even the very smallest, have over the years developed organized relations with other states. As we shall see later, export and import figures, membership in international organizations and other easily available data may give us a rough idea of the extent to which a certain state is involved in exchange and contact patterns with other actors in the international system.

A state is only small in relation to its environment. The interesting thing about such states is not their diminutive size and relative weakness, but the fact that they are able nevertheless to survive and even do well in the international system.

The patterns of external contact will indicate certain trends of involvement – more with some states, less with others. But in most cases such patterns do not tell us how these states developed their *special relationships*, and what were the determining variables. Was their relative success in fulfilling national goals a product of their location, climate, efficiency, diplomatic skill – or just luck? Among the many possible variables, the following seem to stand out as being particularly important for determining the degree of smallness: (1) geography; (2) natural resources; (3) opportunity; (4) protection for trade and territory.

This general proposition might be illustrated by the case of one successful small country – Norway.

Compared to most West European nations, Norway is a relatively young and new country.[2] After several hundred years of Danish rule and Swedish dominance, Norway broke away from Sweden in 1905, less than seventy years ago, and developed a foreign policy of her own.

Today, most people know that shipping and sea transport is a major source of Norway's income and probably the most important single factor in her external relations. It was hardly obvious that this little outlying nation should become one of the world's largest shipping nations. How did she reach this position? How did the small-state variables work to her advantage? The Norwegians have a reputation for being a seafaring people, which might be explained by Norway's long coastline and its proximity to the great seas. This may indicate that Norway's particular pattern of external relations is based on *geography*. The sea was there – so the Norwegians went ahead and used it. But how does one explain the fact that other small (and big) countries have had as much – or more – sea-water around their shores without ever making any attempts to use world shipping as a basis for external influence? Each of the relevant cases would need its special explanation. Some countries may have had natural resources which made seafaring unnecessary. Nature has not endowed Norway with such gifts. Compared to other states in the same region and category, Norway has always lacked most of the traditional natural resources. Whatever there was – and is – could never have carried the weight of external relations in a modern sense.

One might, somewhat paradoxically, say that the *scarcity of natural resources* was as instrumental in forming Norway's pattern of external relations as was the abundance of, for instance, agricultural output in the development of her neighbour Denmark's foreign policy. As there was little else to develop, the Norwegians turned to the high seas as their last resort.

But trade on the high seas was not free for all. By the middle of the nineteenth century, when Norway started clarifying its national goals, sea-transport was a privilege for the then-great nations, primarily Britain. Carrying freight over the seas was dependent upon narrow, British-imposed restrictions, and a given country's naval power to defy them. A small, weak state had no means to claim admittance.

The opportunity came after the 1840s, when Britain abolished her Navigation Acts and opened her domestic and colonial ports for transport services by any nation that could offer cheap and safe sea transport for Britain's increasing industrial output. The Norwegians saw their chance to fill the sea transport vacuum, and they used it. While other nations either developed profitable external relations based on trade with natural resources or industrially refined products, Norway grasped the opportunity to develop and specialize in what others either could not or would not care to do. The earnings from shipping brought enough economic strength to enable her to break away from Sweden and to start out on her own. On her sea-borne savings she built a base for industry and a modern society. Thus, large-scale shipping, as the most prominent trait of Norway's external relations, grew from a combination of these variables: geography, lack of natural resources, and opportunity.

These determinants are important in explaining the economic aspects of Norway's foreign relations. However, perhaps the most important dimension in the development of any small nation is the security aspect, its need for *protection* – not only for its trade but from invasion, war and armed subjugation. A small nation will normally lack the military strength to resist armed aggression or pressures from larger, stronger states.

Two important variables must be present to escape external control and/or foreign domination. One is a favourable strategic location with a low level of attraction. The other is 'protection by a friend'.

Within the Nordic region, Norway had an exposed position. When first the Danes and then the Swedes, through a combination of natural resources, trade, industry and opportunity, rose to European prominence, Norway in turn fell a victim to both countries. With the direct border contact, Sweden became the natural enemy. As long as Denmark controlled the northern seas, Norway was safe from Sweden. With the fall of Danish seapower came Swedish dominance. However, the defence of Norway's enormous coastline was not a feasible task for a small

31

nation. British influence took over from the Danes, and the Swedes were unable to prevent it. Out of these experiences grows a strategic doctrine: *the power which, at any given time, controls the North Atlantic and the North Sea is also in a position to dominate Norway's external relations.* This is the geo-political curse with which she has to live.

The special constellation of powers in the nineteenth century made Britain the dominating force in Europe. On the seas British naval power was absolute. While, after the turn of the century, Norway succeeded in breaking loose from Sweden, from 1905 onward she locked her fate to Britain. Based on the British need for large-scale sea transport from an otherwise weak and dependent state, and the Norwegian need for naval protection for her ships and her homeland, there grew a special Anglo-Norwegian relationship. This became the backbone of Norway's external relations until the 1950s, when the American influence superseded the British one.

Her current national role is still in international shipping. Together with the other Scandinavian states, Norway has professed a great interest in United Nations peace-keeping operations and in the silent diplomacy at the UN headquarters in New York. For the last twenty years, she has been a loyal but unenthusiastic NATO member. Her largest present problem is connected with her European future. The courses she may follow will be as much a product of her internal political and economic systems as of the complexities of her external relations.

STRUCTURE AND PROCESSES

According to the Constitution (art. 26) the King, that is the government, holds the sole prerogative of foreign policy-making in Norway.[3] The parliament (the Storting) maintains a controlling influence through its powers of ratification.[4] However, the Storting exercises considerable influence on foreign policy through the permanent Foreign and Constitutional Affairs Committee. This twelve-member group is the most important of the parliamentary committees, and is made up of party leaders and senior parliamentarians. Dealing with issues that are held to be of special importance, the chairman of the Defence Committee, the Speaker of the Storting and his deputy, together with eight chosen members of the Storting, make up the Extended

Foreign and Constitutional Affairs Committee. This is a highly influential body, and the government's possibilities for opposing its decisions are virtually non-existent.[5] However, clashes and confrontations between this committee and the government are rare. In accordance with the Constitution, the Storting takes a 'back seat' in the day-to-day making of the foreign policy,[6] but plays a decisive role in forming long-term policies and developing trends.

Norwegian public opinion takes relatively little interest in external relations.[7] This observation corresponds to attitudes registered in other Western countries.[8] The general detachment from foreign policy matters is reflected in the Norwegian political parties. Gallup polls and special studies indicate that members of parties, as well as their representatives in the Storting, give low priority to issues that deal with external relations.[9]

It is generally assumed that events during the last decade have brought a change in this picture. Surface observation of the great turmoil and excitement about focal, popular issues such as nuclear disarmament, Vietnam and the dictatorial régimes in Greece and elsewhere, certainly convey this impression. However, comparative studies over several decades do not support such assumptions. The interest and involvement of voters and party members on foreign issues has remained by and large at a low level.[10] This does not mean that all the parties (Norway has seven of them) are equally interested or disinterested. The two small parties on the far left, the Norwegian Communist Party (NCP) and the closely related Socialistic Peoples Party (SPP), take a clear lead in stressing foreign policy issues.[11] There is also a strong correlation between the level of education and social position and strong involvement in foreign affairs.[12]

Both the NCP and the SPP operate on the extreme left and tend to attract support from intellectuals with radical leanings. Though foreign policy takes a relatively high place within the radical ranks, it means little when seen in a national perspective. Neither of the two parties on the extreme left succeeded in being represented among the 159 parliamentarians elected in the 1969 election.

Most Norwegian parliamentarians are still recruited from local politics and have earned their political spurs in municipal assemblies and organizations.[13] As their political future depends on keeping in close touch with their voters and thereby securing nomination and re-election, most of them have neither the incentive nor the opportunity to develop expertise and insight in the external affairs of their country. The fact that the party representatives are inclined to give priority to domestic, not to say local, issues gives the party leadership a limited choice of candidates for top governmental positions, where some familiarity with foreign policy issues and international affairs ought to be a necessary requirement. Consequently, foreign ministers have tended until recently to be non-parliamentarians. This was particularly true of the social democrats. However, the 1965–71 non-socialist coalition government recruited all its foreign ministers from the parliamentary groups.

During the thirty years of social democratic (labour) predominance in Norway, the Labour Party put forward four men as foreign ministers, none of whom had been elected to the national assembly.[14] This practice was continued when Labour returned to government in March 1971. The new Foreign Minister, A. Cappelen, had a wide experience from previous governments and top-level administration, but he had never held a seat in the Storting. Being outside the closed and often very intimate circles of parliamentary relationships, foreign ministers tended to get a remote and somewhat isolated position in the secluded domain of the Foreign Ministry. This was certainly the case with H. Koht and H. Lange – less so with T. Lie, who served most of his time as Foreign Minister in an exile government in Britain, with neither interference nor feedback from a parliamentary body. There is every reason to assume that this relative remoteness had an impact on their conduct of foreign policy. Being generally recognized as experts more than politicians, they achieved a level of authority which gave them a wide range of freedom in the day-to-day making of Norwegian foreign policy. Their opinions on issues in the international field were rarely questioned.[15]

On the other hand, the lack of an intimate contact and a continuous give-and-take with the parliamentarians might bring complications when matters of principle were involved and foreign and domestic issues became intertwined. Halvard Lange became increasingly confronted with this problem during the years of his long 'reign' in the Foreign Ministry. The political factions on the far left whipped up a campaign which tried to make Lange personally responsible for the more unpopular aspects of NATO and of Norway's affiliations with the alliance.[16] The goal of the campaign was clearly to compromise the Foreign Minister to a point where his colleagues in the party leadership became inclined to disassociate themselves from him, in order not to draw the fire on themselves and on the party. Due to Lange's solitary position and relative lack of contacts and supporters on the domestic level, the attempts to push him from the centre of party-leadership into a gradual isolation were by and large successful.[17]

Does a foreign minister of a small country behave and act differently from one who represents a large country? Making allowance for the variations in size, quantity and general implication of decisions, are they faced with different problems in their daily work, in their relations to the parliamentarians, to government colleagues and to the interest groups?

Totally, foreign policy decision-making, for instance in Norway, involves a smaller number of people than in a large country, one such as the United States. But the entire organization does not normally take part in key decisions. There might actually be fewer people behind policy-making decisions in a large country than in a small one, in which the need for consensus often is stronger. On the other hand, as the circle of people and organizations acting on the top level is more restricted, the dangers and consequences of becoming isolated might be greater. A foreign minister of Halvard Lange's calibre might, when unopposed, have a freer hand because there were fewer, if any, other experts on his own level. On the other hand, when exposed to pressure from aggressive political groups, isolation might become more dangerous as there were fewer potential allies, fewer resources to draw on for support.[18]

The Foreign Policy Organization

In a recent study, a research group at Oslo University discovered that although the Foreign Ministry was the most influential single organization in foreign policy decision-making in Norway, it had to share its position with the Ministries of Commerce, Industry and Defence.[19] In functional terms, one might speak of 'four foreign ministries' instead of the traditional and nominal one. In terms of organizational influence, one would have to add *'The Office of the Prime Minister'* (*Statsministerens kontor*) which, however, does not rank as a ministry. There is a very extensive and frequent communication between the relevant departments in the Foreign Ministry and those in the Ministries of Commerce, Industry and Defence that mainly deal with issues concerning external relations. The heads of ministerial departments have a position that in some respects corresponds to Deutsch's 'colonels'.[20]

These, together with the heads of divisions, form the organizational core of foreign policy makers. In terms of accessible information and number of options, the top people at the department/division level in the four ministries probably make more decisions than the ministers themselves. How many, and on which level, will depend more on the character of the individual and of the concrete case than on the formal organizational structure.

In addition to these four identifiable centres in the ministries, there also exists an intermediate level of decision making, or rather influence, a sort of 'mezzanine' made up of a large number of *boards and committees* dealing regularly with problems of foreign affairs.[21] In these officially appointed groups, each assigned to certain sectors, representatives of various interest groups and branch-organizations meet with officials from the administration, mostly heads of departments and divisions in the four foreign policy-making ministries.

This part of the policy-making procedure is becoming increasingly important. The board and committees system enables interest groups to obtain a formal access to levels of information and an insight which they otherwise would have difficulty in getting. By being physically present they can argue their case and the views of their organizations directly to the representatives of the government institutions. On the other hand, because they have these seats on boards and committees, they become involved and, in fact, bound by the courses of action recommended in the joint committees. It is very hard for an organization to come out and protest afterwards when its representatives did not speak up or dissent in the meeting when the matter was discussed.

The Personnel

While organizations provide the structural premises for decision-making, the individuals who run them are largely responsible for the content.[22] The successful outcome of a decision will depend on whether the organization and the official are both of a high standard. Apart from its institutional responsibility and its central location in the hierarchy of foreign policy decision-making, the Foreign Ministry also is the only one of the four ministries that screens and trains applicants for the foreign service. The other ministries usually offer immediate employment after a brief interview.

The Foreign Ministry accepts less than ten trainees a year, gives them one year of regular office work, then sends them through a year-long course for final screening, before they are formally admitted. This period of training and systematized adjustment builds expertise as well as *esprit de corps*. It also strengthens their identification with the organization as well as with their tasks in the diplomatic service.[23]

Through the first decades of independence (after 1905) a stimulating feeling of pioneering and enthusiasm penetrated the whole Norwegian foreign service. The work was often hard, but it was felt to be meaningful.[24] In 1905, when Norway parted from Sweden, only 39 Norwegians had entered the foreign service. By 1910 the number was up to 55, but as late as in 1939 there were still only 100. By 1960 the number of foreign service personnel had doubled. In 1970 there were close on 200. Most of them, 80 to 90 per cent, have an academic background. Before 1905, 77 per cent had a law degree. Throughout the period before the Second World War, the legal profession remained an important means for entry into the foreign service. The lawyers still formed the most numerous professional category among foreign service personnel (1964 – 83 per cent).

The social background of Norwegian diplomats has all along reflected the social structure. In most of the European countries diplomats have often been recruited from the aristocracy. Compared to Denmark and Sweden one notes in Norway a remarkable absence of titles and of *vons* and *des*, which indicate aristocratic descent.

At the beginning of the period, the people opting for the Norwegian foreign service were for the most part raised in the homes of public servants and other representatives of the high middle class. Those whose fathers were farmers and workers have increased proportionally during the post-war period. Since 1950, only one-third of the new diplomats grew up in homes where the fathers had an academic background.[25] In the

37

early sixties about one-fifth were recruited from the business community, as against one-fourth when the service was first established.

Small states tend to have understaffed foreign ministries. If this little 'task force' of a couple of hundred persons were to perform all the tasks that the conduct of Norwegian foreign affairs implies, it would be hopelessly inadequate. Therefore, the officials of the Foreign Ministry should rather be seen as an *avant garde* that spearheads the much larger group of people who, in one way or the other, are actively involved in promoting Norway's external relations. These are, in the first place, the 'external' departments and bureaux of the Ministries of Commerce, Industry and Defence. There is also a number of affiliated agencies; among the larger ones are the Norwegian Export Council, which in fact is a part of the foreign service, and the Directorate of Foreign Aid.

Less conspicuous, but not necessarily less important, are the numerous private non-governmental institutions, representing the larger interest groups. Among them the most influential one is the Norwegian Shipowners' Association. Its prominence is not accidental. As mentioned earlier, Norway's independence and subsequent development grew from the earnings of international shipping. To the average Norwegian this was a fact of life which justified political leadership. It was therefore as natural as unavoidable that the owners of the larger shipping companies also moved into top political positions. Christian Michelsen, a shipowner from the west country, was the man who engineered national independence and became the new nation's first prime minister. During the next two decades other shipping people and industrialists became leaders at the national level.

In fits of democratic euphoria, Norwegians often point out that their society never included an upper crust of nobility. This is true to the extent that Norway did not have an aristocracy *of the land*. Instead it developed an 'aristocracy of the sea'.

In most European nations, political leadership was a function of wealth derived from the possession of land, in pre-democratic times often given by the kings as rewards. In Norway the political leaders acquired national legitimacy from the commercial and communicational exploitation of the seas. While elsewhere in Europe the kings made the nobility – in Norway the 'seaborne nobility' made the king.[26] Under such circumstances the formal structure of titles and privileges serve no useful purpose.

At the beginning of the twentieth century, the shipowners broadened their power base by letting the earnings of shipping spill over into industry. In fact, until the late thirties 'the noblemen of the sea', the élite group of combined shipowners and industrialists, were chiefly responsible for the direction of Norwegian foreign policy, even at times when they did not personally hold key positions in government or in the Storting.[27]

Their political influence became less conspicuous after 1935 when the Social Democrats formed a minority government, but it did not actually wane until after the Second World War. In terms of national policy this means that, through more than half of the sixty-five years when Norway has existed as a sovereign nation, the élite group of 'seaborne nobility' was highly influential in defining the goals and objectives of her foreign policy.

GOALS AND OBJECTIVES

Governments are usually quite vague in defining their national goals. When the non-socialist coalition government took over in Norway in 1965, it announced the following objectives as guidelines for its foreign policy.
It would work for:

1. Peace and harmonious co-operation among states, and support the United Nations in preventing conflict and war.
2. Disarmament and the relaxing of international tension.
3. Stability in Europe through its membership in NATO, with particular reference to a *rapprochement* between Western and Eastern Europe.
4. The improvement of economic and social conditions in developing countries, directly as well as through international co-operation.[28]

An official of the Foreign Ministry, trying to write a general survey of Norwegian foreign policy, was more succinct. The national goals were: to secure Norway's independence and freedom, to look after its interests, and to contribute to peace and international co-operation.[29]

Such statements do, of course, stress the moral implications of foreign policy by including most of the 'right' issues such as peace, stability, disarmament, non-tension and foreign aid. No government will risk domestic difficulties on such a programme. No other country would take offence. Nevertheless, such general statements should not be dismissed as just tactics and verbal exercises. One should rather see them as an array of what a small state would consider optimal goals or a *maximal* fulfilment of its foreign policy. The heavy emphasis on international co-operation is not a pretence. Norway's external relations would indeed be improved by a stronger UN, by comprehensive arrangements for disarmament and by conciliation and international stability. Such goals are all accepted preconditions for small state security and welfare.

One can also speak of a *minimal* goal which is the survival of the nation.[30] Neither of these extremes is what one would call an action policy – the maximal goals because they are too big for a small country to achieve, the minimal ones because the situation in most cases does not imply that bare survival is the only alternative. Decision makers are normally aiming higher than that.

Moving from the declaratory to the action level, one will find that small nations' governments talk much less of goals and objectives than of *problems*. Fulfilment of objectives means problem-solving. The concern is less with what one should do than with what one can do. Neither the maximal goals of assured peace and stability, nor the minimal ones of sheer survival form directives for a small nation's day-to-day making of foreign policy. The real objectives are built into problems that must be solved by the means which at any given time are at its disposal. While the theorists try to sift the goals from aims and objectives and keep them neatly apart, the practitioners in a foreign ministry, who have the responsibility for the making of foreign policy, tend to see ends and means, goals, methods, restraints and capabilities in the same general perspective of problem-solving.

In the Norwegian case, then, how have Norwegian governments perceived the problems of using their external environment to preserve national values and promote a general state of welfare and security for the nation?

Historically, Norway's national policy might be divided into four periods: 65 years of national independence, 400 years of Danish, 100 years of Swedish and 5 years of German domination. The problems for the men who remembered the national liberation in 1905, as well as for their sons who recall the German invasion and occupation forty years later, were: (1) how to prevent another loss of institutional values and national self-determination, and (2) how to preserve and promote economic, social and cultural standards and social security.[31]

MEANS AND METHODS

How does a small nation maximize its use of the external environment for national purposes? A small country, particularly one with such discouraging experiences of foreign domination as Norway, would be very concerned not to become too dependent on a larger and stronger power when formulating its foreign policy. A logical reaction would be to aim for some sort of isolation. But for an industrialized nation, isolation is not an alternative. Lack of natural resources, and a strategic location which is becoming increasingly important to both super-powers, precludes isolation. Therefore, as far as Norway is concerned, interaction is a precondition for national existence.

The corollary of interaction is interdependence. Accepting the existence and the workings of an international system means accepting interdependence. The small states will have to ask, somewhat paradoxically, to what extent they can have interdependence without dependence. In other words, how can they make interdependence advantageously serve the nation's purposes?

For the small nation the crucial matter is not how much one can hope to win, but how little one can afford to lose. A large nation knows that even if it suffers serious setbacks, its national existence is not threatened. A small nation, with insignificant capabilities and perhaps an exposed geographical position, takes a greater risk. If it loses, it may be out for good. It can only misjudge once. Yet it cannot refuse to play.

This is part of the small nation's dilemma. Because of its low capability it will have to generate new assets through the interaction process. It will constantly be looking for new opportunities and exploiting them maximally. The small state will have to develop extra safeguards that may reduce the risks of interaction and provide margins that seem safe enough to prevent disaster.

Lacking a national power base, a small interacting state can seek safeguards either by protection through *international law* and agreed rules of behaviour, or through *'protection by a friend'* in a special relationship, or, finally, through a combination of both law and borrowed power.

Security
Norway is a good example of a small state which has tried all these methods of national problem-solving. Her leaders realized that the marvellous opportunity of large-scale international shipping that had brought Norway back into the rank of sovereign nations was conditioned by *Pax Britannica*, which, as it appeared by the turn of the century, was unlikely to last indefinitely. Norway first attempted to achieve security through a *guaranteed status* on the Swiss model.[32] The 'Treaty of Integrity', which was concluded in 1907 with Britain, France, Germany and Russia, gave guarantees against Swedish aggression, but did not cover her against the great powers.[33]

Norway attempted to give meaning to this policy by adopting legal neutrality based on the 1907 Hague Convention. These were the days when the Norwegian slogan was: 'The best foreign policy is not to have any.' The duties imposed on the neutrals required some degree of military potential, but coupled with a favourable strategic location (which Norway then felt that it had) even a small state might meet the demands successfully. Norway managed to muddle through the First World War,[34] but disaster had been close enough to illustrate the precariousness of neutrality.[35]

Norway then attempted to solve the security problem as a participant in the League of Nations collective security system. But the Norwegian governments quickly discovered that the safeguards of the League were no greater than those of traditional neutrality. Thus, when a Russo-German war became probable and impending, Norway found the risks of involvement too high and reverted to the earlier policy of neutrality – incidentally without giving up her membership in the League. The German invasion in 1940 brought home the fallacies of inadequately armed neutrality in times of crisis. After the complete national disaster in 1940–45, Norway once more opted for collective security arrangements by joining the United Nations and later the NATO alliance system.

What do these vacillations between security organizations and traditional neutrality, both based on legal protection, tell us about Norway's choice of methods in foreign policy? A closer study seems to indicate that the protection aspects were tied more to individual states than to collective security institutions or to the code of neutrality. The search for legal safeguards appeared not so much motivated by hopes of institutional, law-derived protection, but more by the aim of obtaining security through a special relationship. In Norway's case, this meant her special relationship with Britain.[36]

When Norway in 1920 temporarily shelved neutrality and joined the League, the primary motive was not to obtain institutional protection through a law-based organization. With Germany and Russia out of the European power struggle, there seemed in the foreseeable future no discernible threat to her security. Despite a deep and, as it proved, justified, scepticism as to the credibility of the League system, the national leaders felt they could not afford to turn down an invitation to join an organization in which Britain was among the top leaders. Doing so might jeopardize Norway's economic and security interests which depended on British protection.

By the middle thirties, when Britain gradually disentangled herself from active League support, Norway and the other northern states reverted to traditional neutrality. Naturally, the government hoped to stay out of all conflicts, but Norwegian neutrality was conditional. If neutral policies should fail, the rule of impartial behaviour could not be applied strictly to Britain. In a serious conflict Norway had to make sure that she remained on the 'right' side of Britain.[37]

The United Nations experiment presents a slightly different case. The decision to join was made during the war by the Norwegian exile government in London, working very closely with the British government. At this time the special relationship ties were gradually being extended to include the United States as well. When the weakness of the United Nations first became apparent, the Norwegian government once again started moving towards some undefined non-alignment with special connections with Britain and the United States. The search of these two countries for an alternative security arrangement received a positive response in Norway. When, in 1948 to 1949, the British and Americans started preparing for a North Atlantic

43

alliance (NATO), the Norwegian government kept in close touch.

The declaratory explanation stressed the fear of a Soviet attack, particularly after the Czech incident in 1948. In fact, the government was even more concerned about a Soviet-inspired Communist coup in Norway and/or a gradual strangulation of national freedom by increasing political pressures and intimidation. In an isolated neutral position, Norway might end up in a position similar to that of Finland. It was felt that a threat of this kind could not be met with anything less than firm, formal assurance of support from the superior power of large Western states. A Scandinavian defence arrangement (as suggested by the Swedes) would just not suffice. Thus Norway became one of the initial signatories of the North Atlantic treaty. Again, this ready acceptance of the Atlantic treaty idea was not based on an exaggerated belief in the organization as such. It should be kept in mind that until 1951 the Western alliance was not highly developed institutionally. The hopes and the confidence related less to the organizational structure than to Norway's special relationship to the two great sea powers, Britain and the United States. Norway's ties were to *them*, the individual countries, rather than to the NATO organization.

Trade

There is a close relationship between the economic and security aspects of Norway's external relations. For obvious reasons the economic sector presents a more diversified picture. Before the 'great opportunity', with the British liberalization of her maritime transport regulations, Norway's traditional export articles had been fish and timber. The wood products went for a large part to Britain, the fish to Southern Europe. For the past 100 years, ocean shipping has accounted for almost half of all Norwegian exports.[38]

While international shipping brought Norway closer to the British camp, the industry that developed in the later period tended to draw her towards continental Europe, particularly to Germany. Exports to Germany kept growing before the First and the Second World Wars. On both occasions the British demands for the extension of Norwegian trade and other restrictions against Germany brought on the classical conflict between trade and security interests.[39] In 1940 Norway failed to solve this dilemma – with fatal consequences for her national existence.

44

The special relationship was there. The Norwegian preference was clearly with the British. But British ineptness and Norway's inherent lack of relevant capabilities, including political determination, prevented her from making it operational. Her neutrality had a pro-British slant, but the impact of formal trade treaties, the subsequent legal justification of the German case – and, of course, Norway's vain hopes of just sitting out the crisis – caused complications which she was unable to handle successfully.

This tug-of-war between trade and security preferences is one of the constant dilemmas for small states. In more recent times many of them have experienced on one hand the U.S. demand for practising trade restrictions towards Communist countries and on the other the temptation to reap large trade benefits – which someone is going to pick up anyway.

Culture

How do cultural ties between states influence their external relations? Trying to estimate the impact of culture on politics by counting the number of specific treaties and other official arrangements may not answer the question. However, the fact that our means for measuring cultural relations are inadequate should not lead us to downgrade their importance. In the case of Norway we have tried to show that direct, special relationships to individual powers tend to take preference over formal, legal and organizational affiliations.

Are cultural ties the products of trade or protection? Or do they appear at a later stage? Trade and security relations will increase the interactions, which in the next instant may bring about exchange and a mutual respect of values. However, it is also possible to point to cases where this kind of interaction has not worked. One should keep in mind that the Norwegians and the Danes developed a joint, tight cultural pattern during the time when Norway was a Danish protectorate. The hundred years of Norwegian-Swedish coexistence produced very little of cultural sharing and exchange, a fact which may have facilitated their disunion in 1905. On the other hand, it seems that Britain has had an undisputable flair for creating cultural relationships with dependent powers, a trait which the United States apparently lacks. Its special relationships have had few cultural aspects.

45

It appears that, together with trade and protection, the special relationship must also bring out an element of compatibility, whose traits and characteristics are extremely hard to grasp and define. Cultural coexistence requires mutual identification with the sharing of some important values – together with a high rate of mutual tolerance and acceptance. It is not enough to interact, to meet and to see; one must *like* what one sees.

Bilateral and Multilateral Treaties and Agreements: The Impact of Special Relationships

This brief survey of Norway's external relations supports our hypothesis that in her foreign policy she shows a preference for special individualized relationships rather than reliance on organizations. This, of course, is not and can never be an either/or. The optimal situation was, and is, one which combines the benefit of the organization with a special relationship. But so far, 'when the chips were down' and a choice could no longer be postponed, Norway has preferred the latter.

Special relationships would naturally seem to favour bilateral treaties, while multilateral arrangements presuppose an organization. If this is correct, the present trend should favour the multilateral alternative. In 1912, after just seven years of national independence, Norway had concluded 215 bilateral treaties versus only 51 multilateral ones. Half a century later, in 1968, the number of bilateral treaties was 870. During this same period the multilateral ones had risen from 51 to 531. Thus, while the bilateral group had increased by four times, there were now ten times more multilateral treaties. These figures illustrate very clearly the increasing growth of international organizations.

As might be expected, the distribution of Norway's bilateral treaties shows a heavy concentration on Western Europe (see Table 1). Norway had, by 1970, a total of 455 bilateral treaties with West European countries, which is more than half the total number. In addition there were 16 trade agreements and 65 cultural agreements. Arrangements with Eastern Europe were considerably less – 126 bilateral treaties, 7 trade agreements (bilateral) and 2 cultural agreements (bilateral) – but the total number reflects rather the formality of relations. By contrast, only 77 arrangements have been concluded with North America.[40]

In 1970 76 per cent of Norway's exports went to Western

Table 1 *Norwegian Bilateral Treaties 1912–68*

	1912		1921		1930		1939		1950		1960		1968	
	nos.	%	nos.	%	nos.	%	nos.	%	nos.	%	nos.	%	nos.	%
East Europe	21	10	19	8	45	13	53	11	81	13	89	10	126	14
West Europe¹	150	70	181	75	241	68	347	72	456	72	598	70	455	52
North America	9	4	8	3	17	5	17	4	30	5	54	6	77	9
Latin America	8	4	8	3	13	4	24	5	30	5	46	5	63	7
Asia	13	6	13	5	21	6	25	5	20	3	42	5	68	8
Oceania	0	—	0	—	0	—	1	—	3	—	7	—	20	2
Africa	14	6	12	5	15	4	16	3	14	2	27	3	61	7
Total	215¹	100	241²	99	352	100	483	100	634	100	858	99	870	99

¹ Includes Turkey.
² Until 1960 Germany had a special position due to treaties set out force 9 April 1940.
Source: Utenriksdepartementets Kalender, 1912, 1921, 1930, 1939, 1951, 1961, 1969.

Europe, which in turn accounted for 69 per cent of her imports (see Table 2). As can be seen from Table 3, the main European trading partners included Britain, West Germany, Sweden and Denmark. Outside Europe, trade with the United States (imports/exports) and Japan (imports) is particularly important. However, trade with other groupings – the Soviet Union and Eastern Europe, and Africa – has remained relatively low. Whilst the West European emphasis of Norwegian trade will continue, the exact impact of Norway's future economic relations with the EEC on, in particular, trade with countries outside Europe is as yet difficult to estimate.

Table 2 *Norwegian Trade by Area 1960–70*

Percentage of Total Imports

Area	1960	1961	1962	1963	1964	1965	1966	1967	1968	1969	1970
FIN/EFTA	38·4	40·6	40·5	44·2	41·1	42·1	42·1	44·2	43·1	44·2	44·5
EEC	32·9	32·2	31·2	29·8	28·9	29·1	27·8	25·2	24·7	26·9	24·9
COMECON	3·1	3·0	2·9	2·8	3·4	3·1	3·0	3·0	2·5	2·2	1·9
Other European Countries	1·6	1·3	1·4	1·5	2·1	1·3	1·4	1·2	1·6	1·7	1·8
Africa (a)	—	—	—	—	—	—	—	—	2·5	2·4	2·4
Asia (a)	—	—	—	—	—	—	—	—	9·0	5·9	7·6
U.S./Canada	13·2	11·5	11·3	10·6	11·1	10·8	11·4	9·4	11·9	11·7	12·0
Other Countries (a)	—	—	—	—	—	—	—	—	4·7	5·0	4·9

Percentage of Total Exports

	1960	1961	1962	1963	1964	1965	1966	1967	1968	1969	1970
FIN/EFTA	45·6	44·7	43·0	42·5	45·8	44·7	45·4	47·0	45·0	45·0	46·6
EEC	25·6	24·7	26·9	26·9	26·2	25·1	24·3	23·3	23·4	25·5	29·8
COMECON	4·4	4·0	3·9	4·3	4·5	4·4	3·1	2·8	2·5	2·2	2·2
Other European Countries	2·4	2·5	2·9	3·5	3·2	3·3	5·3	4·4	5·2	6·5	6·2
Africa (a)	—	—	—	—	—	—	—	—	5·4	5·1	4·2
Asia (a)	—	—	—	—	—	—	—	—	4·9	3·9	3·1
U.S./Canada	7·2	8·7	11·2	10·3	9·8	9·5	9·7	8·8	8·9	7·5	6·2
Other countries (a)	—	—	—	—	—	—	—	—	4·7	4·3	3·4

Sources: *External Trade 1955–67* (Central Bureau of Statistics of Norway, Oslo, 1969) pp. 56 and 60; and *External Trade 1970* (Central Bureau of Statistics of Norway, Oslo, 1971 (vol. 2, p. 20.

Note: Table 3 provides specific data on the ten main countries to which Norway sent exports and received imports in 1970.

(a) Imports/Exports for the groupings Africa, Asia and other countries were not separately classified for the years 1955–67.

Table 3   *Norwegian Imports and Exports by Main*
          Countries 1970 (in million kroner)

Imports		Exports	
Sweden	3,711·0	West Germany	3,148·3
West Germany	2,673·1	Britain	3,144·5
Britain	2,390·2	Sweden	2,840·3
United States	1,472·9	Denmark	1,262·0
Denmark	1,314·4	United States	1,007·2
Japan	1,140·2	France	633·5
Canada	821·5	Netherlands	572·9
France	650·7	Italy	497·4
Belgium and Luxembourg	638·0	Greece	438·0
Netherlands	615·9	Finland	430·9
Total Imports	26,442·5	Total Exports	17,549·4

Source: *External Trade 1970* (Central Bureau of Statistics of Norway Oslo, 1971) vol. 2, p. 20.

It is hardly surprising that this pattern of external trade corresponds largely to the distribution of diplomatic representation. Of Norway's 45 diplomatic missions in 1968, 15 (45 officials) were located in Western Europe, 2 in North America (11 officials), 5 in Eastern Europe (14 officials), 8 in Asia (16 officials) and 1 in Oceania (1 official). We find a high concentration in Western Europe of Norwegian diplomats as well as stations. It is worth noting that, while North America ranks low in the number of diplomatic representatives, it equals Western Europe in the number of consulates. The combined impact of trade and emigrants is quite evident. Of Norway's 28 consulates, 26 are located either in North America or in Western Europe. Of the remaining two, one is in Asia, the other is in Africa. These figures illustrate the extent to which Norway remains closely linked with Western Europe and North America.

This has been the case for more than a century. In view of this remarkable consistency, can we take for granted that Norway's links with the core countries in the Western world will continue into coming decades as well? Or are there at this point indications of a change? Is it conceivable that Norway may alter or modify the preferences which so far have dominated her foreign policy and set off in new directions, adopting new values, acquiring new capabilities, responding to new opportunities?

Limitations and Alternatives

Degrees of limitations and freedom of action form one of the traditional distinctions between small and great states. Because a large state is less restrained internally as well as externally, it has a wider range of choice in pursuing its national interests. During the fifties and early sixties, this distinction became less obvious. Due to the nuclear stalemate and a number of other special circumstances, the great powers could do less and the small could do more than was generally assumed. In terms of influence on the international system, these two decades might be called the era of the small states.

However, it is doubtful whether this pattern will continue indefinitely. Rather, the trend in the late sixties points toward a greater stress on the factors that limit the freedom of manoeuvre, particularly for the smaller states. With an increase in international violence, the small national units seem bound to suffer harder restraints than the larger ones. And when pressures accumulate, the range of alternatives tends to narrow.

Using the established distinction between internal or 'self-imposed' limitations and those imposed by the external environment, Norway is unfortunately placed.[41] The tangible and intangible capabilities under national, Norwegian control are not of a kind that could secure an easy fulfilment of national objectives. Of the tangible ones, the natural resources, never impressive in any sense, are rapidly being exhausted. Ores, metals, even lumber and cheaply produced water power are gradually being depleted, each in turn increasing her dependence on the external environment. The recent oil discoveries in the North Sea, which now raise such great hopes, may possibly improve the situation. Possession of large oil reserves may give Norway more room for manoeuvre in certain areas. But whilst oil production is likely to ease the economic strain it could create security problems, which may reduce the net effect on the sum of limitations.

The fact that the Scandinavian countries have had a remarkable degree of political stability has often been listed as an important foreign policy asset. National consensus on major issues relating to external affairs increases Norway's credibility and strengthens its general position as a trade and treaty partner. There are, however, indications that the basic agreement on such major issues as the orientation in security policies is being questioned. Triggered by recent developments within NATO and EEC, most of the political parties have splinter groups and factions that express doubts about the traditional alignments with North America and Western Europe. Although as yet unable to change official policy direction, the 'No to Europe' of the national referendum has strengthened the opposition and put stronger limitations on foreign policy moves.

Regulations imposed by international law are often listed as restraints on states' behaviour. To some extent this applies to all states, small as well as big. International legislation aims in the last instance at preventing excessive and arbitrary use of force within the international system. Lack of force is as much a trade-mark of a small state as abundance of usable force characterizes the great ones. By curbing the arbitrary use of force in international relations, effective legislation becomes an equalizer. The elimination of force in the interaction process permits small states to operate on approximately the same levels as the greater ones.

Therefore, the more international legislation, the greater is the relative freedom of action for the smaller nations. Consequently Norway was among the foremost spokesmen for strong restrictive clauses in the UN charter. However, the gradual deterioration of the collective security system and the lack of success in building other legal safeguards might rank as one of the most serious restraints on Norway's freedom of action.

A country hemmed in by natural, built-in limitations, such as Norway, will have to trade to live and to count on borrowed power for protection. Guided by instinct, skill and fortunate circumstances, Norway has been able to overcome the impact of these handicaps imposed on her by internal as well as external limitations. Considering the small population, the lack of natural endowments, the large size of the country and her possessions at both poles, her relative freedom of action with high economic, political and cultural standards is little less than a miracle.

This remarkable achievement cannot be explained by the two alternative orientations in her foreign policy – organizational attachments and neutrality – but rather by the 'special relationship to a friend'. For about a century Britain found it mutually advantageous to play this role of Norway's special friend. The Norwegian shipping services were a valuable and reliable sup-

51

plement to her own needs for ocean transport. In strategic terms, control of Norway's western and northern coastline by a hostile power was almost as intolerable as great power dominance of the Low Countries. To Britain these objectives are still valid, but the attainment of them now depends on power resources which Britain no longer has. This overall decline of British power status, globally as well as in Northern Europe, is for the moment perhaps the most severe limitation on Norway's freedom of action.

There is nothing new about it. The myth of secure British protection received its first blows in 1940, when Britain was unable to prevent the German invasion. The British rather got the blame for having triggered it. Since then every decade has brought new confirmation of the diminished stature of Britain as a power factor in Norway's external environment. In order not to be hamstrung by her accumulating limitations, Norway will have to look for other special friends.

People inside as well as outside the Scandinavian area are sometimes puzzled by the fact that the so-called 'Nordic alternative' does not get more attention. Since 1952 there has been a Nordic Council. After twenty years of existence it can list some achievements in the social and cultural fields. However, as matters of foreign affairs and defence are explicitly excluded from its agenda, its influence on Nordic external relations has been marginal. Why does not Norway look to Sweden or Denmark for some kind of joint arrangement in the crucial fields of economics, security and foreign policy? It is very hard to explain why this is not the case. While the cultural, economic, and political relations satisfy all requirements for a special relationship, there remain, nevertheless, differing conceptions within the three countries on how to achieve security and protection. The largest one, Sweden, lacks now, as at the turn of the century, the naval capabilities and the maritime orientation which in Norway's case is a necessary precondition. Therefore the special friend must be sought outside the Scandinavian region.

The need for protection is stressed by the growth of Soviet military power. The impact of this remarkable and recent development is felt as much in other parts of the world, but, with the great enlargement of Soviet naval capabilities, the change is very noticeable in Northern Europe. Since the early sixties the Soviet Union has launched a whole fleet of nuclear-powered submarines, rocket launchers, landing craft, helicopter carriers and other types of equipment for controlling coasts and waters.[42] The military value of these units is given a psychological component by large-scale manoeuvres. During the past years the Soviet high command has staged naval exercises in the North Sea and the North Atlantic on operational patterns designed very closely on the German invasion model of 1940. For the moment the Soviet objectives are probably not an outright invasion, but demonstrations of Soviet military might. By such manoeuvres the Soviet Union makes its capabilities credible as eloquently as it demonstrated its mental readiness to use them in the 1968 Czechoslovakian affair. The limitations on Norway's external relations grow rather out of the *political* leverage which its military preponderance gives the Russian government in its dealings with next-door neighbours. This is a new situation which Norway is clearly unable to deal with on her own. This recent change in her immediate environment emphasizes strongly the need for a revitalized special relationship.

In view of the established doctrines of North Atlantic and European defence, questions of protection by special friends and 'who is defending who' may sound somewhat unreal and academic. With NATO intact, the defence of West European countries is seen as a joint effort. According to the doctrine, if the need arises, the NATO Council and the national governments will somehow work out an arrangement for the protection of each threatened member.

This may have been satisfactory at the time when the United States held a comfortable margin of superiority over the Soviet Union, at least in strategic forces – which it no longer does. It might even suffice now, provided the threat were conceived primarily in military terms. Today a *political* use of Soviet forces in Europe seems a more likely proposition. This increasingly probable contingency raises demands for a higher degree of immediate preparedness and credibility of Western conventional forces. The psychological effects of Soviet integrated manoeuvres, extending south from the Arctic, can hardly be mitigated by some vague and remote NATO doctrine backed up by declining force capabilities.

The strategic plight in which Norway now finds herself is to some extent of her own making. In order to obtain the protection of a friend, there must exist a certain degree of mutuality. In the early period of Norwegian foreign policy, and particularly before the Second World War, Britain could give such protection because her superiority was still manifest. With virtually no Russian and assumed weak German naval capabilities in northern waters, the costs and risks of protecting Norway were acceptable. Today's situation is widely different. This is due partly to the Soviet preponderance and partly to Norway's ban on allied bases, which has decreased her attraction as a potential friend to be protected by reasonable costs.[43]

Norway's self-denying ordinance on foreign bases must be judged against the background of the situation in the late forties and early fifties. The United States had a monopoly of nuclear weapons and an overall superiority over the Soviet Union. There was a strong domestic pressure on the Norwegian government for a non-committed policy. On one hand there was a general fear of provoking the Soviet Union. On the other the restrictions on bases expressed a precaution against unwanted allied influence and other inconveniences resulting from having forces from the large Western nations stationed on Norwegian territory. The small states' inbred suspicion of great states, even generally friendly ones, makes such a limitation very understandable – if not strategically tenable.

The Norwegian national forces are clearly unable to carry any military or political weight in this northern flank area. Thus the NATO forces that are supposed to provide protection cannot count on being present in the Norwegian (defence area) prior to the outbreak of a crisis. In practical terms, this means that instead of reinforcement and assistance to repel aggression, their most probable task will be liberation – a much less attractive prospect for a potential protector.

The traditional role of 'protecting friend', once played by Britain, could be taken over by the United States and a reorganized Common Market that includes aspects of security as well as of economics and trade. To what extent are these two powers able and willing to play Britain's old role and counterbalance the now accumulating limitations on Norway's external relations? One would think that in the U.S. as well as the EEC case the mutuality and reciprocity which form a major condition for special relationships ought to be present. The United States, both individually and as a NATO member, would be in a worse strategic position if the whole or even parts of Norway were controlled by the Soviet Union. The immediate needs, as in the days of the manned bombers, are probably not felt today, but submarine warfare and surveillance may provide strong motivations for keeping Soviet installations off the North Atlantic 'eastern sea board'. One might, for example, visualize a point in the not-too-distant future when the range of the submarine-borne missiles has increased enough to permit Soviet trans-atlantic launchings against the North American continent from Norwegian fjords and coastal waters, where submerged, Russian launching vessels would be fairly safe from underwater attackers. In straightforward military terms a preventive protection of Norway would seem worth while, even at fairly high U.S. costs.

The incentives for immediate involvement may seem less forceful when seen from a *political* angle. On the one hand there is the possibility of 'Finlandization' – a gradual Soviet political pressure on the Finnish model. Political and social pressure as used against Finland is a slow, piecemeal operation, with little drama or violent action that might cause public concern and raise demands for effective counter-measures. On the other hand, there is the political development within the United States, which is likely to cause major U.S. troop withdrawals and which may discourage future intervention initiatives overseas. On balance, counting these inhibitions and the lack of attraction and incentives to become involved in a vaguely defined political crisis, it should not be taken for granted that the United States would automatically fill the role of what was once the case of the special British-Norwegian relationship. It may—and it may not.

The Common Market alternative is even more imbued with uncertainties. First it is not at all clear whether the EEC members – as they are now, or extended to include the Anglo-Scandinavian applicants – will shoulder the responsibility for bolstering conventional security in Western Europe. If we suppose they will, there are still many unanswered questions. With Britain and West Germany as members, there would be a strong interest in securing the North Atlantic coasts and preventing Soviet military and political influence from encroaching into the North Sea area. But counting in the voices of members such as France and Italy, what costs and risks would seem acceptable for giving effective protection in a political as well as in a military sense? If we assume the validity of the statement: 'The power that controls the Norwegian Sea and the North Atlantic will also control Norway',[44] would there be sufficient West European naval forces to provide a shield or could one count on a satisfactory arrangement being worked out with the American and Canadian forces? Or would possible oil strikes and intensified oil production in the Norwegian continental shelf increase her attractions to a point where both power groups might justify the costs of entering into a special relationship to overcome the limitations in Norway's external relations?

These reflections on the present situation may seem somewhat strained in terms of what in 1972 are the generally accepted versions of the North European situation. They may, however, serve the purpose of illustrating the increasing difficulties which most small states face of establishing a balanced relationship between national objectives and capabilities and internal and external limitations. In order to keep their previous levels of sovereignty and relative freedom of action, they will need the support of special friends. But in times of increased stress and rapidly changing power distributions, such good and special friends may be hard to find.

NOTES AND REFERENCES

Probably the most comprehensive bibliographical guide to Norwegian foreign policy is Nils Ørvik's *Norwegian Foreign Policy – A Bibliography. 1905–1965* (Oslo University Press, 1968). A second volume covering the period 1965–70 will be made available by Oslo University Press in 1972.

The historical background of Norway's relations to other states is mostly included in the standard works of general Norwegian history. This is particularly true of the period before the First World War when foreign policy played a very small role. For the neutrality policies of the First World War, Olav Riste's *The Neutral Ally. Norway's Relations with Belligerent Powers During the First World War* (Oslo University Press, Oslo, 1965) gives a useful survey of the major problems. The foreign and security policies of the inter-war period are dealt with by Nils Ørvik in a two-volume work, *Sikkerhetspolitikken 1920–1939*. Vol. I: *Handelskrigen 1939–40* (Grundt Tanum Forlag, Oslo, 1960) and vol. II: *Solidaritet eller nøytralitet?* by the same publisher in 1961. Both volumes have English summaries.

The post-war period is dealt with in a mainly historical survey of the security policies from the middle forties to the early sixties, provided by

Johan Jørgen Holst in *Norsk sikkerhetspolitikk i strategisk perspektiv* (Norsk Utenrikspolitisk Institutt, Oslo, 1967). This book has a very useful collection of public documents. It presents by and large the official version of Norwegian security policy of the period. The late fifties and the sixties did, however, see an increasing number of books and monographs presenting views that did not conform to the foreign policy directions of the Norwegian government. Most of the non-conforming literature used NATO and Norway's membership in the alliance as points of departure. On one hand, one finds writers arguing that the Norwegian government leads an inconsistent and dangerous policy of semi-neutrality. They are particularly critical of the Norwegian prohibitions against the stationing of allied troops and tactical nuclear charges in times of peace on Norwegian territory. In this category are the present writer's *Europe's Northern Cap and the Soviet Union* (Harvard University Occasional Paper, Cambridge, Mass., 1963) and *Alternativer for sikkerhet* (Ernst G. Mortensens forlag, Oslo, 1970).

Those arguing for intensifying Norway's engagement in NATO and increasing the national defence forces were very few indeed. In the seventies, they by and large gave up and discontinued their open opposition to semi-neutrality. The much larger group of writers that represented the other extreme, campaigning in 'Out of NATO' and 'Ban the Bomb' movements and arguing along revisionist lines have increased in number and continue to put out a fast-growing pile of literature. Among the most well known are: Kari Enholm, *Norge NATO og atomvåpen* (Pax forlag, Oslo, 1965), often quoted in Soviet press commentaries, Johan Galtung, *Norske fredsinitiativ. 20 forslag* (Pax forlag, Oslo, 1964), Harald Lovas and Hans Stokland, *20 Lange år* (Pax forlag, Oslo, 1965) and Nils Petter Gleditsch og Sverre Lodgaard, *Krigsstaten Norge* (Pax forlag, Oslo, 1970).

Partly due to the fact that many who represent the revisionist trend in foreign policy are strongly influenced by behaviouralist methods and views derived from American social science research, partly to the need for a more empirical basis of evaluation, there has been a great emphasis on public opinion and on attitudes to foreign policy. One of the first books to deal with this matter in a systematic way was Henry Valen and Daniel Katz, *Political Parties in Norway* (Oslo University Press, Oslo, 1964). Later works are Theo Koritzinsky, *Velgere Partier og Utenrikspolitikk* (Pax forlag, Oslo, 1970) and Halvor Bjellanes, *Partiene og det politiske lederskap* (Pax forlag, Oslo, 1967).

There has been no really comprehensive study of the Norwegian Foreign Ministry. However, important aspects are covered by Reidar Omang, *Utenrikstjenesten* (Gyldendal, Oslo, 1964) and *Norsk Utenrikstjeneste* (Gyldendal, Oslo, 1955). A comparative analysis of communication patterns and structures can be found in Nils Ørvik, *et al.*, *Departmental Decision-Making* (Oslo University Press, 1972). Erik Colban, *Stortinget og Utenrikspolitikken* (Oslo University Press, Oslo, 1961) deals in a conventional way with the foreign policy aspects of the Norwegian Parliament (Stortinget).

The intense debate on the problems of national sovereignty and European and Nordic integration which raged through most of the fifties and sixties have left surprisingly few marks in Norwegian literature. An important contribution is made by Martin Saeter, *Det Politiske Europa* (Oslo University Press, 1971). Parliamentary attitudes are analysed in *Fears and Expectations in Norwegian Integration* (Oslo University Press, Oslo, 1972), edited by the present writer. While books are scarce, articles in periodicals and major papers provide an ample source through the fifties and sixties. As in most other countries in the same category, NATO and the EEC are the two focal points. There is also a fair amount of written material on the United Nations activities and on foreign aid.

The most important periodicals for Norwegian foreign policy debates are: *Internasjonal Politikk, Norsk Militaert Tidskrift, Pax, Samtiden* and *Kontrast*. Some of the articles are translated into English and presented in the Nordic periodical *Cooperation and Conflict* which, on the whole, tends to reflect the official policies of the four Nordic countries. As such, it is a valuable source.

1. Cf. Oran Young, *The Intermediaries, Third Parties in International Crisis* (Princeton University Press, N.J., 1967).
2. For an overview of the origins of Norwegian foreign policy, see Philip M. Burgess, *Elite Images and Foreign Policy Outcomes: A Study of Norway* (Ohio State Press, Ohio, 1967) pp. 13–43.
3. Johs. Andenæs, *Statsforfatningen i Norge* (Grundt Tanum Forlag, Oslo, 1962) pp. 206, 234–44.
4. Jens A. Christophersen, 'Avgjørelsesprosessen i norsk utenrikspolitikk' *Internasjonal politikk*, no. 7 (1968) pp. 669 ff. (See also other articles in the same issue.)
5. Andenæs, op. cit., p. 243.
6. Cf. Philip M. Burgess, *Internasjonal politikk*, no. 7 (1968) p. 752.
7. Henry Valen and Daniel Katz, *Political Parties in Norway* (Universitets-forlaget, Oslo, 1964).
8. James N. Rosenau, *Public Opinion and Foreign Policy* (Random House, New York, 1961) p. 36, also Roy C. Macridis, *Foreign Policy in World Politics* (New Jersey, 1962) pp. 16 ff.
9. Willy Marthiniussen, 'Velgerne og de politiske stridsspørsmål', *Tidsskrift for samfunnsforskning* (1967) pp. 164 ff. Ottar Hellevik, 'Stortingets utenrikspolitiske spørrevirksomhet', *Tidsskrift for samfunnsforskning*, no. 2 (1965) pp. 91–112.
10. Theor Koritzinsky, *Velgere, partier og utenrikspolitikk* (Pax Forlag, Oslo, 1970) pp. 35 ff.
11. ibid., p. 30.
12. Nils Halle, 'Social Position and Foreign Policy Issues', *Journal of Peace Research*, no. 1 (1966) pp. 46–74. See also Johan Galtung, 'Social position, party identification and foreign policy orientation' in J. Rosenau, *Domestic Sources of Foreign Policy* (Free Press, New York, 1967) pp. 161–93.
13. See Valen and Katz, op. cit., pp. 57 ff.; Halvor Bjellaanes, *Partiene og det politiske lederskap* (Epoke Forlag, Oslo, 1967) p. 20; and Christophersen, op. cit., p. 675.
14. These were: Edvard Bull (1928) (nineteen days in office), Halvdan

Koht (1935–40), Trygve Lie (1940–46), Halvard Lange (1946–65). It is an interesting, although to some extent explicable, contrast on the non-socialist side. The three men whom the non-socialist coalition chose as foreign ministers between 1963 and 1970 were seasoned parliamentarians: Erling Wikborg (1963) (twenty-one days), John Lyng (1965–70), Svenn Stray (1970–71). Significantly, the new Labour Foreign Minister, Andreas Cappelen, who took over in the spring of 1971, was a seasoned administrator with no parliamentary experience.

15. Ministerial colleagues of Halvdan Koht have told me that often, when one of them ventured to ask the foreign minister to clarify and explain his stand on foreign policy issues, he might answer: 'I have given some thought to this matter and this is how it is,' implying that further counselling beyond that point would be unnecessary.

16. H. Lovas and H. Stokland, *20 lange aar* (Pax Forlag, Oslo, 1965).

17. Cf. Nils Ørvik, 'Trygve Bratteli – Med tanke på framtida', *Norsk Militært Tidsskrift*, no. 6 (1970) pp. 281–93. Also in *Alternativer for sikkerhet* (E. G. Mortensens Forlag, Oslo, 1970) pp. 189–206.

18. These problems will be dealt with in more detail in a study on small nations initiated by the Kingston Group for International Relations, Queen's University, Canada.

19. Nils Ørvik *et al.*, *Departmental Decision-Making, A Research Report* (Oslo University Press, Oslo, 1972).

20. Karl W. Deutsch, *The Nerves of Government* (Free Press, New York, 1963).

21. Ørvik, *Departmental Decision-Making*, op. cit., ch. 2.

22. Herbert A. Simon, *Administrative Behavior* (Macmillan, New York, 1957) pp. xii, 123.

23. The special training of 'aspirants' goes back to 1922. It was discontinued during the war, but reintroduced in 1950. Mari Holmboe Ruge, 'Norske utenrikstjenestemenn 1905–65', *Tidsskrift for samfunnsforskning* (1965) p. 216. For more general information, see also Johan Galtung and Mari Holmboe Ruge, 'Patterns of Diplomacy', *Journal of Peace Research*, no. 2 (1965) pp. 101–35.

24. Reidar Omang, *Utenrikstjenesten* (Gyldendal Norsk Forlag, Oslo, 1954).

25. Ruge, op. cit., pp. 221–5.

26. In 1905 the new Norwegian government, headed by Christian Michelsen, went out to 'hire' a constitutional monarch. They finally reached a satisfactory agreement with a Danish prince, who as King Haakon the 7th became one of the most able rulers in Europe.

27. Among the shipowners and industrialists who became prime and/or foreign ministers in this period were Gunnar Knudsen, Nils Ihlen, J. Irgens, Ivar Lykke and L. J. Mowinckel. The shipowner-politician, Mowinckel, was a dominating force in Norwegian foreign policy through most of the inter-war period.

28. Government declaration of 22 October 1965, summarized in the speech from the throne 1966/67, *Regjeringens virksomhet fra oktober 1965 til sommeren 1967*. Issued by the Office of the Prime Minister, 24 August 1967 (mimeographed), p. 180.

29. Knut Frydenlund, *Norsk utenrikspolitikk* (Norsk Utenrikspolitisk Institutt, Oslo, 1966) p. 143.
30. Arnold Wolfers, 'National Security as an Ambiguous Symbol', in A. Wolfers, *Discord and Collaboration* (Johns Hopkins Press, Baltimore, 1962).
31. Thus, even when trying to be specific, there is just a short step to the generalizations of public declarations.
32. In 1902 the Storting requested the government to explore possibilities for 'eternal neutrality'. Trygve Mathisen, 'Nøytralitetstanken i norsk politikk fra 1890-årene til Norge gikk med i Folkeforbundet', *Historisk tidsskrift*, vol. 36 (1952/3) pp. 30–60.
33. The fear of Swedish revenge and a militarily enforced reunion did not subside until the First World War. The North Sea Treaty of 1908, which Norway was not invited to sign, was an indication of the precariousness of Norway's position and of her close relations with Britain.
34. Olav Riste, *Norway, the Neutral Ally* (Universitetsforlaget, Oslo, 1965).
35. Nils Ørvik, *The Decline of Neutrality* (Frank Cass & Co., London, 1971).
36. Cf. Nils Ørvik, *Sikkerhetspolitikken 1920–1939*, 2 vols (Grundt Tanum Forlag, Oslo, 1960–61). See also by the same author, 'Nordic Security, Great Britain and the League of Nations' in K. Bourne and D. C. Watt, *Studies in International History* (Longmans, London, 1967) pp. 385–401.
37. Halvdan Koht, *For fred og fridom i krigstid* (Tiden Norsk Forlag, Oslo, 1957) p. 220.
38. The percentage of total export has been approximately 40 per cent all the time ever since. Statistisk Sentralbyraa, *Trends in Norwegian Economy 1865–1960* (Oslo, 1966) p. 64.
39. In both wars there were formal agreements between the Norwegian Shipowners' Association and the British government, which put a large part of Norway's merchant marine at Britain's service. In addition, however, the British kept pressing for further concessions, such as closing 'the Leads' to German ships and restricting even further Norway's trade with Germany. Cf. Nils Ørvik, *Norge i brennpunktet. Handelskrigen 1939–1940* (Grundt Tanum Forlag, Oslo, 1953).
40. Due to the position of NATO as the major security arrangement, Norway has separate military agreements with only three states, United States, Canada and West Germany.
41. The sale of shipping services, the traditional asset which covers a third of the deficits caused by the nation's import, belongs rather to the list of external factors.
42. See *The Military Balance* (Institute of Strategic Studies, London, 1960–72).
43. Nils Ørvik, 'Base Policy – Theory and Practice', *Cooperation and Conflict*, vol. 2 (1967) pp. 188–204.
44. Nils Ørvik, *Alternativer for sikkerhet* (Ernst G. Mortensens Forlag, Oslo, 1970) pp. 228–31.

Chapter 2

THE FOREIGN POLICY
OF THE NETHERLANDS

PETER R. BAEHR

Throughout their history, the Dutch have
had no foreign policy other than the
advocacy of international law, the protection of their commercial interests, and the
guarantee of their security (mainly by
Britain).[1]

INTRODUCTION

The main part of the Kingdom of the Netherlands consists of
the home territory in Western Europe, which is bordered by the
German Federal Republic, Belgium and the North Sea, and
which has a population of more than 13 million inhabitants
(1972) and an area of 13,053 square miles. It consists further of
the former colony of Surinam in South America, bordered by
Brazil, Guyana and French Guyana, which has a population of
335,000 and an area of 55,144 square miles. Finally there is the
former colony of the Netherlands Antilles, six islands in the
Caribbean north of Venezuela, which has a population of
208,000 and a combined area of 372 square miles; the most
important of these six islands are Curaçao and Aruba.

The foreign relations of the three territories are administered
jointly by the government in The Hague, which for these and
other matters includes a plenipotentiary minister from Surinam
and one from the Antilles. For all practical purposes the day-
to-day foreign policy is made by the Foreign Minister of the
Netherlands, who is accountable to the Netherlands parliament
but not to the parliaments of Surinam and the Netherlands
Antilles. The two former colonies have been self-governing
since the Statute of 1954 was adopted, but they have little to say

61

in the realm of foreign policy; occasionally representatives of the two territories are appointed in the diplomatic service (for example, in permanent missions to international organizations such as the United Nations). Thus, when in this chapter reference is made to 'Netherlands foreign policy', this includes implicitly the two territories in the Western hemisphere.

Successive governments of the Netherlands and a relatively large segment of its population have always been 'international minded'. The development of international law through treaties has received great attention since the time of Grotius. This has even found formal expression in the Constitution which states: 'He [the King] shall promote the development of the international legal order.'[2] Articulate public opinion has shown a permanent interest in developments abroad. This has made problem areas such as the Middle East, Indo-China, Angola and Biafra, in which the Netherlands was not directly involved, into actual or potential issues in Dutch *internal* politics. Symptomatic of this concern with the world outside its borders is the amount of attention paid to the developing nations and the need for closing the gap between the rich and the poorer countries.

A final point that should be made by way of introduction is the fact that recent Dutch foreign policy has more than ever before been dominated by a single political figure: Foreign Minister J. A. H. M. Luns who has been a member of the Cabinet for almost nineteen years (1952–71). This long term of office furnished him with much experience and a certain degree of authority, not only among his Dutch colleagues, but also among his foreign colleagues – witness his appointment as Secretary-General of NATO in 1971. This long experience in addition to a certain comedian-like way of behaviour made him for many years the most popular and admired public figure in the Netherlands (apart from members of the royal family). This popularity plus the fact that he is a member of the Catholic People's Party (KVP) – from 1946 until 1971 the largest political party in the Netherlands – have made his political position unassailable. Moreover, the main lines of Dutch foreign policy have not created great controversy in recent times.

HISTORICAL EXPERIENCE

The history of the foreign policy of the Netherlands is one of declining power. It may seem useful to divide that history into three periods:

1. The Golden Age which lasted from the war of independence against Spain (1568–1648) until the end of the Spanish war of succession (1702–13). During this period the Dutch Republic played a major role in international affairs and the basis was laid for the later colonial empire.
2. A long period until the Second World War, during which Dutch power dwindled and foreign policy became oriented towards neutralism. The same period witnessed also the flourishing of a large colonial empire which was gradually built up in the East and West Indies and which virtually lasted until the conquest of the Netherlands East Indies by Japan in 1942.
3. The area of close Western co-operation which began during the Second World War and was resumed after the war – the Council of Europe and the Brussels Treaty of 1948, the NATO alliance of 1949, the European Coal and Steel Community of 1952, Euratom of 1957, and the European Economic Community of 1958. The colonial empire ended when formal sovereignty over the East Indies was transferred to Indonesia in 1949; the last vestige of Dutch colonial power in the East – West New Guinea – remained a Dutch possession until as late as 1964 when it was transferred to Indonesia.

1. *The Golden Age*

The Republic of the Seven United Provinces, the confederacy that emerged from the struggle for independence of the low countries against Spain, quickly became one of the most powerful nations in Europe. Dominated by Holland – its richest member state – which was in turn dominated by the city of Amsterdam, it developed into a centre of commerce and finance. A strong financial position entailed a strong military position which was defended and maintained against its greatest maritime rival – Britain – in three Anglo-Dutch sea wars. Under the military leadership of the princes of Orange the Republic remained one of the foremost powers in Europe throughout the seventeenth century, while the Dutch East and West Indies companies laid the foundations for what was to become the Dutch colonial empire. In view of its strong commercial interests the maintenance of peace was a foremost goal of the government. Johan de Witt, the famous seventeenth-century statesman, put it in the following terms: 'The interest of the State demands that there be quiet and peace everywhere and that commerce can be conducted in an unrestricted way.'[3] These words can be viewed as the maxim on which Dutch foreign policy has been based ever since.

2. The Period of Decline

After its 'Golden Age' the Netherlands never regained its former position of power. The republic in its final years, the kingdom of the Netherlands in the nineteenth and early twentieth centuries, became a small power in European politics, deriving only some importance from its wealth. Much of this wealth was gained from its possession of the East Indies. The military role of the Netherlands had come to a definitive end, however. Its small territory and population made it by far the inferior of the powers that dominated European and international politics in the eighteenth and nineteenth centuries: France and Britain, Prussia, Austria and Russia. The reunion of the northern and southern Netherlands after the Napoleonic era – intended to create a strong power north of France – turned out to be of only short duration; between 1830 and 1839 Belgium sought and gained independence. From that time dates the peculiar relationship between the two countries. Though closely allied and sharing many political and economic interests, the inhabitants regard each other with a mixture of close understanding and mutual contempt. This is also reflected in the collaboration between the two governments which has never reached the full degree of harmony and understanding which might have been expected.

In view of its military inferiority the choice of a policy of *neutrality* must have seemed a logical one. From the Congress of Vienna until after the outbreak of the Second World War the Netherlands pursued successfully a foreign policy that aimed at staying outside the main international conflicts. Although its neutrality was never formally guaranteed by the great powers, as it had been in the case of Belgium, it was not seriously threatened until 1940. As Vandenbosch has pointed out, Britain, France and Prussia had an interest in maintaining Dutch neutrality:

Should any one of the three violate it, the aggressor would immediately be confronted with the combined power of the other two. In the course of time the Dutch began to look upon this cautious, purely national policy as a positive good and a sacred international duty. In line with this the Dutch began to regard themselves as the great mediator between the various peoples, culturally and in every other way.'[4]

In line with the view mentioned at the end of the quotation, one recent Dutch observer has recalled that the Netherlands was seen as the most unselfish of all states; it was the Joan of Arc among the nations![5]

3. The Western Alliance

The year 1940 meant in many ways a radical change in the premises of Dutch foreign policy. The German attack and the ensuing occupation brought the Dutch policy of neutrality to an end. In looking for help against the superior German forces its government was forced to join the allied powers (which up till 1940 it had always refused to do). During the first years after the Second World War the Netherlands tried to pursue a policy of co-operation with all powers. This policy was based on the hope for successful co-operation between the Western powers and the Soviet Union.[6] When this co-operation failed to materialize, the Netherlands chose a policy of firm alliance with the Western powers. It received its first formal enactment in the Brussels Treaty of 1948, which Britain, France, Belgium, Luxembourg and the Netherlands concluded formally against a revival of the German threat. The NATO alliance of the following year, in which the five Brussels powers were joined by the United States, Canada, Norway, Denmark, Iceland, Italy and Portugal, did not name any enemy, but it was to all intents and purposes directed against the Soviet Union. During the height of the Cold War and afterwards, the Netherlands consistently pursued a pro-Western policy in a strong and loyal alliance with the United States of America. Mr Luns's policies of support for European integration and furthering Atlantic co-operation have found support from all major political parties except the communists and the pacifist-socialists.[7] The policy of self-chosen neutrality had come to what seems to be a definitive end.

CULTURAL IMPACT

If there exists anything like a typical trait that has had an impact on Dutch foreign policy, it may be what Heldring has called the 'moralistic-legalistic attitude' of the Dutch.[8] He calls 'moralistic' the idea that decisions in the realm of foreign policy are taken or ought to be taken not in terms of power politics but on the merits of the issues at stake. This view is also held by many Dutch intellectuals, who feel that the Dutch know not only what is good for themselves but also for the whole world.[9] It is legalistic in the sense that great confidence is put in international law in general and in the binding nature of international treaties and the obligations which they entail. This is at least a partial explanation for the reluctance of the Dutch – which incidentally they share with several other Western powers – to support draft resolutions in the General Assembly of the United Nations containing 'unrealistic' or 'unenforceable' demands on such powers as Portugal or South Africa. On several occasions Mr Luns has publicly rejected support for such resolutions, which the Afro-Asian sponsors often see more as an indication of moral and psychological support for the opponents of Portugal's colonial policies or South Africa's policy of apartheid. When asked in a parliamentary debate why the Netherlands delegation had abstained on a resolution condemning the developments in Rhodesia, Mr Luns said that he considered it premature to condemn possible talks between the Rhodesian government and the United Kingdom before the results of these conversations were known. He added:

> This was not all. There were many unrealistic statements and suggestions. The use of force by the United Kingdom was implicitly and explicitly demanded by the resolution and sanctions were called for not only against Rhodesia, but also against South Africa. *Whatever one may think of such measures it is obvious that they could not be put into effect.*[10]

In fairness to the opponents of Mr Luns's views, it should be added that they claim that the government often advances objections of a procedural or legal nature in order to hide arguments of a far more fundamental nature such as the following: Portugal is a valuable defence partner in NATO into whose affairs we should not meddle; or, Rhodesia is a British problem and the Netherlands should do nothing but support whatever the British government chooses its policy to be.

Machinery and Processes

The formal and actual authority to make and determine foreign policy in the Netherlands rests with the national government. The Constitution states explicitly: 'The King shall have the supreme direction of foreign relations.'[11] In view of the constitutional provision that '. . . the King shall be inviolable; the ministers shall be responsible',[12] it is the ministers, or more precisely the Minister of Foreign Affairs, who is in charge of foreign relations. He heads the Ministry of Foreign Affairs and decides on who represents the country abroad. Since 1965 a separate Minister without Portfolio is in charge of development aid. A separate state secretary for foreign affairs is usually charged with problems of European unification and integration. Initiatives in the realm of foreign affairs usually rest with these officials. It should be noted that such matters as international treaties, the instructions to representatives abroad and other important issues of foreign policy must be submitted to and debated by the Council of Ministers.[13]

The parliament – the 'States-General' – must approve declarations of war, unless '. . . as a result of the actual state of war consultation with the States-General has appeared to be impossible'.[14] It must also expressly or tacitly approve treaties with foreign states.[15] Furthermore, both chambers of parliament have the important right of debating the annual budget, which is always accompanied by an explanatory memorandum for each department in which the minister states the main lines of policy he intends to pursue. The foreign policy debates in the more important second chamber of parliament are usually preceded by public or private sessions of its foreign policy committee. This committee is composed of the foreign policy experts of the different parliamentary parties; it holds no formal constitutional powers, nor can it prevent proposals from reaching the floor for full parliamentary debate. At his own initiative or on request from the parliament, a minister may prepare a formal paper (*nota*) on any aspect of concern to his department, which will be debated in parliament (e.g. the Vietnam paper of 1967). Such debates may or may not lead to further action by either the minister or parliament. Finally, members of parliament can

67

put questions to the minister or the state secretary in either written or oral form; these may also lead to full-scale parliamentary debates.

Another important constitutional provision states that in certain circumstances treaties may deviate from the Constitution; such treaties need a two-thirds majority of the votes cast in each chamber of parliament.[16] A unique feature is the provision in the Constitution that treaties, once approved, have the force of law and can be invoked by citizens in the national courts. They have priority over national laws and even the national Constitution itself.[17]

The Foreign Minister is unquestionably *the* dominating figure in the field of Dutch external relations. Members of parliament often complain of their lack of influence in this field and show signs of frustration when confronted with their powerlessness. This may help to explain why the role of the opposition in this respect is also rather limited. It must limit itself to putting critical questions to the minister, whenever an issue arises that merits such questions. Another reason for the weakness of the opposition is the fact that, apart from the small communist and pacifist-socialist parties, there exists no fundamental disagreement among the major Dutch political parties on the main lines of foreign policy.

The Foreign Ministry
The Foreign Ministry is headed by the Minister of Foreign Affairs. He may be joined by a Minister without Portfolio and one or two state secretaries. These officials often do not belong to the same political party; under Dutch coalition practices it is quite common to divide these posts among different political parties. The De Jong Cabinet (1967–71) was a typical example of this practice. Mr Luns (Catholic People's Party) was the Foreign Minister, B. J. Udink (Christian Historical Union) was Minister without Portfolio charged with problems of development aid, and H. J. de Koster (People's Party for Freedom and Democracy – the Liberal Party) was State Secretary for European Affairs. The decision whether a certain area of specialization will be entrusted to a state secretary or to a minister without portfolio depends on the ratio of posts held by the various parties within the government coalition rather than on the importance which is attached to the subject. For instance, in

1967 Mr Udink was put in charge of development aid as a minister rather than as a state secretary as his predecessor had been, because his party was entitled to a second minister's post in the Cabinet.[18]

The highest permanent civil servant under the political leadership is the Secretary-General. He is in charge of the personnel of the department and the foreign service, which in 1970 amounted to almost three thousand persons.[19] There are three Directorates-General: European co-operation, political affairs and international co-operation. The largest of these is the Directorate-General for International Co-operation (247 civil servants), which deals with international organizations, financial-economic development aid, technical aid and the Dutch equivalent of the American Peace Corps. The Directorate-General for Political Affairs (114 civil servants) comprises the geographical and functional divisions: Europe, NATO and the Western European Union, the East, Africa and the Middle East, and the Western hemisphere. The Directorate-General for European co-operation (34 persons) deals mainly with affairs connected with the European Communities and the Council of Europe. Apart from the three Directorates-General there are several divisions which are directly supervised by the Secretary-General such as the diplomatic service, the protocol division and the treaty division.

The fact that the diplomatic service is a division that is separate from the other divisions of the department has been a permanent bone of contention. It has its own entrance examinations, which are more formal and supposedly more strict than the usual application procedures for the remainder of the department's divisions. Above all, the diplomatic service has a tradition and an *esprit de corps* of its own, which serves as a source of irritation for other people, both inside and outside the department. It still tends to attract members of the aristocracy and it has often been suspected that they could more easily enter the service than people of lower-class background. A more recent form of antagonism between the diplomatic service and other divisions in the department was expressed in a public letter by twenty-one young civil servants who complained that they were given insufficient opportunities to occupy positions abroad and that they did not receive enough chances for promotion at home.[20] On the other hand, it is regretted by some that the foreign service officers get the opportunity of working in the department only once or twice during their thirty years of service. This tends to widen the gap between the people who write the instructions at home and those who have to execute them abroad.[21] It seems obvious that from the point of view of achieving the highest standards of efficiency and morale in the department, the separation of the foreign service from the other divisions of the department is a bad thing. Mr Luns – a former member of the diplomatic service himself – and the leaders of the department have so far refused to change this situation.[22]

There is a standing rule that all departments conduct their contacts with foreign governments through the channels of the Ministry of Foreign Affairs. Nevertheless, numerous frictions have occurred concerning matters of competence. This is particularly the case with problems that arise on the level of the European Communities. Problems such as the harmonization of fiscal policy, European traffic regulations and the reorganization of the agricultural structure of Western Europe, affect other ministries much more directly than the Ministry of Foreign Affairs. Nevertheless, the latter has always insisted on the supervision or co-ordination of whatever negotiations took place on the European level. The permanent representative of the Netherlands at the European Communities in Brussels is appointed by, and, in first instance, accountable to, the Minister of Foreign Affairs. The friction between the various departments has led to the allegation that in negotiations at the European level the Netherlands delegation is usually the largest as it has to accommodate representatives of all the various interested ministries.[23] The strongest conflicts of interest have occurred between the Ministry of Foreign Affairs and the division for foreign economic relations of the Ministry of Economic Affairs. This division was created in 1946 as an interdepartmental co-ordinating agency and put under the direct supervision of the Minister of Economic Affairs.[24] This has led in practice to conflicts with the Ministry of Foreign Affairs, as both agencies claimed the right to co-ordinate foreign economic affairs. Van der Beugel – a former state secretary for foreign affairs – has suggested such problems should be solved during the formation of the Cabinet. Once the Cabinet has been formed, it is too late to solve such questions. His proposal to entrust the co-ordination to the Minister of Foreign Affairs has not been followed up so far.

FREEDOM OF MANOEUVRE

Internal Limitations

Among the internal factors which limit the options which the government has in deciding its foreign policy the following may be considered: the size of the country, the availability of sufficient information, the power of the parliament and the activities of pressure groups.

Many people in the Netherlands are convinced of the rather limited freedom of manoeuvre in foreign policy for a small nation like the Netherlands. Numerous are the references in newspaper articles and similar sources to the fact that '. . . we as a small country cannot expect to carry much influence in the world councils of state'. When challenged, Mr Luns showed himself an exception to this usage, as appears from the following excerpt from the 1970 parliamentary debates on the budget for foreign affairs:

Mr *Hoekstra* (Communist): Mr Chairman, every time the government speaks about foreign policy, they tell us the story that the Netherlands is only a small, powerless small wheel in the world.
Mr *Luns*: That has never been said by me – never, never, never. I have never said that the Netherlands is a small, puny country. The Netherlands is a very important country.[25]

Nevertheless, it is felt by many – possibly including Mr Luns – that the military and economic power of the Netherlands is too small to carry great weight in the world. Nor can the giving or withdrawal of foreign aid by the Netherlands alone even carry the faintest expectation that it might lead a receiving country to change its policy. Such action by the Netherlands can be of any importance only if it takes place in conjunction and co-operation with other countries.

It is by no means true that there would be any information inadequacy through lack of overseas diplomatic representation. The Netherlands is represented in eighty-five states. Any news from or about the other states can be obtained through major international newspapers or from reports by Dutch diplomats in neighbouring countries. There is no reason to assume that

71

there would be any lack of information within the Ministry of Foreign Affairs on any part of the world.

Mr Luns's ability to survive internal political crises has become almost proverbial. This factor, combined with his tremendous popularity in the country, has made attacks on his foreign policies an almost hopeless affair. The customs that rule the formation of coalition cabinets in the Netherlands may help to explain the strength of Mr Luns's position. Cabinets since 1945 have usually included members of the two Protestant parties (ARP – Anti-Revolutionary Party and CHU – Christian Historical Union) and either the Liberals (VVD – People's Party for Freedom and Democracy) or the Socialists (PvdA – Labour Party); they *always* included members of the Catholic party (KVP – Catholic People's Party). It was usually for the leaders of the KVP to decide whether the predominant direction of the government's policies would be 'left' (with the PvdA) or 'right' (with the VVD). Mr Luns is a member of the Catholic People's Party. Since 1952, when he joined the Cabinet, the country has had coalitions with the PvdA or with the VVD, but they always included Mr Luns (see Tables 1 and 2).

On several occasions members of parliament have expressed their dissatisfaction with the kind of information they received and with the general way in which Mr Luns handled the foreign policy debates. Mr Luns has repeatedly claimed that he has

Table 1   *Party Affiliation of Ministers in Dutch Cabinets since 1952*

1952–56: KVP (6), PvdA (5), CHU (2), ARP (2)
1956–58: KVP (5), PvdA (5), CHU (1), ARP (2)
1958–59: KVP (6), ARP (2), CHU (1)
1959–63: KVP (6), VVD (3), ARP (2), CHU (2)
1963–65: KVP (6), VVD (3), ARP (2), CHU (2)
1965–66: KVP (6), PvdA (5), ARP (3),
1966–67: KVP (7), ARP (5)
1967–71: KVP (6), VVD (3), ARP (3), CHU (2)
1971–72: KVP (6), VVD (3), ARP (3), CHU (2), DS'70 (2)
KVP: Katholieke Volkspartij (Catholic People's Party)
PvdA: Partij van de Arbeid (Labour Party)
VVD: Volkspartij voor Vrijheid en Democratie (People's Party for Freedom and Democracy)
ARP: Antirevolutionaire Partij (Anti-Revolutionary Party)
CHU: Christelijk Historische Unie (Christian Historical Union)
DS'70: Democratische Socialisten '70 (Democratic Socialists '70)

Table 2 *List of Ministers and State Secretaries Charged with Foreign Affairs, with Party Affiliation, since 1952*

Period	Minister of Foreign Affairs	Minister without Portfolio charged with Foreign Affairs	State Secretary of Foreign Affairs
1952–56	J. W. Beyen (no party)	J. M. A. H. Luns (KVP)	—
1956–58	J. M. A. H. Luns (KVP)	—	E. H. van der Beugel (PvdA)
1958–59	J. M. A. H. Luns (KVP)	—	—
1959–63	J. M. A. H. Luns (KVP)	—	H. R. van Houten (no party affil.)
1963–65	J. M. A. H. Luns (KVP)	—	L. de Block (KVP) I. N. Th. Diepenhorst (CHU)
1965–66	J. M. A. H. Luns (KVP)	Th. H. Bot (KVP)	L. de Block (KVP) M. van der Stoel (PvdA)
1966–67	J. M. A. H. Luns (KVP)	Th. H. Bot (KVP)	L. de Block (KVP)
1967–71	J. M. A. H. Luns (KVP)	B. J. Udink (CHU)	H. J. de Koster (VVD)
1971–72	W. K. N. Schmelzer (KVP)	C. Boertien (ARP)	Th. Westerterp (KVP)

spent more time in parliamentary debates than any of his foreign colleagues. Yet many members of parliament complain that the information they receive is insufficient to control foreign policy. This type of complaint, which is heard every year, has resulted for instance in the request that the Minister of Foreign Affairs should report to the parliament on each major internal conference that he has attended and on each foreign country that he has visited.[26] This problem has never found a satisfactory solution. Moreover, on several occasions the chamber and the minister have clashed on substantive points of foreign policy. In 1967 the second chamber adopted a motion asking the government to convey to the American government its conviction that the bombardments of North Vietnam should be stopped without prior conditions. Mr Luns thereupon gave a speech in the United Nations in which he said that such was the view of the Netherlands *parliament*, but he very carefully left out the view of the Netherlands *Cabinet* in the matter. The issue of Portuguese treatment of its overseas African territories has also caused conflicts between a majority of the Dutch parliament and its Foreign Minister. However, in view of the strong political position of Mr Luns, mentioned before, there was never the slightest possibility that he would be forced to resign if he failed to carry out the parliament's wishes.

The Foreign Minister has further strengthened his position by appointing members of parliament to official delegations to international conferences and international organizations such as the United Nations. In contrast to the practice of governments like those of Britain and Canada, who appoint only members of their own party to such positions, Dutch delegations often include members of the opposition as well. These parliamentarians, who for the time being are given the same duties and responsibilities as the regular members of the diplomatic service, are then put in the strange position of having to carry out instructions from the Cabinet which at home they normally oppose. Although it may be understandable that the Foreign Minister employs this technique to bolster his position, it seems strange that members of the opposition allow themselves to be manipulated in this manner.[27]

Numerous pressure groups are active in the field of foreign affairs. These include both economic interest groups and goal organizations of a more or less idealistic nature. Among the interest groups are agricultural organizations, trade unions and employers' organizations, which concentrate their activities mainly on the European Communities.[28] The goal organizations include groups such as the European Movement and the Netherlands Society for International Affairs who count many members of the 'Establishment' in their ranks. They tend to support the government or at the most push it gently in the desired direction. On the other hand there is also the 'non-parliamentary opposition' which tends to concentrate on such issues as South Africa, the Portuguese colonies, Vietnam and the Middle East. Some of them are quite active in distributing documentary material and occasionally organizing demonstrations. However, so far they have not been very successful in changing the government's policies. Again the strength of the political position of Mr Luns – whom most of the latter groups have bitterly opposed – may serve as an explanation for the apparent failure of their activities.

External Limitations

It seems likely, though it is difficult to prove, that the alliance with the United States imposes rather severe limitations on the freedom of the Netherlands government to decide its own foreign policy. It has been alleged that it would have been much more open in its criticism of American policy in Vietnam or the Portuguese treatment of its African territories, had the United States and Portugal not been members of NATO. Even in the case of the Greek colonels' régime it is often assumed that stronger criticism would have been voiced, if there had not been fear of American disapproval. The Netherlands government limited itself to joining the Scandinavian complaint against the Greek régime at the European Human Rights Commission; a Dutch socialist member of parliament, Mr Max van der Stoel – a member of the opposition at the time – was active in demanding the expulsion of Greece from the Council of Europe in 1969.

The best-known case of United States pressure on the Netherlands has been its activities in 1961 with regard to West New Guinea (West Irian). Lijphart is quite explicit in this regard:

> ... pressure was put on the Dutch government by other countries, notably the United States. Under the prodding of the United States and with the mediation of American diplomat Ellsworth Bunker on behalf of the United Nations, Dutch-Indonesian negotiations took place near Washington in March and again in July 1962. The Bunker Plan, which was the basis for the Dutch Indonesian pact, was a product of the UN mediator and had the backing of the Kennedy Administration.[29]

It is hard to establish clear evidence of the application of pressure by the Americans on other aspects of Dutch foreign policy. It may well be that such pressure is hardly ever exercised in fact. Dutch foreign policy has very clearly been inspired by the wish not to antagonize the United States. Moreover, the American government may have found more subtle ways of expressing its wishes, without having to exercise crude forms of pressure.

In European affairs the Dutch government has moved very

carefully with regard to the German question. Although there seems to be a rather widespread desire within several political parties to 'normalize' relations with East Germany and officially to recognize the German Democratic Republic, the Dutch government has so far heeded the wishes of the West German government and refused to do so. The West German neighbour is clearly a powerful ally and trade partner, which should not be antagonized needlessly. This is the view which has also been shared by some of the opposition parties. Although the congress of the Dutch Labour Party had adopted a resolution favouring recognition of the G.D.R., socialist members of parliament refused to support a parliamentary motion with the same intention.

PRINCIPLES AND OBJECTIVES

A firm policy of anti-communism and of alliance with the Atlantic nations on the one hand, a strong commitment to European co-operation on the other hand – these have formed the foundations of the foreign policy of the Netherlands since the Second World War. The first of these two aspects of foreign policy has considerable military overtones and has found its expression in membership of such alliances as the Western European Union and the North Atlantic Treaty Organization. The second has found its expression through membership in the Council of Europe, the European Coal and Steel Community, Euratom and the European Economic Community.

Mr Luns has repeatedly expressed his firm support of Western policies, especially *vis-à-vis* the Soviet Union. In a government paper on NATO and defence policy, issued in 1968,[30] the Ministers of Foreign Affairs and of Defence stressed – as they had done before – the common historical, cultural and political ties of the North Atlantic nations. They stated their conviction that, in view of the policies of the Soviet Union, the course followed by the Western nations after the Second World War was the only available alternative:

> It would seem to be of little use – and it is certainly not the purpose of this discussion – to blame any one party [for the failure of East–West co-operation after the Second World War]. However, if one would try to do so, one should not only pay attention to the actual performance of the Soviet Union – so very much in conflict with Western expectations

and with everything that according to Western norms in the field of foreign policy is permitted and acceptable. One should also pay attention to the rashness with which people in the West put confidence in this ally, who as a powerful state had its own interests and was governed by a totalitarian régime, operating on the basis of a doctrine which justified co-operation with states of a different social structure only on opportunistic grounds.[31]

It was admitted in the paper that the Soviet Union had changed its tactics in the meantime, which had resulted in a lessening of tensions in the world. However, in the realm of European security the views of the Western governments and those of the Soviet Union remained far apart. The West could not tolerate an Eastern European supremacy in Europe, whereas a definitive settlement should not be reached without full recognition of the right of self-determination for the entire German nation. The paper then continued:

> In contrast with this, the policy of the Soviet Union continued to be directed in the first place toward a consolidation of the *status quo*, on the basis of which a settlement could be sought which in fact would change this *status quo* in favour of the Soviet Union, leaving Western Europe insufficiently protected against the superior forces of the Soviet Union.[32]

These and similar arguments, which were repeated in the explanatory memorandum to the budget for 1971,[33] led the authors of the paper to the necessary conclusion that the role of NATO should be strengthened both militarily and politically.

At various times the Netherlands government has expressed its confidence in NATO and in its American ally. It has apparently never felt that these Atlantic ties should or could interfere with its striving for European integration. In the government paper of 1968 explicit reference was made to the conception of the late President Kennedy, who viewed Western Europe and North America as fully equal and responsible partners in the world. The paper then continued as follows:

> In anticipation of the ultimate realization of a United Europe and an Atlantic Community, the Government considers it of the utmost importance that the co-operation within the Atlantic alliance should be maintained and made stronger.

77

In doing so full account should be taken of the demands that must be made and fulfilled – precisely in order to ensure the harmonious growth of relations within the alliance – with a view to the development of a greater European unity. On this basis only will it be possible that Atlantic co-operation will maintain its natural and healthy character.[34]

Whenever the Dutch government dealt in public with permanent aims and principles of foreign policy, it always emphasized these dual facets – European integration *and* Atlantic co-operation. Repeatedly, Mr Luns has denied that these two aims might conflict. His prolonged dispute with the French government of President de Gaulle was partly based on the conviction that the two would *not* conflict; that in fact European integration – a desirable aim in itself – could best be realized together with a strengthening of the Atlantic community. Nor has the Dutch government ever publicly shared the French doubts whether the United States would in the future always remain prepared to defend Western Europe. On the other hand, as Russell has pointed out, the Dutch attitude toward national nuclear forces other than those of the United States has been openly hostile. This is true of the French *force de frappe* as well as the British nuclear forces.[35]

Part of the argument for Mr Luns's continual championship of British entry into the European communities can be found in his wish to create a counterweight against French–German domination in Western Europe.[36] Moreover, there has always been a more widespread conviction in Dutch governmental and intellectual circles that the democratic nature of the European institution would be more assured with the British than without them. An additional factor has certainly been Mr Luns's often-expressed personal affection for the British people and the British way of life.[37] Finally, for some Protestant members of the government and the parliament – Mr Luns not being one of them – the idea of balancing the overwhelmingly Roman Catholic population of the European Communities has been an attractive one.

As compared to these two main principles – Atlantic co-operation and European integration – other objectives seem to have been of less importance. The Netherlands government has usually expressed full support for the aims and actions of the

United Nations. This is in accordance with the traditional concern of the Netherlands with the building of an international legal order. Some of its representatives and private citizens[38] have played and are playing an important role in the work of agencies of the United Nations. However, the Netherlands delegation to the UN carries the stigma of representing a NATO member and close ally of the United States, which limits its effectiveness among the majority of Asian and African states in the realm of political and security affairs. Moreover, the record of the Netherlands delegation on matters of colonialism and self-determination has been somewhat ambiguous. Although it did vote in support of the anti-colonialism resolution of 1960 (resolution 1514 (XV)) it often abstained on later resolutions on questions such as the situation in the Portuguese colonies, Rhodesia and South-West Africa. Dutch attitudes and policies towards its NATO partner Portugal have often come under attack, particularly from domestic critics. They feel that the Netherlands government, for military strategic reasons, is too soft in its criticism of both the colonial policies of Portugal and the internal political situation in that country.

Finally, a word should be said about the leading role of the Netherlands in the field of international development co-operation. The Netherlands government has been foremost in its efforts on behalf of extending social and economic support to developing countries. It has been very active in getting the Second Development Decade off the ground and, together with such countries as India and Yugoslavia, it has played a major role in the United Nations in this field. The Netherlands was one of the first countries to adopt 1 per cent of the GNP as the norm for annual expenditure in the field of development aid. Aid by the Netherlands in 1971 amounted to 970 million guilders, 34 per cent of which went to bilateral programmes, 16 per cent was supplied via international organizations and 22 per cent went to Surinam and the Netherlands Antilles. The main receiving countries of Netherlands' aid during the past decade have been India, Pakistan, Indonesia, Nigeria, Kenya, Tanzania, Uganda, Sudan, Tunisia, Peru, Colombia and Turkey. Despite the efforts made by the Netherlands government to strengthen the United Nations and to expand the development aid programmes, these policies have remained of secondary importance to those of Atlantic co-operation and European integration.

79

Military, Economic, Cultural and Diplomatic Ties
Whether one looks from the military, economic, cultural or diplomatic point of view, it is obvious that the closest ties of the Netherlands are with the countries of Western Europe. This is most obvious in the military field where the Netherlands is one of the founding members of NATO. NATO is mainly a military alliance but it is also used for purposes of political consultation and, to a limited extent, for cultural co-operation.

The Netherlands has permanent diplomatic representatives in eighty-five states and at six international organizations. Some of these diplomats are also accredited to the governments of other states where no permanent representatives are stationed. The number of diplomats which is posted in a particular country may serve as a rough indication of the importance the Netherlands government attaches to relations with that country. By far the largest number of Dutch diplomats is stationed in the United States; in addition to seventeen officers at the embassy in Washington D.C., diplomatic and consular officers are stationed in New York, Chicago, San Francisco, Los Angeles and Houston. Second in importance is the German Federal Republic; thirteen officers are stationed at the embassy in Bonn

Table 3   *Countries Where Ten or More Dutch*
Diplomats (Including Consular Officers) are
Posted 1971

Country	Number of Dutch Diplomats
United States of America	35
German Federal Republic	24
France	18
United Kingdom	16
Canada	15
Belgium	15
Indonesia	13
Italy	11
Australia	10
South Africa	10
Brazil	10

Source: *Rijksbegroting voor het Dienstjaar 1972*, hoofdstuk V, Buitenlandse Zaken, bijlage II betreffende de bezetting van de Buitenlandse Dienst ('National Budget 1972, chapter V, Foreign Affairs, appendix II concerning number of personnel of the Foreign Service') pp. 33–9.

and others at consular offices in Berlin, Düsseldorf, Frankfurt, Hamburg, Stuttgart, Munich, and Kleve. The other countries where ten or more Dutch diplomatic and consular officers are stationed are France, United Kingdom, Canada, Belgium, Indonesia, Italy, Australia, South Africa and Brazil (see Table 3). Apart from the serving of political and commercial interests, immigration is an important factor in determining the size of foreign missions, as in the case of the United States, Canada, Australia and South Africa. Of course the fact should be taken into account that in larger countries a larger diplomatic staff can be expected. Thus the fifteen representatives in Belgium may be considered as much more significant than the sixteen in the United Kingdom. A system to weight these factors would be needed for purposes of refinement. The Netherlands maintains a diplomatic post in almost all old-established nations. This becomes evident if one looks at the list of member states of the United Nations where *no* Dutch diplomatic representatives are stationed (Table 4).

Table 4 *List of UN Member-States Where no Dutch*
Diplomatic Representatives or Consular
Officers are Stationed 1971

Western Europe	Cyprus, Iceland, Malta
Eastern Europe	Albania
America	Barbados, El Salvador, Haiti, Honduras, Nicaragua, Panama, Paraguay
Africa	Botswana, Burundi, Central African Republic, Chad, Congo (Brazzaville), Dahomey, Equatorial Guinea, Gabon, Gambia, Guinea, Lesotho, Madagascar, Malawi, Mali, Mauritania, Mauritius, Niger, Rwanda, Sierra Leone, Somalia, Swaziland, Togo, Uganda, Upper Volta
Asia	Afghanistan, Bahrain, Bhutan, Burma, Cambodia, China (Taiwan), Jordan, Laos, Maldive Islands, Mongolia, Nepal, Qatar, Southern Yemen, Yemen

It appears that especially the French-speaking African states receive a smaller share of Dutch diplomatic representatives than the other states. Apart from the North African countries, the Ivory Coast and Cameroon are the only French-speaking African states where Dutch diplomats are stationed. This is caused by the relative lack of importance of most of the former

French colonies for the Netherlands. Also in the cultural field ties with Western European nations predominate. In 1971 the Netherlands had cultural agreements with twenty-two nations. Nine of these were members of NATO (Belgium, Luxembourg, France, the German Federal Republic, the United Kingdom, Italy, Norway, Greece and Turkey); South Africa was another Western country with which a cultural agreement existed. Furthermore, there were cultural agreements with three Latin American countries (Brazil, Colombia and Mexico), with five Eastern European countries (the Soviet Union, Yugoslavia, Rumania, Hungary and Poland) and with four Afro-Asian nations (Indonesia, Iran, Tunisia and the United Arab Republic).[39] The principal trading partners of the Netherlands, as shown in Table 5, are mainly Western European states. Imports as well as exports are dominated by West Germany and the Belgian-Luxembourg economic union. In 1970 27·1 per cent of all imports came from West Germany, 16·9 per cent came from Belgium and Luxembourg, 9·8 per cent from the United States, 7·5 per cent from France and 5·7 per cent from United Kingdom. Among the top ten states from which the Netherlands receives its imports, there are furthermore, next to Italy and Sweden, three oil exporting states: Kuwait, Libya and Saudi Arabia.

Table 5 *Main Trading Partners of the Netherlands 1970 (Value in Millions of Guilders)*

Exports		Imports	
1. German Federal Republic	13,894	1. German Federal Republic	13,155
2. Belgium-Luxembourg	5,943	2. Belgium-Luxembourg	8,186
3. France	4,247	3. United States	4,736
4. United Kingdom	2,979	4. France	3,641
5. Italy	2,305	5. United Kingdom	2,766
6. United States	1,832	6. Italy	2,105
7. Sweden	1,061	7. Sweden	1,087
8. Switzerland	829	8. Kuwait	841
9. Denmark	605	9. Libya	778
10. Spain	453	10. Saudi Arabia	739

Source: Centraal Bureau voor de Statistiek, *Maandstatistiek voor de Buitenlandse Handel per goederensoort, aanvullende gegevens over December 1970* ('Monthly statistics of Foreign Trade by Commodities, supplementary data for December, 1970').

Of the ten principal import partners seven are also among the ten most important export partners of the Netherlands. In 1970 32·6 per cent of all Dutch exports went to West Germany, 14·0 per cent went to Belgium and Luxembourg, 10·0 per cent to France, 7·0 per cent to United Kingdom and 5·4 per cent to Italy.

The principal export commodities of the Netherlands were in 1970: metal wares (30·3 per cent), food and table luxuries (17·9 per cent), chemical goods excluding oil (15·5 per cent), raw agricultural products (8·6 per cent), oil products (7·4 per cent) and textiles, clothes and shoes (6·9 per cent). If one looks at the trade between the Netherlands and the main regions of the world over the last decade (Table 6), one finds a constant increase of the percentage of trade with the countries of the European Economic Communities and a corresponding decrease of the percentage of trade with the countries of EFTA. Exports to

Table 6   *Trade Between the Netherlands and Regions of the World 1960–70*

Percentage of Total Imports

Area	1960	1961	1962	1963	1964	1965	1966	1967	1968	1969	1970
EFTA	23·7	22·8	23·0	20·9	19·4	19·0	18·2	18·1	17·1	16·1	14·8
EEC	45·9	47·6	49·2	53·3	55·7	55·7	55·5	54·9	57·4	60·1	61·5
COMECON	1·3	1·5	1·3	1·1	1·0	1·2	1·2	2·0	1·5	2·1	1·8
U.S./Canada	5·7	5·2	5·1	4·7	4·5	4·7	5·3	5·4	5·9	5·2	4·8
Middle East/ Africa	5·6	4·9	4·7	4·1	3·9	3·9	3·9	3·7	3·4	3·7	3·3
Asia	3·7	3·9	3·4	3·5	3·3	3·3	3·3	3·4	2·9	2·3	2·1
Other Countries	14·1	14·1	13·3	12·4	12·2	12·2	12·6	12·5	11·8	10·5	11·7

Percentage of Total Exports

Area	1960	1961	1962	1963	1964	1965	1966	1967	1968	1969	1970
EFTA	14·0	14·4	14·4	13·9	13·7	13·2	12·6	11·6	11·4	11·5	11·2
EEC	45·8	49·2	50·2	51·6	52·0	53·4	54·0	54·5	55·4	56·5	55·9
COMECON	1·2	1·7	1·6	1·8	1·5	1·7	1·7	1·7	1·8	2·0	1·6
U.S./Canada	14·0	11·7	12·0	11·6	11·7	11·1	12·3	11·4	11·7	11·0	11·1
Middle East/ Africa	9·3	9·4	9·2	8·8	8·2	7·6	7·5	7·6	8·5	9·0	10·1
Asia	3·5	2·6	2·0	1·9	2·8	2·9	3·5	3·6	3·0	2·7	2·6
Other Countries	12·2	11·0	10·6	10·4	10·1	10·1	8·4	9·6	8·2	7·3	7·5

Sources: *United Nations Year Book of International Trade Statistics;* Centraal Bureau voor de Statistiek, *Maandstatistiek van de Buitenlandse Handel per Goederensoort, aanvullende gegevens over December 1970* ('Monthly Statistics of Foreign Trade by Commodities, supplementary data for December 1970').

North America, the Middle East and Africa, Asia and other regions decreased percentage-wise, while exports to the Soviet Union and Eastern Europe remained at the same relatively low level (between 1 and 2 per cent). Imports from North America, Asia and other regions decreased somewhat percentage-wise, while those from Eastern Europe, the Middle East and Africa remained at about the same level.

It would be hard to say whether economic or cultural relations predominate in the external relations of the Netherlands. Analysis of cultural and economic data would seem to indicate a somewhat greater emphasis on trade agreements than on cultural agreements (30 *v.* 22). This is even more so as trade relations with many additional countries are developed on the basis of a most favoured nation clause, membership of GATT, or membership of or association with the European Communities. On the other hand, the absence of a cultural agreement may not preclude strong cultural relations with other countries. The strong cultural ties between the Netherlands and the United States through the exchange of Fulbright scholars and television programmes may serve as an example.

An Empirical Illustration: Dutch Opposition to the French Plans for Political Union in Europe
An illustration of to what extent a small country can pursue an active foreign policy and, in this particular case, thwart the plans of a more powerful state, is offered by Dutch opposition to President de Gaulle's plans for an intergovernmental political union of the six members of the EEC.[40]

The establishment of the so-called Fouchet Committee, which was to study the problems of European political co-operation, was in itself the result of a conflict between France and the Netherlands. At the Paris conference of February 1961 President de Gaulle had proposed a system of regular political consultations between the governments of the six members of the EEC. This plan was not adopted mainly on account of Dutch fears that it would lead to a weakening of the already existing European Communities and that it would tend to widen the rift with the United Kingdom. Instead, the Fouchet Committee was established. In this committee the Dutch representative offered several suggestions to make the proposed consultations occasional rather than regular and to exclude all defence matters, as belonging properly to a field in which NATO was competent. Despite the hesitations of the Dutch, it was decided at the Bonn conference of European government leaders in July 1961 to have consultation meetings at regular intervals and to let the Fouchet Committee draw up proposals institutionalizing the meetings of the Six. This resulted in the first Fouchet plan of October 1961 in which a 'Union of States' was proposed whose main feature would be a council of heads of governments, whose unanimous decisions would be binding on the member states; a European Political Commission consisting of senior officials of the foreign affairs department of each state would be seated in Paris. Objections to this plan focused on the lack of an explicit guarantee to Community institutions and an Atlantic orientation, the weakness of the powers of the European Parliament and the vagueness of the review clause.[41]

The Netherlands was strongly opposed to this proposal, as it feared that this institutionalization would give the 'Union of States' a degree of permanency which, in view of the absence of the United Kingdom, it considered undesirable: the wrong kind of political union was considered worse than no union at all.[42] The Netherlands gradually acquired allies in its opposition to President de Gaulle's plans: Belgium refused to agree to this unless first the problem of British entry to the Common Market had been solved. The German Federal Republic and Italy became more hesitant when a second Fouchet plan was laid before them in January 1962 in which explicit powers were given to the new authority in the field of foreign policy, cultural affairs, defence and economics, thus calling into question the competence both of NATO and of the EEC. Although Italy suggested some alternatives by which NATO and the EEC would be better protected, the second Fouchet plan was not adopted, as no sufficient guarantees could be given to the Netherlands and Belgium about the position of the United Kingdom. Thus the meeting of the foreign ministers of the EEC of 17 April 1962 failed to adopt the French proposals. This negative result can be considered as a success for the Dutch who had never liked the idea of having intergovernmental political consultations by the Six next to the supra-national Communities. Since then the Dutch remained steadfastly opposed to a resumption of the talks about political union without the participation of Britain. While the other EEC members were not over-enthusiastic about

85

the French plans, Bodenheimer makes it quite clear that it was mainly due to Dutch opposition that these plans were never realized.

There was a curious apparent paradox in the Dutch position. While they insisted on keeping the supranational character of the Communities, they made the entry of Britain – not known as a strong advocate of supranationality – into a condition for further talks about political union. In view of the great importance attached to British entry, Bodenheimer's conclusion seems valid that '. . . the "cornerstone" of Dutch policy would have been more accurately phrased as "British participation or *no* institutions of political union".'[43]

In looking for an explanation for the basically negative Dutch attitude to the French proposals, Bodenheimer argues convincingly that Dutch policy was governed mainly by considerations of national security, which, it was felt, would be best guaranteed by preservation of the Atlantic alliance under the military and political leadership of the United States. The French plans for an intergovernmental political union were intended as a challenge to American leadership, which would inevitably lead to conflicts with the United States. While not in principle opposed to French leadership, the Netherlands felt that France lacked the necessary military power to guarantee European security. Only the United States was considered powerful enough to perform this function. Insisting on British participation thus helped to prevent the realization of de Gaulle's plans, while in a more positive way British participation was also seen as a guarantee for a continued interest of the United States in European security.[44]

The successful opposition by the Dutch to the French plans was made possible thanks to tacit support from the United States and the fact that some of the other European governments privately agreed with the Dutch arguments. The example may indicate, albeit in a rather negative way, the possibilities for a small country in the right circumstances to pursue a relatively independent foreign policy.

CONCLUSION

The foreign policy of the Netherlands since the Second World War has been characterized by a close alliance with the United

States. This alliance has strongly influenced all aspects of its foreign policy – even those that had no direct relationship to the Cold War. Long-serving Foreign Minister Luns has become the symbol of this pro-American foreign policy. As foreign policy has not been a factor of controversy among the major political parties, it seems unlikely that Mr Luns's departure will cause major changes in the foreign policy orientation of the Netherlands.

NOTES AND REFERENCES

Those interested in making an exhaustive study of Dutch foreign policy are strongly advised to begin by acquiring a reading acquaintance of the Dutch language. This would give access to the public documents published by the Ministry of Foreign Affairs and the proceedings of the parliamentary debates, which are indispensable sources for such a study.

Below, the principal studies in English as well as in Dutch are listed dealing with the foreign policy of the Netherlands.

There does not exist a recent elaborate study dealing with Dutch foreign policy problems. Foreign as well as Dutch readers are referred to Amry Vandenbosch, *Dutch Foreign Policy since 1815: A Study in Small Power Politics* (Martinus Nijhoff, The Hague, 1959); this study is, however, rapidly becoming outdated. Students interested in the role of the Netherlands within the Atlantic community should read E. H. van der Beugel, *Nederland in de Westelijke Samenwerking: Enkele Aspecten van de Nederlandse Beleidsvorming* ('The Netherlands in Western Co-operation: Some Aspects of Netherlands Foreign Policy Making') (E. J. Brill, Leyden, 1966), and S. I. P. van Campen, *The Quest for Security: Some Aspects of Netherlands Foreign Policy, 1945–1950* (Martinus Nijhoff, The Hague, 1957). More recent is the excellent article by Robert W. Russell, 'The Atlantic Alliance in Dutch Foreign Policy', *Internationale Spectator*, vol. 23, no. 13 (8 July 1969) pp. 1189–1208. The best book in English dealing with the political role of the Netherlands within the European Communities is Susanne J. Bodenheimer's *Political Union: A Microcosm of European Politics* (A. W. Sijthoff, Leyden, 1967). Samkalden's article deals with both the Atlantic and the European aspects of Dutch foreign policy: I. Samkalden, 'A Dutch Retrospective View of European and Atlantic Co-operation', *Internationale Spectator*, vol. 19, no. 7 (1965) pp. 626–42.

Excellent accounts in English of Dutch-Indonesian relations are found in Arend Lijphart's *The Trauma of Decolonization: The Dutch and West New Guinea* (Yale University Press, New Haven and London, 1966) and L. H. Palmier's, *Indonesia and the Dutch* (Oxford University Press, London, 1962). The role of the Netherlands in the United Nations is dealt with in P. R. Baehr's *The Role of a National Delegation in the General Assembly* (Carnegie Endowment for International Peace, New York, 1970).

Discussions of the principles governing the foreign policy of the Netherlands are found in A. L. Constandse, J. L. Heldring and Paul van 't Veer, *Gelijk Hebben en Krijgen: Commentaren op Nederlandse Buitenlandse Politiek* ('To Be Right and to Be Accepted as Right: Comments on Netherlands Foreign Policy') (De Bezige Bij, Amsterdam, 1962); J. C. Boogman and others, *Nederland, Europa en de Wereld: Ons Buitenlands Beleid in Discussie* ('The Netherlands, Europe and the World: Our Foreign Policy in Discussion') (J. A. Boom en Zoon, Meppel, 1970); L. G. M. Jaquet and others, *Nederlandse Buitenlandse Politiek: Aspecten and Achtergronden* ('Netherlands Foreign Policy; Aspects and Backgrounds') (Nederlands Genootschap voor Internationale Zaken, The Hague, 1970); L. G. M. Jaquet, 'The Role of a Small State within Atlantic Systems', in August Schou and Arne Olav Brundtland (eds), *Small States in International Relations* (Almquist and Wiksell, Wiley Interscience Division, Stockholm, 1971) pp. 57–70.

More specialized studies are: J. H. Leurdijk, 'Nuclear Weapons in Dutch Foreign Policy' – a paper prepared for the conference on the role of nuclear weapons in the politics and defence planning of non-nuclear weapon states, organized by the Norwegian Institute of International Affairs, March 1971; H. F. van Panhuys, 'The Netherlands Constitution and International Law: A Decade of Experience', *The American Journal of International Law*, vol. 58 (1964) pp. 88–108; Alan D. Robinson, *Dutch Organised Agriculture in International Politics, 1945–1960* (Martinus Nijhoff, The Hague, 1961).

An excellent bibliographical article in Dutch is G. van Roon's 'Europa en de Wereld: Ons Buitenlands Beleid in Discussie' ('The Netherlands, Europe and the World: Our Foreign Policy in Discussion'), *Antirevolutionaire Staatkunde*, vol. 41, no. 2 (February, 1971) pp. 70–93.

1. Susanne J. Bodenheimer, *Political Union: A Microcosm of European Politics 1960–1966* (A. W. Sijthoff, Leyden, 1967) p. 166.
2. *Netherlands Constitution*, article 58.
3. Quoted by J. L. Heldring, 'De Invloed van de Openbare Mening op het Buitenlands Beleid' ('The Influence of Public Opinion on Foreign Policy'), *Internationale Spectator*, vol. 24, no. 1 (8 January 1970) p. 25.
4. Amry Vandenbosch, *Dutch Foreign Policy since 1815: A Study in Small Power Politics* (Martinus Nijhoff, The Hague, 1959) p. 4.
5. J. C. Boogman and others, *Europa en de Wereld: Ons Buitenlands Beleid in Discussie* ('Europe and the World: Our Foreign Policy in Discussion') (J. A. Boom & Zoon, Meppel, 1970) p. 16.
6. See S. I. P. van Campen, *The Quest for Security: Some Aspects of Netherlands Foreign Policy 1945–1950* (Martinus Nijhoff, The Hague, 1957) pp. 30 ff.
7. In 1968 the Second Chamber of parliament rejected a motion of the pacifist-socialists by 121 votes to 5, in which the government was asked to leave NATO (*Proceedings of the Second Chamber*, 21 November 1968, p. 642).
8. Heldring, op. cit., pp. 28–9.
9. Cf. Robert W. Russell, 'The Atlantic Alliance in Dutch Foreign

Policy', *Internationale Spectator*, vol. 23, no 13 (8 July 1969) p. 1208:

If the Dutch become sufficiently frustrated with the immorality of international politics, and sufficiently enamoured with the pursuit of utopian causes (like peace?), the Netherlands might pursue a pseudo-foreign policy based upon solemn exhortations to the rest of the world to save itself. The Netherlands would leave security matters to the rest of the world, trust in the Common Market for its economic welfare, and conduct a foreign policy based upon the distribution of foreign aid to the needy of the world. In short the Netherlands might engage in futile exercises in international morality in place of a responsible foreign policy.

10. *Proceedings of the Second Chamber of parliament*, 32nd meeting, 10 December 1970, p. 1741; translated from the original Dutch, italics added.
11. *Netherlands Constitution*, article 58.
12. *Netherlands Constitution*, article 55.
13. *Rules of Procedure of the Council of Ministers*, articles 2b, c and d.
14. *Netherlands Constitution*, article 59.
15. Article 61 of the Constitution reads as follows:

Approval is given either expressly or tacitly.
Express approval shall be regarded as having been given, unless, within thirty days after the submission of the agreement, a statement has been made by or on behalf of either of the Chambers of the States-General or by at least one fifth of the constitutional membership of either of the Chambers expressing the wish that the agreement shall be submitted to the decision of the States-General. The period referred to in the previous paragraph shall be suspended for the time of adjournment of the States-General.

16. *Netherlands Constitution*, article 63.
17. *Netherlands Constitution*, articles 65 and 66; see H. F. van Panhuys, 'The Netherlands Constitution and International Law: A Decade of Experience', *The American Journal of International Law*, vol. 58 (1964) pp. 100–6.
18. For relevant accounts in English of the Dutch political system, see Hans Daalder, 'Parties and Politics in the Netherlands', *Political Studies*, vol. 3 (1965) pp. 1–16; Arend Lijphart, *The Politics of Accommodation: Pluralism and Democracy in the Netherlands* (California University Press, Berkeley, 1968); P. R. Baehr, 'The Netherlands' in Stanley Henig and John Pinder (eds), *European Political Parties* (Allen & Unwin, London, 1969) pp. 256–81.
19. Real strength of personnel on 30 June 1970. Of these persons, 1,062 were civil service officers within the department, while 1,921 persons were foreign service officers or lower administrative personnel abroad. See *Rijksbegroting voor het Dienstjaar 1971*, hoofdstuk V, Buitenlandse Zaken ('National Budget 1971, chapter V, Foreign Affairs') appendix III, p. 52.
20. Significantly, the diplomatic service people use the verb 'to parachute' to indicate the rare member of the domestic ministerial staff who

succeeds in obtaining a temporary position abroad, instead of working himself up through the ranks of the foreign service.

21. Cf. H. N. Boon and C. J. Schneider, 'Binnendienst en Buitendienst' ('Inner Service and Outer Service'), *Internationale Spectator*, vol. 24, no. 17 (October, 1970) pp. 1553–65. They conclude that in this respect the situation in the Netherlands principally and practically differs from that in *all* other Western powers (p. 1561). See further 'Insider', 'Uitvoering en Democratisering van het Buitenlandse Beleid' ('Executing and Democratization of Foreign Policy'), *Internationale Spectator*, vol. 24, no. 9 (8 May 1970) p. 859.

22. In a parliamentary debate Mr Luns promised, however, that he would 'study' the problem; he stated that he had no firm convictions in the matter which he would keep forever (*Proceedings of the Second Chamber of Parliament*, 32nd meeting, 10 December 1970, p. 1735).

23. A similar allegation has been made with regard to the Netherlands delegation to the first UNCTAD conference in 1964; cf. E. H. van der Beugel, *Nederland in de Westelijke Samenwerking: Enkele Aspecten van de Nederlandse Beleidsvorming* ('The Netherlands in Western Co-operation: Some Aspects of the Formation of Netherlands Policy') (E. J. Brill, Leyden, 1966) pp. 23–4; the same author, 'Vaststellen en Uitvoeren van Buitenlandse Politiek: Verhouding Buitenlandse Zaken-Vakministeries' ('Determination and Execution of Foreign Policy: The Relationship between Foreign Affairs and the Specialized Ministeries'), *Internationale Spectator*, vol. 24, no. 1 (8 January 1970) pp. 67–75.

24. Van der Beugel, *Nederland in de Westelijke Samenwerking*, p. 18.

25. *Proceedings of the Second Chamber of Parliament*, 21st meeting, 9 December 1970, p. 1658; translated from the original Dutch.

26. See, for instance, *Proceedings of the Budgetary Committee for Foreign Affairs of the Second Chamber of Parliament*, 1st meeting, 1 December 1965, pp. C 602–8.

27. See Peter R. Baehr, *The Role of a National Delegation in the General Assembly* (Carnegie Endowment for International Peace, New York, 1970) pp. 79–90.

28. See, for instance, Alan D. Robinson, *Dutch Organised Agriculture in International Politics, 1945–1960* (Martinus Nijhoff, The Hague, 1961).

29. Arend Lijphart, *The Trauma of Decolonization: The Dutch and West New Guinea* (Yale University Press, New Haven and London, 1966) p. 278.

Mr Luns said repeatedly that he held Robert Kennedy responsible for what he considered a turnabout in United States foreign policy with regard to West New Guinea. In an interview, Mr Luns stated, for instance, the following:

I have always had the feeling that if he [President John Kennedy] had not been so much under the influence of his brother Robert, his policies would have been better. Also with regard to the Netherlands. The president has turned around in the question of New

Guinea at the advice of his brother. Robert Kennedy has been three or four days in Indonesia during the period of conflict. He became so much impressed by Mr. Sukarno's charm that after his return he was firmly convinced that Indonesia would immediately become an ally of the United States, if only New Guinea was turned over to Sukarno. Obviously, as happened to so many others, he has been deceived by Sukarno. Moreover, he assumed that he could do anything to the Netherlands without us protesting or drawing the consequences from it. He was right in that assumption, by the way.

Han J. A. Hansen (ed.), *Luns, Drees, De Quay, Marijnen, Cals over Luns* (Paul Brand, Hilversum/Maaseik, 1967) pp. 44–5; see also p. 51. Translated from the original Dutch.

30. *Nota inzake het NAVO- en Defensiebeleid 1968* ('Memorandum concerning NATO- and Defence Policy 1968'), *Proceedings of the Second Chamber of Parliament*, 1967–68, No. 9635.
31. ibid., p. 12; translated from the original Dutch.
32. ibid., pp. 20–1; translated from the original Dutch.
33. *Rijksbegroting voor het Dienstjaar 1971*, hoofdstuk V, Buitenlandse Zaken, Memorie van Toelichting ('National Budget 1971, chapter V, Foreign Affairs, Explanatory Memorandum') p. 8.
34. *Nota inzake het NAVO- en Defensiebeleid 1968*, p. 31; translated from the original Dutch.
35. Russell, op. cit., pp. 1191–2.
36. See Bodenheimer, op. cit., pp. 158–9.
37. See, for a somewhat different view, Bodenheimer, op. cit., p. 160 (note), who reports Luns stating in an interview that he had a personal propensity toward *France*. She adds: 'In Luns' mind, this did not by any means mitigate the *political* differences between the two countries.'
38. Former delegates such as Van Kleffens and Schürmann; private citizens such as Van Pelt (UN representative in Libya), the late Van Heuven Goedhart (High Commissioner for Refugees), Tammes (member of the International Law Commission), Boerma (Director-General of FAO) and Tinbergen (in an advisory capacity on problems of development aid).
39. *Jaarboek van het Ministerie van Buitenlandse Zaken 1970–1971* ('Yearbook of the Ministry of Foreign Affairs 1970–1971') (Staatsuitgeverij, The Hague, 1971) pp. 143–5.
40. These plans have been extensively described and analysed by Susanne J. Bodenheimer in her study, *Political Union: A Microcosm of European Politics 1960–1966* (A. W. Sijthoff, Leyden, 1967): this section relies strongly on the results of that study.
41. ibid., p. 60.
42. ibid., p. 89.
43. ibid., p. 158.
44. ibid., pp. 157–68 *passim*.

Chapter 3

THE FOREIGN POLICY OF SWITZERLAND

JACQUES FREYMOND

THE SMALL STATE AND THE INTERNATIONAL SYSTEM

The definition of a small state, the kind of state whose very existence and viability were called in question in the aftermath of the Second World War, is now being considered afresh. At that time only the super powers, the colossi of the world, counted; for their possession of atomic weapons was going to give them the power of life and death over all the other nations of the world. We were living, or so we were assured, and would go on living for a long time, in a bipolar international system whose transformation could be brought about only through the formation of major economic blocs. The trend at that time – as now – favoured the concentration of means and of power. As they became industrialized, the political societies of the world were expected in the natural course of events to bring down their frontiers and thereby destroy the nation-state.

Little attention was therefore paid to the vitality of certain small states, and the persistence of particularist groups. We underestimated not so much the extent as the authenticity of a centrifugal tendency which nevertheless represented the irrepressible ambition of individuals and ethnic groups to secure recognition of their own individuality – itself a condition of freedom. The process of modernization which we see taking place, at varying rates, throughout the world, in fact affects only the surface, changing the colour but less frequently the structure of

Author's note: I wish to express my gratitude to Mr Thierry Hentsch for his assistance in the preparation of the bibliography, and to Mrs Nadine Andréas-Galvani, Secretary. The English translation was by Mrs Anne Napthine.

political institutions, for, as we know, the choice of forms of government is limited. The transformation, basically technical in nature, affects the mechanisms, the ways in which trade is carried out, and the methods of production; it has sometimes brought about a change in production, and thus in social relations. But to what extent has it altered behaviour? To what extent can the most revolutionary scientific advances, those concerning communications, which, in the hands of biologists and psychologists, could lead to a genuine manipulation of mankind, result in a new social and political science, and in the development of new criteria by which the conduct and organization of political entities can be judged? It can only be said that, when faced with this kind of projection into a future dominated by technical requirements and by technocrats, men at present react with rejection or indifference. The open resistance, the neo-romantic escapism and rejection of social constraints of minority groups, and particularly the young, exist alongside the contrasting silence of the majority who allow technical progress to pass over them – making use of it meanwhile.

Hence the surprised reaction of our technocrats to the apparently 'primitivist' nature of the youth revolt, the proliferation of 'anomalies' such as nationalism and regionalism, the persistence of ethnocentric reactions, and the absurdity of the mini-state. And indeed who can say, nowadays, who is really moving, or living, against the stream?

The small state continues to exist. Perhaps it even has a future. But what *is* a small state? When does it begin to exist as a state? From what size? And when does it cease to be 'small'? This goes back beyond criteria of sovereignty on which we shall not dwell here, to an old and insoluble problem, the measurement of power. At the Congress of Vienna, the task of the Statistics Commission was to assess the relative values of the territories which were to be redistributed as one of the primary objectives of the coalition powers. The area and number of inhabitants were taken into account, together with the geographical situation and certain natural resources. A somewhat primitive procedure. The inability to evaluate the ingenuity of men and the long-term effects of their activities opened the way to surprise developments, particularly those produced when the industrial revolution opened the way to the exploitation of a subsoil as yet unexplored at the beginning of the century.

Statistics today, as then, offer little help. The area of land, the number of inhabitants, the population density, the economic potential, the military apparatus, fail to provide, either separately or together, criteria for a classification of states in order of magnitude: large – medium – small. It is sufficient to consider the changes which have taken place in the international system since 1945, and to examine, carefully if not necessarily systematically, the combinations of factors conditioning the power relationships of China and Japan, the U.S. and the Soviet Union, to realize that in a dynamic system the power of a state, and hence its political dimension – by which we mean its capacity for independence and its potential influence – can be measured only in terms of relations with other states, whatever their size. The relations between states are governed as much by motion, or its resultant energy – in other words the 'dynamism' of any political society, which is a product of its vitality, cohesion, ingenuity, intellectual qualities and adaptability – as by physical size.

This is no doubt valid for relations in time of peace, even as quarrelsome a peace as that we are now experiencing. As soon as we come to military confrontation, a large state has the means to impose its will and create a hierarchy. That is, to the extent that it dares to go as far as war, and, in war, to use all its available resources. But the most recent disputes opposing states of unequal power have not benefited the party which appeared to be militarily superior; Algeria held out against France, and the Democratic Republic of Vietnam against the United States. This is not just because the people of Algeria or Vietnam were not fighting alone, and because their military activities took place within a system of forces which France and the United States had to take into account, but also because they had the will to survive, an energy which increased their striking capacity and thus their relative power. The world has taken in the implications of these two examples and the case of Czechoslovakia cannot be cited as a counter-argument. Now, as before, a large state commands respect or fear. The existence of a hierarchy of powers is acknowledged, and is, moreover, manifest, in institutional terms, in the composition of the Security Council and the retention of the veto. But we are just as aware today as in past centuries – and this represents an evolution in thinking since 1945 – that the great powers have no wider freedom of action than the small states. In our period of concentration of resources and of means of production, in which the gap between developed and under-developed nations is said to be constantly widening, and science and technology frequently refer to an irretrievable time-lag, the great powers have no decisive authority.

PERMANENT OBJECTIVES[1]

So Switzerland is not the anachronism she was thought to be just after the Second World War. She is no longer an isolated small state, symbol of a disappearing world and way of life, amid the growth of empires. She is one of many small states of unequal size which are today scattered over the surface of the globe and play, with varying degrees of success, a more or less active, positive role in the international system, which is roughly based on three levels of decision: those of the great powers, the regions, and the individual states.

The changes which have taken place in two world wars, the removal from Europe of the 'centre of gravity' of the decision-making process, have not fundamentally altered the basis of her external policy. Situated in the heart of Europe, outside the path of the major migrations and, equally important, off the main strategic routes, moderately, or even poorly, equipped with natural resources, a multilingual community of 6 million people can survive only by its cohesion, its capacity for work, its inquiring spirit (a condition of adaptability to change), and above all by the daily reiteration of its intention to continue life in common. Switzerland is the product of a marriage of reason, constantly called in question by the lure of the outside world, the desire to escape, the cultural attraction of neighbouring communities and irritation over the many trivial concessions imposed by the maintenance of links forged in the past.

And yet this past is still very much present. A striking feature of Switzerland, despite the speed of modernization, is its historical continuity. The fundamental facts have hardly changed. Inadequate natural resources resulted in an opening to the outside world; by intensifying trade, a vital condition for the development of an industry in line with the limited resources of the country, a suitable standard of living can be provided for an over-numerous population which, in earlier times, had to emigrate or seek work abroad on a temporary basis. The heritage of three of the dominant cultures of Western Europe involves permanent discussion, constant mediation to quell heady and dangerous tensions, and also participation in the intellectual and cultural life of neighbouring countries. Possibly it is at this level that the opposing centrifugal and centripetal trends are most apparent, and the vulnerability of this confederation of cantons at its greatest: for despite their gradual relinquishment of sovereignty the cantons still consider themselves as 'states' based on political communities, aware of their own personality and their mission as preservers of tradition.

Neutrality, another constant factor in Swiss policy, can be explained only by the need to ensure that no commitment abroad should divide the Swiss and upset the internal balance. Today, as in the sixteenth century, the maintenance of the status of neutrality is in the interest of the Swiss, before any consideration of conformity with the interests of Europe. Just as federalism – i.e. a policy basing its unity on the recognition of diversity – is an essential counterweight to the perversion of democracy by totalitarianism, so does neutrality make it possible to temper the missionary spirit which sometimes offers a tempting remedy to the frustrations of being small.

Strategically, the facts are likewise unchanged. Switzerland is now, as in the past, enclosed in Europe, with no access to the sea, committed, by her determination to remain neutral and to meet, in this respect, her obligations to other states, to rely first and foremost on her own forces for her defence. This does not mean merely training and equipping an army, but ensuring that it, and indeed the rest of the population, is supplied. In the event of a European war Switzerland is caught in a trap, and the last two wars have provided harsh proof of the need for economic as well as military preparedness. This is a task of a size which may seem beyond the means of a small state, and doubt has sometimes been cast on Switzerland's ability, if not her determination, to maintain her policy of neutrality, in view of the sacrifices it involves, which increase with the improving standard of living of the Swiss people. The development of atomic weapons has also induced pessimism: why bother to resist? War is now unthinkable, and thus impossible.[2]

Nevertheless, the unthinkable has had to be thought about, and this lengthy consideration, doomed to continue interminably, has not called in question the basis of Swiss strategy. As long as the nuclear threshold is not crossed, a war in Europe would involve Switzerland, even if not directly concerned, in total mobilization of her resources, and mobilization in turn would involve every individual in tasks varying not only in terms of his capacities or potential, but even more in terms of the country's need. The inadequacy of Switzerland's resources, the small size of her territory, the nature of modern war, demand total mobilization, which itself is made possible only by the prior organization of a total national defence. It is along these lines that surveys have been conducted,[3] decisions adopted, and measures taken. To the threat of possible war, Switzerland has not replied by abandoning her neutral status, or by any relaxation of her policy of neutrality. She has not considered any alliances which would enable her to renounce an overall strategy, cover her supplies or finance the modernization of her equipment and her arms. She has intensified her efforts and increased, as far as possible, the 'density' of mobilization, an action not without effect on the daily life of the Swiss, or on the external economic policy, particularly the agricultural policy, of the Swiss Confederation.

FORMULATION AND CONDUCT OF FOREIGN POLICY

Switzerland's political continuity is reflected in the conduct of the Swiss Confederation's foreign policy. Now, as previously, the responsibility for the conduct of external relations belongs to the Federal Council – and the reference to the Federal Council, rather than just the Political Department[4] is deliberate. However hard the tasks which fall, in their several departments, to the lot of the seven ministers making up the government, and however clearly defined their individual responsibility, by a method of appointment which involves a personal vote of confidence, the Federal Council is a corporate body. Its decisions are binding not on such and such a minister, but on the whole government. Of course, on relatively minor matters, heads of departments obtain the consent of their colleagues without difficulty, certain rules of non-intervention in the affairs of others are tacitly observed, and personality plays its part in the weighing of arguments and in decision-making. But when it comes to a fundamental problem, and more particularly a

D

question of foreign policy, it is a corporate decision and a corporate commitment. Reference to the discussions about EFTA, the successive approaches made to the EEC, the debate about a possible application to join the United Nations, the principle, extent, and conditions of technical and financial co-operation with developing countries, Swiss policy as regards the GATT, monetary policy, or incidents such as the Zerka incident,[5] is enough to show that it is the Federal Council which takes the final decision – although not always easily.

This decision is taken – except in emergencies – at the end of a lengthy and wide-ranging process of consultation; within the administration, first of all, where the custom of inter-departmental meetings chaired by one of the departments has become general. The change in the actual content of international relations, the interdependence of economic, political, and cultural factors, and the fact that governments are gradually losing their monopoly of relations with other states – as the involvement and interdependence of political societies increase – have rendered a permanent form of co-ordination of external relations increasingly necessary in Switzerland as elsewhere.

This has not resulted in any change in structure, but in intensified interministerial exchanges. The Political Department is responsible for the conduct of affairs at political level, via its ambassadors, whose number has grown in line with requirements, although not to the extent of equalling those sovereign states with whom Switzerland maintains diplomatic relations. Here, and it is not necessarily a matter of regret, the limited means of a small state make it impossible to be everywhere at once. Switzerland has diplomatic relations with 124 countries and maintains embassies in 84 of these. Thus for example the Swiss ambassador to Mexico is accredited on a non-residential basis to Haiti and the Swiss ambassador to Italy is also accredited to Malta. Swiss embassies, although quite numerous, have few officials, as do Swiss delegations to international conferences.[6] At headquarters in Berne, work is carried on with a staff strength whose distribution is, moreover, indicative of Swiss political trends in recent years.[7] The development of the International Organizations Division, or the service of Technical Co-operation, will cause no surprise.

Alongside the Political Department, and still answerable to the Department of Public Economy, is the Division of Trade.

The decision to make it subordinate, taken during the First World War, has not been reversed, although the status of this increasingly influential body is under constant discussion. Its independence, i.e. the fact that it takes on responsibilities exceeding those of a mere administrative division, is sometimes the subject of reproach. It is also criticized as being an incarnation of the socio-economic system characteristic of Switzerland. But nobody disputes its usefulness, efficiency, or the quality of its staff. As a result of a highly selective recruitment policy and, even more, the creation of an intellectually demanding working climate, the Division of Trade has indeed achieved the respect and trust of those who have no ideological objection to its existence. The Division of Trade is, in fact, permanently engaged on the only genuinely active foreign policy front; there has never been any respite in the economic struggle for existence of this small state. Indeed, fronts have progressively hardened, and problems become more complex. The inter-war period was not easy, for barely had the after-effects of the First World War been settled than it became necessary to prepare for a new conflict, which was foreshadowed although its extent could not be measured; and meanwhile the world was disrupted by a general crisis which ripped apart the network of economic relations still left intact by the First War. Then, after 1945, came a succession of major problems, involving the restoration of trade, the integration of Europe, the revision of customs tariffs, and the negotiation of tariff agreements. Considered from outside, in terms of Swiss foreign policy, and disregarding the normal internal rivalries and stresses of any administration, it must be acknowledged that the work of the Division of Trade has been in the general interest, as defined by the government and the majority in parliament. And the subordination of the Division to the Department of Public Economy cannot be said to have prevented the Political Department from stating, or indeed carrying, its point. Several members of the Division of Trade, including its present head, have a long diplomatic career at the Political Department behind them, or will be returning there. In major decisions concerning Swiss economic policy, such as Swiss participation in OEEC, the Political Department conducted the negotiations, and although the relative influence of the heads of the two departments concerned may have varied with their personality, and the general trend of their interests, the feeling nevertheless exists that basically co-ordination – sometimes in the form of a division of work – is assured. At most we should perhaps stress the need, in view of the influence of organized economic interests, for a clearer statement of the primacy of the political side in matters as essential to the future of Switzerland as co-operation with the countries belonging to a Socialist system and with the developing countries.

The preparation of this economic foreign policy cannot be left to the resources of the administration alone. Here again we see, through a process of consultation which has expanded and intensified with the years, the continuation of a historical trend. In every field, whether agricultural policy, social insurance, scientific policy, aid to universities, revision of the penal code or the Swiss code of obligations, or the basic options of foreign policy, the work of the administration is subject to a permanent process of consultation linking, alongside the experts, the representatives of organized interests who are themselves in certain respects regarded as experts – and, of course, the cantonal governments. At this point the big associations representing major economic interests come into the picture: the Union Suisse de l'Industrie et du Commerce, Union Suisse des Arts et Métiers, Union Suisse des Paysans, Union Syndicale Suisse and many other trade organizations representing specific sectors of industry or trade. They act primarily through the Permanent Economic Delegation, consisting of high-ranking federal officials representing the departments concerned, on the one hand, and on the other the representatives of the four organizations we have mentioned. But however important the role of this permanent delegation, it cannot be said to hold any kind of monopoly of relations between representative economic sectors and a federal administration which maintains continual contact with economic circles and with representatives of both industrial and farmers' unions through the network of consultative committees or through personal exchanges of views. [8]

Some observers of Swiss policy and of this process of consultation have concluded that the Confederation's foreign policy was, so to speak, determined by the dominating influence of organized vested interests. It is certain that in the planning and implementation of Swiss policy towards EFTA, that is to say, towards an international association which is essentially economic, economic circles have played a role of capital importance.[9] The same applies to Swiss policy towards the European Economic Community and also, though to a lesser degree, to the planning and implementation of financial policy. Nevertheless, it would be a serious error of judgment to believe that on the whole Switzerland is governed by organized vested interests and particularly – according to one simplified theory – by high finance. The recent controversy concerning the revaluation of the Swiss franc is significant in this respect. Indeed in this pluralist state in which divergent schools of thought are continually at loggerheads, and where vested interests, parties, and trade unions are almost daily engaged in a conflict which contact with life in a microcosm makes inevitable, the government, if in firm hands, can hold the position of arbiter.

As for scientific and cultural relations, although left for a very long period in the hands of individuals, universities, learned societies, cultural associations and the separate cantons, an increasingly systematic and sustained campaign has been undertaken, under the direction of the Federal Department of the Interior, which acts in Switzerland as Ministry of Education. It is of course well known that education at all levels comes within the competence of the cantons, who have endeavoured to prevent any encroachment by the federal state in this field in which they can express their individuality. The Swiss Confederation, therefore, can do no more than adopt a modest policy of encouragement of the arts, literature, and science, and is unable to sign bilateral cultural agreements.

The increasing pressure of foreign propaganda, which was felt particularly keenly on the eve of the Second World War, when German Switzerland watched, powerless, over the disintegration of the German intellectual community to which she belonged; the development after 1945 of state-organized cultural exchanges, fostered and largely co-ordinated by UNESCO; the growing fear in Switzerland of being cut off from the outside world, excluded from cultural exchanges, isolated from the main intellectual stream, and outstripped in science, released the federal government from the restraints imposed by tradition, and induced it, under the increasing pressure of opinion, to take on the task of co-ordinating the cultural policy of the Swiss Confederation. The working group Pro Helvetia, transformed into a Foundation in 1949 with the aim, among others, of 'maintaining cultural relations with foreign countries and making known Swiss work and achievements in the realm of thought and culture'[10] opened the way. The Fonds National de la Recherche Scientifique, set up in 1952, and the Conseil Suisse de la Science, founded in 1965, together with the Commission Nationale Suisse pour l'UNESCO, complete the group of federal institutions responsible for encouraging scientific research in Switzerland and formulating a Swiss scientific policy in an international context. Here again, steps have been taken to ensure co-ordinated action by the Federal Department of the Interior and the Political Department both at cantonal level and at the level of diplomatic representation abroad. The permanent administrative apparatus has also been limited to that strictly necessary, and reliance placed instead upon Swiss citizens who are regarded as particularly representative or likely, by their personality and skill, to make a valuable contribution, not only in terms of the groundwork but also the actual conduct of cultural and scientific relations abroad. This is indeed the expression of a tradition, but it also represents the determination of the government to secure as wide as possible a participation from the Swiss community as a whole.[11]

It may well be asked, after this sketch of the process by which the foreign policy of Switzerland is formulated, what part parliament has to play; and indeed at first sight this part seems very unobtrusive. But in fact it is not so; first, because the major problems of Swiss politics are debated publicly, and press, radio and television vigorously supply fuel for the discussion, subjecting both government and administration to searching criticism. There are many newspapers, and some of them, through detailed research, make contributions of a scope and quality equivalent to those generally found in journals devoted to political science or economics; extremely jealous of their independence, they give the government only very qualified backing.

Members of parliament, however – even if they do not exercise their parliamentary functions as a profession – are constantly in contact with the administration, and, in the case of many of them, with professional circles. They are in a position to follow the various stages of development of projects subjected to their scrutiny. The documentation they receive from various government and private sources is ample, and the only real problem they have to confront is that of finding sufficient time for consultation and for assimilation of information, for they are still lacking the secretarial assistance with which members of parliament are provided in other countries. The meetings of parliamentary committees, however brief, still offer the opportunity for a valid confrontation of ideas and alternative solutions; even in the field of foreign policy, where the executive must have some margin for manoeuvre, the proportion of what politicians call 'closed session' decisions is low. The Foreign Affairs Committee of the two chambers of the Federal Assembly is frequently taken into the government's confidence and consulted, for instance, on such awkward questions as the recognition of new states. A government proposal cannot, therefore, be assured of parliamentary approval on completion of the process of consultation conducted by the administration; and the Federal Council is aware, after some disagreeable failures, that it may suddenly find itself faced with a parliamentary opposition which is resolutely against certain international commitments it considers should be accepted. It must, therefore, act very cautiously in matters such as the arrangements for entry of foreign workers, and their status. Secret diplomacy is impossible on so difficult a subject. And this is not an exceptional case, however violent the emotional reactions to the introduction of a high proportion of foreign workers into the Swiss community. The fact that a motion was filed in June 1969 for the amendment of the Article of the Federal Constitution relating to an optional referendum on international treaties concluded for an indefinite period or for more than fifteen years, so as to 'strengthen the influence of the people and the cantons on basic foreign policy decisions', indicates a certain mistrust of the executive, and some degree of anxiety. The fear exists that Switzerland will enter, in Europe or through the major international organizations, into irreversible commitments which would result in a fundamental transformation of Swiss economic and political structures.

These expressions of parliament's determination to be associated with the conduct of foreign policy, and the repeated reminders of its prerogatives where major political options are concerned, should be taken seriously – as they doubtless are. The freedom of action of the Political Department and the

Federal Council in matters of foreign policy is thus diminishing – a tendency in line with that of most Western parliamentary democracies.

PRINCIPLES AND OBJECTIVES

In its report of 5 May 1969 to the Federal Assembly concerning the outline of government policy during the period 1968–71, the Federal Council declared:

> Our external relations are still governed by the basic requirements of independence, neutrality, solidarity, and universality. Switzerland is prepared, within the limits of her permanent neutrality, to contribute to the strengthening of European co-operation; we hope to be immediately associated with all new efforts which may be deployed to bring about a *rapprochement* between the countries of the EEC and those of EFTA.
>
> Switzerland has accepted the need for a co-ordinated strengthening of international aid to stimulate the economic growth of the developing countries; she will continue her efforts on both a bilateral and a multilateral basis.
>
> Switzerland hopes to take an active part in international scientific co-operation.

After a paragraph summarizing the steps to be taken concerning national defence, the Federal Council adds the following remark:

> The Federal Council will continue to give very careful consideration to the matter of immigration, which is of considerable political importance. In the short term, it is advisable to prevent a further increase in the number of immigrant workers.

The striking feature of this passage, devised and presented as a summary of the main items in the section 'The existence and independence of the Swiss Confederation', is the choice of subjects, following the reminder of the basic objectives of Swiss policy: Europe, the developing countries, scientific co-operation, immigration.

The summary is, however, only a pale and not entirely accurate reflection of a more elaborate government programme.

Careful reading of the whole of the Federal Council's declaration clearly reveals the three major directions in which the Swiss government intends to develop its external relations: strengthened co-operation with Europe, intensified Swiss participation in the activities of the international organizations forming part of the United Nations system, and encouragement of co-operation with developing countries.

On the European level, the stress was placed on a *rapprochement* between the EEC and EFTA. Since then, the further boost to European hopes given at The Hague has opened up new prospects of co-operation between the EEC and the members of EFTA; Switzerland took advantage of the opportunity to declare her intention of establishing special links with the European Economic Community, within the limits imposed by her permanently neutral status, and her understanding of the resultant policy of neutrality. But Europe does not stop at Switzerland's eastern frontiers, and the government's declaration emphasizes this, in expressing the hope that economic and cultural exchanges can be developed with the Eastern European countries and those belonging to the Socialist bloc. The Federal Council made a move along these lines early in 1971, encouraged by the increasing interest shown by the leaders of the Socialist countries in developing trade. The experience of certain European private concerns is so far sufficiently encouraging for a gradual expansion of commercial relations to be envisaged. Cultural relations, of course, touch on a sector which is politically much more sensitive.

More generally, the government declaration stresses Swiss determination to take an increasingly active part in the work of the international organizations. However, the fact that Switzerland is not a formal member of the UN has created certain difficulties. These were referred to in a government report[12] which stressed the real advantages to Switzerland of joining the UN and pointed out the limitations and difficulties of her present position, as a result of the increasing concentration within the UN system of discussions and negotiations on certain matters. It is not, for instance, a matter of indifference to the Swiss government that modern international law is increasingly evolving within the framework of the UN, and that Switzerland, as a non-member of the Committee on International Law, is no longer 'invited to give her opinion on the reports prepared by the Committee, but merely to attend the Codification Conference responsible for preparing the final text'; nor is the fact that the codification of international law, previously undertaken by international conferences open to all states, is increasingly entrusted to the Sixth Committee of the General Assembly, whose discussions Switzerland can follow only as an observer.[13]

The report develops a number of arguments in favour of Swiss participation, but nevertheless concludes on a cautious note: it is better to wait, if only to ensure first of all that Swiss public opinion is in favour of joining – which is not at all certain at the moment – and that the members of the UN will not raise objections to the neutral status which Switzerland intends to retain.

We must not be misled by these reservations; the Swiss government, and with it a large section of Parliament, favours Swiss entry to the UN. An analysis of the evolving structure of diplomatic relations in recent years has shown that multilateral relations are gaining in importance, if only because the small states and those of the Third World in particular find in a multilateral approach an additional protection of their sovereignty, a means of avoiding a *tête-à-tête* bilateral negotiation with a richer and more powerful partner. From this observation, the Swiss government has concluded, without for the moment being put off by the increasing expression of ill temper directed by a sector of American opinion and of Congress against certain international organizations, that Swiss activity must be developed on a multilateral basis.

This change of stress is particularly noticeable in matters grouped under the general title of 'co-operation with the developing countries', whether involving technical co-operation or financial aid. Possibly it is in this sector that a political purpose is most apparent, in the strengthening of activities favouring the developing countries, and the shifting of the centre of gravity of multilateral operations.

It is fair to say 'political purpose', for consideration of the extent of public effort on the one hand and the increase in the proportion of multilateral aid on the other shows that the changes are still small; despite the multiplication of activities, a token of the interest among the young[14] in the development of relations with the Third World, there is still resistance, based on

Table 1 *Distribution of Public Swiss Aid According
to Geographical Sector*

Areas	Payments (million francs)		
	1968	1969	1970
Africa	24·4	36·7	30·2
Technical co-operation[1]	10·7	13·9	14·1
Financial aid	—	—	—
Alimentary aid	5·0	10·4	5·9
Humanitarian aid	8·7	12·4	10·2
Latin America	−1·1	0·1	9·7
Technical co-operation[1]	3·7	5·0	5·9
Financial aid	−5·5	−5·5	−5·5
Alimentary aid	0·6	0·6	8·9
Humanitarian aid	0·1	—	0·4
Asia and Oceania	26·7	26·5	31·4
Technical co-operation[1]	7·2	6·8	9·7
Financial aid	7·9	13·1	11·1
Alimentary aid	6·4	5·1	6·4
Humanitarian aid	5·2	1·5	4·2
Europe	7·2	1·5	2·1
Technical co-operation[1]	1·4	1·0	1·5
Financial aid	5·5	−0·6	−2·4
Alimentary aid	0·3	0·7	2·3
Humanitarian aid	—	0·4	0·7
Unclassified by geographical sector[2]	22·9	37·9	32·7
Technical co-operation[1]	13·0	14·3	15·8
Financial aid	−0·1	1·9	4·0
Alimentary aid	5·1	15·3	5·4
Humanitarian aid	4·9	6·4	7·5
Total Swiss Confederation	80·1	102·7	106·1
Technical co-operation[1]	36·0	41·0	47·0
Financial aid	7·8	8·9	7·2
Alimentary aid	17·4	32·1	28·9
Humanitarian aid	18·9	20·7	23·0
Cantons and Communes[3]	1·2	1·6	3·6
Total public aid	81·3	104·3	109·7

Source: FF, 1971, II, pp. 1657–1770.
Notes: [1] Including academic grants of the Federal Department
of the Interior.
[2] UNDP, ADI, IBRD.
[3] Distribution is not available.

107

unfortunate experiences or, more frequently, aroused by the increasingly radical nature of certain movements which link aid to developing countries with a revolutionary transformation of the structures of capitalist society. This reluctance, clearly visible in industrial circles previously favouring a policy of economic co-operation with and technical assistance to the Third World, could, when added to the indifference of a large percentage of Swiss citizens, impose severe restraints on the growth of Swiss aid to the countries of the Third World.

It is none the less true however that the government seems determined to overcome that resistance to technical assistance and to other forms of co-operation with developing countries. This is because it sees ever more clearly the interests of the two parties involved. That is why there is an observable tendency in the context of technical co-operation and financial aid to distribute the overall benefits equally among the various continents. Although statistics show that Africa has been in the forefront of recipients of technical co-operation, due to certain traditional links like those which were forged by missions, the shares going to Asia and Latin America are tending to increase. It should be mentioned, however, that the nature of benefits differs from one continent to another.[15] (See Table 1.)

The criteria adopted by the Confederation in the selection of countries with which it signs agreements are clearly revealed in the Federal Council's statement in November 1971 on the subject, namely:

> In choosing the developing countries to whom the confederation extends aid, we take into consideration, on the one hand, the universality of Swiss international relations, in accordance to which no developing country is, in principle, excluded from developmental aid, and on the other hand, the practical necessity of concentrating aid on some countries in order to make it more effective. In selecting these countries, we take into consideration their level of development in the sense that we grant an important part of the aid to the least developed countries; which are, at the same time, those countries where technical assistance is the most useful. We consider further whether or not a country is consciously pursuing a responsible policy of development and whether it is making efforts by itself, because it is only then that aid from abroad can have the optimum effect.[16]

Technical assistance to the developing countries is, however, merely one gesture of solidarity, of Switzerland's desire to transcend her neutrality and assert herself on the international scene. The report of the Federal Council on the outlines of policy for the legislative period 1968–71 sets out, in a list which also includes technical aid, the very varying fields in which the government proposes increased activity. This list offers some help towards an understanding of its intentions, and of the political approach:

Development and codification of international law.
Trade policy.
Humanitarian ventures, including disaster aid.
Prevention of hunger.
Control of air and water pollution.
Technical assistance.
Acceding to the Convention on Human Rights and other conventions of the Council of Europe.
Scientific and technological co-operation on international level – primarily satellite communications and CERN.
Strengthening of the position of Geneva as an international centre.

Here again, the stress is placed on multilateral diplomacy within a fairly wide framework which excludes, as far as possible, commitments of a political nature.

But however decisive the role of the Federal Government might be, it is not the only channel through which the Swiss citizen gives expression to his concept of the international role his country plays and of an international vocation transcending neutrality. This determination to contribute is, of course, manifest in cultural and scientific exchange, so individualized that no statistical expression can be given to its intensity. It is also evident at the humanitarian level, through many organizations which represent all social strata and trends within the population. Is it explained by a natural generosity? Is it sometimes due to selfconsciousness about one's own success? Swiss citizens try to outdo each other in their zeal for charitable works, praiseworthy in so far as they are effective. And the difficuties of co-ordination are further proof that that determination to contribute is general.

Consequently, the International Committee of the Red Cross

should be considered only as one among Swiss humanitarian organizations, though the largest and oldest, along with the Swiss Red Cross, which continually affirms its international vocation. But can we, indeed may we, consider the ICRC as a Swiss institution? Does it not rather belong to that international community which we all hope will one day be formed? Is it not an element of the international system which should, as a *uni-national international organization*, assume certain functions, remedy certain defects, and intervene where the multi-national international organizations cannot?

Be that as it may, it is a Swiss institution which, without being an instrument of Swiss foreign policy, nevertheless bases its independence and ability to go into action on Swiss neutrality.

THE INFLUENCE OF SWITZERLAND

What part is there for a small state such as Switzerland in the international system?

A modest view must be taken, and the first thing is simply to exist. It is no disgrace to keep alive a nation in which men, according to Jacob Burckhardt's famous saying, can enjoy the status of citizen. It can exist for the benefit of those who live in Switzerland, a task which in itself demands a constant search for social justice and permanent willingness to accept a reforming policy which adapts structures to changing situations; and exist without being a source of trouble for others, and without bringing trouble to others.

But once this has been said, and without reconsidering the aims of ensuring Swiss independence and neutrality while offering concrete evidence of her sense of solidarity and desire to participate, how can we define the scope and limitations of Switzerland's role?

From the military point of view, Switzerland can contribute only by demonstrating her determination and ability to protect her own territory. This already involves considerable effort, and a personal contribution which goes beyond the merely financial. The Swiss idea of a militia has stood the test of time, although it has been and still is contested, usually in the form of doubt or irony rather than open opposition. And indeed, whatever the assessment of the risk of war, the contribution of the Swiss army to the country's protection, to the training of executives and the integration of Swiss society, should not be underestimated. Experience acquired within this body, which is still today a social melting-pot, is of real value in the case of humanitarian action both inside and outside Switzerland. And it must be pointed out that the assertion of a determination to defend its territorial integrity and national independence in all circumstances, however powerful the potential aggressor, and whatever sacrifices may be required, represents a positive contribution to peace on the part of a small country. It is a capital error to leave the task of policing the world to the great powers alone. For the great powers consider their own interests first of all, and history is there to bear witness that they cannot be expected to sacrifice themselves for others. A system of collective security cannot operate unless each country, at its own level and in its own sector, is not only prepared to make a contribution but also to provide the means.

The influence of Switzerland is most apparent in the economic field. It is true that the turnover of General Motors exceeds the Swiss GNP; but it is beginning to be realized that this kind of comparison is not of any great value, nor is the amount of the GNP particularly significant. What counts is, first of all, the fact that Swiss *per capita* income is one of the highest in the world (10,800 francs in 1969). The important thing is the constant improvement in the standard of living of the wage-earner. It is interesting to note that in the household accounts of both white-collar and other workers the proportion of expenditure on 'essentials' has fallen from 60 per cent of the total budget in 1936–37 to 45 per cent in 1969. This improvement in the standard of living is therefore a reflection of the prosperity Switzerland is now enjoying; but this prosperity is, as we have said, the result of cumulative work, and can be maintained only by intensive effort and by a very careful management of Swiss interests. Switzerland is rich, but on her own small-country scale. She plays an unobtrusive – indeed a deliberately unobtrusive – part among industrial nations. Despite her relative financial power, she is not a member of the Group of Ten and has so far refrained from applying for admission to the International Monetary Fund, in order to limit the risks which inclusion in a permanently crisis-ridden monetary system might involve for the Swiss franc.

What we might call a form of mythology, having its source

111

mainly in the doubts and criticisms aroused by the maintenance of bank secrecy, has exaggerated out of all proportion the power of Swiss banking circles and their influence throughout the world. But those who raise the spectre of the 'gnomes of Zurich' would be well advised to review the history of the 1971 international financial crisis: they would see how marginal was the role played by Switzerland and would then be able to draw up a more realistic hierarchy of world financial powers. Switzerland is rich on its own small scale and can never play more than a *marginal* role.

This desire to limit the risks, or spread them, is also reflected in the distribution of her foreign trade. (See Tables 2 and 3.) Switzerland's disinclination to be enclosed in the European

Table 2   *Swiss Trade by Area (1960–70)*

	Percentage of Total Imports										
Area	1960	1961	1962	1963	1964	1965	1966	1967	1968	1969	1970
EFTA	11·7	12·5	13·3	13·7	15·0	14·9	15·6	16·5	16·5	18·1	18·3
EEC	61·0	62·6	63·1	64·0	62·0	62·2	60·4	59·5	59·5	58·1	58·3
COMECON	2·2	2·3	1·9	1·9	2·0	2·2	2·4	2·2	2·0	2·0	2·1
Other European Countries	1·5	1·4	1·6	1·6	1·8	1·8	1·8	1·7	1·8	2·0	1·9
Africa	2·6	2·7	2·0	2·1	2·4	2·6	2·5	3·3	3·4	3·0	2·9
Asia	3·7	3·3	3·4	3·5	3·5	3·6	4·0	4·2	4·2	4·7	4·8
U.S./Canada	13·1	11·6	11·0	9·6	9·7	9·5	10·0	9·2	9·7	9·3	9·2
Latin America	3·9	3·4	3·5	3·3	3·3	2·9	3·0	3·1	2·7	2·6	2·3
Oceania	0·3	0·2	0·2	0·3	0·3	0·3	0·3	0·3	0·2	0·3	0·2

	Percentage of Total Exports										
Area	1960	1961	1962	1963	1964	1965	1966	1967	1968	1969	1970
EFTA	17·0	17·2	17·9	17·8	19·5	19·8	19·6	21·6	21·0	20·7	21·2
EEC	40·9	41·5	42·0	42·3	40·5	39·8	38·0	36·5	36·5	37·4	37·4
COMECON	3·3	3·2	2·6	2·6	2·4	2·8	3·4	3·6	3·5	3·7	4·1
Other European Countries	3·9	3·7	4·2	4·8	4·9	5·0	4·9	5·0	4·9	5·3	4·9
Africa	3·6	3·6	3·6	3·7	3·6	3·6	3·6	3·2	3·5	3·6	3·9
Asia	10·0	10·3	9·9	10·1	10·5	10·2	10·3	10·6	11·0	10·9	10·9
U.S./Canada	11·7	10·9	11·0	10·6	10·4	11·2	12·3	11·9	11·7	10·9	10·2
Latin America	7·8	7·9	7·2	6·5	6·5	5·9	6·3	6·0	6·5	6·1	6·0
Oceania	1·9	1·7	1·6	1·6	1·7	1·7	1·6	1·6	1·4	1·4	1·4

Source: *Annuaire statistique de la Suisse 1969*, pp. 176–9; and *Annuaire statistique de la Suisse, 1971*, pp. 176–9.

Note: For specific data on the ten main countries to which Switzerland sent exports and received imports in 1970, see Table 3.

Table 3   Swiss Imports and Exports by Main
Countries 1970 (million francs)

Imports		Exports	
West Germany	8,349·2	West Germany	3,288·6
France	3,362·0	Italy	2,073·7
Italy	2,622·8	United States	1,962·8
United States	2,371·9	France	1,806·5
Britain	2,166·8	Britain	1,584·8
Austria	1,250·6	Austria	1,151·7
Belgium-Luxembourg	987·2	Sweden	742·3
Netherlands	964·1	Japan	698·5
Sweden	870·8	Netherlands	593·3
Japan	615·0	Belgium-Luxembourg	507·6
Total Imports	27,873·5	Total Exports	22,140·3

Source: Table 1.

Economic Community is not only due to her desire to preserve her neutrality or to protect her agricultural production and peasant population, but also to her far from negligible overseas trade: although EFTA and the EEC absorbed 58·6 per cent of 1970 exports, the trade with regions outside Europe, 22·2 per cent, and almost 9 per cent with the United States, is important.

The presence of Swiss traders and manufacturers throughout the world helps to strengthen the position of the Swiss government. Although they do not exert any political influence, indeed take care not to do so, they still represent part of the goodwill which is so difficult to build up and so easy to lose. The range of Swiss influence is to a large extent dependent on their conduct and their contacts. They often settle in their adopted country without losing contact with their homeland, and have gradually organized themselves throughout the world in an awareness of their role as intermediaries not only in their economic activities but also in the field of politics and cultural relations.[17]

There is likewise no doubt that industry, by its investments in the countries of the Third World, makes a valid contribution to development. The amount of this investment, although large, is not easy to assess, nor is the overall impact of industrial activity on a given region. This form of private participation in development is of course vigorously opposed by those who prefer to take into account only public 'aid', and would like to subject Swiss private investment to political criteria. Such private 'investments' should not be ranked with 'aid' or with deliberately impartial 'assistance' operations, for they are decided in terms of commercial criteria. The determining factor in assessing the extent of the contribution made by private investment in the developing countries is the interest shown by the governments of these countries, which may well coincide with those of the private investor. This is indeed the view, and the practice, of private investors, and it is also the policy of the Federal Council, which states in its message of 10 September 1969 concerning guarantees against investment risks that 'the primary condition for granting the guarantee is that the developing country approves the investment in question'. This message shows the importance which the Swiss government attaches to private investment, and the role allocated to it within the context of a Swiss policy on financial transfer[18] which Ambassador Probst summarized as follows:

> To provide for the developing country, or facilitate the provision of, the maximum amount of public and private finance, taking into account the need to prevent too heavy a burden of debt; for this purpose, *on the one hand*, to channel private capital towards sectors of production capable of servicing the debt and *on the other hand* to provide assistance in the form of public capital for economic sectors, such as the infrastructure, which require the provision of capital on concessionary terms.[19]

With this combination of private and public resources a Swiss contribution of a size more in line with the needs of the developing countries can be provided. This is a further example of co-operation between the private sectors and the authorities to give greater size and weight to the Swiss commitment. A small state can utilize its economic potential to the maximum only by very careful management of its resources and co-ordination of all available means. And the liberal system which Switzerland boasts does not prevent a very advanced degree of integration of Swiss action, which is possible in the long term only to the extent that a desire for compromise – failing a consensus – prevails among the various elements making up the political society concerned – whether divided according to social classes, age groups, occupations or parties, or according to ideology.

114

A valid foreign policy, one capable of ensuring both the independence and the influence of the country, is based on this consensus or will to compromise, which itself is the result of a determination to continue life in common as a nation. The early and more recent history of all peoples, both great and small, proves that neither military nor economic power can shore up a failing national will.

Switzerland has not escaped the general crisis caused by the scientific and technical revolution in modern societies. Prosperity does not engender stability, but rather fosters dissatisfaction and demands. Public feeling, in a world as integrated as ours does not stop at frontiers, any more than does inflation. Anxiety about a future which is both uncertain, and in some ways all too certain, results in escapism and rejection; what is the purpose of studies which virtually condemn you to becoming an intelligent but dehumanized cog in too highly mechanized a society, unless to dissuade you from grasping what life has to offer before a catastrophic war destroys the whole world?

Escapism, rejection – and indifference as well. Many people are too busy with their own success and their pursuit of a better life to feel concerned. Among the young, however, indifference is a political attitude: what you, the adults, do, does not concern us! We have other spiritual and political ambitions which can be achieved only in a different society, and not even a Socialist society on the Russian or Cuban model. Our kingdom is of this world, they would seem to say, but a world which is not your world, and with which we alone can communicate.

In Switzerland as in many other countries this attitude is that of a minority whose electoral weight is still negligible, but whose influence is real, because of the intransigence of its refusal to participate, and because at a certain age level the resulting community can transcend class barriers.

This non-participation, sometimes moving into open opposition, which arises in the most varied environments, worries thinking people and generally leads to a more searching examination of political conscience. The moralist tradition which sustains doubt despite, or perhaps because of, material success, is complicated by a systematic questioning of institutions which are held to be not truly democratic and by irritation over the pragmatism, attitude of compromise, and the cautious approach characteristic of Swiss political society. At all levels, and par-

115

ticularly of course among intellectuals, there is a certain impatience, a desire for change which does not always relate to
any specific ideology, and a more widespread discontent which
is still basically an expression of egoism aggravated by generally
inflated wants.

This change of climate may not have any immediate political
repercussions, electorally speaking, but its long-term effect will
probably be far-reaching, unless some jolt from abroad provides
distraction from minor personal problems or dreams of a new
'New Harmony'.

This discontent has already shown itself in the success achieved
by the signatories to the Schwarzenbach initiative against foreign
immigration, who almost overturned the system of established
parties and professional organizations. On a major matter of
foreign policy affecting both principle and vested interests, the
freedom of choice of the federal government is, as we have said,
limited. On the whole policy of development aid opinions are
very much divided, and the Federal Council, caught between
intransigence and indifference, is conducting its policy only
with considerable difficulty. As for the result of the debate on
admission to the United Nations, uncertainty still prevails.

The freedom of choice of governments in foreign policy
matters is never, as we have said, very wide, whatever the size
of the state and whatever its means. It is limited, naturally, by
the necessary consideration for the interests of other states; but
it is still further limited by conflicting interests at home which
the government must settle before any commitment abroad.
This process of arbitration is difficult, but it is possible where the
interests involved can be clearly defined and a majority comes
out in favour of one alternative; it is virtually impossible in a
climate of mixed intransigence and indifference.

To conclude these possibly over-pessimistic comments,
Switzerland must re-establish, through a process of internal
discussion which is indeed now taking place, the basis of a
foreign policy which cannot, in any case, differ very greatly from
that conducted hitherto.

NOTES AND REFERENCES

Direct Sources
1. Of the readily accessible sources of information on Swiss foreign policy,

the most important are to be found in the *Feuilles Fédérales* (FF) which regularly publish the *Messages and Reports of the Federal Council to the Federal Assembly*. These documents cover, in particular, matters such as: cultural policy (FF, 1948, II, p. 909; FF, 1970, I, p. 1013); *Switzerland's relations with the UN* (FF, 1962, I, p. 1250; FF, 1969, I, p. 1457); *trade policy* (FF, 1948, II, p. 1113; FF, 1960, I, p. 869; FF, 1961, I, p. 937; FF, 1966, I, p. 725; FF, 1971, I, p. 41); *technical assistance and development policy* (FF, 1964, I, p. 1083; FF, 1969, II, p. 961; FF, 1971, I, pp. 253 and 705, and II, p. 1657); *humanitarian policy* (FF, 1968, I, p. 45; FF, 1969, I, p. 1407). Although dealing in all these cases with very specific questions (such as the Swiss Confederation's grant to the International Red Cross Committee or *Pro Helvetia*) the Government often takes the opportunity to define or to recapitulate the broad lines of its foreign policy in the field concerned. 2. The speeches of the Federal Councillors who have in turn headed the Federal Political Department since 1945 provide an illustration of the slow and cautious evolution characteristic of Swiss external policy over this period. Mr Wahlen's speeches have been published: Friedrich T. Wahlen, *L'Ambassade permanente* (Editions de l'Age d'Homme, Lausanne, 1966). Those of Messrs Petitpierre, Spühler and Graber, with certain exceptions, have not so far been published, but they can be obtained in mimeographed form from the Federal Political Department in Berne. The theme of neutrality and Switzerland's place in the world are generally the chief concern of the speakers.

Written Works
Books on Switzerland abound. Of the few we have selected for this short bibliography, three are standard works, and essential reading:

Edgar Bonjour, *Geschichte der Schweizerischen Neutralität: Vier Jahrhunderte eidgenössischer Aussenpolitik* (Helbing & Lichtenhahn, Basel, 1965–70) 6 volumes (2nd edition), now being translated into French (three volumes have already been published in French, in Neuchâtel, at the Baconnière, 1970–71, volumes 4, 5 and 6, under the title *Histoire de la neutralité suisse*. Quatre siècles de politique extérieure fédérale) (translation by Charles Oser).
André Siegfried, *La Suisse, démocratie-témoin* (La Baconnière, Neuchâtel, 1948).
Denis de Rougemont, *La Suisse ou l'histoire d'un peuple heureux* (Hachette, Paris, 1965).

For anyone who aims at a thorough grasp of the sources of Swiss neutrality, and wishes to understand the influence which these remote historical origins still exert on the foreign policy of the Confederation, Bonjour is essential reading. Siegfried gives the view of an outside observer. A specialist in the study of peoples and their political systems, he analyses Swiss life and institutions through geography and history, and in contrast with other Western nations, in a book which is both complete and succinct. Written just after the Second World War, this book, although still topical, gives a picture of Switzerland which may seem somewhat idealized today. The last chapter deals at greater length with foreign relations. De Rougemont traces the history of the Confederation with a semi-didactic purpose. A convinced European and federalist, his knowledge of Switzerland and his skill as a writer make him the eloquent spokesman of a certain proselytizing trend in Switzerland.

Paul Chaudet, *La Suisse et notre temps: Du souvenir à la réflexion* (Robert Laffont, Paris, 1970) is of particular interest as a personal testimony.

Gustav Daeniker, *Strategie des Kleinstaats: Politisch-militärische Möglichkeiten schweizerischer Selbstbehauptung im Atomzeitalter* (Huber, Frauenfeld, 1966) analyses the political and military position of Switzerland in the atomic era, and attempts to assess her chances of retaining her autonomy.

Peter Dürrenmatt, *Der Kleinstaat und das Problem der Macht* (Helbing & Lichtenhahn, Basel, 1955) provides an excellent view of a small state confronting the problem of power.

The work in English of E. Bonjour, H. S. Offler, and G. R. Potter, *A Short History of Switzerland* (Clarendon Press, Oxford, 1952) gives an efficient summary of Swiss history.

Finally, two basic publications which are of considerable value to those who wish to follow Swiss political developments from abroad:

L'annuaire de l'Association Suisse de Science Politique (1961) (known since 1965 as *Annuaire Suisse de Science Politique*) and *l'Annuaire de la Nouvelle Société Helvétique* (Berne, 1930).

1. The basic work of reference in any study of Swiss foreign policy is Professor Edgar Bonjour's *Geschichte der Schweizerischen Neutralität*, 6 vols. (Helbing & Lichtenhahn, Basel and Stuttgart, 1965–70). A French translation is in preparation, and vols, 4, 5 and 6 were published in Neuchâtel by La Baconnière, 1970–71.
2. Cf. Gustav Daeniker, *Strategie des Kleinstaats: Politisch-militärische Möglichkeiten Schweizerischer Selbstbehauptung im Atomzeitalter* (Verlag Huber, Frauenfeld, 1966).
3. Cf. *Bases d'une conception stratégique Suisse*, Rapports de la Commission d'étude des questions de stratégie, 14 November 1969.
4. 'Political Department' is the translation for *Département politique fédéral*, the expression by which Swiss people name their Foreign Ministry.
5. One remembers the political crisis which, in September 1970, resulted from the hi-jacking by Palestinian guerrillas to a Jordanian desert airstrip of three airliners, one of which was Swiss.
6. Apart from the following, most Swiss missions have 4 or less personnel: Paris (14 diplomatic staff, 3 commercial and 2 cultural attachés); London (14 diplomatic staff, 2 commercial attachés and 1 cultural attaché); Washington (10 diplomatic staff, 3 commercial attachés and 1 cultural attaché); Rome (7 diplomatic staff, 2 commercial attachés and 1 cultural attaché); Paris (OECD) (7 diplomatic staff); Brussels (EEC) (6 diplomatic staff); Buenos Aires (5 diplomatic staff, 1 commercial and 1 cultural attaché); New York (UN) (5 diplomatic staff).

7. There are 137 diplomatic and consular staff at the Political Depart ment in Berne, who are supported by 328 other personnel. Abroad there are 512 Swiss diplomatic and consular staff assisted by 1,143 other personnel (1971).
8. The conditions in which the external economic policy of the Confederation is formulated are covered by many surveys. Cf. in particular the overall picture given by Jean Meynaud in collaboration with Adalbert Korff in *Les organisations professionnelles en Suisse* (Payot, Lausanne, 1963) and an article by Dusan Sidjanski, 'Les groupes de pression et la politique étrangère de la Suisse', *Annuaire Suisse de Science politique* (1966) pp. 28–45.
9. See Paul Veyrassat, *La Suisse et la création de l'AELE: Une page d'intégration européenne, 1958–1968* (La Baconnière, Neuchâtel, 1969) and Eric Roethlisberger *La Suisse dans l'Association européenne de libre échange, 1960–1966* (La Baconnière, Neuchâtel, 1969).
10. On this point, cf. *Pro Helvetia 1939–1964* (Orell Füssli, Zürich, 1964), and *Pro Helvetia, 1964–1966* (Orell Füssli, Zürich, 1967).
11. Denis de Rougemont, in *La Suisse ou l'histoire d'un peuple heureux* (Hachette, Paris, 1965), shows the cultural significance of the Swiss political society. Cf. also Alfred Zehnder, *Politique extérieure et relations culturelles* (Institut universitaire de hautes études internationales, Genève, 1957), publication no. 27.
12. 'Rapport du Conseil fédéral à l'Assemblée fédérale sur les relations de la Suisse avec les Nations Unies', 16 June 1969. The debate on this report in the National Council took place on 8 October 1969.
13. On this very important point, see 'Rapport du Conseil fédéral', op. cit., pp. 121–2.
14. Gerhard Schmidtchen, *Schweizer und Entwicklung Hilfe: Innen Ansichten der Aussenpolitik*, vol. 1 (Haupt, Bern, 1971).
15. The *Fondation Suisse pour l'Assistance Technique*, set up in 1959, was financed solely from the donations of Swiss industry, which amounted to Fr. 18,500,000 by 1969. These sums have been allocated to the training of technical executives, specializing mainly in minor mechanical fields.
16. For details of Swiss development and technical co-operation policy, see bibliographical guide at the end of the chapter.
17. Cf. René Bovey, 'La Cinquième Suisse' in *Aspects du devenir helvétique* (Annuaire de la Nouvelle Société Helvétique, Berne, 1964) pp. 300–21. In this article René Bovey quotes a declaration made on 1 October 1918 by Gonzague de Reynold, founder of the *Secrétariat des Suisses à l'Etranger*, which provides an eloquent description of the contribution to their country's influence which can be made by the Swiss abroad:

They are the channels through which our ideas are spread throughout the world, and through which ideas and experiences reach us from abroad. We must not forget that whatever the outcome of the war, vast economic blocs will be formed, among which our country will have to fight to maintain its industrial and commercial independence, against this form of competition, it will have to co-ordin-

119

ate and to mobilize everything it possesses in the way of talent, productive capacity, experience and knowledge of other countries.

Finally it is worth noting that, conscious of the contribution made by the Swiss abroad, the people and cantons voted on 16 October 1966 for the inclusion of a new article in the Constitution, Article 45 *bis*, which states:

1. The Swiss Confederation is authorized to strengthen the ties binding Swiss nationals abroad to each other and to the homeland, and to support institutions created for this purpose.

2. It may, taking into account the special situation of Swiss nationals abroad, issue regulations determining their rights and obligations, particularly as regards the exercise of political rights and the fulfilment of military obligations, and as regards assistance. The cantons will be consulted before such measures are adopted.

See *Assemblée fédérale du 19 décembre, 1966, Recueil Officiel des lois et ordonnances de la Confédération suisse* (1966) p. 1730, *Feuille Fédérale*, vol. II (1965) p. 401, and *Feuille Fédérale*, vol. II (1966) p. 645.

18. It is worth recalling in this connection the various messages in which the Swiss government has defined its policy of encouraging trade with the Third World: *Message du Conseil fédéral à l'Assemblée fédérale du 10 septembre 1969 concernant un projet de loi fédérale sur la garantie contre les risques de l'investissement; Message du Conseil fédéral à l'Assemblée fédérale du 25 janvier 1971 concernant l'aide économique et financière aux pays en développement notamment l'ouverture d'un crédit de programme pour l'aide financière; Message du Conseil fédéral à l'Assemblée fédérale du 24 mars 1971 concernant la politique commerciale de la Suisse envers les pays en développement et plus particulièrement la participation de la Suisse au système généralisé de préférences tarifaires en faveur de ces pays.*

19. Cf. statement by Ambassador Raymond Probst in *Les investissements privés suisses dans le Tiers Monde*, Genève, Institut universitaire de hautes études internationales, 2–3 juillet 1971 (mimeographed document).

Chapter 4

THE FOREIGN POLICY OF ZAMBIA

MARION BONE

The former British colonial territory of Northern Rhodesia became the independent Republic of Zambia on 24 October 1964, led by President Kenneth David Kaunda. The capital is at Lusaka. Zambia is a small state in economic terms and conventional power, but she is also a new state which is relatively inexperienced in world politics. Seven years is a short period over which to study Zambia's foreign policy, but the outlines have already been traced with remarkable clarity as the country has made considerable impact on African and world affairs.

IMPACT OF HISTORY

A number of influences from Zambia's history are important in shaping contemporary attitudes and policies.[1] Pre-twentieth century movements of African peoples result today in an area where several tribes may be distinguished by varying cultures and frequent mutual antagonisms. Their first contact with non-Africans was provided by Arab and Portuguese slave-dealers who left sharp memories of violence and double-dealing. The Christian missionaries, following in the wake of the explorer David Livingstone, began some early education, social work and Christian government. Then, in the last two decades of the nineteenth century, white settlers spread north from South Africa; they searched for gold, but found rich copper deposits and some productive agricultural land. They also initiated the characteristic separation of white and black people in Zambia and the territory's first links southward.

The British Protectorate of Northern Rhodesia had been defined by 1900 with little regard for local geographical or

121

social factors, leaving long borders which are difficult to guard. Until 1924 the country was administered by Cecil Rhodes' Chartered company which 'left as its monument one of the most neglected territories in Africa.'[2] The subsequent thirty years of direct rule by the British Colonial Office brought only slow advance to the indigenous peoples, and encouraged negligible contact with those outside her borders.

In 1953 the territory became part of the Federation of Rhodesia and Nyasaland, whose capital was in Salisbury in Southern Rhodesia. Northern Rhodesia and Nyasaland became hinterlands which were neglected for development and political life but were used for their financial and labour contributions. It would be difficult to overestimate the impact of this period which created resentment at the economic drain on the northern territories, the political subjugation of the Africans and the subordination to Southern Rhodesian priorities.[3] Though Africans were powerless to prevent the Federation in 1953, the triumph of the pressures which brought independence to Zambia and Malawi in 1964 encouraged belief in the ultimate triumph of majority rule throughout the continent. Hostility to white rule, reinforced by the Unilateral Declaration of Independence (UDI) in Southern Rhodesia on 11 November 1965, was inevitable.

African education was neglected during the colonial and federation periods so that, in 1964, there were a mere one hundred Zambian graduates and about a thousand secondary school certificate holders. Though the country inherited a functioning administration, it was heavily dependent on ex-patriate staff. The African political and civil service leaders were inexperienced, for the first African ministers had only taken office in 1962. The Zambian people, too, were politically immature after years of colonial tutelage.

IMPACT OF ECONOMIC FACTORS

The economy has experienced boom conditions since Independence, but not without accompanying problems of inflation, rising costs and import bills, urban unemployment and high cost production. Agriculture contributes little to the national income on most of the 290,410 square miles, although 50 per cent of the population lives by subsistence farming. Efforts to modernize this sector are much needed but have been largely unsuccessful.

It is the copper mining industry which dominates the Zambian economy by supplying an average 95 per cent of export earnings, 64 per cent of government revenue, and 40 per cent of GDP.[4] The major companies involved are Anglo-American Corporation (AAC) and Roan Selection Trust (RST).[5] In 1969 the government introduced the Matero mining reforms, which requested the companies to yield a controlling 51 per cent of their shares to the state while retaining management and marketing control, and which changed the system of taxation, royalties and mining titles.[6]

Although copper provides substantial revenue, a recession on the world market could have disastrous effects on future development. External aid is still considered necessary and the attached political conditions cannot be ignored; neither can the fact that Western aid tends to perpetuate capitalist structures. Some principles are inevitably compromised while the government must concentrate on internal development to satisfy the aspirations of the people.

Initially, non-Zambians controlled most of the ownership as well as the business and technical skills in industry. Reforms were introduced in 1968 to encourage Zambian participation[7]; the changes are slowly taking effect and employment of expatriates has been strictly limited. The government, at the same time, acquired a controlling interest in a number of enterprises, but this development is in the nature of state capitalism rather than socialism. The economy is still marked by income disparities between urban and rural workers and between expatriate and African employees.

Developments during the years of federation left Northern Rhodesia dependent on Southern Rhodesia and South Africa for 60 per cent of her trade, coal from Wankie, technical skills and management, power from Kariba hydro-electric station, and for communications and import/export routes. Meanwhile copper revenue had been paid into federal treasuries, and it is conservatively estimated that Zambia suffered a net loss of £70 million in the ten years.[8] This historically unequal relationship causes much present resentment.[9]

IMPACT OF GEOGRAPHY AND STRATEGIC FACTORS

Geography is perhaps the most crucial determinant of Zambia's foreign policies. The country is entirely landlocked in Central

Africa, the towns being a thousand miles from the coast. All trade routes and communications must pass through other countries to reach the rest of the world. The distances make all the routes vulnerable and every year there are several breaches of communications through bad weather, accidents or sabotage. Zambia's neighbours are the friendly, African-ruled Tanzania, Botswana, and Democratic Republic of the Congo (Kinshasa); Malawi, with whom relations are equivocal but mainly friendly; and Rhodesia, South-west Africa and Portuguese Mozambique and Angola whose white minority governments Zambia opposes.

In global terms Zambia is strategically insignificant for she does not control international air or sea routes, though she does export important quantities of the world supply of copper. The great powers are not immediately interested in fighting for control of southern Africa. However, Zambia is one of the southernmost territories which firmly oppose the minority governments: she could become a battleground for future conflict in the area.

IMPACT OF CULTURE

Opposition to colonial rule forged a national consciousness and a pride in things black and African, a rejection of alien culture. Kaunda was able to focus these feelings in the continental ideology of Pan-Africanism meaning African personality and unity, common enemies, sufferings, experiences and hopes; and in the fierce determination to see the whole of Africa free of European (white) rule. Understanding the further need for a local idea to guide the people (similar to Tanzania's Arusha Declaration), Kaunda formed the concept of a 'man-centred society' – believed to have been the norm in pre-European Africa – which he called Humanism.[10] These concepts together are held to show Zambia released from the cocoon of colonialism by contributing distinctive African ideas of equal value.

Zambia could never be isolated since the colonial boundaries had divided tribal groups between different countries. This contributes to border problems but makes Zambians aware of developments in neighbouring areas. The country has had little time to develop its own national identity so the six main tribes are still distinguished by their own cultures and languages;

Zambian nationalism is very much on the surface. Within the tribes are Westernized élites who are divorced from tribal culture but remain attached to it.

Of Zambia's 4 million inhabitants, some 70,000 are non-Africans who are influential in the economy and for their ideas. They spread Christianity, Western customs, capitalism, and the English language which, as the *lingua franca*, spreads a veneer of uniformity; most external influences at first were British but a great variety has been subsequently introduced. Some Zambians prefer Western ways, realizing that a more advanced society may be necessary to achieve development. 'In cultural questions, the problem was ... how both to assimilate and preserve, how both to be universal and to be oneself, how to modernize without being western.'[11] Zambia needs advanced techniques for its modernizing economy but cannot accept these without some accompanying culture.

Racial divisions are cultural and economic. Early white farmers, miners and colonial officers practised social separation and economic discrimination. Zambians rejected both, but their pervasive influence prevails sufficiently for tensions to be easily aroused. This explains demands for Zambianization (replacing expatriates with Zambians), wage equality, and rejection of relations with southern African countries which practise discrimination. Zambia's sensitivity on this issue is often underestimated.

MACHINERY AND PROCESSES

The roles of Head of State and Head of Government are combined in the office of President, which has been occupied unchallenged since 1964 by Kenneth Kaunda. Parliament consists of the President and a National Assembly of 105 (75 before 1968) elected members plus a maximum of five nominated by the President to represent special interests. Until 1968 there were ten European members elected on a restricted non-African roll which gave this group representation quite disproportionate to their population size.[12] Members of Parliament are normally elected every five years in single member constituencies on a franchise based on universal suffrage for all citizens of Zambia over eighteen years of age. The President is elected simultaneously but separately. In addition there is a House of Chiefs,

125

totalling about 230 members, with an advisory role and entitled to debate designated matters of public importance.

Kaunda is also the President of the ruling United National Independence Party (UNIP) which has a substantial majority in the National Assembly. The parliamentary opposition, consisting of the African National Congress, the European and Independent members, does not exert much influence on policy but it continually raises important issues for debate. In his first Cabinet, Kaunda combined individuals from various tribal groups, long-time party workers and younger intellectuals. That initial balance was disturbed by the defeat of some key members in the 1968 general election though UNIP's parliamentary strength was not seriously affected.

Outside the National Assembly opposition to the government is focused on economic policies because the business and mining communities are wary of criticizing political actions while their sector is so expatriate-dominated. By obtaining controlling shares in some companies, the government has brought this opposition more within its own compass but has not eliminated it – rather it has become part of internal government and party politics. Other criticism comes from disgruntled tribes and groups who feel they have not fully shared in the expected fruits of independence. There are recent signs that the students in higher education may try to force the government towards more radical policies.

FOREIGN MINISTRY

President Kaunda has always taken a direct interest in foreign affairs. In the first five years there were three ministers of foreign affairs, although the rapid changes were not due to incompetence in this specific job. In August 1969 the President himself assumed responsibility for this portfolio, but a year later he handed it back to the minister who had held the post before him.[13]

The Minister of Foreign Affairs is supported by the Permanent Secretary, Under-Secretary, and the assistants for administration, protocol, economic and political affairs; a special department handles African affairs. The Foreign Affairs Committee discusses policies and makes recommendations to the Cabinet. Kaunda uses a number of informal advisers, both Zambians and non-Zambians, in his own office and round the world. The Ministry itself combines personnel from most regions and tribes, though nearly all belong to UNIP and are part of the modernizing élite of Zambian society, educated abroad. Considering the national shortage of trained manpower, this Ministry includes a high proportion of college-educated staff.

Links with other ministries are informal and co-ordinated through the Cabinet. Despite the interlocking nature of Zambia's economic and political foreign affairs, it appears that the relevant ministries are poorly linked at the lower levels. Defence is handled by the President's office which implies better co-ordination by reason of Kaunda's own involvement in foreign affairs. While he acted as Foreign Minister there was inevitably even closer association between defence and the Ministry of Foreign Affairs.

DIPLOMATIC SERVICE

There was no external representation (other than that handled by Britain or the federal government) before October 1964, but informal contacts were developed by UNIP representatives in Tanzania, Ghana, Egypt, Britain and the United States. The new Ministry of Foreign Affairs had to project a Zambian image but it had scarce resources, in money, manpower or experience, to accomplish this. Inexperienced staff could easily damage Zambia's reputation or make costly mistakes of interpretation. Early telecommunications between missions and Zambia were poorly developed and routed at first through Southern Rhodesia. Mission heads often had to be their own press officers and are required to exhibit individual initiative of a kind rarely demanded by bigger and more experienced countries.

Envoys are moved frequently between different capitals and Lusaka which, though spreading their expertise widely throughout the service, prevents them from becoming familiar with any one country. Most missions have had more than one head in the first six years, and there have been six high commissioners in London. The Ministry headquarters does organize frequent Lusaka meetings for heads of missions in order to keep them in touch with developments at home, to bring together first-hand knowledge and co-ordinate policies and to maximize the efficiency of the service. After 1968 the limited resources were further strained by a new emphasis on economic and technical functions which require more specialized staff.

Nevertheless, the diplomatic corps is rapidly becoming an experienced professional class representing almost every tribal group in the country. About fifty per cent of the thirty heads of missions have had some formal higher education, though almost exclusively in Western countries. Half the diplomatic representatives have at some time been MPs, of whom three also held Cabinet posts which, incidentally, compounded a growing tendency to communicate directly with the President, bypassing the Ministry, and especially while he was the responsible Minister. The President's interest has been very important for he has made twenty-three state visits which supplement the lack of permanent representation. Though such visits do not provide opportunity for daily study of events in other countries, they do have added prestige and bring extended press coverage.

CLASSIFICATION

In 1970 Zambia had sixteen overseas diplomatic missions of which ten were in Africa, three covered Europe (London, Bonn and Moscow), and the remainder were in Washington, Peking and at the United Nations which is a vital mission for continuing contact with many other countries. Some overseas representatives are accredited to several states non-residentially, while elsewhere another Commonwealth country may handle Zambia's affairs for her. By 1970 there were twenty-seven envoys accredited to and resident in Zambia, plus seven others who are resident in neighbouring countries. In addition the UN maintains regional offices in Lusaka for UNDP, UNHCR, WHO, UN/ECA, ILO and UNESCO.

Zambia's foreign representation is limited by lack of finance and manpower and by the government's assessment of where its important interests lie. The greater number of envoys accredited to Zambia gives some indication of the importance with which the country is already regarded by reason of her geographical position in Africa's racial confrontation, the country's and Kaunda's international influence and African leadership, and the fast-expanding economy.

Economic foreign relations may be classified by reference to the trading patterns described later, trade agreements, financial loans and technical aid agreements. Zambia has about fifteen general trade agreements which are, however, little more than expressions of intent to increase mutual trade without any formal commitments. A few are more detailed. Following the £167 million loan from the People's Republic of China in 1967 for the construction of the Zambia to Tanzania railway, the Zambian government agreed to purchase an equivalent quantity of unspecified consumer goods. Another agreement, evidently politically motivated, to sell £1 million worth of maize to China when Zambia was herself a net maize importer, was the subject of considerable controversy. There are agreements for purchases of beef from Tanzania, Botswana and Swaziland, of wheat from Lesotho, and for the sale of copper to India and China. The Zambian government has deliberately refused to enter any agreements with Rhodesia, Angola, Mozambique or South Africa which could have been potentially important trading partners.

Financial loans and technical aid are received from a wide variety of states of which the Soviet Union and its satellites, Britain and the United States are important contributors. The government prefers its more neutral sources which include the UN agencies, the World Bank, Canada, Yugoslavia and the Scandinavian countries, but links have also been made with controversial states such as both nationalist and communist China, East and West Germany, and Israel. Some agreements provide for particular types of assistance such as organization of co-operative agriculture by the Scandinavian states and Israel, railway management by the Sudan and then Canada, and the Tanzam Railway construction which makes Zambia an important object of the Chinese aid programme to Africa. Educational co-operation enables Zambians to train in as many as thirty other countries, but teachers in Zambian schools are mostly British in order to retain consistency. The government has established important links with the copper mining countries of Congo (Kinshasa), Peru and Chile. The biggest impact, however, by any foreign country (other than Britain) has been made by Tanzania in the joint governmental transport and communications projects, and by Italy in a wide variety of commercial undertakings and aid to Zambian state organizations.[14]

The Zambian government has been reluctant to compromise

its non-alignment by joining military pacts despite the dangers to which the country feels exposed. An African or East African defence command has occasionally been suggested but never adopted as government policy. The existing defence agreements provide for the training of Zambians abroad and for expatriate officers who join the Zambian forces on contract or secondment. Britain, Italy, Canada and Ireland share aspects of these preparations while necessary equipment is bought in commercial transactions. Israel has helped in organizing the Zambia Youth Service which includes defence training, but that arrangement terminated after the Middle East Six Day War in 1967.

Zambia identifies herself with African culture, but co-operation has so far been hindered by the distances and the divisive effects of different colonial rulers and languages. The aim is to emphasize Zambia's African past and to reject much of the imported Western cultural influence. So, Zambians took enthusiastic part in the first Pan-African Cultural Festival in Algiers in 1969. Exchanges with both African and non-African countries are often arranged bi-laterally to encourage communication and understanding between peoples as well as governments. A National Dance Troupe has been formed to present Zambian cultural ideas both at home and abroad, including the 1970 Tokyo World Fair. The country is thus projecting both her own image in process of formation and her own view of what it is to be African.

INTERNAL POLITICAL INFLUENCES

Foreign policy is not directly restrained by internal political factors, but some domestic problems could ultimately affect external relations. The African National Congress controls two substantial regions which happen also to be the most distant from the new communications towards East Africa, and the ANC representatives are vocal critics of the government intentions of breaking relations with southern Africa.[15] They are joined in this view by sections of the business community.

Rivalries within UNIP have weakened the government and occasionally caused the President to act to divert the conflicting domestic forces and incidentally affect some foreign interests. The 1968 Mulungushi economic reforms to give Zambians a greater share in business proved politically popular and helped to diffuse mounting tribal conflicts. Kaunda announced the Matero mining reforms in 1969 when a government conflict with the mainly white judiciary led to increasing racial tension which was coupled with continuing tribal rivalry. The announcements were made without prior Cabinet knowledge (though the changes had been previously discussed); the timing was a direct response to the crises and designed to divert attention.

Some white residents in Zambia opt out of political affairs, but there is reason to doubt the loyalties of many who still have contacts in South Africa and Rhodesia; this hostile minority leaves little doubt of its support for those countries. Some people have been discreetly deported and others tried on espionage charges which show unmistakable connections with the white minority governments. Ugly racial incidents which may affect relations with Europe occur quite frequently when local emotions are aroused by this provocation.

The country needs firm control to contain these latent conflicts. Rhodesia's UDI provided a useful focus for nationalist feelings when the unifying goal of ending colonial rule had gone, enabling Kaunda to call for sacrifices on the altar of opposition to minority government and leaving the Zambian government more free to act positively and carve out a name for principled action. It is possible that, having achieved international prominence, Kaunda has neglected domestic affairs. His absences abroad leave Zambia vulnerable to radical elements capable of precipitating an irretrievable crisis. Kaunda's world reputation, after all, rests partly on the overall calm and internal progress which his country has achieved.

PRESIDENT KAUNDA

The presence of a Head of State who commands widespread respect certainly eased the early days of independence. Kaunda[16] astutely balanced the factions in party and government, and mediated in national and international disputes. Foreign policy is almost entirely identified with him, at least in its theoretical outline. His Christian faith colours his words and actions with sincerity and human kindness, while his conviction that all men are equal regardless of race, colour or creed adds the influences of justice and dislike of discrimination in any form. He is easily upset by displays of inhumanity and tribal conflict, and often

131

seems unprepared for the cynicism of politics or some acts of professional politicians.

Although Kaunda had a scanty formal education, he has supplemented that by continuous study including the works of the Koran, Bertrand Russell and Mahatma Gandhi. Before becoming a national leader, he had already taught outside Zambia and worked in the tough Copperbelt mining communities. Then he travelled widely as President to gain firsthand knowledge of the world, to publicize his views and influence others towards peace. Throughout he has been influenced by close personal friendships with African statesmen and some lesser known Europeans, but it is Julius K. Nyerere, President of neighbouring Tanzania, who is closest to Kaunda. They meet regularly for informal discussions and their hopes for Africa are very similar, though their methods may differ.

PRINCIPLES AND OBJECTIVES

President Kaunda takes care to make his views well known, for this is one of the few available ways of influencing governments which he cannot coerce economically or militarily. While his basic principles have not changed, some have been bent in the harsh reality of international politics.

The first concern is 'that political independence is meaningless without economic independence.'[17] The government has sought to establish Zambian control of the domestic economy, to diversify contacts with the world and to end economic dependence on the countries to the south which are also ruled by minority groups. Owing her political independence, in part, to encouragement from other parts of the continent, Zambia now intends to pursue economic development in conjunction with other African states. This expresses the practical Pan-Africanism which Kaunda feels is so important. The near objectives are better communications, trade and understanding, while the distant goal is a United States of Africa.

Kaunda's overall aim has always been to prevent suffering and to promote peace through moral persuasion. He opposes coercion which seems to prevent the common man (defined without regard for race or colour) from expressing his preference. It follows naturally from this and the recent colonial history of the continent that Kaunda opposes oppression in the world and the particular evil of apartheid in South Africa. He says: 'We cannot hold our heads high before the rest of the world unless we take our full part in helping those of our brothers and sisters currently struggling to free themselves from racial oppression and minority exploitation.'[18] In this Zambia is determined to show no lack of commitment, and only in the context of Rhodesia does Kaunda reluctantly condone violence as a method.

Being in a landlocked state, Zambians soon appreciated the need to retain friendly relations with neighbours at government and individual level. The primary focus is East Africa and possible federation, but there are strong pressures to ensure that Zambia's national interests are not sacrificed in the idealistic effort to promote African unity. Outside the immediate region there are strong feelings of affinity to all the continent and the desire to make it a strong and independent unit in world configurations.

Kaunda believes that Zambia should be firmly non-aligned and he is prepared to accept friendship from a wide range of states with varying political systems and cultural backgrounds. Non-alignment is susceptible of many interpretations but for Zambia it means a positive involvement in world affairs. By reserving the right to judge international issues on their individual merits where Zambia is not directly involved, the government seeks to find peaceful solutions to conflicts. Non-alignment is 'a positive contribution to peace'[19] but 'it does not mean expediency.'[20] It is 'a policy which basically sets out to defend the interests of the common man wherever he may be – west, east, north or south'.[21]

Consistent with these goals, Zambia aimed at first to support the United Nations, the Commonwealth and the Organization of African Unity (OAU), and their associated agencies' efforts to encourage the development of the poorer two-thirds of the world. They were all believed to be based on the principles of equality and justice, and provided a forum where Zambia's voice could be heard. Loyalty to the OAU has continued unabated apart from one or two disagreements which, however, failed to shake Zambia's confidence in that organization's usefulness.

It was not felt that Commonwealth membership infringed the commitment to non-alignment or constituted any predetermination to support Britain which has often been criticized, in fact, through the medium of the Commonwealth. Disappointment at the latter's failure, despite frequent discussions, to persuade Britain to end Rhodesia's rebellion or to prevent with certainty the Conservative government's arms sales to South Africa has weakened support for the Commonwealth. Zambians now seriously question the benefits of membership, though the government has not made good several threats to leave the organization.

ECONOMIC ASPECTS OF FOREIGN POLICY

The nature of Zambia's economy and geographical position requires emphasis on economic acts – with all their political implications. The southern African economic region would have been a logical focus for the new state in 1964 and connections with Botswana, Lesotho, Swaziland and Malawi have been developed while relations with South Africa and Rhodesia also persist. Principles and political events, however, drew Zambia closer to eastern Africa in ideological sympathies and economic associations followed. Zambia thus maintains a dual role in the two regions but inclining more towards East Africa.

The most important task was the reorientation of communications in which work has progressed with remarkable speed but at considerable expense. An oil pipeline to bring 90 per cent of Zambia's needs from the Dar es Salaam refinery was opened in 1968. The parallel Great North Road will have an entirely bitumen surface by the end of 1973 and it is used extensively by the jointly owned Zambia–Tanzania Road Services Ltd, formed in 1966 to operate a freight service. The Chinese are helping to build a thousand-mile railway to Dar es Salaam which should be operative by the mid-1970s. Zambia has provided finance to expand Tanzania's port facilities for their joint use, and has joined Kenya, Uganda and Tanzania in the East African Shipping Line.[22]

These developments were mostly conceived soon after Zambia's independence, but were given great impetus by UDI in November 1965. Their political importance lies in the joint responsibility and finance for every project provided by the Zambian and Tanzanian governments. This was facilitated by Tanzania's willingness to share the burden of Zambia's response to UDI and by the personal friendship of the two presidents. However, eastward communications are not yet adequate and Zambia is still forced to use the Rhodesia railways and other southward routes: to end this use immediately would cause unacceptable damage to the Zambian economy. The government cannot afford to be too provocative to South Africa, Rhodesia or Portugal for fear of their damaging retaliation.

High copper prices have facilitated sustained growth *and* the realignment of external economic relations. Though some early domestic projects had to be curtailed, a more self-sufficient economy has developed. Some domestic changes, such as partial nationalization, Zambianization, redefined sources and import routes, affect the interests of other countries but that is not allowed to limit the pursuance of Zambian control and economic non-alignment.

Zambia's foreign trade policy is 'to establish mutually advantageous trading relationships with as many friendly countries as possible and to move right away from the heavy dependence on southern Africa as a source, and a transit route, for imports and exports which was a feature of Zambia's pre-Independence trading pattern'.[23] Those objects are being pursued effectively considering the supposed inability of small states to influence their trading patterns.

In 1964 Zambia's exports totalling £167·8 million (mainly copper) went primarily to Britain (30 per cent), West Germany, Italy, France, Japan and South Africa. By 1968 total exports had risen to £270·2 million and the pattern had changed so that, while South Africa's imports from Zambia had absolutely declined and Britain's percentage of the increased market had remained constant, Japan's share rose from 10 per cent to 21 per cent, the other three countries increased their percentages, and a large number of other states began to buy significant quantities of copper. However, although the number of buyers increased, the share of Britain, Western Europe and Japan together actually rose from 77 per cent to a dominating 90 per cent in 1968. (See Tables 1 and 2.)

The country's import pattern showed far more significant changes between 1964 and 1968, while the total import bill rose from £78·2 million to £162·5 million. First, Rhodesia's share declined, as a result of deliberate Zambian policy, from 37 per cent to an insignificant 6 per cent. Second, sources were so

Table 1 *Zambian Trade By Area 1964–69*

Area	Percentage of Total Imports					
	1964	1965	1966	1967	1968	1969
Sterling Area	81·6	77·3	70·3	63·6	62·1	63·1
EEC	5·7	7·4	8·2	12·2	12·7	9·9
EFTA (exc. U.K.)	1·6	1·9	2·3	2·5	3·1	3·0
COMECON	0·1	0·1	0·2	0·7	0·9	0·7
Dollar Area	5·1	7·6	11·9	12·0	11·0	10·4
Asia	2·1	3·7	3·8	6·4	5·9	7·8
Middle East/Africa	3·4	1·9	2·8	1·5	3·4	4·0
Other Countries	0·4	0·1	0·5	1·1	0·9	1·1

Area	Percentage of Total Exports					
	1964	1965	1966	1967	1968	1969
Sterling Area	45·9	48·0	40·5	35·1	33·6	29·7
EEC	30·3	29·7	34·0	26·6	32·2	30·3
EFTA (exc. U.K.)	2·8	4·1	5·5	5·8	5·8	5·5
Other European Countries	1·9	2·0	2·8	2·4	2·9	3·4
COMECON	1·6	2·3	2·0	1·4	1·0	0·8
Dollar Area	2·6	0·6	0·1	5·1	2·0	0·1
Asia	11·4	12·1	14·2	21·7	21·6	24·9
Middle East/Africa	0·7	1·1	0·7	1·0	0·6	0·3
Other Countries	2·8	0·1	0·3	0·8	0·3	1·2

Source: *Statements of External Trade* (Central Statistical Office, Lusaka, 1964–69).

Table 2 *Imports and Exports By Selected Countries 1964 and 1969 (£'000s)*

	Imports		Exports	
	1964	1969	1964	1969
United Kingdom	13,416	35,703	54,486	99,104
Rhodesia	30,869	10,886	6,912	219
South Africa	16,203	34,973	13,117	3,836
West Germany	2,108	6,076	21,823	48,035
France	—	2,580	9,316	34,997
Italy	—	3,385	12,127	40,061
Japan	1,597	11,294	18,550	90,158
United States	4,025	15,041	4,454	4,345
Sweden	—	2,177	3,830	88,970
Zambian total	78,219	155,898	167,759	383,245

Source: Table 1.

diversified that, while only eight countries supplied more than £1 million in 1964, twenty-one were in that category in 1968, of which the most important were West Germany, Italy, the United States and Japan exporting over £10 million worth each and doubling their percentage of the total market. Third, South Africa and Britain increased their exports from 21 per cent and 17 per cent respectively to 25 per cent each. It is a continuous concern that Zambia must compromise her principles by remaining a captive market for South Africa and thus vulnerable to pressure from there. Government measures attempt to force the reluctant business community to conform with the policy of reduced trade, but that engenders ill-will and has caused costs to rise.

Trade patterns did not change significantly in 1969. The import total fell slightly to £156 million but was still dominated by Britain and South Africa, supplying 23 per cent each, followed by Western Europe (12 per cent), the United States (9 per cent), Japan (7 per cent) and Rhodesia (7 per cent). Exports rose very satisfactorily to £383 million of which Britain, Western Europe and Japan still took 90 per cent though Britain's share actually fell to 26 per cent.

Britain remains an important economic partner, buying 30 per cent of Zambia's exports and supplying a fair proportion of imports, financial aid and skilled manpower. Relations were disturbed, however, by resentment after November 1965 at the failure of Mr Wilson's government to compensate Zambia adequately for the economic losses incurred through support of the sanctions policy against Rhodesia. Zambia maintained that Britain was solely responsible and should use force because sanctions would be ineffective. Nevertheless, Zambia supported the sanctions campaign, believing that Wilson might otherwise blame her in the event of a failure to end the rebellion, and the country's economy suffered accordingly in higher import prices, disrupted copper exports, costly fuel imports, expenditure immediately on new import routes and higher defence costs. Britain's proffered £13 million compensation was considered quite inadequate to meet Zambia's conservative estimate of £30 million.[24] Further reassessment of relations with Britain, including possible sanctions against the latter, followed the Conservative government's reconsideration of the ban on arms sales to South Africa in 1970. However, strong basic

137

factors – economic and cultural – and the inability to apply effective pressure to Britain seems to indicate that links will be maintained even under severe political strain.

Relations with some countries, especially Japan, Italy, West Germany and the United States, have centred on economic partnerships. This is satisfactory for Zambia as no such wide links pertained before independence. Less dependent on any one source, the country is more free to pursue independent foreign policies and has an entrée to many more political circles.

Formal relations with South America opened in 1966 with a series of state visits, but the significant event was a conference in Lusaka in August 1967 when Zambia joined with Peru, Chile and Congo (Kinshasa) in setting up the Council of Copper Exporting Countries. There is a permanent secretariat in Paris and the intention is to co-ordinate prices and policies. The co-operation is an important step in jointly protecting the interests of less developed states against the exploitation of the richer countries. It is a general policy which Kaunda re-emphasized at the Conference of Non-Aligned States in 1970: 'It is essential for non-aligned and developing countries to seek an effective strategy for their own development . . . What we seek is unity through economic and technical co-operation to prevent the stronger nations from imposing their will on us separately or collectively.'[25] From that early economic base, relations with South and Latin America and the West Indies have broadened considerably in more general political directions.

Out of the immediate responses to UDI which pushed her towards East Africa, Zambia has developed more permanent structures. In December 1967 the government made a formal application to join the East African Economic Community. Detailed studies and negotiations have not progressed with any great speed and the Community itself is far from being a cohesive organization. It is not altogether clear that the association would be economically beneficial to Zambia, but political arguments are forceful in urging the assured support against South Africa and for practical Pan-Africanism. Official policy is based on the commitment to join the Community; association in posts, telegraphs, harbours and research will probably be accepted first while other aspects are still being considered. The change of government in Uganda in early 1971 shook the unity in East

Africa and will adversely affect the prospects for Zambian membership of the original Community.

RELATIONS WITH THE UNITED STATES AND THE SOVIET UNION

Africa is on the periphery of the interest of the two great powers which seek mainly to influence rather than to gain exclusive control of any region. Zambia does not have strategic importance nor control of air or sea routes; the United States and Soviet Union both have alternative sources of copper. Zambia herself, observing non-alignment, avoids direct conflict with either power but was ready to condemn the Soviet invasion of Czechoslovakia (indeed, was very apprehensive at the implications for any African state which came under similar control) and American actions in Vietnam. Kaunda commands a sympathetic audience in the United States but he wields little influence in their important policy decisions which are usually carried out through aid to Africa; Zambia has not been a major recipient.[26]

Only in accepting communist Chinese aid to build the northeast railway does Zambia challenge Russian and American interests since both are suspicious of Chinese influence in Africa. However, if a war with South Africa developed, Kaunda would be reluctant to invite Russian, Chinese or American help. He prefers neutral sources and fears that the United States might act to protect white South Africa and her own investments there. He believes the result would be a racial war with Cold War involvement and a Zambian battleground.

BI-LATERAL ISSUES

President Kaunda misses few opportunities to appeal publicly for world peace and racial tolerance, hoping thereby to influence the more powerful states. He has personally attended many international gatherings,[27] and he has visited more than thirty-five countries. Many of these visits have been reciprocated. Zambia supports, for the most part, the organizations – United Nations Organization, Organization of African Unity and Commonwealth – dedicated to peaceful co-operation between states. Zambia's leaders have become respected spokesmen for

Africa and the Third World, although the practical achievements are harder to assess. The real influence may be very small, for Kaunda is believed by some to exaggerate the dangers of a racial war in southern Africa; certainly the great powers have not yet acted at all decisively to end racial discrimination or conflict in the area. However, lacking economic and military power, Zambia must rely on moral pressure alone until she is self-sufficient and strong enough to make her influence more effectively felt.

Finding that constructive dialogue with white minority governments is ineffective, Kaunda has endorsed a policy of violent change in Rhodesia, Angola and Mozambique: for the moment South Africa is considered a different case.[28] To this end the various African nationalist movements engaged in that violent struggle are allowed transit through Zambia, have headquarters in Lusaka and live there with refugee status. They are forbidden to train in Zambia for guerrilla war and they are prevented from disrupting the political life in Zambia. Funds are channelled through the OAU Liberation Committee of which Zambia is one of the few paid-up members. The government is aware of the consequences of these actions. A Bill allowing special powers to the government is presented to the National Assembly every six months, and declares 'that a situation exists which, if it is allowed to continue, may lead to a state of public emergency'.[29] This is justified on the grounds of incidents on the borders with the minority-ruled countries, continuing hostile relations with Rhodesia, the presence of many refugees in Zambia, and the ex-Lumpa exiles over the border in the Congo.[30] Zambian territory has been violated many times from Angola, Mozambique and Rhodesia. Still Zambia offers bases for a British military attack to end the Rhodesian rebellion; Britain has consistently declined the offer.

In contrast to these bad relations, Zambia has acted positively to reinforce friendship with the northern neighbours. Various ministers, officials and private delegations have met regularly with their counterparts in East Africa and the Congo to share common experiences and problems. The inter-communication is now extremely varied compared with the complete lack of it before 1964. Recently the government has cultivated increased relations with West African states, both English and French-speaking, which could become useful economic partners in the future when communications and language barriers are overcome.

Good relations with neighbouring Tanzania were a predictable priority in 1964 as the foundations had been laid during the independence struggle; possible federation and a railway had already been discussed. UDI provided the crucial impetus to faster integration which became important in freeing Zambia from limitations imposed by historical and geographical factors. Tanzania proved ready to share the burdens of Zambia's response to UDI even to the extent of breaking diplomatic relations with Britain, when Zambia did not, in late 1965 as demanded by an OAU resolution. Relations with Tanzania have been the most specific, wide-ranging and friendly of all Zambia's contacts in the first six years.

Diplomatic relations in Africa are frequently disrupted by changes on the domestic political scenes. Kaunda retains a strong admiration for the early leaders who inspired African nationalism, and he is reluctant to acknowledge their political overthrow especially where military forces are responsible. He refused to recognize the legitimacy of the military successors in Ghana, Algeria and Congo (Brazzaville). While this affirms his belief in democratic processes and mistrust of military government, it also hinders relations with several countries where contact would be useful. However, the OAU has provided a valuable channel for maintaining relations meanwhile, and latterly the objective of strengthening relations between African states seems to be prevailing over boycott of the military forces.

The military régime in Ghana was not recognized by Zambia but relations were restored when civilian rule returned in 1969. In that year when Kaunda toured West Africa, he avoided all countries with military governments. By contrast, the Zambian High Commission remained open in Lagos, Nigeria, after the two coups in 1966. It was only closed when Zambia recognized the secessionist state of Biafra a year later.[31] Relations were then restored after the defeat of Biafra in 1970 as Zambia is anxious to maintain friendship with this potentially powerful African state and Commonwealth member, rather than to practise rigid non-communication with military régimes.

Similarly, the government of General Mobutu in the Congo (Kinshasa) has always been recognized.[32] Compromise prevailed because the authoritarian military government offered

141

the best solution to the prevailing chaos in the Congo in 1965, it ended the rule of the disliked Moise Tshombe, and it was in Zambia's interest to support stability to the north when the coup occurred in the same month as UDI in Rhodesia. After all, the Congo provides one of Zambia's outlets to the sea and, of all African countries, trades the most with Zambia.

In relation to another area of Africa Kaunda proved his preference for mediation. In September 1967 he provided the chairmanship, under OAU auspices, for a successful agreement in the Kenya–Somalia border dispute. Certainly the respective leaders had been anxious to end the fighting but Kaunda provided the opportunity to reach a formal agreement.[33] Somali–Zambian friendship flourished as a result. Both countries are firmly non-aligned and have applied to join the East African Community. Prime Minister Ibrahim Egal and President Kaunda exchanged official visits in 1968 but the association came to an abrupt pause in late 1969 when President Shermache of Somalia was assassinated and a military régime imprisoned Egal and assumed control of the country shortly afterwards.

Undoubtedly the single most important issue faced by Zambia has been Rhodesia's UDI which created overnight a long hostile southern border: physical security became a vital consideration. Before 1965 relations with Southern Rhodesia were unfriendly but not without communication. Zambia had aimed to reduce relations to a minimum gradually, but now felt required to end all formal communication despite the very difficult consequences since the economies were so closely related. Zambia twice considered a total break with Rhodesia but was dissuaded by Britain who feared the direct confrontation this would provoke.

The hardest dilemma was the extent to which Zambia could support the African nationalist movements. It is their actions which will provoke retaliation if the guerrilla fighters become even minimally effective in Rhodesia or South Africa. Zambia's support is cautious; South Africa is the most powerful state on the continent and maintains a co-ordinated military front with Rhodesia and Portugal. Conventional attack and delicate sabotage have already been proved effective in disrupting the Zambian economy, and South Africa has often warned of a possible pre-emptive strike to the north of the Zambezi. Zambia remains undeterred by the threats because Kaunda's determination to end minority rule is strong. He has authorized heavy expenditure to expand his armed forces, though they cannot hope to challenge the white fortress and even the long borders are inadequately patrolled.

South Africa's non-military offensive employs an extensive public relations network and formidable economic means to create a buffer ring of acquiescent African states. She would like to include Zambia, a prospect that Kaunda will vigorously resist. Some contradictions have already been forced on Zambia which does business with states heavily committed in South Africa too.[34] The best defence, however, is to reduce Zambia's dependence on South Africa and to offer an example of stability to undermine white complacency about the inevitability of violence and political disruption in black Africa. Successful democracy in Zambia challenges the white rulers far more effectively than physical proximity or a military threat.

Generally the government declines any contact with the South African government which is not considered strictly necessary for economic survival. However, in the spirit of the Lusaka Manifesto, Kaunda undertook private communications with Mr Vorster in 1968[35] which indicate his personal desire to get change there without violence if possible. Yet he is not free to act alone for he is caught in a trap of conflicting desires and restraints, hoping for peace but change, unified African action but lacking the requisite power, and decisive policies but held back by domestic political considerations.

South Africa's policies also brought Zambia into conflict with Malawi on the eastern border. Malawi's President, Dr Hastings Banda, has accepted considerable sums of aid from South Africa and the two countries exchanged diplomatic representatives in 1968. This was considered a betrayal of the Africans in South Africa. At first it brought ostracism in the OAU until some states swung round to Banda's view by 1970. Subsequent differences of opinion about the attempt to form a dialogue with South Africa are crucial to the future of the OAU and to its effectiveness in ending white rule which was one of the primary goals in its formation in 1963. The Zambian government does not agree with Malawi's policy and feels strongly that there should be a common OAU policy.

Prospects for relations between Zambia and Malawi had seemed good in 1964 and Malawi gave helpful assistance in the post-UDI months. High commissioners were not exchanged but less formal contact was maintained and developed. Relations deteriorated when Banda made claims to some Zambian territory, some political refugees fled to asylum in Zambia, and then Malawi's friendship with South Africa flourished. Nevertheless, negotiations continued intermittently between Lusaka and Blantyre and resulted in an exchange of high commissioners in 1971. Though Zambia gains few economic benefits from compromising her principles to retain Malawi's friendship, it is clearly unnecessary to provoke conflict here when other borders are far more vulnerable. The High Commission in Malawi can now, also, continue surreptitious communication with Portugal through its mission there.

Association with Tanzania brought Zambia into contact with the People's Republic of China and thereby aroused Western and South African fears of communist infiltration. In 1964, when China first offered to build the railway from Tanzania to Zambia, Zambia was apprehensive (and still is) of communist influence. Kaunda would have preferred Western aid but, when it was not forthcoming, he accepted the Chinese offer which has already brought seven thousand Chinese workmen to the area and into close contact with the local employees:[36] so far their movements have been strictly controlled in Zambia. In accepting the aid the government has deliberately calculated the advantages of finally being free from southern control against the possible Chinese influence which could fetter future independence. Zambia is definitely anxious to avoid communist involvement in any conflict in the area.

Zambia had expected to continue in friendly co-operation with Britain since independence had been achieved with relative ease. Rhodesia's UDI quickly thrust Zambia into conflict when the rebellion was not quelled immediately, and continued as the Zambian government disagreed with Wilson's methods of handling the situation. The whole UDI crisis, and Kaunda's misplaced trust in Wilson's intentions to act firmly, well illustrate the Zambian leader's instinct to believe in others' sincerity, even persuading his Cabinet to agree. Disillusion has been keenly felt as the continuous unproductive negotiations lead Zambians to believe that Britain will abandon the Africans to the rule of the white minority. This view was further compounded by Wilson's reluctance to endorse the pledge of no

144

independence for Rhodesia without majority rule, and then by the Conservative victory in the 1970 British general election. It seemed likely that Zambian pressure for an honourable settlement would be ignored by Britain.

Already ill-disposed to continue friendly relations, Zambia found further cause to criticize the British role in the Nigeria–Biafra war. It seemed abhorrent that Britain should range alongside the Soviet Union whose aggression in Czechoslovakia had been criticized. Kaunda believed that force could not achieve a lasting solution; while Britain's supply of arms helped General Gowan to resist pressure, Zambia's recognition of Biafra was thought to help to force him to negotiate. No sooner had differences over Nigeria faded in 1970 with the defeat of Biafra than Zambia was roused again by Mr Heath's apparent willingness to consider selling arms to South Africa which is Zambia's enemy: a new conflict of opinion was certain.

The Conservative government's negotiation with Smith's régime in Rhodesia in November 1971 was decried as a 'sell-out' by the Zambians who recognized that African majority rule would not be achieved for three decades at least. Though neither trade nor transport southward will rise to pre-UDI levels while white government remains in Rhodesia, South Africa and Mozambique, Rhodesia's return to legal international status will allow Zambia to re-establish some economic relations to ease her domestic problems. Support for Zimbabwe (Rhodesian) freedom fighters will become more problematical as Zambia tries to normalize relations and reduce the pressure on her southern border; this could be an opportunity either to force the Rhodesian Africans into action to win their freedom or to abandon support for their ineffective divided factions. The agreement reinforces Zambia's disillusion with Britain's role in southern Africa. The result could be further cuts in relations between the two countries or a clearer way for renewed mutual activity now that the Rhodesian issue is being put aside by Britain.

RELATIONS WITH CERTAIN GROUPINGS

Zambia is involved in a multiplicity of groupings both inside and outside Africa. The pre-independence Federation of Rhodesia and Nyasaland which has been mentioned left some early distaste for another binding relationship, but not for long. At that time, UNIP had also joined other African nationalist groups in the Pan-African Movement of East, Central and Southern Africa (Pafmecsa) of which Kaunda was the chairman in 1962.[37] This had provided support in the achievement of independence, but was disbanded in 1963 in favour of the Organization of African Unity.

The OAU has been faithfully supported; Kaunda attends almost every summit meeting and was elected chairman for 1970. Zambian support for Biafra in 1968 had caused some estrangement for only three other states joined Zambia in recognition of the secessionist state.[38] Kaunda subsequently refused a Vice-Presidency of the OAU when Algeria's President called Biafra's supporters (imperialists). This was a low point of isolation in 1968, but relations never reached complete non-communication and reconciliation with Nigeria followed the surrender of Biafra in 1970. Zambia's support for the Organization returned and the OAU proved itself resilient in the crisis.

A number of functional organizations operate under the OAU umbrella including the African Development Bank, the Association of African Airlines, the Conferences of African Labour Ministers and many more which Zambia works actively to support. International events are beginning to force the realization that Zambia's political influence is limited; Africa must be made strong by her own economic development and especially by better communications and inter-African trade. For instance, it was believed that pressure could have been used against Britain (over the arms to South Africa issue) but only if the action was co-ordinated.

Kaunda has always believed that regional associations are the best basis for African unity, so the significant post-independence relations have been focused on eastern Africa. The core is the informal Mulungushi Club of Presidents Kaunda, Nyerere and Obote (Uganda) initiated in 1967. They were closely identified in their hopes for Africa; they all firmly opposed white rule in southern Africa, though Kaunda appears to have moved further on his own towards seeking an accommodation with the South African government. In 1968 they were joined by President Mobutu of the Congo (Kinshasa), but the unity was upset in January 1971 when military forces overthrew President Obote in Uganda. Kaunda and Nyerere refused to recognize the Amin régime, but Mobutu appeared to support the coup. This event is potentially disruptive of all the previous moves towards regional unity and brings much closer to Zambia the problem of attitudes to military governments.

A more formal extension of the Mulungushi Club group is the fourteen East and Central African states which have met annually since 1966 to discuss local and world issues and to co-ordinate policies. The 1969 conference appointed study groups to investigate scientific and technical co-operation in the attempt to move away from wordy resolutions towards positive joint action. The same meeting produced the Lusaka Manifesto[39] which attempted to offer grounds for joint peaceful negotiations with the South African government on the basis of intended progress to majority rule there. Though well received by many UN members, the document was ignored in Pretoria.

Zambia's application in December 1967 to join the East African Economic Community is important in this context. Preceded by informal co-operative action in the region, this new step draws Zambia towards East Africa in an institutional form designed to survive changes in leadership and to aid the development and strength of the region. The resultant growth and stability is expected to contribute to the ultimate unity of the continent. More significantly for Zambia, the political backing of formal association would counterbalance the disturbing isolation which the government was feeling by 1969 as world interest in Rhodesia waned. African support in the early crisis had been valuable, as had extra-African practical assistance, but at the 1969 Commonwealth Conference Kaunda alone still demanded force to end the Rhodesian rebellion. However, the following year found a resilient Zambia leading renewed activity at the Non-Aligned Conference, the OAU, the UN and on bi-lateral diplomatic levels.

Though committed to the principles of the UN and the Commonwealth Zambia recognizes their limitations and is becoming aware that these are not necessarily the most effective organs for bringing pressure to bear on the larger states. While political action seems to be bringing few results, the technical bodies of the UN and Commonwealth provide valuable services for Zambia. The UN assists in development projects which include road improvements, a power station on the North Bank at Kariba, fighting malnutrition and developing better agriculture.

Meanwhile, diplomatic deficiencies are partially remedied through representation at the UN in New York, and special experience and opportunities for influence were gained during Zambia's term as the African representative on the Security Council in 1969. Informal discussions, personal meetings and the multi-racial character are all compatible with Zambia's methods.

The final, and perhaps more significant, grouping to which Zambia belongs is the amorphous congregation loosely called the Third World, and its more specific manifestation – the group of states which base their foreign policies on non-alignment. Though unrepresented at the 1961 Belgrade Non-Aligned Conference, and only just independent when attending the Cairo conference in 1964, Zambia was the venue in September 1970 for the Third Conference of Non-Aligned States, with sixty participants. This is a measure of the remarkable growth in international stature of the country and its President in particular, and of his activity in furthering the aims of this group of states. Zambia gains contacts, support and prestige by this leadership, but incurs the responsibility of maintaining her non-alignment under pressure. There have been few opportunities to utilize the solidarity in practical ways, though verbal sympathy for Zambia's position is often expressed. The association with this group serves best to indicate the deep commitment to an independent and moral foreign policy.

CONCLUSION

Zambia has been very active in foreign affairs despite her lack of conventional military or economic power and despite her youth in the world community. Border relations are crucial since, in a landlocked position, associations with neighbours are a first priority; other policies towards Africa have often been an extension of these. However, historical and economic factors ensured that the country would have a role which stretched far beyond the continent. The character of President Kaunda further emphasized the international activities by adding depth and personal involvement.

Kaunda is the dominant figure though there are others very willing to take his place. No other leader has achieved the same national support nor expressed his views towards foreign policy so comprehensively. However, it is crucial that internal affairs are not very settled. Zambia is a small state but also a new one which is potentially unstable if domestic political change occurs in the near future at which time foreign policies might change radically. Kaunda cannot afford to ignore this when stability is part of Zambia's defence.

Economic development is equally important to satisfy the demands of the Zambian population who are not greatly concerned about events outside their borders. Furthermore, a weak economy is too vulnerable to pressure from outside at a time when the government wishes to pursue independent foreign policies. The fairly advanced nature of certain sectors ensures that worldwide links are necessary but must, in the government's view, be diversified.

A strong theme in the seven years has been the attempt to match principles to practice when survival and development are also paramount. Doubtless Kaunda's ideals are sincerely held but his goals are high. There are those in Zambia who would not hesitate to trade with South Africa, for instance, if it would benefit them and Zambia and they felt strong enough to defy the government. It has been suggested that Kaunda's principles will stand the biggest test if copper prices fall so that Zambia is short of financial resources – and South Africa offers aid.[40]

The Zambian government has been preoccupied with the problems in and relations with South Africa, Rhodesia, Angola and Mozambique. Those are and will be major issues, but it would be wrong to leave the impression that they are the only concerns. A firm foundation of association with northern neighbours, other African states and many non-African countries has been laid. These should assume more importance in the next decade together with the internal problems which will consistently demand thoughtful attention.

NOTES AND REFERENCES

The most comprehensive study of the historical context of modern Zambia from the earliest times is found in R. Hall, *Zambia* (Pall Mall, London, 1965). Other authors have investigated specific aspects of Central African history before Zambia's independence. R. I. Rotberg examines the development of African nationalism in *The Rise of Nationalism in Central Africa: The Making of Malawi and Zambia, 1873–1964* (Cambridge University

Press, London, 1965); W. J. Barber's *The Economy of Central Africa* (Stanford University Press, Stanford, 1961) explains the regional economic patterns at the end of the Federation of which the political history and its implications are elucidated in C. Leys and C. Pratt, *A New Deal in Central Africa* (Heinemann, London, 1960), and in P. Keatley, *The Politics of Partnership: The Federation of Rhodesia and Nyasaland* (Penguin, Harmondsworth, 1963). At that same period, Northern Rhodesian Africans were struggling for their own political rights and the independence of Zambia as comprehensively described by D. Mulford in *Zambia, the Politics of Independence, 1957–1964* (Oxford University Press, London, 1967), and were also helping to establish practical Pan-Africanism in eastern Africa as R. Cox explains in *Pan Africanism in Practice, Pafmecsa 1958–1964* (Oxford University Press, London, 1964). That other Africans throughout southern Africa were in similar struggles is made plain by the participants at the conference of which *Southern Africa in Transition*, J. A. Davis and J. K. Baker (eds), (Praeger, New York, 1966), is a record.

Kenneth David Kaunda is the dominant figure in Zambia and his early life and character are well described by R. Hall in *Kaunda, Founder of Zambia* (Longmans of Zambia, Lusaka, 1964) from the vantage of one with close acquaintance and sympathetic observation. However, the President speaks for himself in his autobiography, *Zambia Shall Be Free* (Heinemann, London, 1962), in C. Legum's collection of Kaunda's speeches up to 1966 entitled *Zambia, Independence and Beyond. The Speeches of Kenneth Kaunda* (Nelson, London, 1966), and in *A Humanist in Africa* (Longmans, London, 1966) which is a series of letters to Colin Morris providing a clear view of Kaunda's dearest principles. The alignment of these principles with Zambian control of the economy is the subject of B. de Gaay Fortman's *After Mulungushi* (East African Publishing House, Nairobi, 1969), while M. L. O. Faber and J. G. Potter give a scholarly account of the early role of the mining companies and the 1969 nationalization of the industry in *Towards Economic Independence* (Cambridge University Press, London, 1971). Finally, in *The High Price of Principles: Kaunda and the White South* (Hodder and Stoughton, London, 1969), R. Hall analyses the diverse domestic and external pressures facing Kaunda by reason of Zambia's geographical position and opposition to continued minority rule in Africa.

Some aspects of Zambian foreign policy are best illuminated by articles dealing with specific areas but not always focusing directly on Zambia. Many authors have examined the links between Zambia and the white south after 1964: 'Zambia and Rhodesia: Links and Fetters' by R. Hall *Africa Report*, vol. 11, no. 1 (January, 1966) pp. 8–12, indicates the various problems arising out of Rhodesia's UDI, while F. Taylor Ostrander gives more details of the consequences of an immediate breakaway in 'Zambia in the aftermath of the Rhodesian UDI: Logistical and Economic problems', *African Forum*, vol. 2, no. 3 (Winter, 1966) pp. 50–65. L. W. Bowman, J. K. Nyerere and A. Rake indicate in their articles under the joint title of 'Three Years after UDI' that there were still many aspects in the Rhodesian situation with enormous consequences for the neighbouring African countries (*Africa Report*, vol. 13, no. 9, December, 1968, pp. 16–25).

The impact of the Rhodesian crisis on the Commonwealth, its member states and Britain is an interesting aspect of Zambia's affairs, and is examined by B. Lapping in 'Wilson's Crucible: The Commonwealth and Rhodesia', *Africa Report*, vol. 11, no. 7 (October, 1966) pp. 10–14, and by J. Day in 'The Rhodesian African nationalists and the Commonwealth African States', *Journal of Commonwealth Political Studies*, vol. 7, no. 2 (July, 1969) pp. 132–44. Moving further south, it is useful to look at how South Africa's foreign policies are developing, as in V. McKay's article on 'South African Propaganda: Methods and Media', *Africa Report*, vol. 11, no. 2 (February, 1966) pp. 41–6, and in the article by J. E. Spence on 'South Africa's "new look" foreign policy', *World Today*, vol. 24, no. 4 (April, 1968) pp. 137–45.

Meanwhile, one has realized that southern Africa is not the only area of concern to the Zambian leaders. Relations with East Africa and the East African Economic Community are highlighted by A. Hazlewood in 'The Kampala Treaty and the accession of new members to the East African Community', *East African Economic Review*, vol. 4, no. 2 (December, 1968) pp. 49–63, and I. Wallerstein's article on 'African Unity Reassessed' contributes to discussion of the most acceptable and possible future policies for Zambia (*Africa Report*, vol. 11, no. 4, April, 1966, pp. 41–6). And beyond the continent, it is evident that the influence of the major world powers cannot be ignored by Zambia, such that the series of articles on the 'African–American Dialogues', *Africa Report*, vol. 14, no. 1 (January, 1969) pp. 8–41 is helpful in seeing what options are open for relations with the west.

1. For pre-independence history in detail, see R. Hall, *Zambia* (Pall Mall, London, 1965).
2. ibid., p. 96.
3. P. Keatley, *The Politics of Partnership: the Federation of Rhodesia and Nyasaland* (Penguin, Harmondsworth, 1963).
4. The figures are from the Central Statistical Office, Lusaka, Zambia.
5. AAC is primarily South African and British owned, whilst RST is British and American.
6. M. L. O. Faber and J. G. Potter, *Towards Economic Independence* (Cambridge University Press, London, 1971).
7. These are often called the Mulungushi reforms. See B. de Gaay Fortman, *After Mulungushi* (East African Publishing House, Nairobi, 1969).
8. The Central African Statistical Office gave a figure of £98 million.
9. For details of the economic distribution of the federation, see C. Leys and C. Pratt, *A New Deal in Central Africa* (Heinemann, London, 1960) pp. 59–97.
10. K. D. Kaunda, *Humanism in Zambia and a Guide to its Implementation* (Government Printer, Lusaka, April, 1968).
11. I. Wallerstein, *The Politics of Independence* (Random House, New York, 1961) p. 122.
12. Members in the National Assembly, 1964: United National Independence Party 55; African National Congress 10; National Congress

Party (reserved roll) 10; Nominated 5. In 1968 the distribution of seats was: United National Independence Party 82; African National Congress 22; Independents 1; Nominated 5. For an analysis of pre-1964 politics, see D. Mulford, *Zambia, the Politics of Independence, 1957–1964* (Oxford University Press, London, 1967).

13. Ministers of Foreign Affairs: Simon Kapwepwe October, 1964–August, 1967; Reuben Kamanga August 1967–April 1969; Elijah Mudenda April 1969–August 1969; President Kaunda August 1969–November 1970; Elijah Mudenda November 1970– .

14. Stirling Astaldi and others in construction, Fiat in a car assembly plant, Total in fuel distribution, Fiat in ZamTan Road Services Ltd, ENI in Tanzama Pipelines Ltd, Alitalia in Zambian Airways, and the Italian Air Force in Zambia Air Force are some of the bigger involvements by Italian groups.

15. The ANC leader, Harry Nkumbula, sympathizes with the policies of co-operation with South Africa pursued by Malawi's Hastings Banda.

16. For a sympathetic view of Kaunda, see R. Hall, *Kaunda, Founder of Zambia* (Longmans of Zambia, Lusaka, 1964).

17. Addressed to a meeting of African Labour Ministers in Lusaka, *Background* no. 18/70 (Zambia Information Services, Lusaka, 9 March 1970).

18. Zambian *Hansard*, no. 6, 3 March 1966, p. 10.

19. C. Legum (ed.), *Zambia, Independence and Beyond. The Speeches of Kenneth Kaunda* (Nelson, London, 1966) p. 192.

20. Zambian *Hansard*, no. 2, 12 January 1965, p. 4.

21. Legum, op. cit., p. 141.

22. For a more detailed account of Zambian–East African links, see M. Bone, *An Investigation of the Relations between Zambia and East Africa*, M.A. thesis, University of Sussex, England, 1968.

23. Report by Zambia's Trade Commissioner in London, *Annual Report* (Ministry of Commerce, Industry and Foreign Trade, Lusaka, 1967) p. 5.

24. R. B. Sutcliffe, 'Zambia and the Strains of UDI', *World Today*, vol. 23 (December, 1967) p. 506, and *Zambia and Rhodesia: Effects of the Sanctions Policy* (Central African Research Office, London, March, 1968).

25. K. D. Kaunda, *Our commitment to a world of genuine freedom, peace and development through co-operation* (Government Printer, Lusaka, September, 1970) pp. 11–12.

26. Zambia benefits peripherally from U.S. aid to regional projects: the Great North Road to Tanzania, the East African Community, the projected Botswana–Zambia highway.

27. Such gatherings have included the United Nations in 1964 and 1967, the Commonwealth Prime Ministers' meetings in 1965, 1969 and 1971, the International Labour Organization in 1969, almost every annual meeting of the OAU and the group of fourteen East and Central African states, and the Non-Aligned Conferences in 1964 and 1970.

28. However, see p. 143 on the Lusaka Manifesto.

29. Zambian *Hansard*, no. 17, 18 April 1969, p. 2320.

30. R. Hall, *The High Price of Principles: Kaunda and the White South* (Hodder and Stoughton, London, 1969) p. 45.
31. This was a decision based on humanitarian considerations, despite the implications for latent secessionism in Zambia. See G. L. Caplan, 'Barotseland: The secessionist challenge to Zambia', *Journal of African Studies*, vol. 6, no. 3 (1968) p. 343.
32. Some people in Zambia have reservations about official friendships with Mobutu. See Hall, op. cit., p. 227.
33. The venue was Arusha in Tanzania and Nyerere was present as an observer. See C. Hoskyns (ed.), *The Ethiopia–Somali–Kenya Dispute, 1960–1967* (Oxford University Press, Nairobi, 1969) and J. Drysdale, *The Somali Dispute* (Pall Mall, London, 1964).
34. Italy, whose role in Zambia is rapidly increasing, West Germany, France and Japan are among the states in this category.
35. *Dear Mr. Vorster . . .* (Zambian Information Services, Lusaka, 1971).
36. J. K. Nyerere, President of Tanzania, *Another Link is Forged* (Government Printer, Lusaka, 1970) p. 21.
37. R. Cox, *Pan Africanism in Practice, Pafmecsa 1958–1964* (Oxford University Press, London, 1964).
38. Tanzania, Gabon and the Ivory Coast also recognized Biafra.
39. For the text see *The Times*, London, 22 May 1969.
40. Hall, op. cit., p. 249.

Chapter 5

ASPECTS OF ISRAELI
FOREIGN POLICY

JACOB REUVENY

INTRODUCTION

Background

The roots of the State of Israel may be traced back to ancient history, i.e. the Old Testament and the Second Temple periods.

In modern history, the development of the Zionist Movement in Europe since the end of the nineteenth century and the Balfour Declaration of 1917 were major events leading to the eventual establishment of a Jewish state in Palestine.

The Balfour Declaration, which was a pronouncement in favour of a Jewish national home in Palestine, raised great enthusiasm among Jewish communities. Following the occupation of Palestine in 1917/18, Great Britain was granted a mandate over Palestine by the League of Nations in July 1922.

The pronounced policy favouring the establishment of a Jewish national home brought about intensive expansion of Jewish immigration and settlement. New towns and villages were established and the Jewish community developed political, social and economic institutions of its own. The early thirties saw an increase in Jewish immigration due to persecution of Jews in Europe following the rise of the Nazi régime in Germany.

The period between the world wars also marked a growth of an Arab nationalist movement in Palestine and a growing Arab-Jewish conflict.

Strong Arab resistance to further expansion of the Jewish community brought about a new British policy expressed in a White Paper of 1939, limiting Jewish immigration and settlement in Palestine.

This policy came at a time when Jews in Europe were des-

154

perately seeking refuge because of imminent danger resulting from German expansion in Europe.

The tragic events, ending in the holocaust in which 6 million Jews perished in Europe, stimulated Jewish leadership in Palestine and the world Zionist movement in its activity for establishing an independent Jewish state. The claim for political independence gained much support in the United States as well as in Britain, where the Labour Party proclaimed its support for establishing a Jewish State in western Palestine. However, after the Labour Party assumed power in 1945 almost no change in British policy followed.

The most urgent issue was the immigration problem. Hundreds of thousands of Jewish refugees in Europe were barred from entering Palestine due to limited quotas. In 1946 President Truman appealed to Prime Minister Attlee for permission for 100,000 Jewish refugees to enter Palestine. The appeal was rejected. In Palestine itself, Jewish military resistance movements and illegal immigration harassed the British army, police and civil administration.

International as well as local pressure made the British role in Palestine untenable and in 1947 Britain presented the Palestine problem to the United Nations, with the declared intention to vacate Palestine the following year.

In November 1947 the General Assembly of the United Nations adopted a partition plan whereby two states, Arab and Jewish, would be created in Palestine.

This decision was favourably accepted by the Jewish leadership but was rejected by the Arab side. It opened a wave of military clashes between Jews and Arabs. With the departure of the British and the proclamation of a Jewish state on 14 May 1948, neighbouring Arab states invaded Palestine with the aim of preventing the establishment of a Jewish state. Following the war, the State of Israel found itself with new boundaries. On the other hand, no Arab state, as recommended by the UN, was established. Most territories allocated for the Arab state were occupied by Transjordan (later Jordan) and Egypt.

In 1949 Israel signed armistice agreements with her Arab neighbours. These agreements, which ended the war, left many issues unsettled. Some of these issues, such as the refugee problem, stir up the Arab-Israeli conflict from time to time and give it a lasting nature.

155

Foreign Policy of the First Years of Independence

The history of Palestine was largely determined by its strategic location at the territorial crossroads of three continents, Asia, Africa and Europe. Due to this position Palestine was a natural object for the domination of larger empires. In most of its history Palestine was a province of such empires, such as the Persian, the Roman and the Ottoman.

A common feature in the establishment of independent political units in Palestine was that their establishment took place during periods of recess in the activities of great empires, somewhere in the twilight between the decline of one power and the rise of another. These intervals were usually short.

If one were to look for recurrent historical traits in the establishment of the state of Israel one could find at least that Israel, like its counterparts in history, was established under similar conditions. The state of Israel was established during the political twilight which came after the decline of the Ottoman and later British Empires and before a new major power has taken over control of the Middle East, all in a manner resembling ancient historical developments.

However, in one sense history does not provide parallels. The long separation of the Jewish people from Palestine during almost 2,000 years of exile has deepened the cultural gap between the Arab nation, of Palestine and the neighbouring countries, and the Jewish nation, far beyond what happened on the return to Judea from the Babylonian exile. This cultural gap, perhaps no less than any real conflict of interests, should be counted among the roots of the present Arab-Israeli conflict.

On the other hand, stronger ties exist between the state and the Jewish communities abroad. The state was explicitly founded with the aim of providing shelter to any Jew who desires to immigrate. The relationship with the Jewish communities – both in terms of adapting foreign policy to the needs of Jews in foreign countries and of asking for their support, economic and political – is one of the foundations of Israeli foreign policy. It also underlies the relations with the big powers; Israel was established by common support of the U.S. and the Soviet Union, two states that also have the largest Jewish communities in the world.

The formal aims of Israeli foreign policy found their expression in one of the first foreign policy statements made by the

Knesset (Parliament). The initial five principles of Israeli foreign policy as approved by the Knesset on 11 March 1949 were:[1]

1. Loyalty to the fundamental principles of the UN Charter and friendship with all peace-loving states, especially the U.S. and the Soviet Union.
2. Efforts to achieve an Arab-Jewish Alliance based on economic, social and cultural co-operation within the UN framework.
3. Support for all measures strengthening peace and the rights of men.
4. Insistence on the rights of Jews to settle in Israel and to leave their present state of residence.
5. Effective preservation of the sovereignty of Israel.

Close study of this statement reveals the great emphasis put on relations with the Jewish nation. This is reflected not only in paragraphs 3 and 4 but, to some extent, even in the first paragraph, namely 'friendship with all peace-loving states, especially the United States and the Soviet Union'. This paragraph reflects a sincere desire for non-identification with one side in the Cold War. This was perhaps due, *inter alia*, not only to the decisive role of the Soviet Union in providing both political and military support for the establishment of the Jewish state, but also to the hope that its Jewish community would take an active role in the development of the country.[2]

THE FOREIGN POLICY MACHINE

The Ministry for Foreign Affairs
With the establishment of the state of Israel the Political Department of the Jewish Agency (which was the 'shadow foreign office') was transferred to the government of Israel, constituting the foundation of the Foreign Ministry. A common trait of many of its diplomats was their Anglo-Saxon or Central European origin and mastery of foreign languages. Very few of its members had previous diplomatic experience. A considerable number of persons transferred from the Jewish Agency are still occupying leading positions in the diplomatic service. The first eight years of the foreign service – 1948–56 – were years of creative growth. During this period many promising diplomats, now holding leading positions, made their steps with the close

157

guidance of the first Foreign Minister (and for some time Prime Minister), the late Moshe Sharett.

With the resignation of Mr Sharett the process of growth (in terms of development of a professional foreign service) began to recede. Besides personal reasons, the process could be attributed to a number of other factors. First, the general weakening of the role of the Ministry for Foreign Affairs in foreign policy-making; second, inadequate attention on the part of the heads of the Ministry to personnel development and the building of a professional foreign service. To this should be added personnel problems owing to the small size of the Ministry as a whole and the great number of missions abroad.

According to the *Israeli Government Yearbook* of 1971/72, Israel had 93 permanent missions – 66 embassies, 4 legations, 3 other missions, 18 consulates general and 2 consulates; with a geographical distribution of 11 in Asia and Oceania, 27 in Africa, 13 in North America, 17 in South America, 24 in Western Europe and 1 in Eastern Europe.[3] In 23 cases Israel was represented by a non-resident ambassador, minister or consul general.

The number of foreign diplomatic missions in Israel was 54, including 8 'non-resident'.

The relatively large number of Israeli missions abroad is due to both the Arab-Israeli conflict and the relations with the Jewish communities overseas.

As a result of the Arab-Israeli conflict, the government of Israel was keen on establishing diplomatic or consular relations with as many countries as possible, not always on a reciprocal basis (e.g. India, Cyprus). This meant, in most cases, maintaining an Israeli presence in a country with the aim of helping to oppose Arab hostile activity in the political, economic or propaganda spheres. In some instances Israeli legations were established with the aim of maintaining relations with remote Jewish communities.

The multifarious system of foreign relations and relatively large number of Israeli missions abroad hindered the growth of a professional foreign service. For many assignments abroad persons are recruited for short terms from diverse sources (other government ministries, the army, political parties, etc.). This arrangement has an obvious administrative advantage since the Ministry for Foreign Affairs bears no responsibility for the placement of personnel after the termination of the assignments

Structure of the Israeli Ministry for Foreign Affairs (1972) if it is unable to find suitable new posts. The negative aspect of this arrangement rests in the fact of inadequate experience and professionality. The rapid turnover of personnel, both permanent and temporary, leaves much to be desired in terms of the capacity of personnel to carry out the heavy and complicated duties of the Ministry.

If we distinguish between 'functional' departments such as the International Co-operation Division and regional (geographic) departments such as the African Division, the inadequate professionality affects primarily (though not exclusively) the functional units. (See Organizational Chart, p. 159.)

One ministerial activity which came under strong public criticism since the June 1967 war was that of the information services. A special government committee under Reserve General Elad Peled recommended, in 1969, the establishment of an independent information agency which would unite internal and external information functions, including the major functions which had been within the jurisdiction of the Ministry for Foreign Affairs. Due to obstinate resistance on the part of the Foreign Ministry this suggestion did not materialize. It did, however, constitute a strong stimulus for introducing some changes in the structure of foreign information organs.

The Institutional Setting

The institutional setting of Israeli foreign policy reflects the patterns of an 'open' system.[4] This is manifested on the one hand in organizational pluralism and on the other in the influence of parliament, public opinion, a free press, and organized interest groups on the formulation and execution of foreign policy.

Beside general 'open' traits of the foreign policy machine, Israeli policy organs, their relative impact and their internal relationship, are largely affected by the basic characteristics of Israeli external relations, i.e. the constant Arab-Israeli conflict on the one hand and the relationship with the Jewish communities abroad on the other.[5]

The Arab-Israeli conflict has increased the role of the military in foreign policy decisions both on the Cabinet and the executive levels.[6] In some cases this process culminated in sharp rivalries between the Ministries of Defence and Foreign Affairs. The growing role of the military has largely resulted from the mere fact that Israel has been involved in a struggle for its very existence. It has had, however, more concrete manifestations. For example, Israeli relations with its surrounding neighbours were conducted until 1967 through Mixed Armistice Commissions which were predominantly military bodies.

Formally, these commissions, established under the 1949 Armistice Agreements (composed of officers of Israeli and Arab armies and presided over by UN officers) were bodies designed to safeguard the strict fulfilment of the Armistice agreements. However, being the only formal framework for Arab-Israeli contact, they sometimes performed political roles exceeding their formal assignments.

The military control of intelligence activity adds another dimension to its role in foreign policy decision-making. In a state with vulnerable boundaries as Israel was prior to the 1967 war, intelligence appraisals were bound to play a major role in foreign policy.

Another more personal manifestation is the absorption of ex-army officers into the diplomatic service (e.g. ambassadors to the U.S. and the United Kingdom, and a growing number of heads and members of diplomatic missions in the developing countries).[7]

In the field of relations with the overseas Jewish communities, the role of the Ministry for Foreign Affairs is limited by its very nature. Most of these relations are carried out by non-governmental institutions, some of which were established in the pre-independence era, including the Jewish Agency, the Jewish National Fund and numerous other Jewish institutions, some operating on a voluntary basis. In some cases there is a considerable overlapping between activities of the Ministry for Foreign Affairs (as well as of other government ministries) and of non-governmental public institutions with functions related to the Jewish communities overseas.

Another area where foreign relations are conducted on a pluralistic basis is the field of technical assistance to the developing countries. Although the International Co-operation Division in the Ministry for Foreign Affairs is the central unit charged with formulation of foreign aid policy, some ministries – including the Ministries of Defence and Agriculture – conduct a somewhat independent policy. This activity is assisted by numerous non-governmental scientific, educational and medical organizations.

F

Similar plurality exists in the realm of scientific, cultural and other non-political relations (e.g. relations with foreign labour unions).

The plurality in terms of the execution of foreign policy is not paralleled in a plurality in terms of participation in decision-making process.

Although the Israeli political system makes it possible for various groups through parties and other representative bodies to influence foreign policy, the actual impact of groups outside the government establishment is limited to secondary issues. Decisions on vital issues are made by a small élite group composed of the country's top leadership.[8]

ISRAEL AND THE ARAB WORLD

The relationship between Israel and the Arab world[9] focuses attention upon three points: (a) basic factors shaping the relationship between Israel and its immediate Arab neighbours, (b) Israel and the Palestinians, (c) aspects of analysis of the Arab-Israeli conflict.

(a) *Basic Factors Shaping Relationship with the Arab World*
The fathers of Zionism including Herzl did not foresee the intensity of the future possible conflicts between Jewish nationalism and the Arab world. In his novel *Altneuland* Herzl expected that amicable relations would prevail between the Arab people and the Jewish immigrants, who would be accepted as Middle Easterners returning to their historical homeland. First steps in Zionist experience after the Balfour Declaration tended to confirm some of these aspirations, e.g. the Weizmann–Feisal contacts in 1918.[10] Soon after, however, in 1920–21, in 1929 and in 1936–39, Arab uprisings against both the British Mandate and Jewish settlement in Palestine upset the hopes of Arab-Israeli peaceful co-existence.

Arab resistance persisted. It was expressed in the Arab opposition to the partition of Palestine decided upon by the General Assembly of the United Nations in June 1947 and in the military invasion of Palestine by the neighbouring Arab states in 1948.

The dominant factor of Arab-Israel relations is the reluctance of the Arab neighbours to acquiesce in its very existence as an

162

independent state in the midst of the Arab world. This tendency of 'non-recognition' of Israel as part of the Middle Eastern family of nations has undergone several changes. It became stronger at certain periods (e.g. prior to the June 1967 war) and it has also had periods of recess as was the case in the early fifties. It should, however, be regarded as a background factor which was never absent in Arab-Israeli relations. This attitude is mostly illustrated by Arab proclamations and attitudes in international organizations.

One could also discern that the Arab claims towards Israel were made on two levels: claims which are directly related to its very existence – which could be defined as 'radical' or 'by root', as opposed to 'incremental',[11] such as claims for the return of some Arab refugees. These 'incremental' claims played a dominant role in international institutions particularly in the realm of the refugee problem. Some of the Arab 'incremental' claims gained international support. Basic Israeli policy has been not to separate between 'radical' and 'marginal' issues. Thus, Israel expressed its readiness to admit to its boundaries a certain number of Arab refugees, but only as a part of a peace agreement.

One of the basic Israeli claims has been that the Armistice Agreements of 1949 were conceived by the Security Council and the General Assembly of the UN as a basis for a peace settlement.[12]

Besides this basic trend, general Israeli policy towards its Arab neighbours between 1949 and 1967 could be characterized by the following tenets:

1. Strict adherence to the spirit and content of the 1949 Armistice Agreements.
2. Retaliatory action in cases of breach by the Arab parties of these agreements. (This policy was dominant in the three years prior to the 1956 Sinai Campaign and found new manifestations after the Six-Day War.)
3. Maintaining a policy of military deterrence towards possibly aggressive Arab states, particularly post-revolutionary Egypt.

A basic feature of Arab-Israeli relations was the fluctuation of the issues in conflict between 'radical' and 'incremental' spheres. Different periods could be characterized by the intensity of one sphere or another. The intensity of the radical sphere

163

reached its peak after the Six-Day War of 1967 when – due to the Israeli victory – Israel took control of large Arab territories. As opposed to Arab 'incremental' claims to return to the 4th of June positions, Israel insisted on a radical solution, namely, the signing of permanent and lasting peace agreements as a condition to a settlement of the border problems and other undecided issues. Israel, on its part, showed readiness for solving basic issues, such as the Palestinian refugee problem, as part of a general peace agreement.

(b) *Israel and the Palestinians*
In terms of lasting human consequences of the Arab-Israeli conflict, the problem of the Palestinians remains the gravest and most tragic. The term 'Palestinians' refers at present to two categories of Arabs: Inhabitants of the western bank of the River Jordan and the Gaza Strip occupied by Israel, and Arab refugees who left the western bank on the establishment of the state or during the June, 1967 war and have not been permanently settled.

There are conflicting views both on the conditions which created the Arab refugee problem and the exact number of refugees.[13]

There is, however, less controversy about the stages of the Arab exodus of 1947–48. The first to leave after the 29 November 1947 Partition Resolution were about 30,000 upper- and middle-class Arabs who constituted the Arab Palestinian élite.[14] The unorganized mass exodus which followed was largely due to the lack of a responsible Arab leadership.

Objective observers could not deny that during the 1948 war Israeli policy favoured the maintenance of an Arab population within its boundaries as a means for future normalization of Arab-Israeli relations and easing of immediate tension.

Israel's Declaration of Independence contains the following passage:

> We appeal – in the very midst of the onslaught launched against us now for months – to the Arab inhabitants of the State of Israel to preserve peace and participate in the up-building of the State on the basis of full and equal citizenship and the representation in all its provisional and permanent institutions.[15]

164

The relations between Israel and the Palestinians have, however, two aspects: first, the attitude towards Palestinians as individuals; second, the policy concerning Palestinians as a political entity. In this discussion we are concerned with the latter issue.

From the signing of the 1949 Armistice Agreements up to the occupation of the western bank of the Jordan and the Gaza Strip in 1967, Israeli foreign policy as well as that of its Arab neighbours preferred to ignore the Palestinians as a direct partner to negotiations, though much lip-service has been paid to them by the Arab side. The Kingdom of Transjordan (later Jordan) annexed the western bank of the River Jordan not without Israeli acquiescence; a similar arrangement – though not amounting to full annexation – happened in the Gaza Strip, which was included in the Egyptian orbit. Amid strong anti-Israel instigation and fostering of guerrilla activity, the Arabs of the western bank of the Jordan gave up their right to an independent state of their own, a right accorded to them in the 1947 UN Resolution.

Although some views in Israel favoured coming to terms with the Palestinians as a practical and just solution to the conflict, the official policy was to strive for a settlement with the Arab neighbouring countries and to try to solve the Palestinians' (and particularly the refugee) problem as part of a general peaceful solution with the Arab world.[16]

The disintegration of the Palestinian population and lack of organized indigenous leadership has facilitated this policy.

Israel started facing the 'Palestinian problem' after its occupation of the western bank of the Jordan, when it had to meet a large Arab population. A parallel 'political awakening' has recently emerged among part of the Arab leadership in the western bank. The problem has generated an internal Israeli discussion as to whether Israel should recognize a 'Palestinian entity' as a future partner in negotiations with its Arab neighbours. A strong proponent of recognizing the Palestinian entity is Professor Jacob Talmon, professor of Modern History in Jerusalem. In an article in the evening paper *Ma'ariv* of 16 May 1969, in the form of an open letter to the Minister in Charge of Information, he emphasized the normative aspect of the recognition of the existence of a Palestinian 'entity' or 'identity'. In his view, lack of recognition of the Palestinian 'entity' is identical with anti-nationalist movements in modern history and cannot be justified before world public opinion.

In his reply published in the same newspaper on 22 May 1969, Mr Galili, representing the government view, maintained that the existence of a political 'entity' or 'identity' should be decided upon empirical rather than normative grounds. Israel has neither the ability nor the duty to create artificially a Palestinian identity which does not exist in reality. In his view, recent Arab history clearly proves that Palestinian Arabs never regarded themselves as a separate political entity. Some came under the orbit of Syrian nationalism, others regarded themselves as owing allegiance to the Hashemite crown, another part was more affiliated with Egypt.

The basic Israeli view concerning the 'Palestinian entity' is pragmatic in nature. It seems much more convenient to regard as partners for negotiations established states rather than a fragmented population which has no institutionalized political representation. Moreover, the inclusion of Palestinians as partners for negotiation may complicate relations with Arab states and make lasting solutions impossible.

(c) *Aspects of Analysis of the Arab-Israeli Conflict*

Numerous books and articles have been written on the Arab-Israeli conflict. In trying to classify the different approaches, probably the most useful criterion is the extent to which a given approach emphasizes the conflict in terms of rational interest as opposed to approaches which try to look for deeper cultural and ideological foundations. One should note, of course, that both interpretations are not mutually exclusive. The problem is mainly an issue of relative emphasis. Recent literature has shown a greater consideration of the cultural-ideological component in the Arab-Israeli conflict, emphasizing the fact that *inter alia*, the mere existence of Israel as a common (real or imaginary) enemy helped in fostering Arab unity.

In an article presenting a model designed to explore the role of the cultural component in international relations, Edmund S. Glenn and his associates write[17]:

Let us look, for example, at the conflict in the Middle East. Is its main cause a conflict of interests, i.e. the loss of territory (with all that territory represents in an 'objective' context of

166

economic and military considerations) by an Arab state which did not then exist? If so, the solution might be suitable compensation, possibly in the form of economic aid capable of increasing the productivity of the land to an extent over-compensating any loss, and of political guarantees against external aggression. Or, is the conflict one of understanding due to the implantation in a culturally associative area of a predominantly abstractive state whose very way of life threatens the associative understanding of legitimacy and sense of identity? In the latter case the solution would be harder to come by. In fact it might be suggested that there is no likely permanent solution, short either of the complete disappearance of Israel or of the westernization of the Palestinian refugees.

Unfortunately, discussion of the Arab-Israeli conflict often tends to ignore one or the other aspect of the dilemma, often with the aim of manipulating arguments so as to favour one or another partisan view of the problem. This ambivalent nature of the Arab-Israeli conflict is of much significance in terms of the political manoeuvring of the parties directly involved in the conflict as well as of external powers who have become involved in it. The exploration of the cultural-ideological dimension of the Arab-Israeli conflict provides support to both 'radicalist' and 'incrementalist' views of the issue. The 'radicalist' view could be supported by the fact that the Arab-Israeli conflict has deep roots and that no solution is possible without cultural and ideological change. An 'incrementalist' view may benefit by the same argument in another form. Namely, since any basic solution calls for cultural and ideological change, policies intended to solve the conflict should therefore be short range and pragmatic, since there is no other feasible alternative.

ISRAEL AND THE FOUR GREAT POWERS

As noted above, due to its geopolitical location Palestine and its neighbours attracted much attention of world powers or of powers striving to attain hegemony. In the middle of this century this potential interest was reinforced by the discovery of rich oil resources in the region.

A significant fact was that Israel was established with the help, political and military, of both the United States and the Soviet Union.

Due to this support, as well as to the fact that in both states there exist the largest Jewish concentrations outside Israel itself, the nascent state adopted a policy of non-identification. This policy in its original form lasted until the Korean War, when Israel sided with the Western (or United Nations) cause, due to the obvious need for some form of security alignment against a possible aggressor. Israel did not, however, take an extreme position at that stage. The Israeli government did not strive to attain formal alliances with Western states.

At this stage the Middle East was within the orbit of Western influence.

One of its formal expressions was the Three-Power Declaration of 25 May 1950[18] which affirmed the armistice lines and international frontiers of the area and the maintenance of the armaments balance between Israel and its Arab neighbours.

Being excluded from its share of responsibility, the Soviet Union exerted pressure from the outside. Its main objection was to Western-oriented mutual defence arrangements such as the Baghdad Pact. Since 1950 Soviet political support for Israel has declined. This process of deterioration of Soviet-Israeli relations in the fifties culminated in the Czechoslovak-Egyptian arms agreement of 1955, which brought about the supply of large quantities of modern arms to Egypt and upset the delicate military balance between Israel and its Arab neighbours.

Israeli relations with the United States were conducted on a different level. Due to the basic preference of an American political orientation by most Israelis and the strong Zionist movement within the United States Jewish community, relations with the United States were on a much more solid ground. It was the United States and its Jewish community which provided most of the economic support needed by Israel in its period of growth. During the first fifteen years of independence direct U.S. government grants and loans totalled $880 million; private gifts (tax-free) and bond purchases, approximately $1,500 million. The United States did not, however, extend an adequate supply of arms prior to 1967, though this was an urgent need in view of the Czechoslovak-Egyptian arms agreement.

Israeli participation in the Suez War of 1956 constituted a turning point in Israeli foreign policy. Due to a decline in the relations of France and Britain with the Arab world (in the case of France, because of the Algerian war; in the case of Britain, because of worsening of relations with Egypt, which culminated in the nationalization of the Suez Canal on 27 July 1956), these powers found it useful to enter into an *ad hoc* alliance with Israel in an attempt to regain a power position in the Middle East.

The Suez Campaign ended in the convergence of Soviet and American policies against the United Kingdom, France and Israel. Israel's main gain was the opening of the Straits of Tiran as a waterway to East Africa and the Far East.

Another result of the alliance with Britain and France was the opening of the French arms market for Israel. France became the major source of supply of military aircraft, an item of crucial importance in Israeli defence.

With the resolution of the Algerian conflict and attempts at a *rapprochement* between France and the Arab world, French support to Israel gradually declined.

Since the June 1967 war there has been a growing Israeli dependence, economic, military and political, on the United States. The constant flow of Soviet arms to Egypt and Syria and the French embargo made dependence on the U.S. inevitable. Moreover, Israel alone could not bear the heavy economic burden of the armaments race. It had to receive grants and credits from the United States totalling hundreds of millions of dollars. The Israeli dependence on the United States – particularly as a source of supply of military aircraft – gave the United States a powerful lever in its bargaining process with Israel. It has undoubtedly contributed towards important concessions by Israel, such as the formal acceptance of the American 'peace initiative' in the summer of 1970 as well as agreement to the idea of an 'interim settlement' involving a withdrawal of Israeli forces from the Suez Canal and the opening of the Canal before a final settlement is attained. In both cases Israeli action, following American pressure, involved considerable concessions in terms of policy principles, such as the principle of direct negotiations and the principle of no retreat before attainment of a peaceful settlement.

Paradoxically, the supply of military aircraft has been used by the United States as a lever not only in the bargaining process with Israel but also in the implicit bargaining with the Arabs too. Manifest readiness to supply Israel with Phantom aircraft

169

seems to be a useful means to counteract Arab intransigence.

In the bargaining process with the United States, Israel leaned heavily on the support it gained from United States public opinion.

In 1971, Egypt attempted a *rapprochement* with the United States, following an unsuccessful *coup d'état* in the Sudan and the conflict of President Sadat of Egypt with the left-wing leadership, which ended in a purge. The fear of total dependence on the Soviet Union led the Egyptian leadership to greater moderation in relations with the West, an attitude which undoubtedly affected relations with Israel. The cease-fire on the Israeli-Egyptian border since August 1970 is undoubtedly a manifestation of this attitude.

It is the purpose of Israeli foreign policy to gain more support for its position from the great powers. The main objectives are recognition of Israel's right to secure and defendable boundaries (a claim based on the vulnerability of the 1967 boundaries), a constant supply of arms in order to maintain effective deterrence, and – in the case of the Soviet Union – a change in attitude towards its own Jewish community. Israel does not look for foreign protection against its Arab neighbours but regards itself as entitled to support in deterring direct Soviet military intervention in the Middle East.

In attempting to enlist support for these objectives, Israeli foreign policy faces severe obstacles. The Arab world enjoys overwhelming superiority – in terms of control of natural resources and strategic crossroads, political power (as expressed in fifteen votes in the UN) and the Arab position in the Afro-Asian block. Israel's position is aggravated by the Soviet and Chinese extreme support of the Arab cause. How can Israeli policy convince Western powers that *rapprochement* with one party should not be bought at the expense of equal alienation of the other? In a conflict where one party strives to exist in relatively modest but secure conditions whereas the other denies this fundamental right to exist, it is nevertheless hard for Israel to convince even its friends that the case is not a usual one, where justice lies somewhere in between.[19]

In such a situation Israel must bring every possible source of political energy into play, ranging from mobilization of Jewish influence in the West to skilful political manoeuvring in the international arena.

170

FOREIGN ECONOMIC RELATIONS

The most salient feature of the Israeli foreign economic relations is the lack of almost any trade with her Arab neighbours which are potentially her ideal trade partners. Arab hostility towards Israel has brought about an economic boycott which is aimed at preventing both Arab and foreign trading with Israel. Since the June 1967 war, trade relations exist between Israel and the occupied areas on the west bank of the River Jordan. Arab states import goods from the west bank and there is a tourist movement across the Jordan.

Due to the lack of economic relations with its neighbours, Israel has had to foster trade relations with more distant partners. At present more than half of Israeli trade is with European countries, followed by North America. Table 1 shows the value of Israeli trade in 1970 with the first ten countries by value. For the last ten years the highest increase of trade relatively has been with France and Japan on the export side and with Italy in imports. As Table 1 indicates, Israel has a negative trade balance. In 1970 exports (consisting mainly of polished diamonds, industrial products, leather goods and citrus fruits) totalled $775 million and imports $1,451 million. Although exports have increased at a higher rate than imports, the gap has been widening in absolute terms. This trend was intensified after the 1967 war, mainly due to military imports. Political obstacles to her foreign trade added to the economic difficulties and increased Israel's dependence on foreign aid. The maintenance and development of foreign trade is therefore a major objective of Israeli foreign policy. In this context the *rapprochement* with West Germany has been of considerable importance.

Israel, Germany and the European Community

On 10 September 1952, in Luxembourg, representatives of Israel and the German Federal Republic signed a reparations agreement. This act was the first step in the process of reconciliation between Germany and the state of Israel, a process which culminated in the establishment of diplomatic relations in the summer of 1965.

At present the Federal Republic is Israel's strongest supporter in the European Community. This support is of special signifi-

171

Table 1   *Israeli Imports and Exports by Main*
           Countries 1970

Imports		Exports	
Country	Imports ($ thousand)	Country	Exports ($ thousand)
1. U.S.A.	323,458	1. U.S.A.	149,114
2. United Kingdom	228,237	2. United Kingdom	81,118
3. Germany F.R.	174,250	3. Germany F.R.	64,729
4. Italy	75,661	4. Netherlands	45,177
5. Netherlands	71,488	5. France	39,585
6. Belgium and Luxembourg	62,641	6. Belgium and Luxembourg	38,168
7. Japan	62,120	7. Hong Kong	37,206
8. France	60,942	8. Switzerland	33,202
9. Switzerland	48,946	9. Japan	32,299
10. Sweden	28,582	10. Iran	22,291

Source: *Statistical Abstract of Israel 1971* (Central Bureau of Statistics, Government Press, Jerusalem, 1971) p. 229.

cance due to the vulnerability of West European countries to Arab pressure.

West German support for Israel is of special significance in the economic sphere. On the one hand, many citizens of Israel, victims of German persecution during the Hitler era, receive personal reparations, which have become a factor affecting Israel's foreign currency reserves. On the other hand, Western Europe, and particularly Common Market countries, had the major share in Israeli foreign trade, as reflected in Table 2. German support played a major role in the signing of a preferential tariff pact between Israel and the European Economic Community, approved in June 1970.

Under this agreement, to be in effect for five years, Israel's industrial exports to the Community, except some items, enjoy a reduction of 50 per cent in customs duty.

ISRAEL AND THE AFRO-ASIAN WORLD

Since the mid-fifties, Israeli foreign policy has set a new goal of establishing relations – diplomatic, economic and cultural – with emerging nations in Asia and Africa. One major motive for this

172

Table 2   *Israeli Imports and Exports by Area*
(1960–70)

	Imports Percentage of Total Imports										
Area	1960	1961	1962	1963	1964	1965	1966	1967	1968	1969	1970
Europe	53·3	56·3	51·5	55·7	59·8	56·8	54·4	55·1	62·2	61·1	59·6
EEC	29·0	30·5	23·7	23·3	28·8	24·2	23·9	23·9	28·7	30·1	30·7
EFTA	22·2	22·9	25·1	29·3	27·2	29·3	26·8	26·4	30·2	27·5	24·9
COMECON Countries	0·8	1·0	1·3	1·5	2·1	2·0	2·1	2·6	2·0	1·9	2·3
Other Countries of Europe	1·3	1·9	1·4	1·6	1·7	1·2	1·2	2·3	1·4	1·5	1·7
U.S. and Canada	30·4	30·8	34·3	28·8	26·1	26·1	27·2	26·0	23·0	24·2	23·5
Asia and Africa	7·3	5·7	5·2	5·8	5·5	6·8	6·9	7·0	4·6	4·9	7·4
Other Countries	9·0	7·2	9·0	9·7	8·6	10·3	11·5	11·9	10·2	9·8	9·5

	Exports Percentage of Total Exports										
Area	1960	1961	1962	1963	1964	1965	1966	1967	1968	1969	1970
Europe	63·7	62·0	61·6	65·0	62·5	61·6	62·2	60·3	55·7	53·8	53·2
EEC	28·6	28·3	26·1	30·3	28·0	28·3	28·4	28·8	27·1	26·1	26·1
EFTA	28·7	26·0	26·9	27·4	25·3	23·7	23·7	23·1	20·9	19·9	18·9
COMECON Countries	1·8	2·7	3·0	2·8	4·0	3·9	4·5	3·3	2·9	3·1	2·6
Other Countries of Europe	4·6	5·0	5·5	4·5	5·2	5·6	5·5	5·1	4·7	4·7	5·6
U.S. and Canada	14·8	17·3	17·2	14·8	16·2	16·1	16·7	17·7	20·6	21·1	21·2
Asia and Africa	15·9	17·2	15·6	15·3	16·4	18·2	16·9	17·4	17·9	19·4	20·4
Other Countries	5·6	3·5	5·7	4·9	4·9	4·1	4·2	4·6	5·8	5·7	5·2

Source: *Statistical Abstract of Israel 1971* (Central Bureau of Statistics, Government Press, Jerusalem, 1971) p, 228.

policy was Israel's position after independence as a country surrounded by enemy states on all sides except the sea coast. There was an urgent need to break the ring of hostility by establishing friendly connections with developing countries not far from its boundaries. The need for more integration in the Afro-Asian world was felt after the Sinai Campaign of 1956/57 when Israel was identified with ex-colonial powers. In this respect, such integration was aimed at refuting the Arab claim that Israel was a foreign entity 'implanted' in the region by imperialistic powers.

173

There were other objectives which guided Israeli policy in the Afro-Asian world: the gaining of political support in the international arena, as well as economic considerations. The opening of the Straits of Tiran to Israeli navigation between the port of Eilat and the East, following this war, made it necessary to rely on friendly bases along this shipping route.

In reviewing the possible motives, one should not overlook pure altruistic ones, namely helping new states in social-economic endeavours through the application of Israeli experience.

The first ties with Afro-Asian developing countries were established with Burma and later with Ghana. This experience, mainly concentrated in the field of technical assistance, laid the foundation for a wide system of connections with the developing world based primarily on technical aid extended by Israeli experts.

Table 3 *Israeli Experts Abroad* (*by Continent*)
1958–70

	1958–69	1970	Total
Africa	2,237	246	2,483
Asia	368	63	431
Latin America and Carribean	435	95	530
Mediterranean area	479	25	504
Total	3,519	429	3,948

Source: The data in Tables 3, 4, 5 and 6 were provided by the International Co-operation Division, Ministry for Foreign Affairs.

Table 4 *Israeli Experts Abroad* (*by Field of Activity*)
1958–70

Agriculture	1,380
Youth organization	614
Medicine and health	385
Education	319
Technology (including construction and building)	347
Miscellaneous (including management of public services, social work and co-operation)	903
Total	3,948

Table 5   *Trainees in Israel (by Continent) 1958–70*

Africa	7,380
Asia	2,837
Latin America	2,554
Mediterranean area	2,352
Others	351
Total	15,474

Table 6   *Trainees in Israel (by Field of Study) 1971*

Agriculture	5,270
Co-operation	2,810
Community development	1,816
Youth leadership	664
Technical training	994
Public administration	1,942
Health	523
Science and technology	674
Other academic studies	781
Total	15,474

Considering Israel's general economic capacity, the foreign aid programme may be considered disproportionately large. The whole endeavour is due to a special effort guided in the early sixties by Mrs Meir, then Foreign Minister.

The above Tables showing Israeli experts abroad by continent and field of activity, and trainees in Israel, reflect the high priority enjoyed by the African continent in Israeli foreign aid, and perhaps the fact that the Africans were more receptive to such aid. This priority may also be accounted for by pragmatic considerations such as the significance of East African states for Israeli navigation in the Red Sea. Israeli 'presence' in Africa was intended, *inter alia*, to counteract Egyptian attempts to become the dominating power in the Black African continent. And, further, at present more than one-third of the UN members are developing African states.

The Israeli foreign assistance endeavour has had positive results for Israel in most of its aspects, though not in all. Israel was not admitted as a member of the Afro-Asian bloc, mainly

175

due to the predominant weight of Arab and some Moslem countries. Israel is often formally denounced in Afro-Asian conferences. Its policy was not successful in establishing ties with some major Asian states, including India.

The positive side of the balance is Israeli success in creating friendly relations on a more individual basis with a relatively large number of developing countries, including Moslem states. It is reflected in various forms of relations, some of which are not overt or formal. On various occasions Israel enjoyed important political support from developing countries in international organizations, e.g. in the case of crucial votes in the General Assembly of the UN following the Six Day War. Moreover, the relations of Israel with the Afro-Asian world centre around technical assistance, an activity which has proved to be quite successful. This success is partly due to its non-political nature, partly to the applicability of Israel's own development experience to the recipient countries, and in no small measure to the special capacity and cross-cultural adaptability of the Israeli personnel.

One important indirect contribution of Israeli relations with the Afro-Asian world is that the Israeli position was strengthened *vis-à-vis* the great powers, improving its leverage and bargaining position.

Although general experience in relations with the developing world has proved to be a relatively successful sphere of Israeli foreign policy, these relations are extremely vulnerable to the political instability of emergent states in the Afro-Asian world.

FREEDOM OF MANOEUVRE AND SOME TACTICAL ASPECTS OF ISRAELI FOREIGN POLICY

'Freedom of manoeuvre' in a given political situation may be conceived to exist where the foreign policy of a state enjoys a wide range of alternatives as well as a relatively high capacity of flexible choice between alternative courses of action or a combination of them.

Freedom of manoeuvre is crucial for the foreign policy of small states as a way of steering a somewhat independent course between the policies of the larger powers. This is undoubtedly true in the case of Israel, and even more so due to the fact that the Arab-Israeli conflict lends an added dimension to the problem of manoeuvre. In this case freedom of manoeuvre is itself an object of conflict between small states, because an increase in the degree of freedom of manoeuvre of one party is often attained only by limiting that of the opponent.

The need for freedom of manoeuvre seems typically obvious in situations calling for (a) the choice of allies according to changing political objectives, or (b) finding proper adjustment of internal and external policies.

Conditions for manoeuvre may range between 'favourable' and 'difficult'. They are favourable when there exists a free choice between a number of alternatives, each being 'reasonably good'. They are more difficult when manoeuvre is the only solution in case of a severe dilemma. Here selection of one course of action may inevitably result in extremely unfavourable results in another field. The 'difficult' conditions for manoeuvre could be illustrated through the problems of the proper adjustment of internal and foreign policies.

For example, militant policies may be required as a way of boosting morale and national unity, whereas attainment of external military or political support may be contingent on more moderation, demonstration of weakness and other policies which are less acceptable inside the system.

Due to the typical features of the Arab-Israeli conflict as outlined above and particularly its dual nature, cultural-ideological and rational-pragmatic, the problem of reconciling internal (and regional) policies with external ones presents dilemmas to all parties involved, though in different degrees of intensity. Whereas the internal systems are strongly related to the cultural and ideological ingredients, foreign policy towards great powers and international institutions tends to emphasize the pragmatic and rational aspects. Often the most skilful manoeuvre is incapable of overcoming this gap.

An interesting point which deserves much consideration concerns the requirements of the internal system necessary to facilitate effective manoeuvring. Is it contingent upon a strong centralized and co-ordinated machinery? If this were true one could assume that 'closed' systems, by a high degree of centralization as well as a relatively high capacity for separating internal from external policies, enjoy some superiority over 'open' and 'pluralistic' systems. On the other hand, a pluralistic system enjoys some advantages of its own. It is capable of using its own

177

fragmented structure with the aim of applying flexible policies using occasionally components of the system for flexible adaptation to changing needs. This form of 'pluralistic manoeuvre' depends on consensus related to ultimate goals, mutual adjustments[20] and high political skill in non-coercive co-ordination of the diverse components of the system. One may assume that even 'closed' systems apply some form of pluralism (often artificially created) for the purpose of manoeuvring.

The basic Israeli policy since the June 1967 war has been the readiness of Israel to return territories taken during this war as a part of a negotiated peace settlement.[21] Israeli policy was not, however, defined in exact terms either in regard to the boundaries or to the nature of the political settlement envisaged.

Israeli policy following the Six-Day War was orientated towards international public opinion, the great powers and international institutions. It gave less weight to the cultural-ideological context of the conflict. For this reason some observers concluded that the Israeli concept of a peaceful settlement which could gain support in Western public opinion could not be accepted by the Arab side. By refusing to accept the Israeli offer of a negotiated peace settlement, the Arab side provided Israel with a tactical advantage. Since the acceptance by Egypt and Jordan of the American peace initiative in July–August 1970, and moderate pronouncements by President Sadat in the spring of 1971, it may be assumed that Arab policy found a successful response based on outward political moderation. Moreover, Israel regarded a possible enforced solution based on outward moderation as a danger to its very existence. It would require withdrawal from presently defendable boundaries without getting any positive and lasting arrangement in return.

In terms of freedom of manoeuvre, Israel has some advantages as well as disadvantages.

Israel is one state in which, despite divergence of opinion, there is much consensus over ultimate goals, such as peace. Distribution of organized political parties as well as unorganized pressure groups presents a certain balance between forces favouring considerable concessions to the Arab side in case of a peace arrangement and groups favouring the present boundaries. This enables the government to adopt a somewhat flexible policy. This potential flexibility has particularly increased with the withdrawal of the right-wing Gahal (Herut-Liberal block) from the government coalition, in the summer of 1970, following the acceptance of the American peace initiative. Although for the most part the broad coalition which was in existence since June 1967 did not put a heavy strain on Israeli freedom of manoeuvre.

Israeli foreign policy has been governed to a certain extent by internal policy requirements and consideration for various pressure groups, but not to the extent common in the Arab neighbouring states. The basic quest for a solution based on a peaceful negotiated agreement enjoys much internal support as well as the understanding of Western public opinion. On the other hand, Arab militancy at home clearly contradicts some of the moderate manifestations of Arab foreign policy. This is a constant dilemma, which Israel utilizes to limit Arab capacity for manoeuvre between domestic (as well as inter-Arab) policies and policies for external consumption. This requires that the constant Arab militant views be exposed in contrast with outward moderation. Israeli tactics are aimed at manoeuvring Arab systems inside the Middle East into a position where the Arab side would be forced to choose an unequivocal course of action.

The high degree of dependence on one power – the United States – limits Israeli freedom of manoeuvre. One could, of course, argue that Egypt has also become in recent years just as highly dependent on the Soviet Union. However, the Arab block contains pro-Western states such as the Lebanon. The Arab world as a whole is also affiliated with the 'Third World'. It may, therefore, adopt a 'pluralistic manoeuvre' policy. This type of policy is contingent upon skilful co-ordination between conflicting states. The late President Nasser successfully used his political skills for this type of manoeuvre.

In terms of freedom of manoeuvre the Arab guerrilla groups are both an asset and a liability. If carefully controlled, these groups can inflict casualties upon the Israeli side provoking Israel to take retaliatory action against the states (mostly pro-Western) where these organizations keep their bases. The policy increases the leverage of the Arab side. It has brought about severe political setbacks to Israeli foreign policy. On the other hand, these groups, if not controlled, may in some cases severely embarrass the Arab world in terms of political tactics and freedom of manoeuvre. Events in the second half of 1970 have illustrated the second possibility.[22]

179

In terms of relations with the great powers the situation should not be regarded statically. New alliances may emerge and old ones be broken up. On the one hand, U.S. and Soviet attitudes to the conflict are not as clear cut as one might assume. A most significant fact is that the Soviet Union uses the Arab-Israeli conflict as a constant pretext for maintaining a Soviet presence in the area. The Soviet Union with all its achievements has not succeeded in establishing a Communist Arab base in the Middle East. The failure in 1971 of a leftist *coup d'état* in the Sudan further illustrates this point. As a whole, it seems that the capacity of one single power to radically affect the political situation in the Middle East is still limited, and that the struggle for dominating the east coast of the Mediterranean is still undecided. In this regard it is still no-man's-land.

Such a situation makes it possible even for a small state like Israel to increase its freedom of manoeuvre. This type of freedom depends not only on actual power but on much political skill, imagination and inventiveness.

CONCLUSION

The state of Israel conducts a multifarious system of external relations unparalleled by any other country of its size.

This is due, mainly, to the relations between the state and the Jewish communities abroad, and the special nature of the Arab-Israeli conflict. The strategic location of the Middle East and its involvement in global conflicts further increase the role foreign relations play in the life of the state.

The central objective of Israeli foreign policy as a constant long-range goal, is the attainment of lasting peace with its neighbours. More immediate goals are survival in a hostile environment within conditions favourable for social and economic development, and fulfilment of the role of the state as a place of shelter for Jews throughout the world.

The orientation of basic issues of survival has brought about an emphasis on the military aspect of foreign relations rather than on political aspects. Political planning lags behind military in terms of range and intensity.

Though situated with the developing world, Israel was not accepted as a member of the non-aligned nations. This has had a negative effect on the freedom of manoeuvre. The State of

Israel is highly dependent on United States political, economic and military support.

Israeli foreign policy enjoys, however, some advantages *vis-à-vis* its neighbours, resulting mainly from cohesion and other internal conditions favourable for political manoeuvre, which its neighbours do not have. Technological, educational, military and economic advantages *vis-à-vis* its neighbours also play a role in setting off some of the tactical disadvantages of Israeli foreign policy.

NOTES AND REFERENCES

For historical sources on Middle East politics the reader is referred to J. C. Hurewitz, *Diplomacy in the Near and Middle East* (Van Nostrand, Princeton, 1956). It is a collection of 228 documents on major events and agreements relating to the Near and Middle East in the years 1535–1914 and 1914–56. Each document is introduced by editorial notes and contains bibliographical references for further information.

George Lenczowski's *The Middle East in World Affairs* (Cornell University Press, New York, 1962) is another historical source narrating events in Middle Eastern countries since the decline of the Ottoman Empire. The third edition contains a good review of events in the years 1956–61 between the Suez Campaign and the disruption of the United Arab Republic in 1961. As to the history of the Zionist movement before 1948, an interesting and reliable source is Chaim Weizmann's *Trial and Error* (East and West Library, London, 1950). It is an autobiography including a personal account of the events which led to the establishment of the state of Israel. The first years of independence are discussed in David Ben Gurion's *Israel: Years of Challenge* (Holt, Rinehart & Winston, New York, 1963). It is a concise statement of goals and policies guiding Israel in these years. Of special interest is the account of events leading to the Israeli participation in the 1956 Sinai War. *The First Ten Years* (Simon & Shuster, New York, 1958) is a diplomatic history of Israel by Walter Eyton, the former director-general of the Israeli Foreign Ministry. The most valuable part of the book for students of Israeli foreign policy is its discussion of the 1949 Armistice Agreements.

The same period is covered by Earl Berger's *The Covenant and the Sword* (University of Toronto Press, Toronto, 1965). The main thesis of this book is that the 1949 Armistice Agreement failed to preserve the cease-fire and that the 1956 war was inevitable. The author maintains that in 1949 Israelis and Arabs were ready to come to terms and it was the intervention of some great powers that prevented conciliation.

Gamal Abdul Nasser's *Philosophy of the Revolution* (Public Affairs Press, Washington, 1959), being an exposition of Nasserist ideology, provides some clues for the Egyptian policy in the Arab-Israeli conflict.

Analytic works on Arab-Israeli relations are Fred J. Khouri's *The Arab-*

Israeli Dilemma (Syracuse University Press, New York, 1968) and Safran's *From War to War* (Pegasus, New York, 1969). Khouri presents a historical analysis based on comprehensive documentation providing suggestions for a gradual progress towards a peaceful solution of the conflict. Safran's study discusses the Arab-Israeli conflict in relation to the inter-Arab struggle and the big powers conflict in the Middle East.

In *The Soviet Union and The Middle East* (Praeger, New York, 1959), Laqueur discusses Soviet policy towards the Middle East before and after 1955. The book reviews the emergence of the Soviet Union as a major power in the Middle East and the prospects for deeper Soviet penetration in the Arab world.

The United States and Israel (Harvard University Press, Cambridge, Mass., 1963) by Safran is a discussion of U.S.-Israeli relations with some emphasis on domestic politics in the United States on her policies towards Israel. Despite its title, the major part of the book is concerned with the Israeli political system.

Michael Brecher's *The Foreign Policy System of Israel* (Oxford University Press, London, 1971) is a comprehensive and penetrating analysis of the Israeli foreign policy-making process with special emphasis on the role of institutions and personalities in the decision-making process.

For general information on the Ministry of Foreign Affairs, official policy statements and current events, the reader is referred to the *Israeli Government Yearbooks*, published by the Central Office of Information, Prime Minister's Office.

1. See *Jerusalem Post*, 25 April 1950.
2. See statement by David Ben-Gurion on 28 September 1950 in *Israel and the United Nations* (Carnegie Endowment for International Peace, New York, 1956) p. 183.
3. *Israeli Government Yearbook 1971/72*, Hebrew version.
4. For a discussion of the nature of open and closed systems in foreign relations, see R. Barry Farrell (ed.), *Approaches to Comparative and International Politics* (Northwestern University Press, Evanston, 1966) pp. 151–208.
5. The relationship with the Jewish people overseas and the maintenance of good relations with countries in which the communities reside are basic tenets of Israeli foreign policy. See, for example, the government statements outlining basic principles on foreign policy which are contained in the *Israeli Government Yearbook 1969/70*, p. 31.
6. The resignation of Foreign Minister Sharett on 17 June 1956 was a major turning point in terms of the increasing importance of military views in shaping Israeli foreign policy.
7. On the general role of the Israeli army in politics, see Amos Perlmuter, 'The Israeli Army in Politics', *World Politics*, vol. 20, no. 4 (July, 1968) pp. 606–43.
8. For further discussion of the institutional setting of Israeli foreign policy, see Michael Brecher, *The Foreign Policy System of Israel: Setting, Images, Process* (Oxford University Press, London, 1971).
9. For the purpose of this chapter the 'Arab world' may be defined

according to linguistic criterion, namely, states where Arabic is the dominant language.

10. See Chaim Weizmann, *Trial and Error* (East and West Library, London, 1950) pp. 290–5.

11. See Charles Lindblom in his article 'The Science of Muddling Through', *Public Administration Review*, vol. 19 (1959) pp. 79–88.

12. See Shabbetai Rosenne, *Israel's Armistice Agreements with the Arab States* (Tel Aviv, 1951).

13. The official view of the Israeli government on the Arab refugee problem was expressed, for example, on 26 November 1968 by Michael Comay, then ambassador at large and political adviser to the Minister of Foreign Affairs, in the Special Political Committee of the 23rd General Assembly of the UN. See also W. Pinner, *How many Arab Refugees?* (MacGibbon and Kee, London, 1959).

14. Fred J. Khouri, *The Arab-Israeli Dilemma* (Syracuse University Press, New York, 1968) p. 123.

15. Shabbetai Rosenne, 'Basic Elements of Israel's Foreign Policy', *India Quarterly*, vol. 17, no. 4 (October–December, 1961).

16. One should note, however, that Israeli policy was motivated by pragmatic considerations. Not only the Arab states but Israel too had territorial gains through the Armistice Agreements. Whereas under the General Assembly's 1947 Resolution, the Jewish state would have consisted of about 5,700 square miles, as a result of the Armistice Agreements Israel controlled about 8,000 square miles.

17. E. S. Glenn, R. H. Johnson, Paul R. Kimmel, 'A Cognitive Interaction Model to Analyse Culture Conflict in International Relations', *Journal of Conflict Resolution*, vol. 14, no. 1 (March, 1970) p. 46.

18. J. C. Hurewitz, *Diplomacy in the Near and Middle East 1914–1956*, vol. 2 (Van Nostrand, Princeton, 1956) p. 308.

19. See on this subject, Alan Dowty, 'The Middle East Conflict: Problems of Analysis', *International Problems* (Israel) vol. 7, no. 3–4 (December, 1969) pp. 12–22.

20. For a general discussion of this subject see Charles E. Lindblom, *The Intelligence of Democracy* (The Free Press, Collier-Macmillan, New York, 1965).

21. Israeli policy was summarized in a speech by Foreign Minister Eban in the UN General Assembly on 25 September 1967.

22. In the summer of 1972 most of the Soviet military personnel left Egypt amid growing tension between Egypt and the Soviet bloc and the strengthening of Egyptian ties with Libya. Egyptian attempts at a rapprochement with West Germany and Britain, and an interest in Western arms supplies, also suggest that Egypt aims to lessen her dependence on the Soviet Union. Furthermore, the outbreak of Arab terrorist activity in September 1972 against Israeli personnel in Europe again illustrates both the advantages and the strains this creates for Arab freedom of manoeuvre. It has damaged Egypt's attempted rapprochement with the West and hardened the Israeli attitude to terrorism and a political settlement with Egypt. The attacks nevertheless hit at points where Israel is most vunerable and is unable to retaliate without suffering severe political damage. See *Jerusalem Post*, 22.9.72.

Chapter 6

THE FOREIGN POLICY
OF CYPRUS

R. P. BARSTON

The island of Cyprus is located in the eastern Mediterranean, less than one hour's flying time from Athens and forty miles from the coast of Turkey; Syria is sixty miles from the 'panhandle', Cape Andreas, and Egypt some two hundred miles from Cape Gata in the south. The island has a population of 622,000 – approximately one-twentieth that of Greater London and three times that of Iceland. There are two distinct ethnic groups: the majority Greek Cypriots, with 80 per cent of the population, and the Turkish Cypriots, the largest minority group, with 18 per cent. On 16 August 1960 Cyprus became an independent republic, headed by Archbishop Makarios. On 21 September 1960 the republic was admitted to the United Nations and in the following year became a member of the Commonwealth.

BACKGROUND

Throughout most of its history Cyprus has been subject to frequent invasion and foreign conquest.[1] Greek settlement on the island dates back to the late Mycenean period, around 1400 BC. Between 540 BC and AD 1960 there were eight external rulers – Persians, Ptolomies, Romans, Byzantines, Lusignans, Venetians, Turks and British. Nevertheless, Greek culture remained dominant in Cyprus from the late Mycenean period. During the Roman and Byzantine rule of Cyprus, which lasted from 58 BC until the end of the twelfth century AD, Greek culture was modified in two respects – religion and language. After the arrival of Christianity in Cyprus in AD 45, Classical paganism slowly began to decline. By AD 313, when the Edict of Milan recognized Christianity as the official religion of the Empire, most of

184

Cyprus had become Christian. Following the break-up of the Roman Empire into its Western and Eastern parts in AD 395, Greek became the official language of the Eastern (Byzantine) Empire, and in AD 431 the Church in Cyprus became independent of the patriarchate of Antioch. With the collapse of the Byzantine Empire at the end of the twelfth century, Hellenism was extinct, politically at least, until the rise of mainland Greek nationalism in the nineteenth century. Cyprus passed to the Franks, Crusaders and Venetians, and from 1573 until 1878 formed part of the Ottoman Empire. In 1878 the island was ceded to Britain, but did not come under *de jure* British control until the Treaty of Lausanne in 1923. In 1925 Cyprus became a British Crown colony and remained, until the end of the Second World War, a half-forgotten imperial backwater. However, after 1945 the movement for self-determination and *enosis* (Union with Greece) intensified, and in 1955 EOKA, led by George Grivas, began a terrorist campaign to achieve these twin objectives.

After three years of bloodshed, inconclusive negotiations and peace initiatives, the deadlock over the Cyprus crisis was broken on 5 December 1958,[2] at a meeting between the Greek and Turkish Foreign Ministers, Averoff and Zorlu, who continued their talks at the NATO meeting in Paris on 18 December 1958. After further exchanges the following month, the Turkish and Greek Premiers, Menderes and Karamanlis, together with their Foreign Ministers, met in Zürich on 5 February 1959, to draw up a draft settlement. The Zürich proposals were presented to the Greek and Turkish Cypriot leaders at the London conference which opened at Lancaster House on 17 February 1959. The leaders of the two Cypriot communities had not attended the Zürich meetings (although they had been consulted beforehand) and were presented, in effect, with a *fait accompli* at the London conference. Two days later, on 19 February, the London agreements were signed.[3]

FOREIGN POLICY SETTING

During the ten years since independence, the international activity of the Cyprus government has been directed, in the main, to firstly the maintenance of independence and security, of which the most important aspect is the management of the

185

Cyprus problem, and secondly economic development. A further category of activity can be distinguished within which the objectives, based upon the principle of international co-operation, aim to improve the effectiveness of international organization, develop friendly relations with other governments and reduce international conflict. This 'co-operative' activity is pursued through membership of international and regional organizations and the non-aligned grouping, state visits, foreign trade and cultural exchanges.

A number of factors have influenced the framing and implementation of the above objectives. First the terms of independence. The drafters of the Zürich and London agreements were faced in particular with resolving the question of the status of Cyprus in relation to Greece and the method of safeguarding the position and rights of the majority and minority communities. The solutions were necessarily conflicting; for although the Zürich and London agreements ruled out the possibility of a union between Cyprus and Greece, the concept of *enosis* has remained an important factor in Cypriot domestic politics. As an attempt to deal with the second problem, the Zürich and London agreements envisaged that Britain, Greece and Turkey should act as 'guarantors' of the Cypriot constitution. Consequently both Greece and Turkey were permitted under the Treaties of Alliance and Guarantee to station military contingents in Cyprus after independence. In practice the treaties have served to legitimize the direct interest and involvement of these two governments in the internal affairs of Cyprus.

The period of British rule left several legacies. Under the Treaty of Establishment with Cyprus (1960) Britain retained two areas, at Dhkelia and Akrotiri, as sovereign bases. The British bases are a supplementary source of revenue for Cyprus (and therefore tolerated by the government) but the continued British presence has been opposed by extreme left- and right-wing Greek Cypriot groups. There have been other British influences on, for example, the structure of the administration, tourism (English is widely spoken and the island is popular with the more wealthy British tourist and expatriate), and trade.

Despite the close proximity of Cyprus to the Middle East, the government has not developed any extensive political or economic relations with states in this region. In part this may be accounted for by the strong trading relations with Britain and

the links between the two Cypriot communities and Greece and
Turkey. Further, Cyprus has not wished to become involved in
intra-Arab disputes or the Arab-Israeli conflict. This latter
reason suggests the Cyprus government recognizes that it has
limited political influence; that in its external policies it must
proceed with caution and not become involved in disputes or
conflicts to which it can contribute little, if anything, but could
lose political prestige and conceivably incur the displeasure of
either or both great powers.

MACHINERY AND PROCESS

Turkish Cypriot Leadership

Within less than three years the constitutional proposals contained in the Zürich and London agreements had broken down.
The terms of the agreements were in fact far removed from the
original aims of the Greek and Turkish Cypriots and required a
degree of co-operation which, given the events of the Emergency
Period, proved unobtainable. Three areas of difficulty emerged
in attempts to implement the Zürich and London agreements:
the staffing of government posts in the ratio of seventy Greek
Cypriots to thirty Turkish Cypriots; the spheres of competence
of the Turkish Cypriot municipalities; and the Turkish Cypriot
use of the veto in the House of Representatives to block or delay
legislation on customs regulations, income tax and the proposed
Development Bank. Tension continued to mount, and in
December 1963 intercommunal clashes broke out in Nicosia
which quickly spread throughout the island.[4]

Intercommunal relations between 1964 and 1967 were characterized by an arms build-up by both sides, frequent shooting
incidents and the movement of Turkish Cypriots from formerly
mixed villages into Turkish-controlled areas. Those Turkish
Cypriots holding posts in the government and administration
withdrew and set up in the Turkish Cypriot quarter of Nicosia
a separate administration headed by the Vice-President, Dr
Kuchuk. The Turkish Cypriot Communal Chamber and the
fifteen Turkish Cypriot members of the House of Representatives
constituted the second and third 'tiers' of the new Turkish
administration. In order to promote the Turkish Cypriot
position on the Cyprus problem, an extensive information
service was built up and the leadership regularly receives

foreign journalists and diplomats. Members of the leadership have also travelled abroad to seek political and economic support, and the chief Turkish Cypriot negotiator, Raof Denktash, has put the Turkish Cypriot case at the UN.[5] In December 1967 the functions of and relationships between the various parts of the administration were more clearly defined and the administration became styled the Provisional Cyprus Turkish Administration.[6]

Greek Cypriot Leadership

Archbishop Makarios has dominated Cypriot politics since independence, combining religious and political offices to create a highly personalized presidency. He is courteous, shrewd, and above all else an extremely good political tactician. This latter ability, together with his use of appointments and carefully timed, oblique political pronouncements, has enabled him to retain a paramount position. The Archbishop has increased his political prestige by making frequent state and official visits abroad (an indication of the security of his political position), and his numerous interviews with foreign journalists and politicians show his grasp of the value of publicity. His political position was not seriously threatened until mid-1969. Then the challenge, discussed below, came from extreme right-wing pro-*enosis* groups within the Greek Cypriot community.

Foreign policy decision-making is centralized around the presidency and foreign policy matters are not discussed to any great extent by the Council of Ministers. Relatively few persons are involved in the taking of major decisions and these normally will include the President, Foreign Minister, senior officials of the Foreign Ministry and, when required, the Ministers of Finance, Industry and Commerce, and the Attorney General.[7] During the execution of policy, co-ordination between the Foreign Ministry and foreign policy related departments is on an informal basis. Two senior negotiators, former Foreign Minister Kyprianou and UN ambassador Zenon Rossides, have contributed considerably to the success of Cypriot foreign policy; both are highly personable and articulate and as a result of their long tenure of office have been able to establish and maintain a wide range of diplomatic contacts. On domestic matters, amongst the most influential is the lawyer-politician Glafcos Clerides, leader of the Unified Party and House of Representatives. In the absence of Archbishop Makarios at international conferences and on state visits, Clerides has acted as President and was also appointed chief Greek Cypriot negotiator in the inter-communal talks which began in June 1968.

Foreign Ministry

There are some seventy personnel in the Cyprus diplomatic service, of whom twenty-one staff the Foreign Ministry (1971). A further eighty-two auxiliary personnel carry out administrative duties as accountants, cypher officers and clerks. The Ministry, headed by a director-general, has five sections: (1) Political Research, Planning, Cyprus Problem: (2) Political (general); (3) Economic; (4) Protocol; (5) Administration. In 1971 thirty-nine states had embassies or high commissions accredited to Cyprus. The high foreign accreditation can be accounted for mainly by the missions of those states with close or developing economic relations with Cyprus (e.g. West Germany and the Eastern bloc), Cyprus membership of the Commonwealth (e.g. Canada, India, Pakistan, Nigeria, United Kingdom) and non-aligned grouping (e.g. Yugoslavia, Cuba, U.A.R.) and the strategic importance of the island as a military base and communications centre (e.g. United Kingdom, United States and the Soviet Union). Though it must be remembered that of the thirty-nine states, only fifteen had residential accreditation. It is interesting to note that whilst the Eastern bloc maintained four embassies in Nicosia (the Soviet Union, Rumania, Czechoslovakia and Bulgaria), the only Commonwealth residential accreditation was the United Kingdom High Commission. Those states accredited to Cyprus on a non-residential basis generally accredited their embassies in, for example, Tel-Aviv, Beirut, Athens, Rome or Damascus, to Nicosia.

It is clearly beyond the means of the republic to maintain residential accreditation in thirty-nine states. Cyprus in fact has embassies in Greece, Turkey, U.A.R., France, West Germany, the Soviet Union and the United States. A High Commission is maintained in London and a mission accredited to the UN. In addition a Consulate-General is maintained in Alexandria, and in February 1971 a representative with the rank of ambassador was appointed to the EEC in Brussels.

The area of competence of the Foreign Ministry is limited by

189

the small size of its staff and therefore, although the Foreign Ministry contains an economic section, its functions are mainly monitoring and drafting formal agreements. The substantive aspects of external economic relations are usually dealt with by the Ministry of Industry and Commerce. The range and type of information which is gathered is restricted too by the size of the diplomatic service and the location of Cypriot missions. Cyprus has no residential accreditation in Africa, Asia or Latin America. Furthermore, the Foreign Ministry finds it difficult to recruit a sufficient number of adequately trained personnel. This problem is exacerbated by the fact that as yet a university has not been set up in Cyprus. Recruits to the diplomatic service have therefore generally received higher education in Greece, Britain, France or the United States. It is noteworthy that over 50 per cent of the members of the diplomatic service have legal qualifications, whilst a further 25 per cent have qualifications in economics.[8]

Political Parties and Opposition
Within the House of Representatives, President Makarios is supported by the Unified Party, a loosely organized group which held thirty out of the thirty-five Greek Cypriot seats until the July 1970 elections when it suffered major losses to AKEL and the Progressive Front. In the 1970 elections the Unified Party won 15 seats, AKEL 9, Progressive Front 7, EDEK 2 and Independents 2. The electoral losses of the Unified Party reflected the growing dissatisfaction within the Greek Cypriot community at the government's handling of the Cyprus problem and the increasing appeal of AKEL on social and labour issues.

Unlike other Greek Cypriot political parties, AKEL is highly organized and has strong extra-parliamentary links, particularly with the Pan Cyprian Labor Federation.[9] Supported principally by agricultural, unskilled and semi-skilled workers, AKEL's activities are directed mainly at domestic economic issues. On foreign issues AKEL does not substantially differ from the broad outlines of the government's policies relating to the Soviet Union and Eastern Europe, non-alignment and the UN, but it is critical of the U.S. involvement in Cyprus and the British sovereign bases. However, the overall political power and influence of AKEL as an opposition party is limited by two factors.

190

Ideologically the party has difficulty in taking a position, publicly at least, on the question of *enosis* and relations with Greece. Secondly, AKEL has been seriously embarrassed politically by the ambivalent attitudes and policies of the Soviet Union towards the Cyprus problem.

Perhaps the most serious challenge to the political position and power of President Makarios developed out of his decision to open talks with the Turkish Cypriot leadership. Following the November 1967 crisis in which the Turkish government threatened to intervene militarily in Cyprus in support of the Turkish Cypriots, Makarios decided to open discussions with the Turkish Cypriot leadership in an effort to seek a re-integration of the two communities. The intercommunal talks, which opened in Beirut in June 1968 and continued in Nicosia, were opposed by the extreme right-wing, pro-*enosis* National Front. In addition to attempting to discredit the talks, the National Front demanded the removal of the British bases and closer relations with Greece. After a series of arms thefts, bombing and sabotage incidents in late 1969 security measures were taken against the National Front, and the organization was banned at the beginning of 1970. This, however, was not the end of the affair. In March 1970 an unsuccessful attempt was made on the life of the President, and one week later the former Minister of the Interior, Polycarpos Georghadjis, allegedly connected with the National Front, was assassinated.

THE CYPRUS PROBLEM

As noted earlier, the international activity directed to the management of the Cyprus problem has continued to be one of the two most important aspects of the external relations of Cyprus. Let us briefly examine, then, the methods Makarios has employed and the difficulties he has faced.

From the outset it seemed unlikely that the number of external parties involved in the intercommunal conflict would remain limited to the 'guarantor' powers Britain, Greece and Turkey. The possibility of military conflict between Greece and Turkey, both members of NATO, meant that the United States could not ignore events in Cyprus. For the Soviet Union the intercommunal conflict was not of direct interest except in that it might lead to Cyprus coming under the control of the NATO bloc.

Makarios aimed to exploit tactically the competing Soviet and American interests and to 'internationalize' further the Cyprus problem by putting the conflict before the UN.

After the inconclusive ending of the London conference in January 1964, the British government, who had assumed responsibility for internal security in Cyprus, proposed with the United States a NATO peace-keeping force for Cyprus. The plan was rejected by Makarios as he considered it would lead to too close an involvement with a military bloc and could result in the possible loss of Soviet and Afro-Asian support. Makarios preferred a UN peace-keeping force as this could reduce the military dependence of Cyprus on Greece, and UN discussion of the intercommunal conflict would provide an opportunity for recognition of the sovereignty and independence of Cyprus. Indeed, Makarios succeeded in placing the Cyprus problem before the UN partly because the plan for a NATO force was not regarded with any enthusiasm by France or West Germany. In addition, the British government, after the failure of plans for either a NATO or a Commonwealth peace-keeping force, recognized that there was little choice but to place the Cyprus problem before the UN. On 4 March 1964 the Security Council formally authorized the Secretary-General to establish a peace-keeping force in Cyprus.[10]

The geographical proximity and military superiority of Turkey have meant that Cyprus could not rely solely on Greece to prevent a Turkish military invasion. (As a Greek Foreign Minister once said: 'The problem is that Cyprus is dominated militarily by Turkey. Put Cyprus in the place of Corfu and I would solve the problem immediately.'[11]) Thus during the Kokkina crisis (June–August 1964), United States diplomatic initiatives, including pressure on Turkey and the deployment of the U.S. Sixth Fleet, were important factors in limiting the scale of the crisis.[12] In the November 1967 crisis the Turkish government again threatened to intervene in support of the Turkish Cypriots after the Greek-Turkish Cypriot clashes at Ayios Theodorus (Kophinou). The crisis was successfully resolved by the mediation carried out by the U.S. special envoy, Cyrus Vance, between Athens, Ankara and Nicosia.[13]

The diplomatic dimension of the Cyprus problem – the contest for political support – has been fought both within and outside the UN. In mid-1964 the Cyprus and Greek governments began an intensive campaign to publicize and gain support for their position on the intercommunal Cyprus problem. A Greek Cypriot delegation visited the Soviet Union in September 1964 for political consultations and to obtain Soviet arms, and in October President Makarios attended the conference of non-aligned nations in Cairo. The ground for UN support was prepared by the submission by the Cyprus government of a document in October 1965 on minority rights in Cyprus, which in content did not substantially differ from the recommendations of the March 1965 report of the UN Mediator Galo Plaza.[14] The campaign culminated in probably the greatest success of the Greek Cypriots at the UN – the passage of the General Assembly resolution of 18 December 1965 which recognized the sovereignty and independence of Cyprus.

However, the diplomatic successes gained by the Cyprus government during 1964–65 were subsequently offset by the diplomatic and economic campaigns of the Turkish government and the opportunism of the Soviet Union. Though Cyprus steadily developed trading relations with the Soviet Union, consistent Soviet political support was not obtained. The arms agreement of September 1964 was not fully implemented and the visit of N. V. Podgorny to Turkey in January 1965 marked the beginning of a pro-Turkish phase of Soviet policy. The Turkish Prime Minister Urguplu visited the Soviet Union in August 1965 and the communiqué issued after the talks confirmed the shift in Soviet policy to a 'two communities' concept. The improvement in Soviet-Turkish relations was demonstrated the following year with the visit of the Soviet Premier Kosygin to Turkey.[15]

Apart from efforts to improve relations with the Soviet Union, Turkey sought closer trade links with Rumania, Bulgaria and Yugoslavia. Negotiations were also held with those states which had voted for the December 1965 General Assembly resolution. By June 1966 seven states voting for the resolution (Nepal, Uruguay, Syria, Gabon, Ethiopia, Ghana and the Lebanon) had issued statements indicating that their vote was not to be interpreted as favouring *enosis*.[16] In May 1967 a natural-gas agreement was signed with Iraq, which had taken a pro-Turkish position, and a joint communiqué with Rumania in the same month referred to the rights of both communities in Cyprus. Thus by mid-1967, Turkey, aided by its range of politi-

G   193

cal options, important economic and strategic assets and links with states with a Moslem background, was able to counter the Greek Cypriot gains of 1964–65.

The continued Turkish political, economic and military support (short of full invasion) for the Turkish Cypriots led to conflict between the Greek Cypriot and Greek leaderships, particularly on the question of a political solution to the Cyprus problem. Relations between the two governments further deteriorated as a result of the November 1967 crisis. The Greek military government, which had come to power in April 1967, was unwilling to become as heavily involved in the Cyprus problems as its predecessors. Support for the Greek Cypriots between 1964 and 1967 had been a heavy drain on the Greek economy, and, despite the presence of General Grivas and several thousand Greek troops, Greek political influence was minimal. Aware also of its delicate international position, the Greek military government aimed to avoid, if possible, military conflict with Turkey. As part of the agreement negotiated by the U.S. envoy Cyrus Vance at the end of November 1967, both Greece and Turkey were to withdraw those troops stationed in Cyprus which were in excess of the numbers permitted under the Treaty of Guarantee. Though the agreement was bitterly criticized within the Greek Cypriot community, eight thousand Greek troops, including General Grivas, were withdrawn from Cyprus in January 1968.[17]

But probably the main difficulty Makarios has faced stems from the extension of the parties involved in the Cyprus problem to include, in addition to the 'guarantor' powers, the Soviet Union, United States, the Security Council, General Assembly, UN officials and the Political Liaison Committee of UNFICYP. The development of a multilateral decision-making process during the period of overt military confrontation, in which the parties had competing interests, aims and institutional loyalties meant that Makarios was unable to shape personally a political settlement. Makarios, for example, was not present at the meetings held during July and August 1964 in Geneva under the chairmanship of the first UN mediator to discuss the Acheson proposals. Again, Makarios was excluded from the Greek-Turkish talks which commenced after the failure of the Acheson proposals and continued until September 1967. In such circumstances the influence of Makarios was mainly negative. He

194

rejected the Acheson proposals, gave qualified support to the mediator's report of 1965 (which was rejected by Turkey and the Turkish Cypriots) and aimed to avoid a solution imposed by Greece and Turkey. This latter possibility did not become a serious threat to Makarios until after the November 1967 crisis. Prior to this, the outcome of the Greek-Turkish talks had been inconclusive owing to the gap between the negotiating positions and the effect of internal crises in both countries on the progress of the talks.[18]

As a result of the November 1967 crisis the management of the Cyprus problem moved into a new phase. The emphasis shifted from the role of external parties to the 'domestic' management of the problem with the commencement of the intercommunal talks in 1968. However, the failure of the talks to produce a settlement by the end of 1969, despite some improvement in intercommunal relations, resulted in the formation of extremist groups including the pro-*enosis* National Front.[19] More ominous for Makarios is the possibility that the internal political stalemate, combined with improvement after 1969 of relations between Greece and Turkey, will lead to an attempted imposed solution or an Athens-backed coup.[20]

THE ECONOMY OF CYPRUS

The Cypriot economy has three main components. Agriculture remains the most important sector, employing approximately 36 per cent of the total labour force of 262,000 and contributing, on average, more than 20 per cent to the Gross Domestic Product annually. But unlike certain of the small states in, for example, the Caribbean, whose economies are very largely dependent on the produce of a single crop, the agricultural products and by-products exported by Cyprus are varied and include potatoes, carobs, citrus fruits, tobacco, grapes, wine and spirits.

The mining industry (cupreous concentrates, cupreous pyrites and asbestos) has been, traditionally, the next most important sector of the economy. Exports of agricultural products and minerals together account for 85 per cent of the total annual exports. However, by the early sixties mining began to decline in importance as the known copper reserves became exhausted. Between 1959 and 1969, the value of mineral exports

195

as a percentage of total exports fell from 50 per cent to 29 per cent. The slow decline of the mining industry (apart from asbestos) seems likely to continue, as no substantial new deposits were located in the extensive mineral survey completed in 1970.

The third main sector of the economy is tourism. The island's geographic location, climate and low cost of living are favourable factors, but the intercommunal conflict seriously affected the tourist industry from 1964 until 1967. With the return of internal stability after 1967 the tourist industry began to recover.

Considerable economic progress has been made in the ten-year period since independence. The GNP of £64·4 million in 1960 rose to £225·2 million in 1970. But there are three sources of economic vulnerability. The first is the dependence of the economy on agriculture. The low and erratic rainfall furthermore makes agriculture an uncertain source of revenue. Further, the impact of unfavourable prices for the principal export products on the trade balance is another vulnerable aspect. During 1967, for example, the terms of trade deteriorated mainly through a fall in mineral prices. The value of mineral exports fell from £12·2 million to £8·9 million, which more than negated the rise in agricultural exports.[21] Some economic diversification has been achieved since the mid-sixties, but the structure of the balance of payments is such that a substantial part of the visible trade deficit is generally covered by invisible receipts, most of which originate from unstable sources, e.g. foreign military expenditure, expatriate remittances and tourism.

Economic Planning

At the time of independence, the economic position of Cyprus was unfavourable. The preceding five years had seen increasing economic stagnation caused by the dislocation of the Emergency Period, adverse trade terms and rising imports. This situation was exacerbated by the severe droughts of 1959 and 1960 and the economic uncertainty following the withdrawal of foreign capital as the date for the transference of power approached. On achieving independence, the government set up an economic planning commission to construct the First Five Year Plan (1962–66). The Plan envisaged a growth rate of 6·2 per cent and allocated, over the five-year period, 80 per cent of the planned public development expenditure to agricultural and infrastructural projects. By 1966 an overall growth rate of 6·8 per cent had been achieved.

The Second Five Year Plan (1967–71) again made agriculture the primary development sector, but recognized the need for greater economic diversification. Although the contribution of the manufacturing sector increased after 1966, three main difficulties have affected the rate of progress and the type of diversification. First, factors such as the type of natural resources, the availability of skilled manpower, the size of domestic demand and the level of investment, have limited the scale of manufacturing industries. The tendency, therefore, has been for the development of small-scale light industries, e.g. building materials (bricks, cement), sawmills, metal products (except machinery and transport equipment), clothing and leather goods. A second problem has been increasing the competitiveness of manufactured goods for export. In order to re-structure the economy a considerable amount of capital goods and raw materials is imported. In 1969, for example, 57·7 per cent of the total imports consisted of raw materials and capital goods, the largest single item being industrial raw materials, accounting for 22·8 per cent[22] of the total. But the output of the manufacturing sector is, however, as yet relatively low. Consequently a number of manufactured goods for export have to be subsidized or protected by tariffs. Finally, it has proved difficult to increase import substitution because of established domestic preference for imported goods, which remain, in some cases, even with tariffs less expensive than similar locally-manufactured products.

Development Assistance and Trade Policy

Although certain of the economic difficulties facing the newly independent republic were of a short-term nature, its overall resources were such that extensive external financial and technical aid would have to be supplied if development projects were to be carried out. This conclusion was emphasized by a UN economic survey team, headed by Dr Willard Thorp, in its report on the Cypriot economy.[23] A further recommendation of the Thorp Report was the establishment of a development bank to assist in the co-ordination and funding of development projects. In order to implement the planned development projects, the government largely relied between 1960 and 1963

197

on aid from Greece, Britain and, in particular, the United States.[24] In December 1960 the U.S. concluded the first of three agreements to provide low-cost surplus wheat and barley to offset the effects of the droughts of 1959 and 1960. Further agreements in the following three years were signed by the U.S., providing assistance for the development bank, agriculture and the purchase of machinery. By June 1963, U.S. aid in the form of grants, loans and grain supplies amounted to $20 million.[25] But with the outbreak of the intercommunal conflict, U.S. aid to Cyprus was extensively cut. Commodity aid did continue though under the PL 480 programme, and it also remained unaffected by political difficulties resulting from the Cyprus government's refusal to prevent vessels flying the Cypriot flag from trading with North Vietnam.

The reduction of U.S. aid forced Cyprus to find alternative sources of external assistance. At the same time, whilst Cyprus avoided the problems of economic dependence, the subsequent development process has been slowed down to some extent by the need to negotiate a series of discrete agreements with a number of different parties. Since 1963, extensive financial and technical assistance has come from international agencies. Between 1963 and 1970, for example, the UN Development Program (which maintains a permanent mission in Nicosia) and the UN Special Fund provided financial and technical assistance for an intensive survey of the island's mineral and water resources. The IBRD has provided long-term loans for extensions to the Moni power station near Limassol and, in 1965, for harbour development at Famagusta, the only deep-water port of Cyprus. At the island's other ports, large ocean-going vessels have to unload their cargoes off-shore. Extensive port developments were started, though, in 1968 to improve the facilities at the second largest port, Limassol, and at the smaller port of Larnaca. Long-term loans for these projects were negotiated with the IBRD. The completion of the Larnaca-Limassol projects will mean improved cargo-handling times and a reduction in freight costs, thus making exports, particularly bulk products such as carobs, more competitive.

Assistance has also been received from other international organizations, including the ILO, FAO, UNESCO and the Council of Europe. In addition to some financial assistance, these agencies have generally provided technical assistance – statisticlans, economists, agronomists and engineers. Cyprus has also received aid from her main trading partners. West Germany, in particular, has played an increasingly active role since the mid-sixties, providing long-term loans for development projects and seconding technical experts to the Cyprus government.[26] The close relationship with Western Europe as a whole has brought one further important benefit – assistance from universities and specialist institutes. This intellectual contact – maintained by frequent conferences and regular visits by foreign scholars – has meant that Cyprus has not been cut off from important developments and new techniques in such areas as forestry, agriculture and public administration.

Turning to trade policy, we find a close positive correlation between diplomatic representation and major trading partners. Cyprus has trading relations with fifty states, but by far the greatest volume of trade is carried out with countries in Western Europe. Britain is the most important single trading partner, supplying over 30 per cent of the island's total imports and receiving nearly 40 per cent of its exports. Next in importance are the bilateral agreements with members of the EEC; taken together, Britain and the EEC absorbed 68·5 per cent of 1970 exports and provided 59·5 per cent of the island's imports (see Tables 1 and 2). The EEC seems likely to become the major trading group of Cyprus following the re-opening of the British

Table 1   *Cyprus Foreign Trade By Region 1970*

Continent	Imports (excl. NAAFI)		Exports (incl. Re-Exports)	
	Value £000	%	Value £000	%
Europe	77,147	78·5	40,838	90·4
Asia	11,100	11·3	2,346	5·2
Africa	767	0·8	1,116	2·5
America	8,286	8·5	721	1·6
Oceania	596	0·6	74	0·1
Unclassified	333	0·3	94	0·2
Total	98,229	100·0	45,189	100·0

Source: *Analysis of Foreign Trade* (Ministry of Finance, Nicosia, 1971) p. 5.

199

Table 2 *Cyprus Trade with the U.K. and EEC 1962–70*

£000s

	1962	1963	1964	1965	1966	1967	1968	1969	1970
1. Total Imports	44,953	47,141	37,616	51,407	55,368	59,712	70,944	86,462	98,229
2. Total Exports	20,797	21,902	20,549	25,288	29,238	29,697	36,959	40,903	45,189
3. Imports from U.K. (excl. NAAFI)	15,099	15,679	11,392	17,224	17,571	19,044	23,895	28,163	28,874
4. % of 3. to 1.	33·6	33·3	30·3	33·5	31·7	31·9	33·7	32·6	29·4
5. Exports to U.K. (incl. Re-Exports)	9,507	9,100	8,392	7,815	9,471	11,956	13,724	16,028	17,352
6. % of 5. to 2.	45·7	41·5	40·8	30·9	32·4	40·3	37·1	39·2	38·4
7. Imports from EEC	12,520	15,363	11,474	16,778	18,007	17,057	19,861	24,058	27,049
8. % of 7. to 1.	27·9	32·6	29·9	32·5	32·3	28·6	28·0	27·8	27·5
9. Exports to EEC (incl. Re-Exports)	5,660	6,701	6,216	8,447	9,902	6,948	12,288	12,822	13,587
10. % of 9. to 2.	27·2	30·6	29·9	33·3	33·8	23·4	33·2	31·3	30·1

Source: Analysis of Foreign Trade (Ministry of Finance, Nicosia, 1966–71).

application for EEC membership in 1970. The possible reduction of trade with Britain left Cyprus with little choice but to try to formalize its trading relations with EEC. Therefore Foreign Minister Kyprianou opened preparatory negotiations with the EEC Commission in August 1970 to secure some form of association agreement. However, the talks ended without agreement, partly over difficulties on the question of preferential treatment for citrus fruits. After further working papers had been drawn up by the Cyprus Ministry of Commerce and Industry, the Foreign Ministry and the EEC Commission, the talks were resumed in March 1971.

Apart from the trade with Western Europe, trade has been steadily developed with the Soviet Union and Eastern Europe. By 1970 this amounted to 10·3 per cent of total exports (see

Table 3   *Cyprus Trade with the Soviet Union and Eastern Europe 1970*

Country	Imports		Exports		Trade Balance £000s
	Value £000s	% of Total Imports	Value £000s	% of Total Exports	
Grand Total	98,229	100·0	45,189	100·0	− 53,040
Bulgaria	582	0·6	296	0·6	− 286
Czechoslovakia	1,430	1·5	372	0·8	− 1,058
Eastern Germany	506	0·5	1,014	2·2	+ 508
Hungary	114	0·1	36	0·1	− 78
Poland	262	0·3	206	0·5	− 56
Rumania	1,556	1·6	461	1·0	− 1,095
U.S.S.R.	2,027	2·0	2,289	5·1	+ 262
Total (above countries)	6,477	6·6	4,674	10·3	− 1,803

Source: *Analysis of Foreign Trade* (Ministry of Finance, Nicosia, 1971) p. 6.

Table 3) and 6·6 per cent of total imports. In 1971, trade with Eastern Europe was put on a more formal level with the conclusion of clearing agreements under which payments are made

201

through the Central Bank of Cyprus. Prior to this, trade had been carried out on a barter basis between Cypriot traders and Eastern bloc state organizations. Although perhaps the primary reason for Eastern bloc trade was political, it has, nevertheless, helped to reduce the economic dependence on Western Europe and the Eastern European states in particular have been a useful source of capital goods. But difficulties have arisen over the question of import substitution. Thus, trading relations with the Soviet Union (an important supplier of petroleum products to Cyprus) needed careful re-adjustment following the Cyprus government's decision in 1969 to establish an oil refinery at Larnaca, managed by Petrolina (a Cypriot oil company) in conjunction with Shell, BP and Mobil. It seems probable, however, that trade with the Soviet Union and Eastern Europe will continue to increase gradually as an insurance against any future trading problems with the EEC.

Other efforts at increasing trade redirection have been less successful. An examination of exports by value and destination suggests that it has proved difficult to open new markets for primarily agricultural products. A number of transactions are low in value and the market destinations distant. In 1970 exports to Argentina, Brazil, Australia, New Zealand, Japan and Hong Kong amounted to less than 1 per cent of total exports.

CYPRUS AND INTERNATIONAL CO-OPERATION

Makarios established links with the non-aligned before Cypriot independence. In 1955, for example, he attended as an observer the non-aligned conference at Bandung. After independence close relations with the non-aligned and neutrals were maintained via the UN, state visits to, for example, India (1962), Central America (1965), Scandinavia (1968) and East Africa (1970), and Makarios attended the non-aligned summits held at Belgrade (1961), Cairo (1964) and Lusaka (1970). Membership of the non-aligned grouping is regarded by the Cyprus government as a means of emphasizing its sovereignty and its intention not to become part of a military bloc. The periodic non-aligned conferences and UN caucus meetings provide a forum for the discussion of international issues such as disarmament, strengthening international law and the UN, human rights and strategics for economic development.[27] In an interview Makarios assessed the value of non-alignment as follows:[28]

I believe that the countries of the non-aligned world are offering a good service to the cause of international peace. Some people think that since the great powers are at the head of two opposing blocks there is no other middle political road to be followed than the one leading to the Western or to the Eastern camp. I disagree with this view. I do not overlook the fact that war and peace in the world depend, mainly, on the great powers. I believe, however, that countries which are outside the opposing blocks can play an important role in the effort for the restoration and maintenance of international peace. I have the conviction that the international situation would be worse than it is today if many countries did not follow a non-aligned policy, which is bridging to a certain extent the dangerous gap between West and East.

The non-aligned countries do not have at their disposal big armies and material power. They represent, however, a substantial percentage of the earth's population and by assuming on the various international problems an attitude based on principle rather than on military or other commitments, they constitute a great moral force which can play a very constructive role in international problems. I think that some practical ways should be found so that the moral power of the non-aligned world should become more effective.

The UN provides the main arena for Cyprus to play a modest international role through debates, drafting resolutions and committee membership. In general, the contribution of Cyprus on such issues as disarmament, Vietnam and the Arab-Israeli conflict is limited to declaratory statements of principle. However, the legal training of members of the diplomatic service enables Cyprus to play a greater role on procedural questions and issues involving international law. The Cypriot delegation to the UN has been active on, for example, the international régime of the sea-bed and the definition of aggression.[29] Through the initiative of the chief Cypriot representative, Zenon Rossides, the UN Special Committee for the Definition of Aggression adopted a systematic procedure by which the discussion was restricted to direct or armed aggression. Another useful initiative by Rossides led to the introduction of group drafts,

203

representing the main trends of thought in the Committee. The non-aligned Afro-Asian and the Latin-American group joined in one draft definition; the Soviet Union presented another; and the six members of the Western European group presented a third draft definition. In this way the Committee made some progress in narrowing the differences between the various drafts.[30]

Commonwealth membership has brought several advantages to Cyprus including development assistance and educational scholarships. Politically, the Commonwealth prime ministers and heads of state conferences provide an opportunity for international contact and discussion, and give, particularly to the smaller states, a sense of importance. The value of the continued existence of the Commonwealth as a means of furthering international co-operation has been consistently stressed in the speeches of Makarios and the other Cypriot ministers. Makarios has attempted therefore to use his influence to reduce the disruptive effects of intra-Commonwealth disputes on the organization. At the Lagos conference, for example, Makarios supported the British government's policy of ruling out the use of force against Rhodesia, and used his influence to obtain support for this position. But the 1971 Singapore conference clearly highlighted the inherent contradiction between strong links with Western Europe and membership of the non-aligned grouping. The proceedings of the conference were dominated by the Canadian and Indian attack, supported by the non-aligned, on the British government's projected arms sales to South Africa. President Makarios was placed in a difficult position because of the conflict between his pro-British orientation and agreement with the non-aligned group's attitude on the question. Fortuitously, the dilemma was in part avoided because the latter part of the conference clashed with important national celebrations in Cyprus and President Makarios returned to Nicosia. It is worth adding that it took the skilful chairmanship of Singapore's Prime Minister Lee Kuan Yew and the timely passage of a Soviet flotilla off Singapore to maintain some semblance of Commonwealth unity.

Before providing a concluding assessment, we must note the role of cultural diplomacy in the external relations of Cyprus. Unlike more powerful states, Cyprus does not have an extensive range of means to implement its external relations. As we have seen, economically, a large part of Cyprus trade is necessarily directed to markets in Western Europe and, politically, Cyprus has few bargaining assets. Cultural diplomacy is therefore of considerable importance to this small island republic. Much of this work, together with the organization of domestic cultural programmes, is undertaken by the Cultural Service of the Ministry of Education.[31] The Cultural Service co-operates closely with the Cyprus Tourism Organization, the Greek Cultural Services, embassies accredited to Cyprus, UNESCO and the Council of Europe. An important asset for Cypriot cultural diplomacy is the large number of archaeological sites on the island. The excavations, which are supervised by the Department of Antiquities, are opened to foreign as well as Cypriot archaeological teams, and the findings have been widely exhibited in Europe, the Middle East and Asia. Cultural relations have also been developed through overseas exhibitions of Cypriot art, pottery and ceramics. In the field of contemporary art, for example, Cyprus has been represented at major international art festivals held in Bratislava, Venice, Alexandria, New Delhi, Boston and Sao Paulo. The work of the Cultural Service is also closely integrated with trade promotion, and the Service provides exhibitions for the main international trade-fairs at which Cyprus is represented. The bilateral cultural agreements which Cyprus has signed serve two aims: firstly, to develop further relations with states with which there is a high level of interaction, e.g. West Germany, or secondly, to establish links with states with which it is not possible to develop significant political, economic or military relations, e.g. Yugoslavia.

CONCLUSION

The external relations of Cyprus have been dominated by the intercommunal conflict and economic development. In dealing with the Cyprus problem the government has relied to varying degrees on external powers and the UN in order to avoid too great a dependence on a single source of assistance. Whilst this brought certain advantages, it has undoubtedly contributed to the intractable nature of the problem. In the economic sector the progress of development – aided by generally favourable factors such as geographical location, the links between Cyprus and

Western Europe, and assistance from international agencies –
has been impressive. Apart from the international activity
directed to the above areas, membership of the UN, Commonwealth and the non-aligned grouping has given additional freedom of action and enabled Cyprus to make a modest contribution to international co-operation, particularly on international
legal issues and through cultural exchanges. Thus, by the careful
delineation of the limits of its power and international roles,
Cyprus, on balance, has been successful in the management of its
foreign policy.

NOTES AND REFERENCES

There is no systematic treatment to date of the foreign policy of Cyprus;
in general, the available literature deals with various aspects of the island's
political history, social development, architecture and archaeology. The
pre-independence history of Cyprus is well covered in a number of scholarly
works, in particular those of Sir George Hill; a more general historical
survey is provided by Doros Alastos. Both are referred to in footnote 1 of
this chapter. In addition, readers will find useful Sir Harry Luke's *Cyprus:
A Portrait and an Appreciation* (George G. Harrap & Co., London, 1957).
The economic structure of Cyprus between 1950 and 1960 is analysed by
A. J. Meyer and S. Vassiliou, *The Economy of Cyprus* (Harvard University
Press, Cambridge, Mass., 1962).

The literature which touches on Cyprus foreign policy usually does so
through discussions of the Cyprus problem. Perhaps the best work on
Cyprus, part of which is devoted to post-independence politics, is H. D.
Purcell, *Cyprus* (Ernest Benn Ltd, London, 1969). The book contains a
good bibliography, including material on the Emergency Period, sections
on the Cypriot press and a useful list of Greek and Turkish Cypriot
pamphlets. However, owing to the at times microscopic detail, the reader
is advised to consult first Robert Stephens, *Cyprus: A Place of Arms* (Pall
Mall Press, London, 1966), which is a lucid, historical survey of the Cyprus
problem up to 1966 and contains an extensive bibliography. T. W. Adams
and Alvin J. Cottrell carefully analyse the nature of Soviet and American
involvement in the Cyprus problem in their short but very valuable study,
Cyprus between East and West (The Johns Hopkins Press, Baltimore,
1968). The role of UNFICYP is sympathetically dealt with by James A.
Stegenga, *The United Nations Force in Cyprus* (Ohio State University
Press, Columbus, Ohio, 1968). An 'operational' view is provided by Michael
Harbottle, *Impartial Soldier* (Oxford University Press, London, 1970).
There is relatively little detailed literature on the post-independence ideas,
political power and policies of President Makarios. A brief sketch is
provided by Dr P. N. Vanezis, *Makarios – Faith and Power* (Abelard-
Schuman, London, 1971). More interesting is the little-known work of

Stanley Mayes, *Cyprus and Makarios* (Putnam & Co., London, 1960), which contains good chapters on, for example, Makarios's attitudes to the Greek Cypriots, Turkish Cypriots and the British Labour and Conservative parties.

The above literature is supplemented by the official publications produced by both communities. These include the Greek Cypriot *Cyprus Bulletin* and the Turkish Cypriot *Special News Bulletin*. Both provide a useful record of the main political and economic events in Cyprus. The 'besieged' style of the *Special News Bulletin* is worthy of particular note. The quarterly journal of the Ministry of Education, *Cyprus To-day*, deals mainly with cultural matters. In the economic field, considerable information is available through the reports of the Ministries of Finance, Commerce and Industry and the Central Bank of Cyprus. *Biographical details of the Greek Cypriot leaders* (1971) is one of the many pamphlets produced by the Public Information Office.

Finally, no bibliographical note on Cyprus would be complete without mention of Lawrence Durrell's book, *Bitter Lemons* (Faber and Faber, London, 1957), which classically evokes the ethos of Cyprus.

1. For the pre-independence history of Cyprus see Sir George Hill, *History of Cyprus*, 4 vols (Cambridge University Press, Cambridge, 1940–54); Sir Harry Lake, *Cyprus Under the Turks 1578–1878* (Oxford University Press, Oxford, 1921) and *Cyprus: An Appreciation* (Harrap, London, 1957); Doros Alastos, *Cyprus in History* (Zeno Publishers, London, 1955); George Grivas, *Memoirs*, ed. Charles Foley (Longmans, London, 1964); H. D. Purcell, *Cyprus* (Ernest Benn, London, 1969).

2. See Robert Stephens, *Cyprus: A Place of Arms* (Pall Mall Press, London, 1966) pp. 130–67.

3. *Cyprus: The London and Zurich Agreements and Report on the Implementation*, Cmnd. 1093 (H.M.S.O., London, 1960).

4. See, *The Turkish Case 70:30* (Turkish Communal Chamber, 1963); *Cyprus: The Problem* (Turkish Information Centre, September 1967); C. G. Tornaritis, *Constitutional and Legal Problems in the Republic of Cyprus* (P.I.O., Nicosia, 1969), and *Cyprus: The Problem in Perspective* (P.I.O., Nicosia, 1968).

5. For a discussion of the separate Turkish economic development, see *Special News Bulletin*, 16 April and 23 April 1970.

6. See UN Documents, S/8323, 3 January 1968, and S/8446, 9 March 1968.

7. The Attorney-General, Criton Tornaritis, acts as the chief Cyprus representative on international legal matters. In August 1971, for example, the itinerary of the Attorney-General included attendance at the meeting of the Committee on Legal Co-operation of the Council of Europe, held in Strasbourg; the Council of Europe conference at Aarhus in Denmark on the execution of administrative acts abroad, and the International Conference for the Revision of the Berne Convention on Copyright in Paris. *Cyprus Bulletin*, vol. 7, no. 33 (29 August 1971).

See pp. 203–4.

9. For an account of the role of AKEL, see T. W. Adams and Alvin J. Cottrell, *Cyprus Between East and West* (The Johns Hopkins Press, Baltimore, 1968) pp. 14–54.

10. For an analysis of the role and difficulties faced by UNFICYP between 1964 and 1970, see R. P. Barston, 'Problems in International Peace-keeping: The Case of Cyprus,' *International Relations*, David Davies Memorial Institute, vol. 3, no. 11 (May, 1971) pp. 928–40.

11. The remark, attributed to a Greek Foreign Minister, is quoted in Stephens, op. cit., p. 210.

12. See Edward Weintal and Charles Bartlett, *Facing the Brink* (Charles Scribner's Sons, New York, 1967) chapter 2.

13. An account of the November 1967 crisis is contained in the Secretary General's Special Report, 7 December 1967, S/8248 and Add. 1–9.

14. Report of the Mediator, S/6253, 26 March 1965.

15. Adams and Cottrell, op. cit., p. 47.

16. Purcell, op. cit., p. 367.

17. *The Times*, 16 January 1968.

18. Purcell, op. cit., pp. 366–88.

19. See R. P. Barston, 'Cyprus: The Unresolved Problem 1963–70', *India Quarterly* (April–June 1971) pp. 114–21; and *Cyprus: The Problem in Perspective* (P.I.O., Nicosia, May 1971).

20. A further complicating factor is the position of General Grivas who returned secretly to Cyprus in October, 1971. See *Cyprus Mail*, 28 and 30 October 1971; and *The Times*, 8 February 1972. Strong diplomatic pressures, including demands for cabinet changes, were exerted by the Greek government in February 1972 following the visit of Makarios to the Soviet Union and the importation of Czech arms to combat extremist groups. Foreign Minister Kyprianou resigned in May and the Finance Minister, A. Patsalides, took over as acting Foreign Minister. Eight ministerial changes were made in June 1972, including the appointment of a new Foreign Minister, Ioannis Cl. Christophides. See *Cyprus Bulletin*, vol. 9, no. 24 (25 June 1972)

21. See *Economic Report* (Ministry of Finance, Nicosia, 1968) p. 8.

22. See *Analysis of Foreign Trade 1969* (Ministry of Finance, Nicosia, 1970) p. 9.

23. W. L. Thorp, *Cyprus – Suggestions for a Development Programme*, ST/TAO, CYP/1 (United Nations, New York, 1961).

24. Adams and Cottrell, op. cit., pp. 55–75.

25. ibid., p. 60.

26. See *Annual Report* (Central Bank of Cyprus, Nicosia, 1969) p. 39; and *Cyprus Mail*, 4 September 1970. West Germany has also provided finance for UNFICYP. See UN Press Release, PR/66/6 (11 February 1966).

27. See, for example, the speech of Makarios at the non-aligned conference held in Lusaka (P.I.O., Nicosia, no. 12, September, 1970).

28. *Cyprus Bulletin*, vol. 7, no. 25 (11 July 1970).

29. The election of Zenon Rossides as Chairman of the General Assembly

Legal Committee in September, 1971 is an indication of the recognition of the important role Cyprus plays in international legal matters involving the United Nations.
30. For an indication of the Cypriot position, see the speech of Ambassador Zenon Rossides, Sixth Committee of the UN General Assembly on the Definition of Aggression, 25 November, 1968.
31. See *Cyprus To-Day*, vol. 8, no. 3–4 (July–December, 1970) pp. 80–1, and *Cyprus To-Day*, vol. 9, no. 1–2 (January–June, 1971), pp. 60–8.

Chapter 7

THE FOREIGN POLICY
OF CUBA

DAVID STANSFIELD

Of all the small states, few have generated as much international interest as Cuba. Over the past decade or so Cuba has been seen to successfully challenge the American dominance of its economy; it has been at the centre of a crisis which brought the world to the brink of a nuclear war; it has propagated an ideology which has inspired insurrectionary groups throughout Latin America; and its leader, Fidel Castro Ruz, has emerged as an international figure.

This Caribbean island, however, has not always had such international prominence. Until 1959 it was thought of as a small, corrupt and acquiescent adjunct of the United States.

What, then, accounts for this spectacular transformation? Basically it was the result of a radical change in response from the Cuban leadership to the general policy environment. 'Traditional' styles of managing political and economic problems were abandoned in favour of new, previously unthought of, or prohibited alternatives.

In this chapter I wish to do three things:
1. To outline two of the major problems facing Cuban foreign policy-makers and to explain the ways in which they were 'traditionally' dealt with.
2. To ask why and how this response changed.
3. To examine the subsequent problems of a Cuban re-orientation of her external relationships.

THE CONTINUING PROBLEMS OF CUBAN FOREIGN POLICY

Generations of foreign policy-makers in Cuba have had to come

210

to terms with two constraining problems – the size and location of Cuba in relation to the United States, and the dependence of their economy upon one crop and one trading partner. These were the primary problems, and arrangements made to deal with them have determined the main course of Cuba's foreign policy both before and after the Revolution of 1959.

Location
Cuban politicians have always been aware of the fact that they operate on a small island less than 100 miles off the coast of an immeasurably more powerful neighbour. They have also realized, even from the earliest days of the War of Independence against Spain, that the United States takes a direct and active interest in Cuban affairs. Indeed, the first constitution of the Cuban Republic, ratified in 1902, contained a recognition of the United States right to 'supervise' the affairs of the re-public.[1] In the following fifty-odd years, the United States was to translate this formal right into positive action, and the prospect of U.S. intervention in its various forms became a basic fact of Cuban political life.[2]

This 'supervisory' American role had two somewhat contradictory effects on the development of Cuban politics. First the American Embassy in Havana came to be regarded by political groups in Cuba as a focus for political activity. Governments sought approval in order to confirm their own political status and, in extreme cases, requested American military support to deal with recalcitrant opposition. Opposition groups, on the other hand, worked to convince American representatives of the deficiencies of the government and their own qualities as alternatives. The Americans were not unaware of their central position. As Earl T. Smith, a former incumbent, observed, 'the American Ambassador in Havana was the second most important man in Cuba: sometimes even more important than the President.'[3]

American interference also provoked a more negative response. Cuban nationalists had never forgiven the United States for its emasculation of the independence movement; and the constant reminders of its continued pre-eminence generated a fierce but impotent anti-*Yanqui* element within the political culture.

The implications of Cuba's proximity to the United States were not only political. American tourists, taking advantage of good communications, laxer moral standards and a lower cost of living, flocked to the hotels and beaches of Havana.[4] As the tourist business became an important source of revenue, so politicians became more concerned about not upsetting its customers. Traffic between Havana and Miami, however, was not one-way, and the more affluent sectors of Cuban society developed direct ties with the United States. They visited the United States as tourists, sent their children to American schools and universities, invested in American industry[5] and married into American families.

The United States had more than a neighbourly interest in Cuba. Its strategic significance for them had already been pointed out by Alfred Mahan as early as 1894.[6] With the opening of the Panama Canal in 1914 and the development of the Venezuelan oil industry in the twenties, the importance of its location in the Gulf of Mexico was emphasized. Cuban statesmen, however, were unable to capitalize upon this increasing strategic significance. On the contrary it compounded American surveillance of its affairs.

In sum, Cuba's location was regarded by both Cubans and Americans alike as a factor of weakness, which determined its acquiescence to the dictates of its more powerful neighbour.

Economic Dependence

In trying to describe the importance of sugar to the economy, Sartre once described Cuba as a 'diabetic island'. For over 100 years the Cuban economy has been dominated by the sugar industry. An idea of the overall importance of the industry is given by Boorstein:

> Together with its by-products, alcohol and molasses, sugar made up about 80% of the exports and paid for the bulk of the imports. The sugar companies controlled 70–75% of the arable land; they owned two-thirds of the rail-road trackage; most of the ports and many of the roads were simply adjuncts of the sugar mills. The sugar industry employed about 25% of the labour force. The export of sugar and its by-products constituted 20–30% of the gross domestic product. But this last percentage does not give sugar its true importance: most of the rest of the gross product depended upon sugar.[7]

By the end of the nineteenth century Cuba was well on the way to becoming a classic case of the monocrop economy, with its fortunes heavily dependent upon the fluctuations of the world market in sugar. During the first thirty years of this century, however, an important additional factor was to complicate the case. American investment in the sugar industry increased dramatically, swamping local investment.[8] At the same time sugar exporters, taking advantage of tariff reductions and high prices, concentrated on the American market. The American impact on the Cuban economy was not limited to the production and consumption of sugar. American exporters, taking advantage of the 'reciprocity' agreements and the lack of local competition, increased their stake in the Cuban market for manufactured goods. By the 1950s the United States was supplying between 70 and 80 per cent by value of all Cuban imports and receiving over 65 per cent of all her exports. Since by this time American investors had also obtained an important stake in the non-sugar related industries and public utilities, the Cuban economy was heavily dependent upon the United States. To some observers the links were so close that Cuba seemed a mere extension of the American national economy.

For Cuban policy-makers the implications of this economic relationship were many and varied. Although the welfare of Cuba was closely involved with the sugar trade, its governments were severely restricted as to its management. Production policy was, in the main, in the hands of the large U.S.-owned sugar firms, and the market was not susceptible to Cuban pressure. Until the 1930s this situation was not too onerous. World prices for sugar were high and Cuba prospered from its privileged access to the U.S. market. The situation changed after the Depression. U.S. Investment in the Cuban sugar industry was cut back and new competitive sources of sugar began to flood world markets and depress prices. The Cuban share of the U.S. market decreased as the U.S. raised tariffs and established quota systems. Lacking access to alternative markets, the Cuban economy stagnated. These economic problems soon found political expression and by 1933 'the island was the scene of guerrilla warfare, urban tension and a general strike'.[9]

This political instability caused concern in both Havana and Washington. Washington wished to protect its economic and strategic interests in the island. Governments in Havana wanted to be seen to be getting concessions from the U.S.A. for the

213

ailing sugar industry. In fact, for the next thirty years Cuban foreign policy revolved around the problem of improving the conditions of the sugar trade with the U.S. Attempts to diversify the export trade by finding new customers had only limited success. Potential buyers like France or Britain had already developed their own sources of supply. Cuba was forced to make the best of its trade with the United States.

Relations between the United States and Cuba over the sugar trade focused upon the regularly reviewed quota and price levels. The Cuban position was expressed in several ways. Formal diplomatic negotiations between officials of the two governments were supplemented by less conventional ties between sugar producers and the U.S. congressional committees. American firms with interests in Cuba supported a strong 'Cuba-lobby' in Washington.

In short, Cuban foreign policy-makers recognized the restrictions implied by her economic dependence upon the United States. Broadly, their objective was a 'realistic' maximization of Cuba's sugar export potentiality in the U.S. market. No much more and sometimes less.

The massive American stake in the Cuban economy had important political repercussions. As well as its traditional security interests in the Caribbean, American policy was concerned with the protection of American investors in Cuba. Although demands for the annexation of Cuba were ignored by American administrations, military occupations of the island were often justified in terms of the defence of American lives and property. Cuban awareness of this concern inhibited economic policy-making and added fuel to the smouldering fires of anti-*Yanquismo*.

One of the most important effects of this economic development was the cultural one. The injection of American capital into the sugar industry, and later into other sectors of the economy, was accompanied by an influx of American managerial talent. Middle-class Cubans seeking employment in American-owned firms tended to be relegated to the less well-paid and less prestigious middle-level positions. This helped to create a form of schizophrenia. At times, envious of the Americans' salaries and status, many Cubans took violently anti-American postures. At the same time most middle-class Cubans aspired to and did their best to imitate American life-styles. The result was a form

214

of 'cultural dependence' sometimes described as the 'coca-colarization' of Cuba.

The Filter

Inanimate facts like a country's location or economic capability are not in themselves the ultimate determinants of foreign policy. They become important as factors only when recognized as relevant by persons or groups involved in the making of foreign policy. This translation of aspects of the policy environment into the policy process by politicians is not a simple or direct process. By and large politicians see what they want to see, or more accurately, what they have learned to see. The images held by decision makers constitute a 'filter' through which the environment is perceived. The characteristics of the 'filter', i.e. what it cuts out as irrelevant or unsuitable, or what it highlights as necessary and appropriate, are the products of a variety of factors – the political experience of those involved, their understanding of what functions they should perform, and the values of the society in which they operate.

The radical changes in Cuban foreign policy after the 1959 Revolution reflect changes in the characteristics of this 'filter'. Cuba was still economically tied to a very close and very powerful neighbour. What had changed by 1960 was the Cuban response to this situation. In other words the 'filter' had changed drastically. Whereas previous governments, with varying degrees of reluctance, had adjusted to the idea of an unavoidably limited Cuban sovereignty, Castro at the head of the revolutionary government decided that the situation was reversible and that the range of policy alternatives could be expanded.

What brought about this change in the range of feasible alternatives? Why, by the end of 1960, did Castro abandon the traditional diplomatic techniques for dealing with the United States?[10] To explain this 'second Revolution' as Draper calls it, one must concentrate primarily on internal Cuban developments.[11]

Endemic anti-Americanism had long been a feature of Cuban politics. The history of its expression, however, was one of frustration. Nationalist governments had been elected only to falter in the face of American disapproval. Castro, like many of his followers, had had direct experience of this sense of frustration. He could also point to the fact that the U.S. had for several

215

years supported an exceptionally brutal, corrupt and unpopular Batista régime. In addition, he had cause to remember that arms supplied by America had been used by *Batistiano* troops in the Sierra Maestre against his guerrilla band.[12]

When Castro entered Havana in January 1959, his victory must have seemed complete. The survivors of the *Granma* expedition had, in the space of just over two years, defeated a substantial American-equipped army, and had been received in Cuban cities with incredible demonstrations of popular support. According to contemporary reports it was a period of unbounded euphoria, when almost anything seemed possible. Certainly the provisional Revolutionary government, which was dominated by Castro, embarked upon an ambitious programme of agrarian and administrative reform, ignoring the pleas for caution from the older and more experienced ministers.

It is clear that the revolutionary leadership during the campaign in the Sierra Maestre had developed a strong attachment to the depressed peasantry of Oriente province. 'Ché' Guevara gave an indication of this affection and its implications for the development of the ideology of the Revolution when he wrote:

> ... we began to grow more conscious of the necessity for a definitive change in the life of the people. The idea of agrarian reform became clear and one-ness with the people ceased being theory and was converted into a fundamental part of our being. The guerrilla group and the peasantry began to merge into one single mass ... As far as I'm concerned, those consultations with the *guajiros* of the Sierra converted my spontaneous and somewhat lyrical resolve into a force of greater value and more serenity. Those suffering and loyal inhabitants of the Sierra Maestre have never suspected the role they played as forgers of our revolutionary ideology.[13]

A far-reaching agrarian reform aimed at alleviating the plight of the Cuban peasantry thus became an important plank of the revolutionary programme. In fact, one of the first acts of the revolutionary government was the establishment of an Institute of Agrarian Reform (INRA) charged with the implementation of the Agrarian Reform Law.[14] This commitment to a radical change of the land tenure system and an improvement of the conditions of rural life has been a constant feature of revolutionary policy.

The American reaction to the land reform was, as far as Castro was concerned, rather hostile. American diplomats, in urging caution and pressing for 'proper' compensation for the expropriated landowners, seemed antagonistic to a central feature of the Revolution's programme. Castro was also worried by the unofficial American reaction. Whilst some important leaders of public opinion, like the *New York Times*, were more or less sympathetic, Castro was disturbed that other sectors of the American Press, together with the old pro-Batista lobby in Washington, were highly critical of his beloved agrarian reform. Since the land reform was the highest priority of the Revolution, these reservations were regarded as reflections of a basic incompatibility between Cuban interests and American policy. Land reform was not negotiable.

The change in foreign policy can also be explained by organizational developments within Cuba. Although the cities had received the Rebel Army with remarkable displays of support, they had played only a minor role in the overthrow of Batista. Castro's influence in the urban centres had always been tenuous, less strong than in rural areas.[15] With victory the need for a wider political base than that provided by the 26 July Movement was recognized.

Most of the old parties were unsuitable. Many had disqualified themselves through too close an identification with the deposed Batista régime. Others, despite their anti-Batista credentials, were unable to provide the necessary political infrastructure. In this situation the status of the PSP (the Partído Socialista Popular – the Cuban Communist Party) was equivocal. It had a record of collaboration with Batista, had condemned the attack on the Moncada Barracks in 1953 as 'adventurist putschism' and had been cool in its relations with guerrilla forces until very late in the game.[16] Its attractiveness to Fidel, however, lay in its organizational strengths. Its urban and trade union cadres were particularly useful. In addition, with his increasing suspicion of American policy, the PSP's offer of Soviet support must have sounded very tempting. As Draper has written, 'The Communists and Fidel walked towards each other, each with his eyes open, each filling a need in the other.'[17]

Through the interaction of these factors, the backlog of anti-

American feeling, the elation of victory, the ideological importance of the land reform and the organizational requirements of
the Revolution, the filter of 'foreign' policy was transformed.
Traditional foreign policy postures were abandoned and new
international links were pursued. Cuban foreign policy, as well
as Cuban society, was to undergo a revolution.

THE REORIENTATION OF CUBAN FOREIGN POLICY

The implications of this changed way of looking at foreign
policy alternatives were enormous.

The central problem for Castro was not simply breaking
Cuba's economic and political ties with the United States. It
also involved finding a new *patrón*. Cuba's military vulnerability
and economic weakness required that any declaration of diplomatic independence from the United States be guaranteed by a
compensatory set of relationships with another super power.
Despite their brave words, Cuban leaders recognized that Cuba
could not 'go it alone' in the face of American opposition.

In choosing the Soviet Union as the 'protector' of the
Revolution, Castro took a monumental gamble. There was
every chance that the United States would react quickly to meet
this challenge to their hemispheric authority, as they had done
several years previously in Guatemala.[18] In addition, Castro's
initial contacts with the Soviet leadership were none too
promising. Although elements of the Cuban PSP had tried hard
to convince Castro of the eagerness of the Soviet Union to
support the Revolution, Castro's discussions and negotiations
with Moscow brought little encouragement. To the Kremlin
Cuba must have seemed a remote and extremely vulnerable
little island on the periphery of the Soviet Union's security
interests. Khrushchev's immediate concern in 1959–60 was to
arrange a summit conference to solve the Berlin crisis.

Castro's response to this precarious situation was characteristic. He pursued what Suárez has called an 'audacious' foreign
policy, designed to demonstrate Cuba's independence from the
United States and his own Socialist credentials.[19]

This central problem, the restructuring of the pattern of Cuba's
external relations, was complicated by a number of other
factors.

Firstly, there was the question of priorities. What should

218

come first? The reform of Cuban society or the restructuring of foreign policy? Although many believed that the latter was a necessary guarantee of the former, some commentators suggested that the administration of a far-reaching social revolution was the prime commitment. They argued that the leadership should concentrate on the immediate problems of internal reform without complicating the matter through an adventurous and risky foreign policy. Castro took the other view and moved Cuba forward on both domestic and international fronts.

Secondly, this process of reorientation involved certain structural problems. The revolutionary leaders, and Castro the undoubted leader was no exception, were relatively young and largely inexperienced in diplomatic and economic matters. They saw themselves as 'men of action' and had difficulty in adjusting to the strictures of traditional diplomatic intercourse. They had little respect and use for the diplomatic machinery available to them. Many diplomats were Batista appointees and soon deserted their posts for exile in America or Spain. Much of the remainder were ill-trained and ineffectual. Thus Castro embarked upon a new direction of foreign policy aided by a minimum of professional expertise.

The changed attitude towards foreign policy also produced domestic repercussions. The revolutionary leadership was not completely united in its decision to effect ties with the Soviet Union, and Castro faced opposition from within the 26 July Movement and the Rebel Army. The opposition, however, was weak and never really threatened the position of the *líder maximo*. By 1961 opponents of the pro-Soviet policy were either in exile, in prison, or in agreement.

Castro also faced problems within the pro-Soviet lobby. He was particularly concerned with the position and influence of the PSP, which had long-established ties with Moscow, and had been the main channel for communication between Cuba and the Soviet Union after the Revolution. This special access to the new *patrón*, together with its organizational strengths, threatened Castro's own position and had to be controlled. In consequence he developed formal non-party structures to manage relations with the Soviet Union, attempted to establish his own 'socialist' credentials and kept a tight grip on party organization.

Despite all these problems, by 1961 the process of reorientation was well in hand.

CUBAN POLICY TOWARDS THE SOVIET UNION

Cuban relations with the Soviet Union have not been a regular and harmonious pattern. They are best understood as a series of distinct periods or stages: 1959–62, 1962–65, 1965–68, 1968–?

1959–62

Cuban policy in the immediate post-revolutionary situation had two main objectives: first to enlist active Soviet support for the Revolution, and secondly to define the terms of that support.

In order to convince the Soviet Union of Cuba's suitability as an ally, the revolutionary government adopted a two-pronged tactic. This involved, on the one hand, stressing Cuba's ideological sympathies with the Socialist bloc, and on the other hand exploring the possibilities of alternative arrangements within the Third World at large, or with China.

Although the Soviet Union recognized the Castro régime only two days after his triumphal entry into Havana on 10 January 1959, its support for the Revolution was limited for over a year to moral encouragement and vague declarations of solidarity. Unsure of the economic, military and political viability of the régime, the Soviet Union seemed willing to use it merely for short-term Cold War advantages. As González says,

> ... in 1959, Moscow valued the Cuban Revolution insofar as the Castro regime disturbed inter-American solidarity, weakened American hegemony in Latin America, and diverted Washington's attention to the Western hemisphere. Nevertheless, the Soviets evidently hoped to realize these limited cold-war objectives with a minimum of direct involvement in Cuba and with the Revolution retaining its liberationist but non-Communist character.[20]

The Cubans, having doubts about the American reaction to their reforms, wanted something more substantial. Castro, therefore, increased the régime's identification with socialism. Thus the amalgamation of the PSP into the revolutionary régime provided not only a useful political machine but also demonstrated his sympathy for the communist point of view. The appointment of Osvaldo Dorticós as President had a similar utility.[21]

Elements of the PSP itself were also involved in changing the

Soviet attitude. Through their contacts in Moscow they stressed their influence within the revolutionary group and the 'socialist' character of its reform programme.[22]

At the same time Castro adopted a belligerently anti-American stance. He criticized American complaints about the adequacy of compensation for expropriated American assets. He refused American offers of economic assistance for Cuba and referred to the need for revolutions similar to Cuba's elsewhere in Latin America.

As well as courting the Soviet Union with displays of domestic and international complicity, Castro was also exploring the possibility of ties with China and with the 'unaligned' countries of the Third World. Whilst it is unlikely that he ever thought such ties would be an effective substitute for Soviet support, he must have realized that such explorations gave him a certain, albeit limited, leverage with the Soviet leadership.

By the beginning of 1960 this pressure on the Soviet Union had brought results. Mikoyan visited Havana and on 13 February signed a trade agreement which involved Soviet loans worth about $100 million at $2\frac{1}{2}$ per cent interest and a guarantee that the Soviet Union would buy 5 million tons of Cuban sugar over the next five years. Payment for the sugar was to be 80 per cent in Soviet goods and 20 per cent in foreign currency. Similar agreements with East Germany and Poland, on a much smaller scale, followed within the next few months. The scale of Soviet support for the Cuban economy was increased further during the summer when Khrushchev promised that the Soviet Union would buy the 700,000 tons cut from the American sugar quota by President Eisenhower. Cuba had found her economic patrón.[23]

Castro's attempts to get Soviet military support were less dramatically successful. His requests for supplies of arms for the defence of the Revolution against an 'inevitable' invasion brought little in the way of Soviet response. Although Khrushchev is reported to have said on 19 July 1960 that 'in a figurative sense, if it becomes necessary, the Soviet military can support the Cuban people with rocket weapons' he later chastised the Cubans for 'rattling Soviet missiles'.[24] There is also evidence to suggest that weapons of the more conventional type were not supplied to Cuba in any significant amounts until the following year.

221

Cuban pressures for military support persisted. Small-scale invasions and sabotage by American-based Cuban exiles showed no signs of ceasing and the possibility of an all-out invasion was real. In fact the invasion came on 17 April 1961. A force of about 1,400 American-trained Cuban exiles landed in the Playa Girón (the Bay of Pigs) on the south-western side of the island.[25] Fortunately for Castro the invasion was both badly planned and ineptly executed. The invasion was repulsed within fifteen hours and a large number of prisoners taken.[26]

Although elated by victory, Castro realized that Cuba was still vulnerable to an all-out American attack. His forces had performed creditably during the invasion but they were now even more badly equipped than before. He therefore continued to press for arms from his Soviet benefactors. The Soviet Union continued to prevaricate, preferring to underwrite the now failing Cuban economy. The number of Soviet technicians in Cuba increased as did the number of Cubans being trained in the Soviet bloc.

By the late summer of 1962 the Soviet attitude had changed. Medium- and intermediate-range nuclear ballistic missile sites were being constructed in Cuba by Soviet specialists. It looked as though Castro's calls for effective military support had been, at long last, successful. The acquisition of missiles would increase Cuba's military capability enormously.[27]

Cuba's delight, however, was short-lived. In early October American pressure on the Soviet leadership brought a halt to the construction of rocket sites and the 'turn-about' of Soviet ships carrying missiles to Cuba.

The way in which this 'missile crisis' was resolved, i.e. through United States/Soviet dialogue with minimal Cuban participation, left Castro resentful and humiliated. It also left him a wiser man. The 'backing-off' of the Soviet Union in the face of resolute American opposition demonstrated the limits of Soviet support for Cuba. If the defence of Cuba involved a threat to the Soviet Union's most immediate security interests in Europe, then Cuba could and would be sacrificed.

1962–65

After the 'missile crisis', Cuban relations with the Soviet Union were distinctly cool. Castro criticized the Soviet Union for 'capitulation' and, against Soviet wishes, refused to allow a UN team to inspect the dismantled sites. He was careful, however, to avoid making a complete break. Cuba's economic position was causing concern and required increased Soviet support. There was also the possibility that the United States would invade Cuba to prevent a recurrence of the crisis. However bitter the taste, Castro had no alternative but to look again to the Soviet Union as his guarantor.

On the Soviet side Khrushchev was concerned to repair some of the damage caused by the 'missile crisis'. He had lost prestige in many parts of the Third World for having sacrificed Cuba and sought ways of re-establishing his reputation. Mikoyan was despatched to Havana in November 1962 and in the following January a Cuban/Soviet trade agreement was published. This extended the scale of Soviet credit facilities to Cuba, raised the price paid for sugar and allowed the sale on the world market of one million tons of sugar originally destined for the Soviet Union. At the same time the trickle of conventional arms was stepped up.

Whilst Castro realized that Cuba was dependent upon the Soviet Union for economic and military support, he was reluctant to submit to Soviet international policy.[28] He was unwilling to abandon his policy of encouraging violent revolution in Latin America in order to fit in with the Soviet mood of 'peaceful co-existence'. The exhortation of continental revolution was more than an ideological requirement. It distracted local opinion from domestic problems, it reinforced his international status as anti-imperialist and, if successful, might divert American interest away from Cuba. His commitment to this policy, however, was sporadic. His main concern was Cuba's economic health. Policies aimed at industrialization, import substitution and export diversification had met major problems and the Soviet Union as the main creditor was demanding a major re-assessment of Cuban economic policies.[29]

Economic necessity, therefore, brought the two countries together. Castro's penchant for revolutionary rhetoric was subdued and Cuba looked like becoming a loyal, if somewhat reluctant, member of the international socialist community. Castro condemned the Chinese for sowing discord in the world communist movement, thereby taking the Soviet side in the Sino-Soviet dispute. He also accepted a compromise on the policy of advocating violent revolution in the Western hemi-

223

sphere. At the Havana Conference of Latin American Communist Parties in November 1964 it was agreed that Castro would in future direct his calls for revolution only to those areas where local communist parties had judged the popular mood suitable for armed struggle. In the other states he would respect the 'gradualist' views of the local communists.

1965–68

This acceptance of the Soviet policy of 'peaceful co-existence' was short-lived. The minimal Soviet response to the landing of American marines in the nearby Dominican Republic in April, 1965 caused Castro to reconsider his position.[30] It raised doubts about the reliability of Soviet support for Cuba in the face of a similar American invasion. In addition, the new Soviet leadership of Brezhnev and Kosygin might not have the same stake in Cuba as their more impulsive predecessor Khrushchev. It seemed sensible to look for an alternative strategy.

For some time Castro had played with the idea of building alliances between Cuba and the 'unaligned' countries, sometimes collectively described as the 'Third World'. Such alliances, although unlikely to be economically significant, were tempting because (a) they enhanced his international reputation and respectability, therefore making a United States invasion less likely, and (b) they increased his bargaining power with the Soviet Union. A major role within this 'Third World' bloc, however, was unlikely to be achieved if Cuba was regarded as a quiescent Soviet satellite. Castro needed to demonstrate his independence. This he did by abandoning the policy of co-operation with the traditional 'gradualist' communist parties of Latin America and stepping up his calls for a pan-continental revolution against local 'oligarchies' and American 'imperialism'.

This decision to digress from the Soviet international line was aided by domestic dissatisfaction with the terms of Cuba's relationship with the U.S.S.R. Soviet demands that Cuba concentrate upon sugar production rather than experiment with industrialization and export diversification were unpopular within the revolutionary leadership and led to a certain anti-Soviet resentment.

. . . from September 1965 onward, there were repeated signs

224

that Castro was undergoing a strong psychological reaction against past agreements with the Soviets. Indeed, a very strong case can be made for the thesis that Castro's pride had suffered so much under the effects of his apparent sell-out to Moscow after Khrushchev's fall that he was looking for every conceivable opportunity to flaunt Moscow's will.[31]

By the autumn of 1965 Castro's independent line was beginning to take shape. 'Ché' Guevara, previously identified with the abandoned industrialization plans and out of the political limelight for several years, was politically resurrected. Public discussion of the moral/material incentive controversy was reactivated; and the PURS (the United Party of the Socialist Revolution), despite being renamed the Cuban Communist Party, was so organized as to minimize the influence of old-time Moscow-line communism.[32] Castro also reserved the right, on behalf of the new party, to interpret Marxism-Leninism in his own way.

On the international front Castro gave tacit support to the Venezuelan guerrillas led by Douglas Bravo[33] and criticized the Soviet Union for its attempts to improve relations with Latin American governments hostile to Cuba.

The Soviet Union was disturbed by these deviations from the Moscow line, especially with the Tri-Continental Conference planned to open in Havana in January of 1966. For the Soviet Union the conference represented a means by which the AAPSO (Afro-Asia Peoples Solidarity Organization) could be expanded by the inclusion of Latin-American delegations, thus reducing its pro-Chinese potential.

For Castro the conference had a different purpose. Although he went through the motions of attacking the Chinese, his prime concern was to use the meeting to consolidate his 'Third World' reputation, as previous AAPSO hosts like Sekou Touré, Julius Nyerere and Kwame Nkrumah had done. It also provided a safe platform from which to call for increased Soviet support for the various *castrista* 'liberation movements' in Latin America.

It became clear as the conference progressed that although the Soviet Union had been successful in reducing Chinese influence in AAPSO, its Latin American policies were under severe attack. Cuban speeches showed little sympathy for the pro-

Soviet Latin American communist parties and urged material support in the form of weapons and finance for such groups as the Venezuelan FALN/FLN.[34] The Cubans were also successful in getting the permanent Tri-Continental Secretariat established in Havana, in the face of a Soviet preference for Cairo.

Castro's rhetorical bid for Third World prominence was quickly backed up by organizational ploys. The Latin American Solidarity Organization (LASO) was established and its head-quarters located in Havana. A conference for Latin American students was convened in Havana in July/August 1966 which resulted in the formation of the OCLAE (Continental Organization of Latin American Students). Cuban policy as a whole took a more militant tone.

The Soviet reaction was one of embarrassed defeat. To the outside world it played down the status of the conference and made clear its reservations about the militant tone of its pro-nouncements.[35] Within communist circles its critique of the radical Cuban position was made by the Mexican and Vene-zuelan communist parties.

These tactics failed to curb Castro's new confidence. He declared his support for Latin-American liberation movements and condemned pro-Soviet communist parties as 'charlatans' and 'pseudo revolutionaries'.[36] He also criticized openly Soviet trade agreements with the Frei government in Chile.

Relations between Moscow and Havana continued to deteri-orate through 1967. The main responsibility for this lay with Castro, for the Soviet Union pursued a fairly cautious, low-key policy of conciliation.

The split was most obvious during the Havana OLAS con-ference in July and August 1967. Latin American delegations representing the 'armed struggle' point of view clashed with the orthodox communists. Castro himself condemned the orthodox parties as an 'international mafia' committed to the 'destruction of the Cuban Revolution'.[37] The conference, however, did not limit itself to a critique of Soviet agents. A secret resolution castigated the Soviet Union for giving financial and technical assistance to 'oligarchic' Latin American régimes. Castro described aid to countries like Chile and Colombia as 'a sad contradiction' and a 'violation of international solidarity'.[38]

This attitude was worrying for the Soviet leaders. They did not enjoy having their policy of 'peaceful coexistence' attacked.

It represented a way in which tensions between Cuba and its neighbours could be relaxed. Such relaxation held the possibility of a re-establishment of hemispheric trade with Cuba, thereby reducing the scale of the expensive subsidy of the island's economy. On the other hand, they did not want a confrontation with Castro which might push him towards the Chinese or erode their standing in the Third World. They therefore proceeded with caution.

Castro, however, continued with his independent line. The Cuban delegation to the celebrations of the Soviet Union's fiftieth anniversary was distinctly low-key. It took little part in the proceedings and left before the end. The Soviet Union was snubbed in a similar fashion by the Cuban decision not to send representation to the Consultative Meeting of the Communist Parties held in Budapest in early 1968. Events inside Cuba were equally ominous for the Soviet Union. Anibal Escalante was arrested and accused of leading a 'micro-faction' of ex-PSP members hostile to the current policies of the revolutionary government. The group was further accused of attempting to enlist the support of Soviet officials resident in Cuba. Although care was taken to avoid openly implicating the Soviet Union in the discovered plot, the point was clear. Castro would not tolerate Soviet meddling in Cuba's domestic affairs. As Carlos Rafael Rodríguez put it:

> I believe that we should no longer put up with a state of affairs where a whole series of officials and members of socialist organizations – socialist countries – work against the Cuban Revolution here and in their own country.[39]

1968–?

These displays of Cuban independence came less frequently during 1968. There were still public differences of opinion with the Soviet Union over such issues as the war in Vietnam, but the general tone of Cuban policy was moderated. This was particularly true of the policy encouraging 'violent revolution' in Latin America. Insurrectionary propaganda aimed at the neighbouring republics was cut back and material assistance to the various guerrilla groups reduced to a trickle. There were fewer open conflicts with the Soviet leadership over its endorsement of the traditional communist parties of the hemisphere and its moves to improve relations with countries like Chile and Peru.

The reasons for this shift were mainly economic. The delays in delivery of Soviet oil in the winter of 1967/68 had brought home to the Cuban leadership the harsh facts of their dependence upon the Soviet Union for economic survival.[40] They also realized that Cuba's vulnerability to this sort of economic pressure would be increased as the year progressed. The country was faced with pressing economic problems. A drought had cut sugar production to 4 million tons (1 million tons less than the previous year), thereby reducing export capability and threatening plans for industrialization. It was clear that in the forthcoming negotiations over the new Soviet trade agreement the Cubans would be in a weak position. They needed further extensions of credit and could expect to have to give concessions in return.

The shift away from the 'export of revolution' policy was also due to the shortcomings of the policy itself. It had proved unsuccessful in generating 'the second or third Vietnams' in Latin America. In Colombia, Guatemala and Venezuela, Cuban-sponsored *guerrilleros* were on the defensive and in Bolivia they had been decisively defeated.[41] The failure of the Bolivian expedition and the death of 'Ché' Guevara was perhaps the most significant reverse. It was Cuba's most serious attempt to ferment revolution in Latin America, and its elimination caused a major reassessment of strategy. In addition, the execution of Guevara by the Bolivians removed the most committed and influential proponent of 'continental revolution'.

Thus by the middle of 1968 the scene was set for an improvement of Soviet-Cuban relations. This did not mean that Cuba was reduced to the role of a passive client satellite. Castro publicized the efforts of guerrillas in the Portuguese African colonies and declared Cuba's solidarity with North Vietnam and North Korea. Even his well-publicized approval of the Soviet invasion of Czechoslovakia in August 1968 was not without reservations. He regretted the Soviet failure to identify the events in Czechoslovakia with American espionage activities and doubted whether the Soviet Union would be as willing to defend communism in Cuba, Vietnam and Korea as it had been in Eastern Europe.[42] Despite these reservations, Castro's support was welcome in Moscow. The supply of arms to Cuba was stepped up and economic relations moved into a more harmoni-ous state than before.

Since 1968 the pattern of relations between the two countries has stabilized. The Cubans have focused their revolutionary energies on the problems of economic development and national defence. Relations with the Soviet Union, therefore, have been more 'functional' than before, concerned with the details of development credits, trade, military and technical assistance rather than rhetorical exchanges.[43]

The Soviet attitude is problematical. On the one hand, Cuba's continuing anti-American and 'socialist' ideology is a useful source of Cold War propaganda. It also has potential as a 'staging-post' for the Soviet fleet and long-range aerial recon-naissance.[44] On the other hand, it is proving a costly and rather unpredictable dependant. At the moment the Soviet leadership seems interested in resolving this dilemma by urging a reduction of tensions between Cuba and its neighbours. This undoubtedly was a topic in the discussion between Castro and Kosygin during the Soviet Premier's visit to Cuba in October 1971. If Cuba were reintegrated into the hemispheric economic system without conceding its ideological position, the economic burden would be lessened with a minimal loss of Cold War advantage. The recent increases in the number of Latin American govern-ments apparently willing to reopen diplomatic and trade rela-tions with Cuba must have given Soviet leaders great hopes.[45]

CUBAN POLICY TOWARDS CHINA

The Cuban leaders have never really believed that China could provide the same scale and variety of material support as the Soviet Union. Its potential as an economic *patrón* was limited and it was even farther away than the U.S.S.R. In consequence, Cuba's China policy has had a 'residual' or 'complementary' quality, almost always fitting into the more general lines of her Soviet policy.

In the first few years of the Revolution, relations between Cuba and China were quite warm, with each government declaring its admiration of the other's revolution and anti-imperialist stand. This mutual admiration was given a more concrete form by the autumn of 1960.[46] Delegations of Cuban trade unionists and students visited China and a series of trade and technical co-operation conventions were signed. By these conventions the Chinese agreed to buy 1 million tons of Cuban sugar and granted the Cubans $60 million credit for the purchase of Chinese equipment and technical assistance.[47]

These agreements were important to the Cubans for two reasons. First, although the Soviet Union had already agreed to take 1,700,000 tons of sugar, the Cubans were still left with over 2 million tons to dispose of.[48] The opening up of a Chinese market was therefore a very welcome development on purely economic grounds. Secondly, the treaties demonstrated to the Cuban leaders that their apparent *rapport* with the Chinese could be used to their advantage in negotiations with the Soviet Union. They noted that the Soviet leadership reacted to the Chinese agreement by quickly improving the terms of its trade agreements with Cuba.[49] The Cubans had prospered from their first venture into the politics of the Sino-Soviet split.

In 1961 the Cuban attitude towards China was more restrained. The immediate concern was the military defence of Cuba, and Castro decided that his chances of enlisting Soviet military support might suffer from a too-friendly attitude to the Chinese. This was a time for caution, and therefore silence on the Sino-Soviet debate. The Chinese, however, continued to stress the similarities between the Cuban and Chinese revolutionary experiences.

This persistence looked like paying dividends in late 1962 as Cuban relations with the Soviet Union cooled. Throughout the October Missile Crisis the Chinese had supported the Cuban case for retaining the missiles. They had also criticized Khrushchev for capitulating to the 'paper tiger' of American imperialism.[50] Castro's response, however, was still cautious. Peeved by the Soviet withdrawal but fearing a punitive American invasion, he was careful not to alienate his main source of protection and supply. Nevertheless his criticisms of the Soviet international policies had a slight 'Chinese' flavour about them. They were certainly enthusiastically received in Peking.

This brief demonstration of independence by Castro had its desired effect. The Soviet Union, already concerned to repair its international image, could not afford to have Cuba taking the Chinese side in the Sino-Soviet debate. The terms of the 1963 trade agreement with Cuba were consequently improved and the supply of arms stepped up. Once again Castro had exploited the smouldering Sino-Soviet conflict to extract concessions from his Soviet *patrón*.

This improvement of Cuban/Soviet relations did little to cool Chinese enthusiasm for the Castro régime. There were continual declarations of solidarity and admiration. The Cuban attitude to the Chinese, however, became increasingly critical. Major economic difficulties had restricted the Cuban scope for foreign policy initiatives. Care had to be taken not to upset their main creditor – the Soviet Union.

Relations between China and Cuba reached their lowest point yet in November 1964. Mao, clearly worried by Castro's pro-Soviet position, criticized the Moscow-line affiliations of most of the delegations invited by Castro to the Havana conference of Latin American communist parties. His fears proved to be well founded. The conference took a pro-Soviet line, demanding 'an immediate end to the polemic' between the Soviet Union and China and condemning 'fractional activity' within the world communist movement.[51]

In 1965 Castro's criticisms of the Chinese became more open and direct. He criticized them not only for sowing discord in the socialist camp but also for disseminating propaganda in Cuba.[52] Castro, it seemed, had decided to openly back his Soviet allies in the Sino-Soviet split. The Chinese were silent. Reference to Cuba and Cuban developments in the Chinese Press were cut to a minimum. For example, the *People's Daily*, which in the previous two years had published many speeches by the Cuban leaders, ignored the Cuban statements at and immediately after the Havana conference.[53] By the end of the year there are grounds for thinking that this passive line had been abandoned. On 2 January 1966 Castro announced that the Chinese had indicated that they could not meet the conditions of the trade agreement. He had been advised, he claimed, that they could not take 800,000 tons of Cuban sugar nor could they supply the promised 250,000 tons of rice.[54]

If these 'shortages' were intended by the Chinese to persuade Castro to take a more sympathetic line during the forthcoming Tri-Continental Conference, they were misconceived. Castro used the issue to launch a public attack on the ways in which the more advanced socialist countries operate in the Third World.

It was no longer a question of more or fewer tons of rice . . .

231

but a matter of very much greater importance, fundamental to the peoples, namely: whether in the world of tomorrow the powerful countries will be able to take on themselves the right to blackmail, exercise extortion against, pressure, commit aggression against and strangle smaller [*sic*] peoples; whether there will also prevail in the world of tomorrow ... the worst methods of piracy, aggression and filibustering that have been introduced into the world ever since the emergence of class society.'[55]

China was not the only country to be taken to task by Castro at the Tri-Continental Conference. He also attacked the Soviet Union for its failure to assist liberation movements in Latin America. Castro, unhappy with his restricting dependence on the Soviet Union and fully aware of the logistic and diplomatic limitations of alliance with China, was bidding for leadership of the Third World.

The Chinese response was once again muted. Press coverage of the conference was highly selective and the Chinese leaders refrained from the temptation of rebuffing Castro's charges. After all, Castro's policy of encouraging and assisting liberation movements in Latin America was in line with their current international postures. For the moment they were content to shelve the Cuban problem. They withdrew their ambassador in Havana in early 1967 and were absent from the OLAS conference in July.

Although Castro used the OLAS conference as an occasion for opposing the Soviet policy of co-operation with 'oligarchic' régimes in Latin America, he was also careful not to identify himself with the Chinese. His bid for leadership of the *tiers monde* required of him demonstrations of independence from not only the Western 'capitalist' countries but also from his 'socialist' allies.

This period of 'neutrality' in the Sino-Soviet conflict was brief. The Cuban sponsored/approved *guerrilleros* in Latin America suffered severe setbacks; and economic difficulties once again caused the Cubans to readjust their attitude towards their major source of support – the Soviet Union. There is little doubt that the costs to the Cubans of further financial assistance included a requirement that Cuba endorse the Soviet position in the Sino-Soviet debate. Despite the subsequent improvement of relations between Moscow and Havana, Castro has been reluctant to indulge in an anti-Chinese campaign. Apart from some rather oblique criticisms of the Chinese for their 'timidity' in supporting Hanoi in the Vietnamese War, there have been relatively few official references – positive or negative – to China and its affairs. Press coverage has been similarly restricted.[56]

CUBA'S POLICY TOWARDS THE UNITED STATES

The Cuban revolutionary government was recognized by the United States on 7 January 1959. Two years later, on 3 January 1961, President Eisenhower, as one of the last acts of his administration, severed diplomatic relations with the Castro government.[57] The two governments then embarked upon policies of more or less open hostility to each other. Why, within such a short space of time, did relations deteriorate so far?

The break was not sudden. From the very beginning relations between the bearded revolutionaries and the American embassy personnel had been strained. The professional diplomats in Havana were confused by the character of the rebel leadership. The Fidelistas were not only young and inexperienced but also apparently unsympathetic to the traditional styles of conducting political business. Castro's preference for frequent public statements handicapped the process of private diplomatic negotiation. There were also basic difficulties in finding the right man to negotiate with. Lines of responsibility were only hazily drawn in revolutionary Havana. American relations with the new government were, in fact, impeded by a series of frustrating structural or administrative obstacles. The Americans found that diplomatic efficiency is not a common characteristic of revolutionary régimes.

Diplomatic ineptness, however, was not the major factor in bringing about the break. More important was the difference between what the Americans expected Castro to do (or not do), and what he actually did (or did not do). Important sections of the American administration assumed that Castro, like most of his nationalist predecessors in Cuba, would moderate his plans once exposed to the 'realities of the situation'. He would recognize that Cuba's economic weakness and proximity to the United States would not permit him the continuing luxury of an anti-American campaign. Sooner or later he would have

233

to come to terms with his American neighbour 'realistically'. But Castro seemed determined to be 'unrealistic'. He was unwilling to play the role of the leader of a small and economically vulnerable island within easy striking distance of one of the world's super powers. He insisted on his right to confiscate American properties and interests and was a less than enthusiastic negotiator over what constituted 'reasonable' compensation. He even had the audacity to ask for Soviet support for his Revolution. In short, Castro's independent posture came as a surprise to the American administration. Some optimistic diplomats believed that Castro's extremism was negotiable, others preferred to think of him as a romantic but dangerously irresponsible rebel. Few seemed to take his independence as unexceptionable.

Communication was also handicapped by Cuban images of the Americans. The revolutionaries, citing many local and international precedents, feared that the Americans were automatically opposed to all the reforms envisaged. American demands for negotiations over the compensation offered to expropriated American interests were regarded as the 'thin end of the wedge'. The Cubans believed that they had already offered 'reasonable' compensation and that such demands were not only superfluous but infringed upon the right of the revolutionary government to manage its own affairs. In other words communication between the two governments was hindered by the mutually suspicious images each held of the other's motives.

Relations between the two governments were also influenced by developments in American public opinion. Although the influence of public opinion in foreign policy-making is difficult to assess, there is little doubt that increasing hostility towards the Castro régime in the influential American newspapers put pressure on the already embarrassed and confused Eisenhower administration. The American press, initially largely sympathetic to Castro,[58] began to express serious doubts about the character of the Cuban leader and the Revolution he epitomized. Public opinion seemed most disturbed by the trial and subsequent execution or imprisonment of people associated with the deposed Batista régime.[59] This led to more general doubts about Castro, who persisted in making irritating anti-American speeches and who seemed intent on nationalizing American assets in Cuba.

The most significant single factor in bringing about the

rupture in American-Cuban relations was the American realization that Castro was seeking political and economic ties with
the Soviet Union. When Cuba responded to American economic
pressure, not by making the appropriate conciliatory adjustments, but by canvassing compensatory trade relationships with
the Soviet Union, the die was cast. American interests in Cuba
were perhaps negotiable, a major shift in the international
balance of power certainly was not. The break in diplomatic
relations became, for the Americans, inevitable.

Almost immediately the tone and medium of communications
changed. Both countries used both domestic and international
platforms to revile each other. The United States charged that
civil liberties were being violated in Cuba and that her ties with
the Soviet Union endangered the security of the hemisphere.
Castro replied with complaints against the violation of Cuban
territory by sabotage squads and aircraft flying from bases in
Florida.

Despite his brave words and a good deal of international
goodwill, Castro's position was precarious. He was still unsure
about the reliability of his Soviet ally – especially on the vital
question of military support – and he knew that a large-scale
invasion was in the offing.[60] He therefore concentrated on two
lines of action. Firstly, he set out to attract as much international
attention on Cuba as possible, hoping that the new Kennedy
administration might have reservations about ordering the
invasion of an island enjoying frequent and usually sympathetic
headlines in the world's news media. He reasoned that Cuba's
chances of survival were improved by extending the number of
interested parties beyond the Western hemisphere. Second, as a
necessary insurance against the failure of this indirect, propa-
ganda-style defence, he reinforced Cuba's defence forces. This
involved not only the arming of the militia but also a campaign
for boosting civilian morale. Some of the arms came from the
Socialist bloc, fuel for the campaign came from Florida. Groups
of saboteurs recruited from the gusano[61] community and armed
with American weapons made the threat of imminent invasion
more credible. Cuba became a nation in arms.

When the invasion came on 17 April 1961, at the Playa Girón
these tactics proved at least partially successful. President
Kennedy, although sanctioning and equipping the invaders, was
careful to minimize American operational involvement. He

refused to give air-support and resisted the obvious temptation of salvaging the exercise by the landing of American troops. Undoubtedly one of the reasons for this limitation was the fear of world opinion. The Cuban military preparations also proved successful. The invading force was quickly mopped up, thereby confirming Castro as both prophetic and invincible.

The invasion had an international impact. Cuba was now vividly in the world's view with Castro's personal reputation enhanced. It brought improved relations with the Soviet Union and drew expressions of support from throughout Latin America. Following the invasion, Cuban policy towards the United States entered a new and more confident phase. Attacks on American policy were extended beyond its Cuban aspects. Cuban leaders criticized America's role in Latin America, and Radio Havana and the Cuban news agencies disseminated a stream of anti-American propaganda.

The reasons for the development of this new, more confident, wider-angled policy are many, but three are particularly important. As Hennessy has suggested, the Cuban nationalist tradition, of which Castro is a part, has traditionally been expressed in universalistic or pan-Latin American terms rather than in the forms of a narrow Cubanism.[62] There was, therefore, an ideological push towards a more general continent-wide critique of the *Yanqui* enemy. To this motive some commentators have added an individualistic dimension. They argue that Castro saw himself as the new Bolívar – a twentieth-century liberator of the Latin American republics.

This change in Cuban policy was also a response to a change in American tactics. Smarting from the embarrassment of the Playa Girón débâcle, the Kennedy administration abandoned unilateral (i.e. exile-backed) action against Castro, in favour of more respectable, multilateral regional measures, supplemented by the Alliance for Progress. Pressure was applied to the member states of the OAS to enlist their support in 'containing' the Cuban threat. The Cubans, encouraged by opposition in the OAS to the American proposals[63] and enjoying widespread popularity in the various republics, sensed an opportunity for obstructing American intentions. Thus Cuba's American policy became inextricably connected with its policy towards its Latin American neighbours.

The new policy was also important in the context of Cuban

relations with the Soviet Union. Although Cuba was receiving Soviet military and economic aid, there was no real guarantee that it would not dry up. In the event of a *rapprochement* between the United States and her hesitant Soviet *patrón*, Cuba might well prove to be a negotiable strategic asset. It was essential, therefore, that Castro should raise the temperature of the Cold War. His best chance of success lay in stepping up the challenge to the United States, thus increasing the tension between it and his Soviet guarantor.

In pursuing this policy the Cubans were obviously taking risks. The Americans might become so irritated that they would once again consider the possibility of another – this time more comprehensive – invasion. Measures to improve the island's defences were therefore taken. The army was expanded and its officers transferred more and more into civilian posts of authority. Political organizations were strengthened, especially in their 'supervisory' or counter-espionage functions.

These preparations, however impressive in Cuban or even Latin American terms, were unlikely to deter an American attack. By the middle of 1962, however, the Cubans were on their way to getting a massive boost to their defensive capabilities. Soviet technicians were constructing missile sites in Cuba and the appropriate missiles were *en route* for Havana.

Before the sites were completed and the missiles assembled, the United States took decisive action. President Kennedy, ignoring Castro completely, 'persuaded' Khrushchev to withdraw the missiles.[64] The fact that Khrushchev seemed as unconcerned about Castro's views as Kennedy, meant that the crisis was resolved without Cuban participation.

The effect of the 'missile crisis' on United States/Cuban relations is difficult to assess. It demonstrated to the Cubans that Soviet solidarity was dispensable in the face of a direct threat to the security of the Soviet Union. It did not, on the other hand, lead to a moderation of Cuba's anti-American propaganda. After an ill-fated attempt to make the dismantling of the sites conditional upon an American guarantee not to invade the islands, the Cubans returned to the propaganda offensive. The offensive, however, was to vary in intensity from time to time. Towards the end of 1963, for example, the Cubans seemed much more in tune with the Soviet-endorsed 'spirit of coexistence'. In January 1964, Castro offered to consider the problem of compensation for American properties nationalized since the Revolution, if Washington would allow the resumption of trade.[65] Later that month, after his visit to Moscow, he declared that his government was willing to 'do everything necessary to re-establish good relations between Cuba and the United States'.[66] This somewhat reluctant initiative produced only a low-key response in Washington. The State Department refused to heed Senator Fulbright's advice to come to terms with the 'disagreeable reality' of Castro's Cuba rather than hang on to the myth that it was collapsing from the effects of the trade embargo.[67] The State Department would go no further than stating that American efforts to curb Cuban subversive activities would 'fall short of war'.[68]

By the end of 1964 the war of words was resumed, but with a change in emphasis on the Cuban side. American imperialism continued to be condemned, but there was an increase in the publicity and encouragement given to the various guerrilla groups operating throughout Latin America. This, in fact, was to set the pattern for the next three years or so. On occasions the propaganda was supplemented by more concrete forms of assistance like weapons, finance, training or even personnel. The tactical motive was clear. If a series of 'wars of liberation' were to develop in Latin America, the attention of the Johnson administration might be distracted from Cuba.

By 1966, these diversionary tactics had begun to strike nearer home as the Cubans took up the cause of the various American minority groups involved in the Civil Rights Movement. The plight of the negro in American society received particular attention and publicity. In August 1967 the American black militant Stokeley Carmichael was received by the Latin American Solidarity Organization's (LASO) Conference as the 'delegate of honour representing the people of the United States'.[69] In Cuba, with its largely negro or mulatto population, these moves proved very popular.[70] They also struck a responsive chord throughout the Third World at large.

In the United States the reaction was muted. The Johnson administration, committed to the implementation of a civil rights programme and fearful of losing credit in the Third World, could hardly object without seeming to condone racial inequality. President Johnson, however, was not under any great pressure to take action against Cuba. There was more concern with the entanglement in Vietnam than with differences with Castro. In addition, the number of groups in favour of Castro were now as vociferous as those opposed to him. Student groups, for example, were increasingly open in declaring admiration for the Cuban Revolution and its leaders.

Although, following the death of 'Ché' Guevara in Bolivia, the Cuban policy of actively supporting the 'liberationist' forces was phased out, the propaganda offensive against American-backed 'oligarchic' régimes in Latin America was retained. Castro's ambitions for Third World leadership prevented a complete retreat from his revolutionary commitments. The space devoted to international affairs in the Cuban Press, however, was reduced. This did not mean that Castro had abandoned his anti-Americanism. As already noted, his analysis of the events leading up to the Soviet invasion of Czechoslovakia made a laboured attempt to place some of the blame for the Czech 'aberrations' on the United States and its agents.[71] He also refused, despite strong American pressure, to return the growing number of hijackers diverting American airliners to Havana.[72] Instead he gave them political asylum and suggested that the airlines involved should be charged for the use of landing and refuelling facilities.

The Americans for their part seemed more interested in improving relations with Cuba. They stopped short of unconditionally dropping the trade embargo but suggested that a dialogue with Havana might prove valuable.[73] This attitude was no doubt related to the less militant Cuban line in Latin America.

The Cubans refused to be tempted. A *rapprochement* with the United States at this time would not solve her immediate problems. In fact it might complicate them. It might, for instance, give the Soviet Union the excuse for cutting the scale of economic support; and Castro could not rely upon the United States taking over this burden. Ideologically, too, it would be difficult to square. Castro's position as a Third World leader was predicated on his anti-American and anti-imperialist stand. A reversal of this stand would damage his domestic and international credibility irreparably. As a result, he ignored the American hints, preferring to concentrate his attention upon the urgent problems of agricultural and industrial development in Cuba. There seems little chance that this situation will change in the near future. The United States has come to terms with its noisy socialist neighbour, but is in no hurry to reintegrate it into the inter-American system. Castro also seems content. He notes the American mood of toleration but prefers to use its proximity and reputation to mobilize the Cuban population to a range of economic and political targets.

CUBAN POLICY TOWARDS LATIN AMERICA

Prior to the Revolution, Cuban relations with the rest of Latin America were of little importance. There was little trade with the neighbouring republics and Cuban diplomatic concerns in the area were more cultural than political. Real diplomatic activity focused upon the various Pan-American conferences sponsored and usually dominated by the United States.

The situation was changed radically after 1959. Cuban interest in the area increased and changed its style. No longer were Cuban communications with her neighbours characterized by rather vague declarations of cultural and political affinities. Instead, the Revolution was held up as an example to the rest of Latin America. In 1960 Castro declared: 'We promise to continue making the nation [Cuba] the example that can convert the Cordillera of the Andes into the Sierra Maestre of the American continent.'[74]

One of the reasons for this concern for Latin America was, and still is, an ideological one. The Cuban tendency to translate local experience into universalistic propositions no doubt impelled the revolutionaries towards suggesting a wide-ranging applicability of their revolutionary model. This was especially true of those who were familiar with conditions elsewhere in the hemisphere, where poverty and corruption seemed as, or even more, pronounced, than in pre-revolutionary Cuba.[75]

As well as its ideological justification, this attitude brought other more immediate political benefits. Internally it enhanced Castro's reputation. It demonstrated that he was not willing to compromise his revolutionary principles, thereby adding to his moral stature. Nationalistic Cubans were also proud of Castro's (and by implication, Cuba's) leading, somewhat 'superior' role in the hemisphere's affairs. Revolutionary evangelism, therefore, assisted in the consolidation of the régime.

Interest in Latin America can also be explained as a function of Castro's policy towards the United States. Lacking the domestic base to resist the 'colossus of the north' and never certain of his Soviet protection, his encouragement of revolutions throughout the area was intended to divert American attention from Cuba. The exhortation and assistance of revolutionaries was, therefore, a defensive tactic as well as a moral imperative.

Although these reasons may account for Castro's interest in the continent's revolutionary future, they do not indicate the variations in its focus, intensity and style. Until 1962 the Cubans concentrated their efforts on removing the dictatorships and authoritarian régimes of the Caribbean and Central America. By a combination of public encouragement and the clandestine supply of small quantities of arms and/or trained men to local insurgent groups, it was hoped to topple such men as Trujillo in the Dominican Republic, Duvalier in Haiti and Ydígoras Fuentes in Guatemala. Their countries were potential bases for exile-led attacks in Cuba. In addition, their internationally malodorous reputations might deter the United States from coming to their assistance should they be overthrown. As it happened they survived without American help.

As for the rest of Latin America, where he enjoyed wide popular appeal and a certain official respect, Castro tended to speak in broad terms about the need to reduce American influence. His moderation was certainly a factor influencing the Mexican, Argentinian, Bolivian, Brazilian, Chilean and Ecuadorian resistance to American pressure in 1961/62 to make the OAS the vehicle for bringing down the Castro régime.

In 1963 Cuba's attentions focused on Venezuela. Angered by Betancourt's condemnations, Castro took up the cause of the FALN/FLN guerrilla groups in earnest.[76] Their activities and programmes were given publicity in the Cuban press and over Radio Havana broadcasts beamed at Venezuela. In addition, a system for supplying weapons and the occasional guerrilla expert was set up. It is unlikely that the Cubans anticipated a full-scale revolution in Venezuela. Their support was designed to augment the nuisance value of the guerrilla groups in a country whose oil was vital to the United States.

This policy, confirmed by the Venezuelan authorities' discovery of a cache of Cuban arms destined for the guerrillas, disturbed some Latin American 'allies'. This, together with the military *golpes* in Ecuador and Brazil, weakened the resistance to American pressure in the OAS.[77] As a result, in July 1964 the OAS agreed to sever diplomatic, transportation and trade links with Cuba. By the end of the year Cuba's economic and political isolation was almost complete. Only Mexico refused to break her ties with the island.

Table 1   *The Diplomatic Isolation of Cuba*

Year	States Withdrawing Diplomatic Recognition
1959	Dominican Republic
1960	Columbia, Costa Rica, El Salvador, Guatemala, Haiti, Honduras, Nicaragua, Panama, Paraguay, Peru, United States, Venezuela
1961	—
1962	Argentina, Ecuador
1963	—
1964	Bolivia, Brazil, Chile, Uruguay

Source: *The Times* 1959–64.

At first there was little by the way of a Cuban reaction. For some months Castro, due no doubt to Soviet pressure, had been moderating his views on the inevitability of violent revolution and had even hinted at his readiness to reach a *détente* with Washington.[78] The OAS decision forced a reconsideration of this line of thinking.

Within four months the reformulation was decided upon. The generalized *via armada* or 'armed struggle' was abandoned in favour of a more selective commitment to assist the guerrilla groups in Venezuela, Colombia, Guatemala, Paraguay and Haiti.[79] In concentrating on these countries it was hoped to enlist the support of the local communist parties, which in the past had sometimes been very critical of Cuba's stress on the violent road to socialism.

This compromise between traditional communist tactics and *Fidelismo* broke up by early 1966. Concerned by the American invasion of the nearby Dominican Republic[80] and infuriated by the Venezuelan communist party's (PCV) treatment of the FALN guerrilla groups, Castro was ready to embark upon a more militant line again. [81] The Cuban speeches to the Tri-Continental Conference in Havana became increasingly critical of the tactics of 'peaceful coexistence'; and by July Castro was condemning the established communist parties of Latin America as 'charlatans' and 'pseudo-revolutionaries'. He was also seeking to bypass them by sponsoring a number of international organizations to serve as links between Cuba and the 'revolutionary' forces' of Latin America.

The Cuban efforts to speed up the revolutionary process were not limited to ideological posturing. Plans were being made to open up a guerrilla *foco* directed by 'Ché' Guevara in Bolivia. He arrived, to the annoyance of the local communist leader Monje, in November 1966. [82] In May of the following year a small group of Cubans and Venezuelans, trained in Cuba, landed on the Venezuelan coast. These revolutionary ploys, however, proved ill-fated. The Venezuelan expedition was eradicated within hours of landing and the Guevara column in Bolivia lasted for less than a year.

These setbacks, plus the internal economic difficulties plaguing Cuba, caused yet another reconsideration of foreign policy, especially towards Latin America. Despite the naming of 1968 as 'the Year of the Heroic Guerrilla' in honour of 'Ché', that year marked the withdrawal of the Cuban government from active participation or support of guerrilla activities in Latin America. The propaganda offensive was retained, but even here changes were made. The massacre of Mexican students during the Mexico City Olympic Games passed without comment; and the new military junta in Peru was praised for its 'progressive' measures. Clearly Cuba had decided upon a policy of qualified 'peaceful coexistence' towards her neighbours.

Her neighbours, too, were changing. For a variety of reasons a growing number of statesmen began to hint at the possibility of re-establishing diplomatic links with Cuba. Little was done, however, until January 1971, when the newly elected Marxist President of Chile – Salvador Allende – re-opened diplomatic and trading relations with Cuba. By November not only had ambassadors been exchanged and mutual assistance pacts signed but Castro had also arrived in Santiago de Chile at the start of an extended state visit to his new Latin American ally. The diplomatic siege of Cuba had been raised; and Castro's stops in Peru and Ecuador *en route* back to Cuba suggest that her isolation is coming to an end.

Thus Cuban policy towards Latin America can be seen to have undergone several distinct changes in emphasis. It must also be pointed out that the agencies of 'structures' through which this policy has been conducted have also changed. As Cuba's diplomatic contacts with Latin America were steadily cut off, so less formal agencies of policy implementation came into operation. Until their withdrawal in 1965 the various Cuban embassies acted more or less conventionally. They were concerned with the presentation of their government's views and the dissemination of propaganda. Not always by design they also became *foci* for local 'revolutionary' or aspirant 'revolutionary' groups seeking assistance and advice. As a general rule such groups got little more than verbal encouragement. After 1965 official contacts between Cuba and the Latin American states were limited to meetings of the United Nations and its specialized or regional agencies, and through intermediary diplomatic missions in Havana. The most popular embassies for this purpose have been those of Switzerland and Mexico.

The link with Mexico has been of vital importance to Cuba. The flights between Mexico City and Havana have provided, despite the problems of American surveillance at the Mexico City end, the main channel of communication of personnel between Cuba and the continent at large. It has been the means by which Latin American sympathizers travelled to Cuba and, in turn, the way in which couriers and propagandists got out. Its importance, in fact, might explain Castro's seeming unwillingness to upset the Mexican government. It would, for example, explain his silence over the 1968 massacre of students in Mexico City and his delicate handling of the exposure of CIA influence in the Mexican embassy in Havana in 1970.[83]

The lack of formal contacts with Latin America has also led to the development of a comprehensive propaganda machine. From the earliest days of the Revolution, Radio Havana has broadcast – in Spanish, Portuguese, creole French and the Indian languages, Quechua and Guaraní – a steady stream of propaganda extolling the virtues of the Cuban Revolution. It has also publicized the proclamations and successes of pro-Cuban guerrilla groups throughout the continent. The news agency Prensa Latina has operated in a similar fashion, although journalists accredited to it have, on occasions, taken on a more active revolutionary role, taking financial assistance and political advice to the various guerrilla groups sponsored by Havana.

CONCLUSION

Like many revolutionaries the *barbudos* who entered Havana in January 1959 were more aware of the failings of the régime they had deposed than of the details of the system with which they intended to replace it. In these early days the Revolution was defined in negative terms – it would bring an end to corruption, it would punish those guilty of crimes against the nation and would take steps to eradicate injustice.

Revolutionary thinking about what Cuba's external relationships should be was similarly negative and vague. Only one thing was clear. The United States' 'exploitation' of Cuba would be brought to an end. Just how this momentous change was to be effected was not really spelled out. The attempts made to spell out and guarantee this transformation are the pivotal points of Cuba's foreign policy since 1960.

NOTES AND REFERENCES

For a state so frequently in world headlines Cuban foreign policy has received surprisingly little serious academic attention. Commentators have preferred to concentrate upon the internal development of the Revolution, limiting their observations on foreign policy to wide-ranging and unsystematic generalizations.

Of the few authors who have seriously come to terms with the problem of foreign policy, Andrés Suárez stands out. His *Cuba: Castroism and Communism 1959–66* (M.I.T., Cambridge, 1967) is a well-documented description of Cuba's extremely complicated dealings with the Soviet Union. D. B. Jackson's *Castro, the Kremlin and Communism in Latin America* (Johns Hopkins U.P., Baltimore, 1969) and E. González's article 'Castro's Revolution, Cuban Communist Appeals and the Soviet Response', *World Politics*, vol. 21, no. 1 (October, 1968) are less general but provide useful alternative interpretations of specific problems of the developing Cuban/Soviet nexus. Stephen Clissold's *Soviet Relations with Latin America* (R.I.I.A., London, 1970) includes a valuable collection of documents, both Cuban and Soviet, on the changing relationship between the two countries.

Coverage of the internal characteristics of the Cuban Revolution is more comprehensive, though often partisan. Hugh Thomas's attempt at a definitive history of the republic, *Cuba or the Pursuit of Freedom* (Eyre & Spottiswoode, London, 1971) is impressive in scope and its attention to detail. K. S. Karol's *Guerrillas in Power* (Cape, London, 1971) is specifically post-revolutionary in scope and more polemical in style. It is particularly useful in its discussion of the practical difficulties of meshing Cuba – ideologically and technologically – into the Socialist bloc. A less sympathetically critical view of the Revolution and its relations with the Soviet Union is provided by Theodore Draper in his two books *Castro's Revolution: Myths and Realities* (Praeger, New York, 1962) and *Castroism: Theory and Practice* (Pall Mall, London, 1965), and by Boris Goldenburg in his *The Cuban Revolution and Latin America* (Praeger, London, 1965).

What is most obviously lacking in this literature of the Cuban Revolution are descriptions and analyses of the actual political structures evolved since 1959. Alan Angell's 'Castro and the Cuban Communist Party' in *Government and Opposition* (January, 1970) is alone in tracing the development of a political institution. For the most part the student is left with references to the constant state of institutional flux and/or the continuing but idiosyncratic omnipotence of Fidel Castro. In view of this gap in the literature the sometimes unimpressive biographies of the *líder maximo* take on a necessary but regrettable importance. Herbert Matthew's *Fidel Castro* (Penguin, Harmondsworth, 1970) is perhaps the most useful of this type. The other major source of information is the local newspapers and journals. The official organ of the Cuban Communist Party *Granma* publishes the texts of major speeches of the leadership as well as those of visiting foreign dignitaries. It also provides the official view of internal political developments. The quarterly journal *Politica Internacional*, also published in Havana, is a more specialized forum for the Ministry of Foreign Relations.

1. This limitation of Cuban sovereignty, which is known as the Platt Amendment, was appended to the 1902 Cuban Constitution after American pressure. Amongst other things it stipulated that Cuba should allow American intervention for the preservation of Cuban independence, and for the maintenance of a government adequate for the protection of life, property and individual liberty. It also required that Cuba should lease to the U.S.A. 'lands necessary for coaling or naval stations'.
2. Between 1902 and 1934, when the Platt Amendment (except for its provisions for the American naval bases) was abrogated, there were several instances of American intervention, e.g. American occupation and government from 1906 to 1909 and marine invasions in 1911 and 1919.
3. This famous and much quoted remark is part of Smith's evidence to an American Senate sub-committee to investigate the administration of the International Security Act, which met in Washington D.C. in August 1960.
4. Cuba's tourist business, with its traditional attractions of legalized gambling and prostitution, was given a great boost by the American Prohibition legislation of the 1920s.

5. By the mid-1950s, Cuban investments in the United States were estimated to be more than $312 million.
6. Alfred Mahan, *The Interest of America in Sea Power: Present and Future* (Sampson, Low Marston & Co., London, 1898).
7. E. Boorstein, *The Economic Transformation of Cuba* (Monthly Review Press, London, 1968) p. 2.
8. 'American investments in Cuba increased 536% between 1913 and 1928 ... American owned sugar mills produced approximately 15% of the Cuban crop in 1906 and 48·4% in 1920. By 1928 various estimates placed American control of the sugar crop between 70% and 75%.' R. F. Smith, *The United States and Cuba: Business and Diplomacy 1917–1960* (Bookman Associates, New York, 1960) p. 29.
9. D. Seers (ed.), *Cuba: the economic and social revolutions* (University of North Carolina Press, Chapel Hill, 1964) p. 10.
10. There is some controversy about when exactly Cuban policy took a distinctly anti-American line. One side has argued that Castro was basically anti-American and that even his earliest policies were designed to enlist Soviet support and provoke American hostility. This view is put with differing degrees of sophistication by: D. James, *Cuba – The First Soviet Satellite in Latin America* (Avon Books, New York, 1961) and Theodore Draper, *Castro's Revolution: Myths and Realities* (Praeger, New York, 1962). The other side argues that Castro's antagonism towards America was a response to a series of American policy mistakes and misunderstandings. This view is put not very convincingly by D. Scheer and M. Zeitlin, *Cuba: An American Tragedy* (Penguin, Harmondsworth, rev. ed. 1964).
11. Draper, op. cit., pp. 15–20.
12. H. L. Matthews, *Castro* (Penguin, Harmondsworth, 1969) p. 117.
13. E. Guevara, *Reminiscences of the Cuban Revolutionary War* (Allen and Unwin, London, 1969) pp. 96–7.
14. The Agrarian Reform Law was passed on 17 May only six months after Castro took power.
15. Urban resistance to Batista was organized by two, occasionally mutually suspicious, groups – the Civil Resistance Movement and the 26 July Movement. Their relations with the Rebel Army were far from harmonious. It was not until July 1958 that they joined with the Castrista forces to create the Civilian Revolutionary Front. The tensions between the groups developed again soon after Fidel's triumphant entry into Havana, when they competed for the spoils of office. See W. MacGaffey and C. Barnett, *Twentieth Century Cuba* (Anchor Books, New York, 1965) pp. 291–5.
16. Carlos Rafael Rodríguez visited Castro in the Sierra as the representative of the PSP in late July 1958. He returned to Havana to submit his report, then returned to fight with guerrillas. At about the same time other party activists joined the other guerrilla columns of Raúl Castro and of Guevara. The communist party acted with what Andres Suarez has called 'consummate prudence'. A. Suárez, *Cuba: Castroism and Communism, 1959–1966* (M.I.T., Cambridge, 1967) p. 29.
17. T. Draper, 'Cuba and US Policy', *The New Leader*, 5 June 1961.

18. For a description of the fall of the Arbenz régime in Guatemala and the role of the CIA, see G. Toriello, *La Batalla De Guatemala* (México D. F., Ediciones Cuadernos Americanos, 1955).

19. Suarez, op. cit., p. 81.

20. E. González, 'Castro's Revolution. Cuban Communist Appeals and the Soviet Response', *World Politics*, vol. 20, no. 1 (October, 1968) p. 48.

21. Dorticós replaced Manuel Urrutia on 17 July 1959. Dorticós was an ex-member of the Unión Revolucionaria Comunista (the name of the Cuban Communist Party between 1939 and 1945).

22. See González, op. cit.

23. By December, 1960 a new Cuban/Soviet Trade agreement was signed in Moscow, in which the following were agreed:

    1. The U.S.S.R. was committed to assisting in the construction of industrial complexes in Cuba. Specifically this involved the design and construction of an iron and steel mill and an oil refinery. In more general terms it involved assistance in the development of Cuba's oil and ore deposits and the generation of electric power.

    2. The U.S.S.R. would help to protect Cuba from the effects of the economic blockade. It would, for example, supply Cuba with oil, and take larger amounts of Cuban sugar.

    3. The U.S.S.R. committed itself to rendering to Cuba 'full support in defending its independence against aggression'.

24. Khrushchev's promise was reported in *Revolución*, 11 July 1960.

25. For a description of the United States role in the Bay of Pigs invasion, see H. Johnson, *The Bay of Pigs* (W. W. Norton, New York, 1964), and Arthur M. Schlesinger Jnr., *A Thousand Days: John F. Kennedy in the White House* (Houghton Mifflin, Boston, 1965) p. 226.

26. See Matthews, op. cit., p. 204.

27. There is some confusion as to who took the initiative in getting the missiles installed in Cuba. Khrushchev has claimed that the U.S.S.R. was responding to Cuban pressures in order to defend the Revolution. Castro, on the other hand, has said that Soviet missiles were installed 'not to assure our defence but first of all to reinforce world socialism', *Le Monde*, 22 March 1963. For a brief summary of this debate, see Suárez, op. cit., pp. 161–2.

28. He refused, despite Soviet pressure, to sign the Nuclear Test Ban Treaty of 18 November 1963.

29. Many of the economic programmes criticized by the U.S.S.R. were closely identified with 'Ché' Guevara. His disappearance in the spring of 1964 after returning from a tour of Africa is regarded by many as being the price of the January 1964 Cuban/Soviet trade agreement. Some Trotskyites even went so far as to suggest that Guevara had been liquidated by Castro in return for the trade concessions. It is more likely that Guevara withdrew from the scene when policies directly opposed to those he had propounded became inevitable.

30. For a description of the invasion, see T. Szule, *Dominican Diary* (Delacorte Press, New York, 1965). Soviet action took the form of two protests against the American policy in the UN.

31. D. B. Jackson, *Castro, the Kremlin and Communism in Latin America* (The Johns Hopkins Press, Baltimore, 1969) p. 65.

32. The revolutionary party has undergone several changes in name and structure since 1959. The 26 July Movement was integrated with PSP (Communist party) in July 1961 to form the ORI (Integrated Revolutionary Organizations). ORI was gradually faded out and replaced by the PURS in early 1963. PURS was replaced by the PCC (Cuban Communist Party) in October 1965.

33. For a description of the split within the Venezuelan Communist Party (PCV), which led to the establishment of the FALN-FLN faction led by Bravo and Ojeda, see R. Gott, *Guerrilla Movements in Latin America* (Thomas Nelson, London, 1970) pp. 108–65.

34. For a fairly comprehensive, if somewhat biased, summary of the proceedings of the Tri-Continental Conference, see Council of the OAS *Report on the First Afro-Asian-Latin American Peoples Solidarity Conference and its Projections*, 2 vols (Pan American Union, Washington D.C., 1966).

35. Communist leaders meeting in Prague in May 1967 denounced the forthcoming OLAS conference as 'divisionistic' and declared their support for the Venezuelan PC, which had previously been denounced by Castro.

36. *Granma*, 27 July 1967.

37. *El Mundo*, 11 August 1967.

38. *Granma*, 14 July 1967.

39. ibid., 1 February 1968.

40. It is not being suggested that these delays represented an effort by the U.S.S.R. to 'discipline' Castro, merely that the delays and subsequent need for petrol rationing demonstrated to Castro and his lieutenants the possibility of such 'disciplinary' action.

41. Gott, op. cit., pp. 297–356.

42. Castro's attitude in August 1968 cannot be explained simply in terms of cynical opportunism. He was ideologically opposed to the Czechoslovak reform movement, as he had been to developments in Yugoslavia in the past. He was committed to the idea of moral rather than material incentives as the motor of the Cuban economy. As he said, 'we must not translate money or riches into awareness, but awareness into riches'. *Analysis of Events in Czechoslovakia* (Department of Stenographic Translations, Havana, 23 September 1970).

43. The scale of Soviet support of Cuba can be gauged from the following estimates (1970): economic assistance – credits, loans etc. = $ U.S. 300–370 million p.a.; military assistance = $50–60 million p.a.; between 5,000 and 10,000 Soviet technicians working in Cuba, about 1,000 of which are attached to the armed forces. *The Times*, 27 July 1970.

44. In July 1970 Cuba was visited by Soviet ships and the United States warned against Soviet plans to build a submarine base at Cienfuegos.

45. By the beginning of 1971 the governments of Bolivia, Peru, Trinidad and Venezuela had all expressed 'serious' interest in re-establishing diplomatic and trade links with Cuba. The first government to actually

reopen diplomatic relations was that of President Allende of Chile in November 1970.
46. Diplomatic relations were established in September, 1960.
47. *Hoy*, 4 (December 1960).
48. ibid., p. 15.
49. ibid., p. 15.
50. Suárez, op. cit., p. 162.
51. *Revolución*, 19 January 1965.
52. *Granma*, 6 February 1966.
53. See D. Tretiak, 'China and Latin America: an ebbing tide in trans-Pacific Maoism', *Current Scene* (1 March 1966), quoted by C. Johnson in *Communist China and Latin America 1959–67* (Columbia University Press, New York, 1970) pp. 163–4.
54. *Bohemia*, 10 January 1966.
55. *Peking Review*, 25 February 1966.
56. Recently Sino-Cuban relations seem to have taken a more positive turn. A Chinese delegation attended the 1970 '26 July' celebrations in Havana and a Cuban mission visited China in October. In December a Chinese ambassador returned to Cuba after an absence of almost two-and-a-half years.
57. Ostensibly, the break was caused by the Cuban demand for a severe reduction in size of the American embassy staff in Havana. In fact, this incident provided the excuse for the Americans to withdraw recognition of the troublesome Castro régime.
58. The attitude of the American press towards Castro was far from uniform. The *New York Times*, however, was not alone in declaring its editorial approval of his government on the fall of Batista.
59. The Cubans could not understand the American objections to the trial and execution of well-known Batista henchmen. There had been no such protests at the untold number of political executions ordered by Batista without benefit of a trial.
60. See H. Matthews, op. cit., pp. 199–203.
61. The term *gusano*, meaning 'worm', is used derogatively to describe those Cubans who have left the island for exile in the United States.
62. C. A. Hennessy, 'The Roots of Cuban Nationalism', *International Affairs*, vol. 39, no. 3 (July, 1963) pp. 345–59.
63. By the autumn of 1961, Castro was charged by the American representatives to the OAS Council with conducting subversive activities against his neighbours and with violating the human rights of Cuban citizens. The American call for a meeting of consultation to consider these charges brought an interesting vote. Excluding Cuba, six countries – Mexico (which opposed the proposal), Argentina, Bolivia, Brazil, Chile and Ecuador (which abstained from the vote) – refused to support the motion. The six states involved accounted for over half of the total population of the continent.
64. For a description of the way in which the crisis was handled by President Kennedy, see Robert Kennedy, *13 Days: The Cuban Missile Crisis* (Macmillan, London, 1969).
65. *Revolución*, 3 January 1964.

66. Joint Cuban–Soviet communique printed in *Hoy*, 23 January 1964.
67. *New York Times*, 26 March 1964.
68. Speech by Under-Secretary of State George W. Ball, at Roanoke, Virginia, on 22 April 1964, quoted by Suárez, op. cit., p. 192.
69. See Council of the OAS report, op. cit.
70. For a detailed description of the racial composition of the Cuban population, see W. MacGaffey and C. R. Barnett, *Twentieth Century Cuba; the background of the Castro Revolution* (Anchor Books, Garden City, 1965) pp. 34–67.
71. *Granma* (English edition), 25 August 1968.
72. The first hijacking of a plane to Cuba took place on 21 February 1968. This drastic way of breaking the restrictions on hemispheric travel escalated rapidly, in 1968 there were seventeen such hijackings and in 1969 over twenty.
73. See K. S. Karol, *Guerrillas in Power* (Jonathan Cape, London, 1971) p. 521.
75. The revolutionary régime of the early 1960s had a distinctly international flavour. Most of the leadership group had travelled extensively in the Caribbean and Central American area and it included the Argentinian 'Ché' Guevara, an advocate of the international nature of Cuba's commitments. In addition, the régime was served by a number of exiled Latin American left-wing intellectuals and politicians. There was, for example, a fairly large contingent of Chilean economists working within the bureaucracy.
76. Fuerzas Armadas de Liberación Nacional – the guerrilla offshoot of the Communist Party (PCV).
77. President Arosemena of Ecuador was replaced by a military junta in July 1963; and in Brazil, President Goulart was deposed by the military in April 1964.
78. See Richard Eder's interview with Castro in the *New York Times*, 6 July 1964.
79. See *Revolución*, 19 January 1965.
80. The American marines invaded the Dominican Republic in April, 1965, thus preventing the 'constitutionalist' forces of the ousted President Bosch from taking power.
81. For descriptions of the ideological differences between the PCV and the FALN, see Jackson, op. cit., pp. 40–67 and Gott, op. cit., pp. 139–65.
82. See R. Scheer (ed.), *The Diary of 'Ché' Guevara: Bolivia, November 7 1966–October 7, 1967* (Bantam Books, New York, 1968).
83. *Granma* (special supplement to the English edition) 15 December 1969.

Chapter 8

THE FOREIGN POLICY OF SINGAPORE

FRANK H. H. KING

Singapore's population is three-quarters Chinese, her national language Malay. Singapore is a non-aligned member of the Afro-Asian People's Solidarity Organization with close ties with Israel and a defence policy based on the co-operation of extra-regional powers. Critical of the United States, Singapore has recently advised against time-tables of withdrawal from Vietnam, viewed with apparent calm growing Russian interest in the Indian Ocean, and helped save the Commonwealth. Dominated politically by the People's Action Party traditionally espousing a militant socialism, Singapore is establishing itself as an Asian financial centre and as a base from which overseas industry may penetrate the Southeast Asian market. A parliamentary democracy in which one party legitimately won all seats, Singapore's world image is dominated by the personality of her brilliant but hardhitting Prime Minister, Lee Kuan Yew, softened by the understanding of S. Rajaratnam, the Foreign Minister.

Having sought and achieved 'independence through merger' with the Federation of Malaya in 1963, Singapore was forced to accept a sovereign independence in 1965. Though Lee Kuan Yew once declared that in the Southeast Asian context island nations were political jokes, Singapore today is regarded seriously by all – yet, and this is basic to all understanding, the dream of a reunited Malaysia remains.

The republic's foreign policy is dominated by her special ties with the Federation of Malaysia, by her strategic economic siting – a 'Chinese' enclave in a Malay world, by the impact of her special history – including the vital Commonwealth political orientation and defence links, and by the necessity of non-

252

alignment. Based solidly on a successful domestic administration, Singapore's policy may be judged against these goals: full recognition of her sovereign status and preservation of independence, close relations with Malaysia, access and co-operation within the region for her economic requirements, and, less precisely, furtherance of 'socialistic' goals of freedom and justice. Since independence her status has been recognized and her position, as one may judge such matters at the moment, is secure. Relations with Malaysia are in constant flux and sufficiently complex to prevent a summary conclusion. Singapore's economic foreign policy, while not achieving all goals – some of which, e.g. textile export agreements, were unrealistic – has furthered the state's high growth rate. Her foreign policy, while consistent and to a considerable degree independent, has been contributory without being 'aggressive', especially in regional and Commonwealth co-operation.

This essay is a description and assessment of Singapore's foreign policy attitudes, achievements and methods. Having first considered the resources and their organization which are available for the administration of policy – a key limiting factor for a small state – the approach is historical, since the origins of her policy precede independence in a significant and unique manner. There follows then a description of independent Singapore's policy in the context of her present situation and heritage.

FOREIGN POLICY FOR THE BUSINESS STATE

After eight years of independence, the island republic of Singapore has a fast-developing society of over 2 million people, an area of 225 square miles, a gross domestic product (GDP) increasing at more than 9 per cent per annum, and a *per capita* income second only to Japan in Asia. In 1970 Singapore's total overseas trade was $12,290 million, or more than double the GDP estimated at $5,565 million. (All values in Singapore dollars: S.$1·00 = U.S.$0·38) Although the population growth rate has been steadily declining and in 1970 was only 1·5 per cent, the population is young and with 21 per cent of GDP allocated to capital investment, employment opportunities are still but barely adequate.[1]

Singapore's continued prosperity depends, therefore, on the preservation of her entrepôt trade – still responsible for some

25 per cent of GDP despite the growth of the manufacturing sector – the securing of overseas capital for industrialization, and the continual probing for new markets for Singapore-originating exports, despite the suspicion of the primary producers. In 1971 the petroleum discoveries in the Indonesian-Malaysian region may provide an opportunity for Singapore to act both as base of operations and chief supply depot, but an opportunity qualified by the difficulty of maintaining a position which, while economically sound, may run counter to economic nationalism.

Singapore's world economic role is disproportionate to her size. Situated on one of the world's strategic shipping lanes, where the oil for Japan's miracle economy must pass through the narrow Malacca Straits, where Soviet shipping must pass to reach the Indian Ocean, Singapore, even as she industrializes, remains a world market for tin and rubber, a developed port with facilities for trans-shipping, processing and packaging operations which are still essential to the region's economy.

But Singapore also remains a small nation with limited resources, especially in manpower. What foreign policy must such a nation develop? Indeed, what foreign policy can such a nation afford?

There are two aspects to Singapore's foreign policy, neither of them luxuries in themselves, although certain of the contents might be judged superfluous to immediate needs: first, the economic measures necessary to the state's economic growth – double taxation agreements, textile quota arrangements, financial arrangements, trade treaties, air traffic agreements, and second, the political measures necessary to ensure independence, a world position, and defence. But cannot a government rely on some great power for its independence and remain passive in defence? On all other matters a business state especially might be expected to be silent. The present government of Singapore would argue, however, that independence must be asserted and that defence must be provided for, partly by Singapore's own efforts, partly in the context of its historical Commonwealth associations – certainly not passively. And, finally, for that luxury of the small state, a world position, Singapore has its dynamic leader whose reputation is based to some degree certainly on his own personal image but more importantly on the leadership he has provided a successful domestic administration. Beyond the leader, there are his colleagues and his People's Action Party, long-standing spokesmen against colonialism and imperialism, long associated with the Afro-Asian nations and the international socialist movement with positions taken some time before the independence of the state whose policies they now determine.

There have been conflicts in priority between the economic image and the assertion of independence, between the economic necessities and the world image. In all cases the economic needs have suffered at most only a temporary setback; the independent impetus of the economy has smoothed out the foreign policy ruffles.

Singapore's relatively active foreign policy, the creation of a distinctive international style, is a consequence of her economic needs, the personality of Lee Kuan Yew, the politics of the People's Action Party, and the historical accident that Singapore has been twice on the defensive in the Third World. This particular situation is reinforced by the very structure of international society; a United Nations member is yearly confronted with the need to vote on a series of issues beyond its immediate concern; its record in the United Nations affects other and more vital aspects of its foreign policy whether it wills this or no. For Singapore this has meant particularly the need to comment on United States Asian policy while attempting to attract American investments, and the necessity of voting on the Middle East crisis while valuing both Egyptian and Israeli associations. Such policy dilemmas make particularly attractive the basically regional associations, the Colombo Plan and the Association of Southeast Asian Nations (ASEAN), and the club to which nations in the British tradition may belong, i.e. the Commonwealth. The Commonwealth particularly provides close policy-free association in a multi-state world without the need for too close a relationship with the great powers. It is precisely because Great Britain is no longer a world power that the Commonwealth is attractive to Singapore.

And yet underlying this vigorous exercise of established sovereignty, there are factors which interplay and limit internal and foreign policy, an understanding of which may help to explain a certain tenseness of mood, an apparent tendency to over-react to opposition, and a sudden change from assertiveness to passivity, at least in policy speeches.

For all Singapore's insistence on independent action, the PAP government accepts the verdict of the 1971 Five Power Defence Conference that the defence of Malaysia and Singapore is 'inseparable'. Singapore faces policy dilemmas in the Middle East, but error of judgement there would not be fatal, and in Southeast Asia Singapore can react almost as an equal in the routine of international relations; but there remains China.

Even here Singapore can maintain some independence of policy. While Malaysia declares for one China, despite Peking's support of the remaining bands of communist terrorists, Singapore argues the right of Taiwan to a United Nations seat. Passively accepting the growth of Russian activity in the region and the Indian Ocean, Singapore can declare itself unconcerned with the Russian-Chinese rivalry – Singapore is not a third (or fourth) China, but an independent state of Singaporeans.

But China is still there.

Despite the government's attempts to demonstrate a Malay base, to use English as the language of administration, and to minimize the Chinese cultural orientation of the majority community, ties remain both with the mainland and with other overseas Chinese communities.[2] Indeed each group in their particular way denies Singapore's independence. The overseas Chinese particularly have not fully recognized that an independent Singapore is no longer a colonial, a political trading outpost, one of many among which the overseas Chinese once moved relatively freely and without political commitment.[3] A Chinese identity for Singapore which is based on relations with people outside the republic, whether Taiwan, Peking or the non-assimilated overseas Chinese in other Southeast Asian nations, endangers both the internal security of the state and the foreign image Lee Kuan Yew and the PAP government are attempting to develop.

This policy of disassociation from other Chinese, while some Singapore Chinese-language newspapers still write as if China were home and their cultural inspiration, while overseas Chinese invest in key industries, and while relatives in China and elsewhere contest for the political loyalties of a large proportion of her citizens, is a continuous one; but the policy is one likely to explode in periodic crises which mar Lee's image as a 'statesman', but which he considers essential for the long-run independence of Singapore.[4]

256

And although the ultimate foreign-policy goal may be the hoped-for 'neutralization' of Southeast Asia, Singapore realizes that it cannot act on this Malaysian dream until the unlikely event of great power agreement and acceptable assurances. In the meantime the policy of 'disassociation', which is a recognition of Singapore's limitations within a Malay sea, must continue. And, finally, this negative China policy reflects in part Singapore's careful relationship with Malaysia – the analysis thus returns as always to the dominant power immediately north of the Johore Causeway.

FOREIGN POLICY FORMULATION AND IMPLEMENTATION

Foreign Policy and the Constitution
The republic of Singapore is a unicameral parliamentary democracy, with a chief of state elected by parliament for a fixed term of five years.[5] The Prime Minister is the head of the government, presiding over a Cabinet having joint responsibility to parliament. In early 1971 there was only one party, the People's Action Party, represented; the chief legal opposition party, the Barisan Sosialis, had renounced participation in the electoral process and had declared its intention of political action outside parliament. There have been no primarily foreign policy debates in the parliament, the formulation of foreign policy is a cabinet matter and prime responsibility rests with the Foreign Minister, since independence S. Rajaratnam, and the Prime Minister, Lee Kuan Yew.

Both Lee and Rajaratnam, who is also Minister of Labour, lend their character to the tone of Singapore's policies. Nevertheless it is obvious that others in the Cabinet are involved – especially Goh Keng Swee and Lim Kim San, the alternating Defence and Finance Ministers. Indeed, certain technical negotiations and agreements are carried out by the several ministries, and there would not appear to be a single collected list of Singapore's international undertakings – from World Bank loan guarantees and cotton textile agreements, double taxation agreements, to full trade agreements – presently available.[6]

Public opinion undoubtedly plays a permissive but passive role in the formulation of foreign policy, and inclusion of foreign policy comments in local political speeches reflects more an

I

257

attempt to explain the reasons for internal situations rather than seek reactions to foreign policy *per se*. Singapore's citizens of Chinese descent are undoubtedly supporting Singapore's moderate attitude to the People's Republic and there is no effective, purely Kuomintang sentiment in Singapore, whatever conservative attitudes to the government on Taiwan may be. Malay feelings undoubtedly support the *rapprochement* with Malaysia and the close ties with Indonesia, welcoming official visits from Islamic groups. All policies expanding economic opportunities would be supported; those involving Indonesia would have Malay communal support in addition. The British cultural orientation has support among all but the Chinese chauvinists – a not inconsiderable group – and Lee Kuan Yew's efforts on behalf of the English language show his desire to obtain a consensus on the emotional subject of communal education.

The actual conduct of foreign affairs, formally understood, is the responsibility of the Foreign Ministry, and there do not appear to have been cases of jurisdictional conflicts. Rather, the overseas representatives of the Economic Development Board or the trade representative of the Singapore government's international trade company, INTRACO, supplement the resources of the Ministry in a clearly defined field. Information on vital issues is received from Singapore's overseas missions, commissions, embassies and consulates, trade representatives and Economic Development Board Staff, is processed in the Foreign Ministry, referred to the Cabinet when of sufficient significance to any consequent policy, and implemented usually by the Ministry but also by specialized departments if within the economic sphere, e.g. air traffic agreements.

The Foreign Ministry and Service
To accomplish its tasks the Foreign Ministry's Singapore-based staff has grown since 1965 to 100, of which only 25 are 'desk' or senior officers. Overseas the ministry has 91 posts, including personal assistants – at the end of 1970 there were 12 vacancies. This breaks down to 47 Branch 'A' officers, 19 attachés, and the rest junior staff.[7] Parliamentary contact is maintained through political secretaries; there is a single political, economic and consular division headed by a deputy secretary with five functionally oriented assistant secretaries; there are also training,

administrative and protocol divisions with seven posts at the assistant secretary level or above. With this Singapore directs its fifteen overseas missions and maintains relations with the forty-five foreign missions of all levels in Singapore. Singapore did not rush precipitately to send permanent missions to all countries; priority was given to the United Nations and to Kuala Lumpur, then to London, Canberra and Auckland. Then again, Singapore had experience in dealing with governments other than its own, including Kuala Lumpur. Nevertheless, the task of setting up the Foreign Ministry and the first missions was formidable. There were three further factors which eased this task, however: firstly, there were already foreign missions in Singapore; secondly, Singapore's state civil service understood administrative procedures; thirdly, with the then retirement age at fifty to fifty-five, there were experienced senior civil servants, e.g. S. T. Stewart, one-time head of the civil service, then High Commissioner to Australia and now permanent secretary in the Foreign Ministry, who were 'retired' but, in an age of air-conditioning, still available. Foreign Ministry recruitment was not confined to Singapore citizens, and those from the Federation and, marginally, Hong Kong, are eligible. For overseas mission chiefs, Singapore has relied on Singapore businessmen long resident in the country, e.g. Ho Rih Hwa in Thailand, Lim Lee Chin in Hong Kong, senior politician-statesmen, e.g. former Speaker of the House Punchardsheram Coomaraswamy in India, and academics, e.g. Professors Wong Ling Ken and his successor, Ernest S. Monteiro, in the United States and Brazil. No civil servant had been chief of mission by the end of 1970; the highest rank achieved was Counsellor of Embassy. Immediately apparent also is the variety of talent suitable for foreign service, for few small nations can appoint a Portuguese-speaking ambassador to Brazil, a fluent Malay-speaking Chinese to Indonesia, or a Japanese expert to Japan, to cite examples. Singapore has been able to draw from the rich variety of its multi-communal society to select mission chiefs capable of establishing immediate *rapport* with the host nation – e.g. Maurice Baker in Malaysia was a fellow-student of Prime Minister Tun Razak; Tommy Koh is a brilliant young lawyer, impressive in the United Nations and well received in Canada.

There are two views on protocol – that from a leading foreign embassy is a certification that Singapore's conduct of foreign affairs is very professional, its mastery of protocol complete. From the Singapore side one may quote the lesson of a new ambassador overseas: being a university professor he had naturally studied Satow's *Diplomatic Guide* with scholarly care,[8] but on arrival, as the newly trained officer on the battlefield, had to throw away the book, learn the 'new diplomacy' from the Malaysians, British and Australians, and confess himself hugely assisted by the host country's Department of State, whose relevant under-secretary he had no problem in contacting when necessary.

Actual duty priorities will, of course, vary from mission to mission and from time to time.

In Hong Kong the Commissioner is responsible for encouraging skilled workers, of which there is a shortage now in Singapore, to emigrate; he also encourages local Chinese businessmen to invest in Singapore. Secondly, he is concerned with the 'image' of Singapore, and his office functions as an information centre for cultural matters, tourism, and general political and economic affairs. Thirdly, he is uniquely concerned with Singapore's trade with China and with the reality of the Chinese predominance in the republic and therefore with the 'Chinese connection'.[9] As another example: in the United States in those first years the ambassador spent half his time outside Washington lecturing on economic opportunities in Singapore. Experience indicated that this function could not be assigned to a Singapore economic expert – American businessmen wanted to hear the ambassador.[10]

In determining the need for a permanent mission, Singapore has learned that matters of key national concern may be handled when foreign ministers or prime ministers visit; technical matters are best conducted by teams of experts from the relevant Singapore government departments. Where necessary, negotiations can be conducted through the foreign mission in Singapore. Overseas permanent missions can therefore be determined on a strict priority basis and total, even broad, coverage is not essential either for Singapore's world position or for obtaining specific agreements.

Some further generalizations can be made about Singapore's diplomatic representation. There is, first of all, a relationship between trade and representation (the leading trading partners –

Malaysia, Japan, United States, Britain, Republic of Vietnam, Australia and Thailand but excluding China and Kuwait – have received permanent missions). There is no pure sentiment in the scope of Commonwealth representation as the variation between Australia and Canada and the absence of any African mission illustrate. Singapore has confined her European missions to representatives of the Economic Development Board, for China there can only be Hong Kong, for South America there is only an ambassador resident in the United States, and for Eastern Europe only a trade representative with consular status in Moscow—although an embassy was finally established in the summer of 1971. Singapore's representation in the United States was first shared with the United Nations, but the development of trade and tourism alone justifies a separate mission. In Japan and Southeast Asia Singapore is better represented but is still selective. The Khmer mission, perhaps surprisingly, represents the close political and developing trade relations Prime Minister Lee established personally through the former Cambodian chief of state, Prince Sihanouk. Singapore's long friendship with and membership in the Afro-Asian bloc is represented by a mission in Cairo, where the ambassador reaches out to Pakistan, the Lebanon, Ethiopia and Yugoslavia. Indeed Ethiopia and the Lebanon are the only two countries which do not reciprocate Singapore's representation.

Singapore's limitations are reflected in part by the fact that she has felt unable – or possibly, in some cases unwilling – to reciprocate representation with twenty-five countries. The European nations, both East and West, account for the majority in this category. Certain nations, for example, those with interests in trade and shipping, Greece and Panama, need representation in Singapore.

There is a total lack of representation in or from Africa south of the Sahara, and this is interesting in view of Singapore's Commonwealth role, her background of appeals to African nations both during Confrontation and immediately on Independence. It would also seem consistent with the views of those who have suggested that Singapore is 'distant', presumably in attitude to Africa and its problems. There is, however, a wholly pragmatic Singapore explanation. First, note that Singapore has no permanent diplomatic representation in Africa, South America *or* Continental Europe. There is no discrimination; as already stated, Singapore cannot afford permanent missions in order to cover the globe, and Singapore's contacts with Commonwealth Africa are through Commonwealth meetings, including one in Singapore in 1971, and through various specialized organizations.

SINGAPORE'S BASIC FOREIGN POLICY POSITION

Singapore must create an image satisfactory to her Malay neighbours, consistent with the Afro-Asian group's opposition to neo-colonialism and sufficiently non-aligned to permit a close working relationship with the Commonwealth and with capital-exporting nations without provoking serious adverse criticism from the Soviet Union. While keeping the People's Republic of China at a distance, Singapore must attempt to limit her hostility and foster her trade.

The popular image of the overseas Chinese in Southeast Asia – or the image that local politicians can only too quickly provoke – is that of the too clever alien trader and money lender, anxious to make a fortune and return to China, or of the communist subversive preparing revolution from a Singapore base. This is not the place to defend the Nanyang Chinese from such extreme and outdated criticisms. Admittedly communism has been a political force in Singapore, the population of the republic is 75 per cent Chinese in origin, and Singapore's trading connections, through family and communal trading organizations, are spread throughout Southeast Asia. Singapore must, therefore, convince her neighbours that as a sovereign nation she speaks for her own citizens and not for all Chinese. Thus during the aftermath of the coup which overthrew Indonesia's Sukarno in 1966 or after the May 1969 riots in Malaysia, Singapore was unusually restrained in commenting on the Chinese aspects of the disturbances. Rather, Singapore has taken positive action to correct her image by providing technical advice and capital investment in Indonesia and by continuing to attempt economic co-operation with Malaysia.[11] Charges of subversion are countered by the record of a strong, efficient, non-communist government, marred, perhaps, by heavy-handed over-reaction to domestic criticism.

Thus Singapore partially offsets the Chinese prejudice by stressing the functional rather than racial role a developed economy can play in the region. Further, Singapore stresses its multi-cultural composition rather than the Chinese predominance – less than half the chiefs of Singapore's overseas missions are of purely Chinese origin.[12] More important, Singapore is ever conscious of her image in Malaysia: Singapore's national language is Malay, her coat of arms includes the Malayan tiger, the special privileges of Malays granted in the Federation are preserved in Singapore, Muslim custom is given legal recognition, and English (not Chinese) is the usual (and natural) language of administration.

As a non-aligned nation Singapore must present an acceptable front in the United Nations. Singapore's position in the General Assembly is basically low-posture, reluctant to lend support which will enable one side to score off the other or where voting will not help improve the situation. As an example of the former, Singapore did not support the 1968 Afro-Asian resolutions on the Middle East crisis; and of the latter, she has not contributed on the Korean issue.

Further, on the Middle East, Singapore has specifically declared her opposition to Israel keeping any territories on the basis of armed conquest. In fact, Singapore was able to maintain its long-established friendship with President Nasser without fully supporting the Arab position on the Middle East, i.e. by insisting on Israel's right – as a small state – to exist. Israel's close involvement in Singapore's military training programme indeed required recognition, and Singapore stated its sovereign right to do so. Singapore's need to take a complex stand in this emotional situation is an example of the small nation's dilemma – the inability to stand outside major policy disputes.[13]

While not supporting the original Albanian draft resolution on China, Singapore long held that a delegation from the People's Republic should represent China at the United Nations and in the crucial 1971 assembly she voted against the issue being considered an 'important question'. But consistent with her concern for self-determination of small political entities, Singapore has also asserted that the people of Taiwan have the right of self-determination and, if voting for independence, to a seat in the United Nations as Taiwan.[14] Lack of staff has prevented Singapore from keeping abreast of the details of disarmament proposals, but she supported the treaty on non-proliferation of atomic weapons. And, by rotation, Singa-

263

pore has accepted chairmanship of the UN's Afro-Asian group.

Singapore is a non-aligned nation which 'leans to one side', that is, has demonstrable sympathies with, in this case, the West. But to be effective non-alignment must be a reality. On independence, therefore, Singapore countered its Commonwealth image by a mission which visited not only such an acknowledged non-aligned leader as Yugoslavia, but also the Soviet Union, whose representatives and Tass reporters reached Singapore within a year. Trade agreements have been reached with several Eastern bloc nations; the Singapore government's International Trading Company, INTRACO, has been formed primarily, it is reported, to facilitate trade with communist governments. In 1970 some 500 Soviet ships called at Singapore, Soviet naval vessels cruised off Singapore waters during the Commonwealth Conference in January 1971, and the Soviet mission is one of the largest in Singapore – but not as large as that of the United States, which, as the government is quick to point out, is Singapore's third largest trading partner.[15]

There is evidence, then, that Singapore's participation in world events has not been headlong – there are policy reservations and hesitations. This is also true within the region: Singapore's participation in the Association of Southeast Asian Nations (ASEAN) lacks *political* enthusiasm and stresses the primary economic and co-operative role. Singapore was a reluctant participant in the Indonesian-sponsored 1970 conference on Cambodia, probably because she felt the other delegates too committed and unlikely to achieve results. This reluctance was possibly reinforced by the long-standing personal relationship between Lee Kuan Yew and former Cambodian chief of state Prince Sihanouk.[16] And yet Singapore refused on Independence to lift a ban on trade with South Africa and subsequently extended the ban to Rhodesia, despite the political risks and the small chances of success for such policy.

Singapore has also given forthright support to Malaysia against the Philippines over Sabah. The Sabah claim is a complex subject. Although in pressing the claim the Philippines intended to mark the nation's entry into Asian affairs, in fact the Philippines destroyed the effectiveness of the Association of Southeast Asia (ASA: an association with the Federation of Malaya and Thailand) and left the Philippines alone with Indonesia, then a doubtful ally. The difficulty in taking the claim seriously has impaired discussion.[17] In any event Singapore's position extends beyond the immediate interests of a trading and business state. Here is further evidence that the republic has a world position.

Singapore's image has been marred on occasion by a certain brashness, a certain lack of caution in official statements on foreign affairs. This is partially explained by inclusion of such statements in speeches intended for local political purposes, and, since the republic is small, and since national leaders are responsible, such comments are repeated internationally. Singapore politics are tough, and Singapore leaders can speak emotionally. Then, too, the feeling that independence must be asserted, that Singapore's success must be proclaimed and others compared unfavourably, can lead to friction. In August 1965, during the immediate aftermath of independence, for example, Lee Kuan Yew in the course of an anti-American address accused U.S. government agents of trying to recruit him in 1959. This was promptly denied, despite the fact that Secretary of State Dean Rusk had written Lee a letter of apology. Lee released the letter; the first American ambassador was not appointed until 1966.[18] Off-the-cuff comments by Singapore leaders on Malaysia brought protests and consequent apologies.

But the long-run effect of such missteps appears negligible; certainly by 1970 Singapore–U.S. relations were excellent *because* of Prime Minister Lee. Singapore has, for example, felt a need to comment frequently on the Vietnam situation. Lee Kuan Yew's caution on timetable withdrawal, accepted as supporting America's 1970 policy in Southeast Asia, is found in his speech at a banquet in honour of Spiro T. Agnew, Vice-President of the United States, on 10 January 1970. Singapore's Foreign Minister has taken more critical positions, and in general Singapore at the United Nations has supported a solution based on the 1964 Geneva agreements. This concern for Vietnam reflects Singapore's security interests but also her basic non-aligned image, her ruling party's (People's Action Party) socialist international doctrines and the trend towards a stress on neutralism as the United States' withdrawal is gradually implemented.[19]

The assertion of independence has also led Singapore into policy conflicts. There are from time to time the retaliatory measures which in themselves would appear totally justifiable as actions of a sovereign state – but not if a special relationship is their criterion. Immigration control is an example. Two special cases stand out, however.

The first is the failure of Singapore and Malaysia to reach agreement over the continued issuance of a common currency. Malaysia conceded Singapore's rights to management of its own portion of the currency reserves and to immediate access, but Singapore held out for legal ownership.[20] The second involves Indonesia. During confrontation Singapore arrested several Indonesian saboteurs; later those not responsible for loss of life were released. Two marines whose actions in March, 1965, before Singapore's independence, had caused civilian casualties were given death sentences; their appeal to the Judicial Committee of Britain's Privy Council failed. But three years had passed. The new Indonesian government, whose declared policy was improved relations with Singapore, urged clemency; General Suharto despatched a personal representative. But this last move was interpreted as an attempt to exert undue pressure; Singapore's leaders apparently took the position that an independent policy must be maintained. The executions, they decided, had to take place. Both Indonesia and Malaysia reacted communally – the Chinese had executed a Malay. But again the setback was temporary and, while not forgotten, its impact on long-run relations is impossible to detect.

A survey of Singapore's foreign policy statements suggests the following summary over-view.[21] Politics is the art of the possible; Singapore in determining its capabilities realizes that her impact on world events is small, that certain policy roles are pre-empted by the super powers, and that Singapore must in certain economic as well as political issues accept a passive role. Singapore's policy must be directed first at ensuring a sound domestic base; bankruptcy forces dependence. A sound base must be supplemented by a policy of non-alignment to ensure independence: a non-aligned nation may take aid from international organizations or accept country-to-country aid on a short-term, paid basis, e.g. military technical assistance from Israel. Universal recognition and selective contact are essential policy elements, but in a time when sympathy with Western traditions does not require full support for United States anticommunist crusades, Singapore can and must accept trade and diplomatic relations with the Eastern bloc and view with appar-

cnt calm Soviet expansion into the Indian Ocean, while accepting a basically 'Western' defence alliance, a moderating role in
the Commonwealth and a temperate view of United States
Southeast Asian policy. Thus the United States might charac-
terize Singapore's policy as 'friendly and understanding'; the
Soviet Union as 'correct' or, possibly, 'not unfriendly'.

THE CONTINUITY OF POLICY – A SELECTIVE HISTORY

Singapore, founded in 1819, developed as a trading colony in the
era of the imperialism of free trade. Over 150 years the island's
economic links within the region have been close-forged; as a
political entity, however, Singapore developed separately – and
differently. This difference was confirmed when, in 1946,
Singapore was separated even from her sister-settlements of
Penang, Malacca, and Labuan; these could be absorbed into
developing political areas without upsetting the demographic
balance in favour of the Chinese. Singapore, the port, the
financial centre, the trading nexus, was excluded in a policy as
understandable as it was short-sighted. As long as British
imperial power provided the overhead of political co-operation,
formal political union was not necessary for economic co-
operation. The course to independence once set, the dichotomy
was immediately apparent; Singapore's exclusion made the
path of Malay-Chinese compromise easier in the Federation,
the Malay fears of the big city Chinese, of Singapore communism, of Chinese competition and eventual domination were
temporarily exorcized, but the regional resultant was economically untenable and politically unstable.

Singapore's politicians saw from the first the difficulties of the
situation, and they argued, for differing reasons and in differing
ways, integration or merger. Federation leaders, still involved in
the Emergency, that is, in the combating of communist
terrorism, were reinforced in their opinion that there was trouble
enough without involvement in the secret societies, the labour
strife, and the tough political scene of Singapore: the Causeway
must be made a *cordon sanitaire*, the Federation's first chief
minister, Tengku Abdul Rahman, told David Marshall, his
Singapore counterpart.[22]

Until 1963 foreign policy was a reserved subject, that is, one
outside the constitutional competency of the elected Singapore

267

government. But for a trading state at least relations with neighbours are a key political issue, and during this period the government did promote air traffic agreements, arrange with the Federation for continued joint issue of the currency, co-operate on security, and concern itself with the complex details of economic relations with Indonesia. The overriding concern, however, was the People's Action Party's policy of 'independence through merger' with the Federation of Malaya.[23] This was achieved in September 1963; the Tengku had changed his views and, with the Emergency concluded, Singapore seemed safer within than without the Federation;[24] the communal imbalance could be corrected by the inclusion of Sarawak and British North Borneo (Sabah), then Crown colonies. A new nation, the Federation of Malaysia, was established incorporating the city-state of Singapore.

And yet essential to an understanding of Singapore's foreign policy today is recognition that merger *reinforced* Singapore's separate identity; the state was not submerged in the union, and the issues negotiated during the period of merger, 1963–65, are issues today. The international reaction to the merger, that is to the creation of Malaysia, continues to have an impact on Singapore's policy.

On the eve of merger Indonesia, supported by political agents operating from her missions in Kuala Lumpur and Singapore, stepped up pressure for a pan-Malay state, for *Melayu Raya*. Noting the Anglo-Malayan defence pact, Indonesia labelled Malaysia a neo-colonial plot perpetrated against the wishes of the people. This was the origin of 'confrontation', a policy short of war which led to warlike acts, including invasion of the peninsula and involvement with regular Singapore units of the Malaysian army. Malaysia was on the defensive in the Third World, and, on behalf of the Federation government, Lee Kuan Yew, premier of the state of Singapore, led a successful mission of twelve leaders from the three new states of Sabah, Sarawak and Singapore to seventeen African states. Here Lee met the late President Nasser; here too developed Singapore's early involvement in international affairs and Lee's close connection with African leaders and the Afro-Asian group. Malaysia was also on the defensive over the Philippine claim to Sabah, but in this Singapore had no direct interest but unequivocally spoke against the Philippines.

The origins then of Singapore's international position came from its support of Malaysia; continuity of policy arises from the unique nature of the new federation which *de facto* permitted the political identity of Singapore to persist even in the minds of overseas observers.

Malayan leaders had accepted the necessity of the Singapore merger with reluctance and for two years conducted a series of complex and hard-fought negotiations which were as between two sovereign governments.[25] For although Britain was formally responsible for Singapore's foreign relations, the merger negotiations were *de facto* with Singapore's elected, political leaders. The personality of Lee Kuan Yew, the dynamism of his Cabinet colleagues, and their bitter political struggle with communist-infiltrated unions and parties drew world attention – not to a British colony or to the Federation, but to the Singapore government. And did not American Secretary of State Dean Rusk, in his apology to Prime Minister Lee, write in the language of equals of relations between 'our governments'?[26] When, at the request of Indonesia, the Malayan government agreed to a postponement of the federation to create Malaysia, Lee Kuan Yew unilaterally proclaimed Singapore's independence. Although this was recognized neither by the United Kingdom nor by the Federation, the declaration accurately reflected Singapore's mood and its self-confidence. In fact the postponement was brief, and the 'merger', that is, the establishment of the Federation of Malaysia with Singapore as a constituent state, took place on 16 September 1963.

Nor did the final merger arrangements which determined Singapore's position in the new Federation do much to change the 'independent' or, more accurately, 'separate and distinctive' image; there were to be Singapore citizens and Malayan citizens on separate electoral rolls, thus isolating Singapore politically; Singapore was consequently under-represented in the Federation parliament; but Singapore retained state control of certain subjects which were elsewhere under federal jurisdiction. If during the negotiations Singapore gained confidence and identity during the period of merger the continued need to negotiate implementation of the economic agreements, including United Kingdom textile quotas, confirmed and developed the separate identities.

The very nature of the federal agreement and constitution

encouraged Singapore's semi-autonomous attitude and its feeling of equality with Kuala Lumpur; the PAP's exclusion from the federal government gave it political form. Had the problems been confined to economic affairs, this attitude might have been tolerated; merger was accepted as a logical economic development and the Tengku had seen Singapore as the New York of Malaysia. But the political ambitions and differences persisted. The People's Action Party's involvement in Federation politics, the attempts of the United Malay National Organization, encouraged by the party's secretary-general, Syed Ja'afar Albar, of Singapore origins, to discredit the PAP as a Chinese communal party in Singapore, the consequent 1964 riots, and the growing estrangement between Lee and the Tengku, between Chinese socialist leaders in Singapore and conservative Malayan Chinese Association (MCA) leaders in the Federation led to the Tengku's personal and unilateral decision that Singapore must leave the Federation.

Foreign policy differences were partially involved.[27] Lee opposed the establishment of a Taiwan consulate in Kuala Lumpur and the closing of the Peking-owned Bank of China in Singapore. He spoke critically of United States policy in Vietnam, and in 1965 travelled in Australia where, MCA leaders charged, he spoke critically of the Federation itself.[28] There was more than a suggestion that the PAP sought to replace the MCA as the Chinese partner in the Alliance government; more credible still, that Lee Kuan Yew wished to be Prime Minister of Malaysia. Whatever the fears, the facts were already clear: too many were treating the Tengku and Lee as equal, Singapore was tarnishing Malaysia's image as a successful multi-communal state. Lee was summoned to Kuala Lumpur and over the weekend the agreements were reached after all alternatives proposed by Singapore had been rejected; on 9 August 1965, less than two years after the merger, Singapore became an independent nation.

INDEPENDENT SINGAPORE'S FOREIGN POLICY

In the first few months of independence, Singapore established her world position. Sponsored by the Federation and opposed by none, Singapore became the 117th member of the United Nations in September; in October she was admitted to the

Commonwealth. By the end of 1965 the Republic had become a member of the Economic Commission for Asia and the Far East (ECAFE) and specialized UN agencies; eleven ambassadors and high commissioners plus thirteen consular and two trade missions were in Singapore – although, in contrast and reflecting her resources, Singapore had established only two overseas missions, at the United Nations and in Kuala Lumpur. A Singapore mission again visited Africa, Yugoslavia and the Soviet Union. Major contacts had been made by 1968, although Singapore's overseas activities continue to develop.

With the People's Republic of China no formal diplomatic contact could be made since that government supports the Malayan Communist Party and refuses to recognize the separation of Singapore. Singapore did, however, reverse Malaysia's decision to close the Bank of China, thus maintaining unofficial business relations with the People's Republic.[29] Restoration of relations with Indonesia was delayed until 1967 by internal developments in that country and by friction with Malaysia over the pace of the reconciliation.[30] Relations with Japan have been normalized. On the past Lee commented: 'a chapter closed but not forgotten'. Japan's economic role in Singapore is of growing importance.

Disengagement and re-establishment – Relations with Malaysia
Independence did not change the rationale of Singapore's close and special relations with the Federation of Malaysia, but issues which had been the subject of domestic in-fighting had now become matters of foreign policy. Under the provisions of the independence agreement and as a successor state, Singapore entered into close defence relations with the Federation, undertook mutually with the Federation not to enter into any treaty or agreement with a foreign country which might adversely affect the independence or defence of Singapore or the Federation, and accepted responsibilities for all treaties and international guarantees made on behalf of Singapore – including the essential water supply agreement with the State of Johore.[31]

The affairs of the two states were intertwined; the task of both governments was to preserve the essential with due respect to sovereignty. There had to be first disengagement and then re-establishment; there had to be policies constructed between parties which knew each other well – sometimes too well –

against the background of some suspicion and over-reaction, but always the subconscious recognition that the split must not be made irrevocable, that for the next generation the opportunity for merger might again exist.

Economic disengagement began with the collapse of all negotiations for a customs union. Separate currencies were issued in 1967, immigration and work regulations were developed separately for Singapore and Malaysian citizens, postage stamps, business and other licensing and, indeed, economic legislation separated and diverged. Singapore's banking legislation remained unamended, however, and continued to be administered by the Singapore branch of Malaysia's Bank Negara (central bank) under the supervision of the republic's finance ministry and the bank's deputy governor – a Singapore citizen. By 1970 the two nations apparently had only a joint airline, a joint stock exchange and joint banking association in common. The Federation has been developing its ports in competition with Singapore, its industrial promotion policy seeks to attract new industry to the peninsula with the promise of a domestic market which Singapore cannot offer.[32] But as both economies expand, as both governments pursue fiscal and monetary policies in the same tradition, the impact of this economic disengagement, if the potential benefits of the customs union be disregarded, has not been serious. Between any other two sovereign nations the level of economic co-operation remaining would be a sign of achievement, and it is not a criticism of Singapore's foreign policy to conclude that economic arrangements difficult to maintain in the days of merger had to be formally altered after independence.

More obvious disengagement came in the political sphere, where the PAP had to withdraw from political activities in the Federation and their sole Malayan-elected representative, P. V. Devan Nair, organized the independent Democratic Action Party. Until the establishment of a Singapore supreme court, appeals continued to be made to the Federation; the path through the Federation to the judicial committee of Britain's Privy Council ceased only in 1968.

When the Federation's permanent Secretary for Foreign Affairs, Dato Muhammad Ghazali, spoke of a 'special relationship' with Singapore and promised that the two countries would dispense as far as possible with formalities and protocol, and when Tan Siew Sin, the Federation's conservative Finance Minister and leader of the MCA, declared that the two nations had separated as friends and that one day they would come together again, they were undoubtedly totally sincere.[33] But while relations between the two countries have remained informal and close, they have not, however, been smooth; the crisis in Malaysian-Singapore relations is yet to come.

Singapore has retained the formal Malay base of the republic – national language, certain privileges, national motto – and has refrained, after the early emotion had passed, from interference and has co-ordinated certain policies. But the test will come (i) if there is economic depression in either nation, (ii) if Malaysian communal policy should drive the Chinese towards the Malayan Communist Party and so endanger Singapore's internal stability, and, less significant, (iii) if either Sabah or Sarawak should attempt extra-constitutionally to modify their relations with the federal government.

Defence
Singapore's defence rests on agreements reached at the April 1971 Five-Power meeting – Malaysia, Singapore, Australia, New Zealand and the United Kingdom. Although these agreements are based on the assumption that the defence of Singapore and Malaysia is indivisible, the republic, nevertheless, is determined to present a separate military capability, described by the Prime Minister as one appropriate to a small fish wishing if necessary to poison a middle-sized fish. Thus within ten years Singapore will be able to mobilize 140,000 men on short notice, the consequence of an Israeli-inspired and advised universal military training programme which has the additional benefits of keeping youth off the labour market and of fostering a Singapore nationalism.

Despite these well-publicized efforts, the keys to Singapore's defence will remain the ability to maintain close co-operation with Malaysia, an integrated air defence plan to be initiated in September 1971 and controlled by joint council, and the promise of ANZUK support. The course of co-operation will not, however, be easy, and there have already been conflicts over the use of Malaysian facilities not only by the ANZUK forces but also by Singapore.

While welcoming the new agreements as consistent both

273

with traditional defence alignments and also with the new Malaysian policy of neutrality, Singapore and Malaysia stress, in the words of Malaysia's Prime Minister Tun Razak, self-reliance and non-alignment. Whereas the old Anglo-Malayan defence agreement of 1957[34] – extended to cover Singapore on independence – *required* the involvement of the United Kingdom, the new agreements call only for consultations of the five powers if either Singapore or Malaysia is threatened by external aggression. This basic provision is backed up with supplementary arrangements for stationing of forces and standing consultative committees; it is still sufficiently strong to induce unfavourable reaction from the Soviet Union. Moreover, the changes reflect not only the requirements of Malaysia's new policy but also Britain's restricted commitment in the area and the unwillingness of Australia and New Zealand to inherit without modification.

From Singapore's standpoint, Commonwealth-based defence is the only acceptable foreign involvement, and this primarily on the grounds that continuation of the same – or less of the same – is not provocative. Indeed, Prime Minister Lee was responsible for the postponement of the original withdrawal date set by Britain's Labour government, but as the limited British military presence and the modified agreements indicate, the trend of British policy remains unchanged.[35] For in defence matters also Singapore's external and internal policies are intertwined; Lee needed time to convert the British base to civilian use as well as military and naval protection.

The conclusion of new defence agreements reflects the fact that neither Singapore nor Malaysia have accepted Soviet proposals of 'collective security' as of immediate relevance. Nevertheless, Singapore has been careful to keep her defence involvement consistent with her concept of neutrality, that is neutrality with Commonwealth involvement excepted, by declaring on independence she was the sovereign of the bases and by prohibiting their use to SEATO and explaining the presence of foreign, i.e. British, forces in terms of legitimate self-defence.[36]

The success of her defence policy must depend, regardless of all other factors, on co-operation with Malaysia. Past experience is not wholly encouraging. Singapore's independent foreign policy towards Indonesia, for example, caused her to withdraw in 1966 from the joint defence council which had been established under the 1957 agreement.[37] There have already been misgivings over sharing of training facilities, in particular the Malaysian jungle warfare school. Non-defence matters could always cause friction on the joint councils. This could restrict Singapore's foreign policy range of manoeuvre or it could lead again to a Singapore withdrawal from the councils. The delicate balance which fulfilment of sovereignty and the maintenance of sound defence requires may explain the sensitivity of Singapore's government to criticism and is one legitimate factor in its controversial press policy. Matters which in larger countries are of solely municipal concern are likely in Singapore to be matters having a direct impact on sensitive foreign policy issues.

An Asian Financial Centre

Singapore's challenge to Hong Kong and Japan to become an Asian financial centre has had mixed success, partly because of limitations which economic co-ordination with Malaysia impose, partly because of the realities of world financial organization. The key elements are the new gold market, the Asian-dollar market, and a system of Swiss-style numbered accounts. The gold market is operated consistent with IMF rules, is controlled by the government, and is entirely successful. The Asian-dollar market is controversial, although relatively unimportant when compared with the Euro-dollar market, but Singapore operates while London is closed and thus provides a significant facility.[38] The numbered account system has been approved by parliament but had not been implemented by the end of 1970; already objections have been lodged by interested governments, particularly the United States. But, in contrast, Singapore seems reluctant to grant all foreign bank applicants licences to operate, a policy apparently inconsistent with the requirements of an international financial centre.

Singapore cannot, however, operate a foreign exchange market in the Hong Kong tradition since it is unlikely the Bank of England would approve a second exception for a sterling area nation. Singapore is, of course, free to withdraw from the sterling area, but while Malaysia remains a member, such withdrawal would disrupt financial transactions across the Causeway and endanger Singapore's financial role in the Federation's expanding economy. Indeed Singapore's monetary link with the Federation is even closer, despite the issuance of separate

275

currency.[39] Singapore's par-value decision after the devaluation of sterling was pre-empted by Malaysia, which had decided not to devalue; Singapore followed Malaysia. And the present agreement for exchange of the two currencies at par effectively requires, while the agreement lasts, Singapore to take Malaysia's fiscal policies into careful consideration before determining her own domestic economic plans. Such, then, are the financial realities of independence.

Britain, the Commonwealth, and Regional Activities
While the PAP fought for political leadership in Singapore, Britain had no more severe critics than Lee Kuan Yew and his associates. Since independence, however, *rapprochement* with Britain has been a key element in the republic's foreign policy.[40] There have, of course, been disputes, e.g. on textiles and air traffic, but the keys to the relationship are defence and tradition. That Lee himself is politically intelligible to the British is at least partly proven by his general popularity (including 'Lee for Prime Minister' buttons during a Labour government nadir), and his speeches contain references to the benefits of the British legal and educational heritage and especially to the value of the English language for the people of a technically developing economy.[41]

Relations with Britain are not, therefore, based on agreement *per se*. While Singapore accepted Britain's decision of military withdrawal, Lee reacted sharply to the revised time-scale schedule which was the price of Labour Party unity over devaluation, and which brought the promise of £350 million in assistance to Singapore. But the evacuation of Singapore's base opened up new industrial potentials: Singapore experts visited Commonwealth Malta to study her experience in conversion.

The tone of Singapore's relations with Britain is consistent with her Commonwealth policy. The Commonwealth provides certain obvious, specific advantages to its members, but the long-run value is more difficult to assess, if only because the cynical too quickly demand facts or charge sentimentality. First of all, therefore, be quite certain that Singapore's Commonwealth is not the Commonwealth envisaged as the aftermath of Empire, a group of former colonies bound by ties as real as imperial rule, nor is it the Commonwealth as alternative to Britain in Europe. It either is or will be something else; Singapore is involved in the transformation.

The specific advantages are several. First there are the specialized organizations. Of the twenty-three regional and international organizations to which Singapore belongs, including the Asian Development Bank (ADB), ASEAN, WHO, WMO, ILO and IMF, six are entirely Commonwealth in composition. The Colombo Plan itself was Commonwealth inspired, but is now a larger, regional grouping. Secondly, certain British foreign service reports and other internal documents are made available to Commonwealth governments – this and other exchanges are facilitated by membership and are extremely valuable to small Commonwealth nations with limited resources. Thirdly, Commonwealth high commissioners have recognized access to Britain's Prime Minister; ambassadors to the Foreign Secretary. This can be but a formal difference; it can, however, be important for the smaller nation. Fourthly, consular and visa duties may be undertaken for other members – Malaysia does this for Singapore where the former has missions, in other cases, British foreign service officers may act on Singapore's behalf.

Two traditional Commonwealth advantages are, however, disappearing: Commonwealth preference policy is becoming increasingly less advantageous for technical reasons, and Britain's application for entry into the Common Market is requiring renegotiation of economic relationships. Then too Commonwealth citizenship and ease of dual nationality built into the original Commonwealth concept is becoming less attractive as the new nations, including Singapore, find such arrangements tend to be used by expatriates and others not sure of their final allegiance as a hedge against political instability.

But Singapore does not see the Commonwealth as a policy-forming group comparable, for example, to the Afro-Asian People's Solidarity Organization, although Lee Kuan Yew in 1966 helped the African members in their dispute with Britain over Common Market terms of entry. On the arms to South Africa issue, Singapore has been prepared to accept Britain's decision; Prime Minister Lee Kuan Yew was thus an ideal chairman for the January 1971 conference in Singapore. 'The Commonwealth' declared Singapore's Foreign Minister at the close of that conference, 'declines to fall'. As has already been stressed, Singapore views the Commonwealth as a group needed by small nations in a multi-nation world: the United Nations is

277

too large, other groupings either too policy-oriented – there is a separate need for these – or too closely aligned to the super powers. Then, too, Singapore's non-aligned policy does not appear to lean too far to one side if pro-Western policies, e.g. the five-power defence agreements, can be placed in a Commonwealth context.[42] Commonwealth membership excuses the non-aligned member its lapses. Foreign policy is explained in power-bloc terms, but the reference is no longer a power-bloc; it is a free association of nations with a common tradition. Its need is felt as urgently in Singapore's Foreign Ministry as it is denigrated by those British diplomats who remember the descriptions of the early 1950s and no longer recognize the reality or understand its functions.

As the Commonwealth gives Singapore a world grouping, so ASEAN, the Association of Southeast Asian Nations, provides Singapore with a regional association which is consistent with her non-aligned policy position. Singapore is also a member of other regional organizations, including, for example, the Asian Development Bank and the Colombo Plan, but the former is a specialized agency and the latter is concerned primarily with the technical tasks of development. Singapore has rejected membership in SEATO, as a creation of the Cold War long since irrelevant to its original purposes. Similarly ASPAC is openly anti-communist; membership for Singapore would be inconsistent with non-alignment.

The inspiration for ASEAN lies with its predecessor the Association of Southeast Asia, ASA ('hope'), virtually inoperative since 1963 when the Philippines refused to recognize the Federation of Malaysia because of her Sabah claim. Yet ASA had promised to be a low-key, basically non-political organization of states with similar development goals and some commitment to the concept of the open society. ASEAN is ASA with Indonesia and Singapore added to the membership – the Federation of Malaysia, Thailand and the Philippines; it has, however, been able to maintain its general approach, although with the 100 million people of Indonesia it is no longer an association of small states. Singapore's approach to ASEAN is pragmatic, revealing quite clearly again the republic's basic economic requirements and the underlying economic policy needs which play a significant role in Singapore's overall foreign policy. Thus Singapore stresses the economic purposes of ASEAN, and within this field stresses the need for immediate and practical projects. While this has reinforced Singapore's image as a hard-headed business state, Singapore's regional involvement is recognized as significant.

Singapore participates in the Economic Commission for Asia and the Far East (ECAFE), the Regional English Language Centre of the Southeast Asian Ministers of Education Council is located in Singapore and the republic has sponsored a Southeast Asia Fisheries Development Centre; and her Foreign Minister participated in the Southeast Asian Ministerial Conference in Manila in 1967. There have been meetings in Singapore of the Ministerial Conference for Economic Development of Southeast Asia and of the Colombo Plan Consultative Committee. If to these major events are added the meetings of sub-committees, project groups, and technical associations – from national archivists to university vice-chancellors – Singapore's regional participation appears exhaustive; Singapore plays a full role in Southeast Asia.

Singapore's foreign policy is difficult to assess in standard terms. The republic's Foreign Minister and Deputy Prime Minister were born in Malaysia; one declared policy goal is to assert Singapore's sovereignty and independence, but the ultimate – today expressed in non-policy generalities – is reunion. A second priority is development of the nation's international economic contacts, but treaties and agreements reflect as much particular legal problems, even the need for political gestures, as success in economically-significant negotiations.

A full appreciation of Singapore's foreign policy depends on one's ability to grasp the tremendous drive and vitality – reflected, for example, in the speeches of Singapore's leaders – of the citizens of multi-communal Singapore. This energetic tone – the term 'aggressive' has been used but this may be misunderstood in a foreign policy context – touched with the impatience of brilliance but tempered with a genuine concern for non-alignment, for the welfare and problems of Afro-Asian groups, and for the development of her neighbours, reflects the dynamism of Singapore society at all levels.

The foreign policy activities of a small state with international contacts are apparently numerous and varied, taxing the limited resources available to the government, resources urgently needed for domestic development. Yet each small state is peculiarly restricted in the way these foreign policy activities may be implemented and in the scope for manoeuvre in key issues. Singapore inherits an apolitical past and a special relationship with Malaysia. Thus many from outside find difficulty in accepting Singapore nationalism as legitimate; many within, Malays and Chinese, look elsewhere for their ultimate loyalty. Defence requirements run counter to Singapore's overall foreign policy position; the link between domestic politics and foreign policy, activities which require two very different approaches, is dangerously close. In all these matters Singapore is torn between policies of extreme caution and outspoken, sometimes personal, reaction.

The purpose of this essay has been to show that, despite limitations, there is scope both for independent policy and significant contribution, and indeed too often a necessity for involvement in complex international issues of no immediate concern to the interests of Singapore. Thus there is constant need for caution and balance. The history of Singapore's foreign policy indicates she has several times been close to the brink, and the future holds new dangers as Russia moves south, China interests herself again in the world beyond, the West withdraws.

Since independence, Singapore's foreign policy may be described as soundly conceived, for the most part consistently developed, but, given the complexity of the problems faced, not achieving all goals. The overall record, however, permits the conclusion that Singapore's foreign policy has indeed been successful.

NOTES AND REFERENCES

The basic source for information on Singapore is the government's annual report, with the series title *Singapore Year Book*. Especially important are the general review and foreign affairs chapters. Ooi Jin-Bee and Chiang Hai Ding have published a collection of valuable essays on various aspects of the Singapore scene under the title *Modern Singapore* (Singapore University Press, Singapore, 1969). In addition there are the reports of various government departments, parliamentary debates, and an official newspaper, *The Mirror*.

The information in this essay is based primarily on interviews, foreign policy statements from Singapore and from their United Nations spokesman, and those international agreements available. To be practical, however, one should first seek selections of such material. The most useful is P. J. Boyce, *Malaysia and Singapore in International Diplomacy: Documents and Commentaries* (Sydney University Press, Sydney, 1968). Reference may also be made to J. M. Gullick, *Malaysia and its Neighbours* (Routledge and Kegan Paul, London, 1967), and, for material on the Prime Minister, to Alex Josey, *Lee Kuan Yew* (Donald Moore Press, Singapore, 1968) and *Lee Kuan Yew and the Commonwealth* (Cellar Book Store, Detroit, 1969).

The point was made in the essay that there is a continuity to Singapore's foreign policy pre-dating independence. The general pre-independence regional scene is analysed in Russell H. Fifield, *The Diplomacy of Southeast Asia 1945–1958* (Harper Bros., New York, 1958); a more specific and very sound article is P. J. Boyce, 'Policy without Authority: Singapore's External Affairs Power', *Journal of Southeast Asian History*, vol. 6, no. 2 (September, 1965) pp. 87–103. (This entire issue of the *Journal* deals with the Federation of Malaysia.) Singapore's first chief minister, David Marshall, has told his story with references to foreign policy in 'Singapore's Struggle for Nationhood, 1945–1959', *Journal of Southeast Asian Studies*, vol. 1 (September, 1970) pp. 99–104. In 1970 Western concern mounted over Russia's interest in Southeast Asia and the Indian Ocean, but this interest is hardly new and should be placed in perspective by reference to, for example, Charles B. McLane, *Soviet Strategies in Southeast Asia, An Exploration of Eastern Policy under Lenin and Stalin* (Princeton University Press, Princeton, 1966). There is a long bibliography.

For Singapore in Malaysia and the separation, there are several useful studies: J. M. Gullick, *Malaysia* (Ernest Benn Ltd., London, 1964) and Wang Gungwu (ed.), '*Malaysia*', *a Survey* (Pall Mall, London, 1964) are two for beginning – especially note the chapter on 'Malaysia and the Commonwealth' by Robin W. Winks in the latter collection. A briefer account is Robert O. Tilman's 'Malaysia and Singapore, the Failure of a Federation', in his edited *Man, State and Society in Contemporary Southeast Asia* (Pall Mall, London, 1969) pp. 490–505. A more thorough analysis of the separation in Nancy McHenry Fletcher's monograph, *The Separation of Singapore from Malaysia*, Data Paper no. 73 of the Southeast Asian Program of Cornell University (Ithaca, New York, 1969).

The fluidity of regional co-operation usually turns studies designed to describe existing associations into historical monographs, but Bernard K. Gordon, in addition to providing background on ASA, is sufficiently current to have described the transition to ASEAN in his contribution 'Regionalism in Southeast Asia' to Tilman's work cited above (pp. 506–22). *The Far Eastern Economic Review*, a Hong Kong weekly, keeps more up to date, and its *Annual Survey* usually contains a summary on regional co-operation.

Specialized references may be found below. The strictly limited purpose of this note has been to focus on foreign policy studies, but the majority of the books cited contain bibliographies.

The author wishes to acknowledge a research grant from the Centre of Asian Studies, University of Hong Kong and to express his appreciation to officials of the Singapore Foreign Ministry, and in particular Mr S.

Rajaratnam, the Foreign Minister, for their time and assistance in providing background and up-to-date information. Special thanks are extended to Mr J. Lever, manager of the Singapore branch of the Hongkong and Shanghai Banking Corporation, Dr Mary Rayner of the University of Singapore, and foreign diplomats who were generous of their time.

1. A useful summary of Singapore's economic record is found in Dr Goh Keng Swee, *Decade of Achievement* (Ministry of Culture, Singapore, 1970). The Singapore annual reports are a basic source used in this essay. Reference may also be made to the reports of the Economic Development Board. At par S. $1·00 = U.S. $0·33. Singapore's trade statistics are incomplete and omit Indonesia – thus the figures can be used in their raw form only for such generalizations as are made in this chapter. The official reason for the Indonesian omission is that differences in compilation methods have led to unjustified accusations of smuggling and endangered Indonesian-Singapore relations.
2. Chinese cultural activities traditional to the regions from which the several communities migrated are, of course, encouraged – Singapore as 'instant Asia'. But indoctrination in the élite culture – whether it be Confucian, Nationalist, or Maoist – implies exposure to the 'Middle Kingdom' complex and is politically dangerous to Singapore's present policy. It is one thing to sing songs of the 'old sod' and another to support the IRA.
3. This attitude is not confined to overseas Chinese. The role of Singapore as a trading centre independent of the politics of the Malay peninsula has created the image of a non-national, non-political area, which the PAP government does not accept. Hence the frequent outraged comments of expatriates and international businessmen whose activities have been curtailed.
4. One such flare-up occurred in May and June of 1971 and involved Prime Minister Lee's actions against certain Singapore Chinese- and English-language newspapers. The issue was considered internationally in the context of Press freedom, in Singapore in the context of overseas influence with special reference to relations with Malaysia and the overseas Chinese.
5. For the Singapore Constitution, see *Reprints Supplement* (*Acts*), no. 14 (25 March 1966).
6. Though certain trade agreements, usually of the most-favoured-nation type, can be found in the treaty supplements to the government gazette. But, as suggested in the text, actual agreements, or their absence, reflect only a legal position and not the actuality of relationships.
7. Based on information provided by the Foreign Ministry's permanent secretary, Mr S. T. Stewart.
8. Sir Ernest Mason Satow, *A Guide to Diplomatic Practice*, 4th ed. by Sir N. Bland (Longman, London, 1964).
9. Based on an interview granted by Singapore's Commissioner in Hong Kong, Mr Lim Kee Chin.

10. Professor Wong Ling Ken, then Minister of Home Affairs, was kind enough to provide me with an account of his early experiences as ambassador to the United States.

11. See, for example, *Report of the Singapore Technical Fact-finding Mission on the Development of Tourism in Bali* (Singapore, 1968). Singapore investors are in hotels, rubber, and tobacco. Income from Singapore investments to Indonesia is not taxed by the Singapore government. Singapore has received approval to invest long-term in twenty-four projects totalling S.$110 million – not for quick profit. *The Mirror* (Singapore), 21 December 1970, p. 7.

12. Singapore, Ministry of Foreign Affairs, *Diplomatic and Consular List* (July 1970).

13. See especially Foreign Ministry Statement on establishment of diplomatic relations with Israel, Singapore Government release (11 May 1969).

14. Relevant documents are quoted in Peter Boyce, *Malaysia and Singapore in International Diplomacy: Documents and Commentaries* (Sydney University Press, Sydney, 1968) pp. 149–50.

15. Singapore's trade agreements are not necessarily guides to the republic's economic activities nor is there any necessary correlation between trade treaties and trade. Such agreements may be a consequence of legal requirements only or gestures of friendship or proofs of friendly intent and non-alignment. Other bibliographical information may be found in the bibliographical guide at the end of the essay. Russia's ambassador to Singapore, I. I. Safronov, pointed out that the Indian Ocean was no one's lake, but an international ocean – a position difficult for a non-aligned nation to fault. See *The Mirror* (Singapore) 7 December 1970, pp. 4–5.

16. With the overthrow of Sihanouk in 1970, Cambodia became known as the Khmer Republic.

17. See, for example, Michael Leifer, *The Philippine Claim to Sabah*, Hull Monographs on Southeast Asia, 1 (Interdocumentation Co., Zug, Switzerland, 1968), Leigh R. Wright, 'Historical Notes on the North Borneo Dispute', *Journal of Asian Studies* vol. XXV (May, 1966) pp. 471–84, and Philippine government, *Philippine Claim to North Borneo*, I (Manila, 1964). One reason for pressing the claim was said to be the country's need for a buffer against Singapore's Chinese communists! O. D. Corpuz, *The Philippines* (New Jersey, 1965) quoted in Leifer, op. cit., p. 73.

18. Rusk's letter is found in Boyce, op. cit., pp. 158–9. There is no documentary support that the American officials were agents of the CIA, however, and no general anti-American conclusions can safely be drawn from these events. On the strong Malaysian speeches, see ibid., p. 35.

19. For an understanding reference to U.S. Vietnam policy in the context of the overall Asian security situation, see Lee's speech at the opening ceremony of Everton Park Housing Estate, 8 November 1965.

20. This interesting case study may be found conveniently in *White Paper on Currency*, Cmd. 20 (Singapore, 1966). The correspondence confirms

that inter-government relations were conducted informally, see below, but it also reveals a Singapore stubbornness verging on distrust of the Federation's central banking policy. Yet, since the demands of Singapore cannot be called unreasonable, these negotiations reveal that there are limits to formal co-operation between two sovereign states when that co-operation requires *de jure* submission. Singapore, it might be said, was in 1966 giving high priority to the *assertion* of independence and had difficulty assigning a consistently high priority to economic policy requirements. For an account of the basic working of the Singapore–Malaysian currency system, see Frank H. H. King, *Money in British East Asia* (HMSO, London, 1957).

21. Complete sets of the speeches of government leaders are available in the Foreign Office and Prime Minister's Office. The summary which follows is also based on interviews conducted in December, 1970 with the Foreign Minister and several of his colleagues. I wish to acknowledge the very great contribution made by S. Rajaratnam, the Foreign Minister. I must also thank my old friend Mr George Thomson of the Training Division for arranging my schedule in Singapore and for providing background information, including his own essays on foreign policy: George G. Thomson, 'Changing International Scene of the World as it Affects Singapore' and 'Internal Political Developments in the '70's', in Thomson (ed.), *Singapore in the '70's* (Adult Education Board, Singapore, 1970) pp. 1–5 and 46–51 and discussions on subsequent pages.

22. For the Malayan position and the compromises of the 1957 constitution, see Frank H. H. King, *The New Malayan Nation* (Institute of Pacific Relations, New York, 1957).

23. See, for example, Lee Kuan Yew, *The Battle for Merger* (Ministry of Culture, Singapore, 1961).

24. See P. J. Boyce, 'Communist Subversion and the Foundation of Malaysia', in J. D. B. Miller and T. H. Rigby (eds), *The Disintegrating Monolith* (Australian National University Press, Canberra, 1965) pp. 184–202; and N. McH. Fletcher, *The Separation of Singapore from Malaysia* (Southeast Asia Program of Cornell University, Ithaca, New York, 1969).

25. Federation of Malaya, *Agreement Between . . . Malaya and Singapore on Common Market and Financial Arrangements*, Cmd. 27 (1963).

26. Boyce, op. cit., p. 159.

27. P. J. Boyce, 'Policy without Authority: Singapore's External Affairs Power', *Journal of Southeast Asian History*, vol. 6, no. 2 (September, 1965) pp. 87–103, gives the constitutional situation.

28. These issues are discussed in Fletcher, op. cit.

29. A conciliatory, business-first statement by the Bank of China, Singapore branch, is quoted in Boyce, *Malaysia and Singapore*, op. cit., p. 149, but there have been subsequent problems in dealing with the bank.

30. In 1965 the Malaysian-Singapore Defence Council had determined that Singapore should not reopen barter trade with Indonesia; Singapore withdrew from the council. Boyce, *Malaysia and Singapore*,

op. cit., p. 25. However, it was in 1965 also that Indonesia stated its refusal to recognize Singapore as long as the British base remained; this position was subsequently modified. Singapore's position was expressed as a willingness to negotiate with Indonesia at any time, despite Malaysian disapproval. See transcript of a press conference of Lee Kuan Yew to foreign correspondents, 11 December 1965. Singapore-Indonesian relations are officially proper but sensitive, despite better understanding and care.

31. The independence documents – the proclamation of Singapore, the proclamation on Singapore, the Agreement, and the relevant legislation – are collected in Singapore, *Government Gazette Extraordinary*, vol. VII, no. 66 (9 August 1965).

32. Helen Hughes and You Poh Seng (eds), *Foreign Investment and Industrialization in Singapore* (Wisconsin University Press, Madison, Wisconsin, 1969) is a useful commentary on this subject.

33. Quoted in Boyce, *Malaysia and Singapore*, op. cit., p. 34. See also note 20 above.

34. Cmd. 263 (HMSO, London, 1957). Cited as the *Agreement on External Defence and Mutual Assistance between the Government of the United Kingdom and the Government of the Federation of Malaya of 12 October 1957* and relevant annexes, especially Annex F relating to service lands in Singapore. See a bill entitled, 'An Act to amend the Constitution of Malaysia and the Malaysia Act', par. 13, in Singapore, *Government Gazette Extraordinary* (9 August 1965).

35. The Conservative government decision on a continued Eastern presence is outlined in the British Defence White Paper of October 1970. *The Economist* (16 November 1970, p. 6) suggested that the 'presence' was better described as an 'appearance', but Tun Razak commented that it was 'reasonable', adding that Malaysia *and Singapore* (italics added) must be the dominant partners. In London Lee Kuan Yew commented: 'It is enough to be quite credible for disruptive forces both within and without and around the region and not too big to upset the really big ones who may feel that they are being challenged. So I think it is a comfortable presence.' *The Mirror* (Singapore), 2 October 1970.

36. See presentation and S. Rajaratnam's statement quoted in *Singapore Year Book 1965* (1966), the annual review and foreign policy chapters.

37. See note 30 above.

38. A Euro-dollar is a U.S. dollar liability of a European bank; by extension the Asian-dollar market is the market in which dollar liabilities of Asian banks, in this case Singapore banks, are bought and sold. Singapore eliminated the tax on interest on foreign-owned deposits, thus making the market possible; in the view of Hong Kong bankers the market is not a valuable asset, but Singapore bankers feel otherwise.

39. See note 20 above.

40. For example, Singapore's chief of state's memorandum of 8 December 1965:

No memory however bitter of British exploitation in the past should blur our assessment of the capacity of Britain, and other white members of the Commonwealth like Australia and New Zealand ... to make a contribution to our security and to assist us in our economic development.

41. See, for example, Lee Kuan Yew, 'Address to the 75th Congregation for the conferment of an honorary degree, University of Hong Kong', 18 February 1970, in *University of Hong Kong Gazette*, vol. XVII, no. 4 (19 February 1970) pp. 50–3.

42. As, for example, Indonesia's acceptance of the British bases in Singapore and the five-power defence negotiations as Commonwealth affairs. See also note 36 above.

Chapter 9

NEW ZEALAND FOREIGN POLICY

REG HARRISON

Though not formally independent until 1947, New Zealand has just over a hundred years' experience of self-government and of self-concern with external relations. Representative control of domestic affairs was achieved in 1856 and extended in practice very rapidly to external affairs. New Zealand is a small state in the conventional senses of population size, GNP and limited political influence, but these factors of size are themselves much affected by the overwhelming importance to New Zealand of her extreme isolation in the Pacific.

IMPACT OF ISOLATION

New Zealand's isolation in the Pacific affects her climate, culture, economy and politics. Wellington, the capital, whose antipodes are close to Madrid, is 1,233 miles from Sydney, 1,400 from Antarctica, and 1,500 from Fiji. Tokyo is 5,000 miles distant, San Francisco 6,000, and London 12,000. Though the two main islands stretch north to south over 1,000 miles, all climatic influences are modified by ocean distance, and variations from the general sub-tropical to temperate conditions are the effect of the opposition of an almost continuous mountain barrier to the prevailing west winds. The country is approximately the size of the United Kingdom and, though very mountainous, it could support a much larger population than the 2·8 million recorded in December 1969.[1] Known natural resources of hydro-electric capacity, coal, natural gas, oil, geo-thermal power, extensive ironsands deposits, and various industrial minerals could provide a basis for industrialization. However, 'distance looks our way; and none knows where he

287

will lie down at night'. The New Zealand poet, Charles Brasch, thus expressed a strong cultural theme of remoteness and insecurity which has its more mundane declensions. It has, in particular, limited population-growth through immigration by accentuating the strain of separation. In recent years the number of departures from New Zealand has exceeded the number of arrivals so that the small annual increase in population, approximately 2 per cent, is attributable to births in New Zealand. Potential future growth through immigration is limited by the acceptability criterion that applicants should be able to adapt easily to New Zealand society. The European population is overwhelmingly British and emphasis has always, therefore, been placed on attracting more people from the British Isles. The Maoris, a Polynesian people, whose legend and tradition give the country its only non-British cultural flavour, numbered only 225,435 in December 1969 – approximately 9 per cent of the population. Though three-quarters of the population is urban, 50 per cent in the four main cities, and though only 16 per cent is employed in agriculture, the small population limits the potential for economies of scale in industry, commerce and administration; and the maintenance of living standards commensurate with European expectations continues to depend largely on the export of large quantities of pastoral products to very distant markets. A National Development conference convened by the Government in 1968 and 1969, recognizing the importance of the manufacturing sector to the economic expansion and independence of New Zealand, set it a growth target of 6 per cent per year, and unanimously recommended a policy of industrial protection. The statistical evidence which is available suggests that this planned rate of growth was attained, but by the end of March 1970 there was growing concern about the intensification of labour shortages, rising consumer prices, wage increases, and deterioration in industrial relations. The need to achieve an adequate level of net immigration in such conditions was stressed in governmental assessment of the situation.[2] To such effects of isolation upon internal development must be added its profound effect on foreign policy.

PRINCIPLES AND OBJECTIVES

'The fundamental subject of foreign policy,' Lippmann has said,

'is how a nation stands in relation to the principal military powers
. . . to be isolated is for any state the worst of all predica-
ments . . . to be among the many against the one is security.'³

This dictum would be accepted as axiomatic by New Zealand
decision-makers, past and present. The historical development
of New Zealand foreign policy shows that, among the broad
national objectives which have determined specific policies,
security, sought through alliance with a major military power,
is accepted as the only real indemnity for geographical isolation.
Security has not been conceived only in its military aspect.
Economic considerations have ranked high. Progress from the
crudities of pioneering existence, for all its bucolic compensa-
tions, had to be maintained if the country was to attract more
immigrants from Britain. Fulfilment of immigrant expectations
of European standards of living depended absolutely on trade.
To negotiate the conditions of New Zealand's economic security
has always been one of the priorities of external policy. In the
1970s it is paramount.

Other objectives or national values can be seen to have
influenced policy development. New Zealanders place a high
value on the cultural homogeneity of their society. The soupçon
of Polynesia is relished, but a great deal of importance is
attached to the well-being of the so-called 'old country', Britain,
and the link with it through Commonwealth co-operation.
Policies express, too, moral values, vaguely Christian, which in
a rather uncertain way New Zealanders feel should carry over
into foreign affairs.

Fortunately these objectives have usually been compatible
with each other. Until the turn of the century, moral sentiment,
security and New Zealand's colonial status all worked in the
same direction, towards loyal support of and dependence on
Britain. In the nineteenth century Britain had the commanding
position the United States now occupies. Its economic development was in advance of other countries and its relatively cheap,
well-made goods were sold in far-off markets. The lines of its
commercial empire were protected by the world's most powerful
navy. The existence of that navy encouraged British entre-
preneurs to invest and promote settlement overseas. Cheap food
and raw materials from the Empire were readily absorbed in
the British market and, in New Zealand's case, a near-complete
economic dependence on British trade resulted.

K   289

New Zealand and the rest of the Commonwealth, like the United States, accepted, sometimes without being aware of its source, the sense of security which they owed to the Royal Navy. Between Great Britain and New Zealand the strategic relationship was taken so much for granted that New Zealand's viewpoint was often expressed with as much vigour and independence in the nineteenth century as in the first thirty years of the twentieth century when there were challenges to British naval supremacy and when New Zealand was therefore more acutely conscious of how much her military security and her trade lifelines depended on the navy.

HISTORIC CONCERN WITH IMPERIAL DEFENCE AND PACIFIC SECURITY

Even during the nineteenth century, the sense of security was by no means absolute, and the factors which led to New Zealand's first efforts to obtain reassurance within the imperial and Commonwealth framework are those which since the Second World War have suggested wholesale reinsurance with the United States, and concern with the Pacific area. In particular, both New Zealand and Australia showed anxiety from time to time about their remoteness from the source of military strength. It was this which prompted New Zealand to urge upon Britain the annexation of neighbouring Pacific islands in case they should fall into foreign hands. While the strength of other European powers was still more remote than the British navy there was little to fear, but the prospect of having France or Germany on New Zealand's doorstep was cause for alarm. As early as 1848, Sir George Grey, then Governor of the colony, recommended the annexation of Fiji and the Tonga Islands.[4] After him, Prime Ministers Stout, Vogel and Seddon in succession pleaded with the British government either to annex the South Pacific islands or allow New Zealand to do so. The acquisition of New Caledonia by France in 1853 and her activities in the New Hebrides, then the German acquisition of New Guinea and activities in Samoa stimulated strong anxious protest from New Zealand to the British government.

This anxiety, however, was not that Great Britain would not ultimately be willing and completely able to defend the interests of New Zealand. It was merely a quite realistic apprehension about the time it might take for British help to arrive. Smallness, isolation and colonial status had combined to produce, as in Australia, what may best be described as the 'outpost' mentality: dependent, loyal, but insecure.

A change in the nature of the anxiety is noticeable in the twentieth century. In 1899 Britain signed away the island of Samoa to Germany as part of the more comprehensive Anglo-German Agreement. To Australia and New Zealand, this seemed to show blatantly and decisively that Britain attached very little weight to her Pacific and Australasian interests when they conflicted with her European diplomacy. The then Prime Minister, Richard Seddon, was prompted between 1900 and 1902 to make a vigorous, even ruthless attempt to gain control for New Zealand of Fiji and the other British Pacific islands.[5] Though his was not the first such attempt, it was certainly the most concentrated and highly energetic. The vision of an island empire with its prestige and economic advantages was attractive *per se*, it is true, but there is little doubt that the security problem seemed suddenly very much more acute with Germany in Samoa. In Seddon's own words,

> The colonies of Australasia feel keenly the placing in the Pacific – in the central group of the Pacific – fortified positions of foreign powers that may in the future be used as bases of attack upon them and their commerce. This surrender of Samoa will in future be a source of anxiety and entail expense on Great Britain and the colonies in preparing for and providing against eventualities. ... Some definite action of a forward character is required in the Pacific at the earliest opportune moment, for the surrender of Samoa has disheartened the natives in the island, disappointed the people of Australasia and lowered the prestige of Great Britain in this part of the globe.[6]

Seddon's annexation policy can be seen as an attempt, in part, to supply this 'definite action of a forward character' himself. He was largely unsuccessful (though the Cook Islands were handed to New Zealand in 1901), but it is possible to generalize that, from this time, there is an increased sense of the need for New Zealand to make an appraisal of her strategic interests in the Pacific and to make them a part of her general policy objectives.

291

There is abundant evidence of the increasingly Pacific orientation of policy after Seddon's venture. New Zealand's attitude towards the islands in the immediately ensuing years was one of 'Oceania for the Anglo-Saxons'. Thus, a vigorous protest was made when the New Hebrides condominium was agreed upon between Britain and France in 1906. Then, in 1914, New Zealand accepted with alacrity a British request that she render a 'great and urgent imperial service in seizing the German wireless station at Samoa'. An expeditionary force took the island and it remained under military administration until 1 May 1920, when civil government as a New Zealand mandate was established. Prime Minister Massey had made his determination that either Britain or New Zealand should control the island very clear at the Peace Conference.[7] His arguments had been couched primarily in strategic terms.

After 1918 the vision of an island empire died, but the strategic importance attached to the islands can be seen all the more clearly. The Cook Islands and Samoa were soon regarded as, economically, more of a burden than an asset, and little enthusiasm was roused by the transfer of new responsibilities from Great Britain to New Zealand either in 1923 or 1926 when the Ross Dependency and the Union Group respectively were brought under New Zealand administration. But the basic strategic premiss was never really questioned. The islands should not be in the hands of a potential enemy, and if their defence necessitated the exercise of responsibilities by New Zealand, then such responsibilities would be accepted. This was the New Zealand attitude at the Imperial Defence Conference in 1939. When the conference dealt with the Pacific islands, New Zealand was, in a sense, the pacemaker, pressing their strategic importance on the conference.[8] When war did come, 8 Brigade group, a force of 3,000 men, was sent to garrison Fiji. Later, as the development of Nandi airport increased the island's importance, another 4,000 men were sent to bring the garrison strength up to two brigades. Most of New Zealand's anti-aircraft equipment was sent as well.

It is not only in policy towards the islands that the new emphasis on the Pacific can be discerned. Naval policy was affected. As British naval strength declined in relation to other powers in the Pacific, the consciousness of dependence on it became more acute. In 1902, New Zealand welcomed the signing of the Anglo-Japanese alliance, glad to have Japanese strength on the side of the British Empire. In 1903 she raised her contribution to the Royal Navy from £20,000 annually to £40,000.[9] In 1908 the sum was raised to £100,000 and in the following year a battle cruiser for the Home Fleet was presented as a gift from New Zealand.

From time to time, attempts were made to make the British guarantee more explicit through a unified imperial defence system. Richard Seddon, at the Third Imperial Conference in 1902, advocated imperial economic integration and a system of defence by imperial service troops. His proposals did not find favour, but after his death Prime Ministers Ward and Massey advocated a more closely integrated Empire. Ward's idea of a British Empire parliament would have been one kind of affirmation of Britain's responsibility, and would have given the smallest domininion a formal voice in the formulation of imperial decisions.

This integration policy was, of course, motivated very strongly by sentiment for the mother country, but the importance attached to strategic considerations is shown by the fact that, as it continued to prove unsuccessful, attempts were made to reduce the reliance on Britain and the Empire. After the First World War, a change in naval policy decided on before the war was put into effect. A local New Zealand Division of the Royal Navy was formed, vessels of which were stationed in New Zealand waters, partly manned by New Zealand personnel and controlled exclusively by the New Zealand government in peacetime. By 1919 there was some anxiety in New Zealand about Japan. It was true that she had been an ally during the war and was still allied with Britain, but her expansionist mood was unmistakable. In 1915 she had presented the twenty-one demands which would have made China a vassal state. After the war she insisted on staying in Shantung province, which during the war she had occupied as a German sphere of influence. She sent more troops than any other power in the Siberian intervention and stayed in Siberia when the other powers withdrew. Her navy grew rapidly.

New Zealand's anxieties were lulled slightly by the results of the Washington conference of 1921 to 1922, which stabilized the relative naval strengths of Britain, America and Japan, and guaranteed that there would be no change in the status, or fortification, of the Pacific islands. New Zealand welcomed this check to Japanese strength and expansion, but did not find it sufficient cause to neglect another project which would counterbalance Japanese strength – the construction of a great British Pacific base at Singapore. When, in 1924, the British Labour government decided not to go on with the development of the base, the New Zealand Prime Minister, Massey, wrote a strong letter of protest to Ramsay MacDonald.

> I regret exceedingly that . . . the government of the United Kingdom do not intend to proceed with what is looked on as one of the most important proposals connected with the defence of the Empire. India, Australia, New Zealand and a number of Crown Colonies are intensely concerned in this matter and are looking to the present British government to remember that every country of the Empire and every citizen of the Empire are entitled to protection from the possibility of attack by a foreign foe. You say that your government stands for international co-operation through a strengthened and enlarged League of Nations. In reply I must say that if the defence of the Empire is to depend on the League only then it may turn out to have been a pity that the League was ever brought into being.[10]

In 1927, the project having been revived, the New Zealand government announced its decision to contribute £1,000,000 to its cost, although, for New Zealand, 1927 was a depression year.

COLLECTIVE SECURITY THROUGH THE LEAGUE OF NATIONS

The New Zealand Labour Party, which became a political force after 1919, was very critical of these developments in policy. It opposed naval and arms expenditures as a matter of principle, and Mr Harry Holland, leader of the party, was a very keen critic of the Singapore base project.[11] The ideals of the League of Nations, as they were then commonly understood in New Zealand, reinforced these principles.

However, when the party achieved power in 1935, the international situation had so far deteriorated that no fundamental change in policy was made, though a new emphasis was placed on the League as an instrument of collective security. Sir

Samuel Hoare's powerful speech before the League in September, 1935, during the Ethiopian crisis, expressing Britain's determination to co-operate with the League in collective resistance to aggression, had won commendation from both parties in New Zealand. Mr Walter Nash, President of the New Zealand Labour Party, in the first big speech of the general election campaign, made it quite clear that the party, which had always been solidly behind the League, was also solidly behind the idea of collective security. The concept of collective security, still untried, had great appeal for a small state like New Zealand as a way of reducing an increasingly uneasy security dependence on the Commonwealth. A short time after the Labour Party took office, the Hoare–Laval Pact, which would have conceded Ethiopian territory to Italy, was announced. New Zealand promptly advised the British government that it had taken the sanctions proposals seriously and could not associate itself with the Pact. In 1936, against Britain's advice, the Labour government submitted to the League proposals for strengthening it. It advocated that enforcement of League decisions be automatic and overwhelming. New Zealand declared herself willing to take part in sanctions including complete economic boycott and the use of force against an aggressor. She was in favour of an international force. When the Spanish civil war began, New Zealand, in an attitude markedly different from that of Great Britain, advocated at Geneva that the League look into the conflict and do something about it, rather than adopt a policy of non-intervention.[12]

A cynical view of New Zealand policy at this time would have it that a small country, remote from the scenes of trouble and without the responsibilities of power, could afford to take the high moral tone. Such a view may be, in part, justified, but it is not the main explanation of New Zealand's attitude. It overlooks the fact that New Zealand, because she was small and remote, had an interest in making a collective security system effective. She declared herself willing to make the sacrifices which would have been required of her in the application of sanctions.

It is not surprising then that the Labour government adopted a similar attitude towards League responsibilities in the Pacific area. China appealed to the League Council in September 1937 when she was invaded by Japan. New Zealand demanded positive League action. Railwaymen and watersiders proclaimed a boycott on Japanese imports and on goods destined for Japan. New Zealand and Russia alone were still criticizing the weak attitude of the League in 1938. The principles of the League and of collective security harmonized with New Zealand's self-interest in the face of the relative decline in British strength and resolution, particularly in the Pacific. Soviet attitudes to the League and collective security were governed by analogous factors. Russia was isolated because she was as politically distant from the rest of Europe as New Zealand was geographically distant. Like New Zealand, she would have made the League her protection. Like New Zealand, she was disappointed.

The emphasis on collective security did not, however, lead to a neglect of other policies designed to lessen New Zealand's geographic distance from military assistance. The Singapore base, which the Labour party had once strongly opposed, was supported just as strongly by the Labour government. As far as New Zealand's own armed forces were concerned, the emphasis was on defence of New Zealand and of British interests in the Pacific. As late as June and July 1939, the Prime Minister, appealing for recruits, promised that no one would be compelled to serve overseas.[13] By 1939, it was clear that very little could be expected from the League and collective security. New Zealand's only possible source of protection in the Pacific was Britain, and, in the Pacific, Britain was weak in spite of her assurances. As a result, New Zealand concentrated on persuading England to strengthen itself at Singapore while doing everything possible to diminish reliance on help from that quarter.

During the war which followed, two events, occurring within a space of only three years, gave that policy the fundamentally different aspect which it has today.

ALLIANCE WITH THE UNITED STATES

First, Winston Churchill, as First Lord of the Admiralty, had, in 1939, assured New Zealand that Britain, through the Royal Navy, would give high priority to the defence of the Southern Dominions if they were attacked. Accepting this assurance, New Zealand denuded herself of trained soldiers, despatching them to the battlefields. In June 1940 New Zealand was informed by Britain that if Japan came into the war, no British fleet could be sent to the Far East, and the Commonwealth would have to rely on the United States to defend its interests in that area. 'At that time,' observes Professor Wood, 'and for the better part of a year afterwards, the United States Government made it perfectly clear that it would be just too bad if the British communities in the Pacific got into trouble with Japan.'[14] The second event was in 1941. America was, willy-nilly, brought into the war and filled the power vacuum in the Pacific, assuming the role which Britain had perforce abandoned.

In retrospect, these two events mark a turning point in New Zealand foreign policy. From this time New Zealand began to act 'as a nation and not as a colony'. New Zealand had participated in the Versailles Conference at the end of the First World War, had signed the treaty in its own right and had become a member of the League of Nations, but, though rigorously active in the League from 1935 to 1939, there was still a marked tendency to follow a British lead and to pursue New Zealand interests through representations to London. From 1941, the transformation was rapid. Between 1941 and 1942, diplomatic posts were established in the four main Pacific border countries, the United States, Canada, Australia and Russia. In 1943 an act was passed establishing for the first time a separate Department of External Affairs. In 1944 New Zealand signed the Canberra Pact with Australia, announcing that the two countries were qualified for leadership in the Pacific and had a vital concern with the peace, welfare and good government of the area. They declared their right to be associated in the planning of the international organization envisaged in the Moscow declaration, and their readiness to assume responsibility for policing areas of the South-West or South Pacific. In 1947, New Zealand assumed complete formal as well as practical sovereignty by adopting the Statute of Westminster. In 1951, signing a peace settlement with Japan, she felt it necessary, as in the past, to obtain some assurance of assistance in the Pacific from a powerful ally. She turned, not to Britain as she had done before the war, but to the United States, signing the ANZUS Pact, a pact specifically relating to the Pacific area. Subsequently, in 1954, she signed the SEATO Pact, another regional pact whose main strength is that of the United States. Her military commitment to the Commonwealth has been transferred from the Middle East to Southeast Asia. New Zealand has assumed the role of donor member in the

297

Colombo Plan and has joined ECAFE. In the matter of recognition of Communist China, she has followed the lead of the United States rather than that of Britain.

ECONOMIC SECURITY

No comparable transformation has taken place in the economic field, though considerable efforts have been made to diversify markets and products.[15] The effect of the depression after 1930 was the widespread growth of economic nationalism through the raising of tariff barriers. For New Zealand, dependent on trade, too small for self-sufficiency, this resulted in a growing, now preponderant, weight being attached to economic rather than political relationships as a concern of her diplomacy. From the abandonment of British free trade in 1932, trade reciprocity between Commonwealth countries was governed by the Ottawa agreements of that year. During the Second World War, Britain became the sole purchaser of New Zealand's dairy, meat and wool exports under bulk purchase agreements which provided Britain with cheap food throughout the war. These agreements were terminated in 1954, but in subsequent agreements in 1959 and 1966 the supply of high quality, cheap food from New Zealand to Britain has been maintained. New Zealand grants minimum rights of preference for British goods in the New Zealand market and has in practice afforded preferences going well beyond the contractual obligation.

The wartime bulk purchase agreements and the Ottawa agreements have helped to maintain the pattern of trade dependence which now threatens New Zealand's economic prosperity as Britain negotiates entry to the European Economic Community. Uncertainty is compounded by the fact that the agreement of 1966 became renegotiable in September 1970 to govern trade after September 1972. The proportion of New Zealand exports which went to Britain in 1958 was 55·8 per cent. By 1969 it had been reduced to 38·5 per cent. Britain, however, still takes 90 per cent of New Zealand butter exports, 90 per cent of lamb exports, and 80 per cent of cheese exports.[16] The pastoral industry as a whole, including wool, hides, casein, skim milk and various specialty products, which is sustained by the basic British trade, accounted for 82 per cent of all export earnings in 1968–69. Efforts to reduce dependence on the British market

Table 1 *New Zealand Exports*

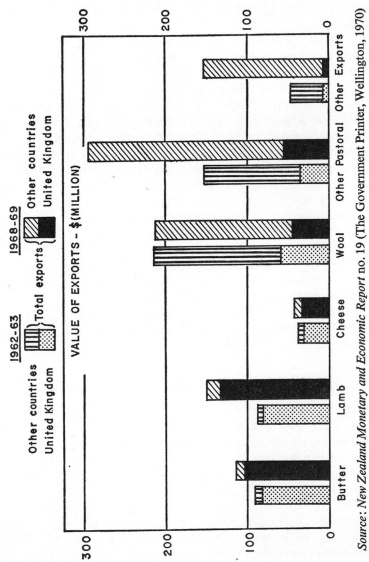

VALUE OF EXPORTS – $(MILLION)

Source: New Zealand Monetary and Economic Report no. 19 (The Government Printer, Wellington, 1970) p. 19.

have been impeded by the Common Agricultural Policy of the EEC. This has effectively eliminated any Community market for New Zealand dairy products and has reduced the potential of other markets by heavily subsidizing competing Community exports.

General agricultural protectionism has been an additional impediment to reduced dependence on the British market. The new strategic guarantor, the United States, shows no signs of being prepared to accept a comparable economic role. She obtained a waiver under GATT in 1955 to impose quotas on agricultural products, including dairy products. This has prevented expansion of New Zealand exports, though beef sales have become important, limited by a voluntary quota system. Japan is protecting and stimulating a domestic pastoral industry, and growth of New Zealand exports there has been mainly in forest products and mutton. Thus the short- and long-term prospects for the vital pastoral sector look very bleak. A recent survey and report summarized the position starkly: 'No prospect exists for the rapid development of significant alternative markets for the present quantities of dairy products and lamb sold to Britain.'[17] Economically New Zealand's relations with Britain remain critical. (See Table 1.)

In the formulation and execution of her foreign policy also, New Zealand still operates within a British institutional framework and political tradition.

MACHINERY AND PROCESSES

Constitutional Setting

New Zealand offers a very pure example of the Westminster constitutional model in something very close to its classic form, a form which partially determines the foreign policy-making process. New Zealand's size, however, imposes its own logic on the operational reality.

The role of the Queen as head of state, represented by a governor-general appointed on the advice of New Zealand ministers, is, in this context, minimal. The governor-general occasionally provides some relief for the Prime Minister in the entertainment of important foreign guests, and some governors-general have been of some assistance to New Zealand through their influential British contacts. However, the constitutional responsibility of the government places the main policy formulating role squarely with the Cabinet. Cabinets are small, being drawn from the majority party in the small, single-chamber parliament with only eighty members (eighty-four after the 1972 election). All ministers, consequently, have several portfolios.

The Prime Minister is ordinarily also the Foreign Minister, though there have been a few exceptions. This is a reflection of the role of the Prime Minister within the Cabinet where, in general, his functions fit in well with the kind of interests he must assert as Foreign Minister. As will be shown below, in common with other small, highly dependent states, there is a very close connection in New Zealand between economic policy, commercial interests and foreign policy and defence policy. The Prime Minister's co-ordinating role in Cabinet must, therefore, also operate in the context of external affairs. The other side of this coin is that other ministers also take an active part in policy-making, in particular the Minister for Overseas Trade and the Minister of Industries and Commerce, portfolios currently held by the same minister – the Deputy Prime Minister. The relations between the Prime Minister as Foreign Minister and the minister with the primary responsibility for external trade will vary with personal factors. Just before and after 1970, the prospect of British entry to the Common Market and the effects it might have on New Zealand trade were a reason for great activity on New Zealand's behalf in Europe by the then Minister of Overseas Trade, Mr J. Marshall. The fact that the Prime Minister, Sir Keith Holyoake, had been in office since 1960, had been ill and was near retirement, accounted, in part, for the range of responsibility on this vital question left to his deputy and prospective political heir, Mr Marshall. In the early sixties Sir Keith took a much more active role in reacting to the Conservative government application for EEC membership.

In the discharge of his responsibility for foreign affairs the Foreign Minister is accountable, constitutionally, to parliament. Two parties, Labour and National (conservative-liberal) dominate parliament. One effect of size in an egalitarian parliamentary democracy is that a substantial, not merely vociferous, 'public opinion' can have considerable impact on policy-making. The small size of parliament makes every member a frequent contributor to debates (which are broadcast in their entirety)

301

and, therefore, a national figure. The short life of parliament, three years, recommends an ear-to-the-ground rather than nose-in-the-air posture for the individual member and makes parliament a responsive body. Full-scale debate on foreign affairs and the raising of foreign issues in general debates are now frequent, but the parliamentary Foreign Affairs Committee is the specialist organ of the House in this respect. Drawn from both parties, with a government majority, it includes the chief spokesman for the Opposition on foreign policy. The Committee's chief significance is in facilitating the flow of information to parliament from ministers and officials. This is supplemented by the visits made by parliamentary delegations to all parts of the world for personal observation and briefing. New Zealand politicians with any substantial parliamentary service behind them are likely to have had an opportunity to meet the leading politicians and government members in areas of major concern and to be given on-the-spot briefings by the local New Zealand mission. This is undoubtedly one of the main reasons for the higher level of interest and informed debate in Parliament in recent years. Within the last two years there has been a marked disposition to discuss foreign policy at a very early stage in decision formulation within party caucus, caucus meetings being a regular weekly affair for both major parties, allowed for in the timetabling of the House. The importance of caucus in every field of policy-making is a function of size. Ministers form just over one-third of the total strength of the government parliamentary party in most parliaments and there is no question of remote ministerial dominance of the rank and file. Parliament is small. Relationships are intimate and egalitarian.

No convention of consultation with, and briefing of, the Leader of the Opposition to a degree going beyond the briefing of the Committee of Foreign Affairs has grown up, though in times of crisis the close personal connections which exist between members of the government and the opposition in the small parliament ensure that if Leaders of the Opposition wanted information on some aspect they would be briefed by ministers or officials.

The major constitutional instrument of foreign policy formulation in New Zealand is, however, the Cabinet and the various committees of Cabinet in which, where appropriate, discussion is initiated. The Overseas Trade Committee, the Cabinet Eco-

nomic Committee, and the Defence Committee are the commit-
tees principally concerned in foreign policy matters – there is no
special committee with an overall foreign policy interest. The
Overseas Trade Committee, which, because of the nature of
New Zealand's overseas concerns, is the main committee with
foreign policy interests, is made up of the Prime Minister, the
Minister of Overseas Trade (in the chair), the Minister of
Finance, the Minister of Agriculture and the Ministry of Cus-
toms. Co-ordination at the official level, through the Officials
Committee, is also very important.

Foreign Ministry: Role
The clear interest of several departments in overseas policy
helps to define the role of the Ministry of Foreign Affairs in the
policy-making process. Because its development is more recent
than that of comparable departments in Western Europe, it is
not difficult to see the Foreign Ministry evolving in response to
a need not met by other specialized departments in the modern
state. It has fulfilled the secretarial function indicated in the
British designation of the minister as secretary: dealing with
correspondence with foreign governments, making contacts
with their ambassadors, and arranging overseas representation.
In comparison with other departments, the Ministry of Foreign
Affairs is a smaller, secretarial operation, conveniently located
in the Prime Minister's office. The total personnel of the department at home and abroad, excluding shorthand typists, was just
over 300 at the beginning of 1971. The degree to which particular
people in the office, because of continuity, personal expertise,
acceptability to their ministers, and contacts they have abroad,
do in fact influence foreign policy in contributing to decisions
that the government takes, can never be accurately stated and it
changes over time. The secretarial-executant function, however,
is probably more important than the policy-influencing function
in so far as it is possible to separate the two, and anything like
a critical overview of long-terms trends in policy was lacking
until the late fifties.[18]

Increasingly, however, by a process of accretion of staff
numbers and range of New Zealand interests, the determination
of priorities and the co-ordination of activities has been added
to the functions of the ministry, and to some degree formalized
inside the ministry by the creation of a small research division

303

in 1969 and by a limited public involvement by officials in foreign policy debate. The important decision taken in 1955 to station forces in Asia is a landmark in this extension of responsibility, in that it was a geographic expression of self-assertion based on a conception of New Zealand's own area of strategic interest. Though the Department of Defence necessarily plays its part in the review and development of this conception, the role of the Ministry of Foreign Affairs as part of the Prime Ministerial office is much more important. The smallness and consequent intimacy of New Zealand government very much reduces the problem of defence, trade and foreign policy co-ordination and lessens the need for formalization of the process, but in so far as it is formalized it takes place within the Foreign Ministry. The Prime Minister's department and the Foreign Affairs Department are run as one unit and the Secretary of Foreign Affairs is permanent head of the Prime Minister's department. During the Second World War the permanent head was also Secretary of the War Cabinet, the Prime Minister's department being responsible for defence co-ordination through its own Defence Secretariat. The functions of the Secretariat have been taken over by the unified Ministry of Defence which was established in 1964. A close relationship is still maintained between Defence and the defence division of the Ministry of Foreign Affairs.

Change in the domestic environment in which the ministry operates has also contributed to the development of the critical role. Without the stimulus of a lively interest in, and debate on, foreign policy in the public domain, a small foreign service is unlikely to be productive of ideas and criticism. Public debate on foreign policy in New Zealand in the aftermath of the Second World War was restricted to a small minority and had little impact. To the professionals, the development of the Cold War presented an apparently unambiguous argument for Western alignment and strong United Nations support – not in practice presenting any conflict while that organization was reacting mainly to American initiatives. The level of activity required in implementing this policy, however, was intensive, and a departmental ethos of hard work and attention to detail prevailed which was not conducive to the critical re-evaluation of the policy necessary in the light of changes in the international system. However, the scope of public debate was extended. The universities, bodies like the Institute of International Affairs, radio commentators and journalists took an increasingly critical view of policy in Asia and, in particular, the war in Vietnam. To this the department eventually responded, joining the debate notably by co-operating with the New Zealand Institute of Public Administration in a symposium on New Zealand foreign policy, the proceedings of which were published,[19] and also undertaking a joint study with a committee of the Wellington branch of the New Zealand Institute of International Affairs on New Zealand policy in Southeast Asia. In 1969, the Prime Minister in his capacity as Foreign Minister, and later the Permanent Secretary and other senior members of the Foreign Ministry, addressed meetings of the New Zealand Institute of International Affairs. In his address the Prime Minister summed up the change that has taken place since 1955:

> In the past too many people have ignored the issues and pretended that there was no problem. They have been content because they believed that New Zealand was tagging along behind Britain and that this was the obvious – the 'loyal' – thing to do. This attitude is clearly irrelevant today and has been irrelevant for years.[20]

Organization, and Relations with Other Departments
The Department of External Affairs, created in 1943, became the Ministry of Foreign Affairs on 1 March 1970. The original name probably reflected practice in other Commonwealth countries – for example, Canada and Australia. Departmental organization[21] makes no distinction between officers serving overseas and members of the department in Wellington. Career planning attempts to ensure that any officer serves one four-year term in three at home, though senior members of the department may find their overseas postings outrun this proportion, diplomatic representation having increased steadily since the war.

The department is broken down geographically into divisions: a Pacific and Antarctic division; African and Middle Eastern Affairs; the Asian division; a Commonwealth and Western Europe division which also deals with the United States. Separate functional divisions for economics, legal questions, information and cultural affairs, administration, communications, consular activities, defence, external aid, libraries, protocol, United Nations and research also exist. Consular posts overseas are part of the Foreign Ministry. Separate trade commissions are part of the Department of Industries and Commerce. Trade commissioners with embassies are part of the diplomatic establishment under the authority of the ambassador. The top appointment to the major posts in the Commonwealth is normally made on political grounds. London, Canberra, Ottawa, and Kuala Lumpur are in this category. Other missions have also at times been headed by political appointees. The practice does not go uncriticized,[22] but is defended as conventional political patronage. In 1970 there were sixteen career and five non-career heads of mission of ambassadorial status. Specialist functions are not accentuated in the recruitment programme, but the economic and legal divisions are staffed by people with appropriate academic qualifications and experience. New Zealand's size has not prevented the development of an excellent educational system which provides ample opportunities for tertiary education. There are six universities, the standards of which are comparable with British universities. The public service as a whole provides an attractive career for graduates in a country where industrial opportunities are somewhat limited. For the Foreign Ministry, the majority are recruited specifically by the department, though there is some cross-fertilization from other departments. In the first few years after the department was formed, a number of academically well-qualified people were recruited who had been servicemen during the war. The first permanent head of the department, who remained in this position until 1966, welded this group into the 'band of brothers' who now fill most of the senior posts at home and overseas. A recruitment programme to meet the expanded needs of the department in the fifties maintained an emphasis on good academic background. Social background has no official importance in the selective process, and in fact plays little part in New Zealand life in general. A tendency, however, to regard the British foreign service as one of exemplary professionalism may be said to have left some mark on the department in assessing the personal qualities of recruits. There is, among other departments in the public service, some disposition to see the Foreign Ministry as a self-consciously 'gentlemanly' body with pretensions to élite status. Relatively rapid promotion within the small but expanding department and the conditions of overseas service also tend to promote the image of privilege. A person who has been in the department for ten years and who has shown exceptional ability could expect to be in the very senior position of first secretary or counsellor in a post of middle-range importance. And after a few years of overseas service he will reappear in Wellington with a smart, duty-free car and some of the other outward signs of the life which Adlai Stevenson summed up as 'alcohol, protocol and Geritol'.

The working relationship between the ministry and other departments is not, however, affected. The fact that some senior people have been brought in from other departments, Treasury, Industries and Commerce, and Overseas Trade, has helped to ensure amicable co-ordination, and there is no sense in which any of the concerned departments is wedded to a particular point of view because it has a departmental origin. The very high calibre of Treasury economists ensures that they play an important part in discussions of foreign economic policy, but it would not be true to say that any one department is dominant. Relations with the producer boards (which exist for the major export products) are close but not formalized. Senior officials of the boards have close personal contacts with members of the Officials Committee, which serves the economic sub-committee of Cabinet, under the chairmanship of the secretary of the Treasury. The producer boards have separate representation overseas and, though contact is close, they are not part of the diplomatic post.

The timing of recruitment and the range of functions performed within the department has not led to the emergence of a particular set of attitudes. Some disillusionment with the United Nations after the first high hopes which led New Zealand to take such an active part at San Francisco undoubtedly set in, but, as the range of activities and interests, particularly of an economic kind, developed, there has been no difficulty for career officers in finding interests which absorbed their energies and which they have found worthwhile. If, for some, professional cynicism has led to a preoccupation with technical competence, there remain 'ideas' men for whom wider issues are important.

METHODS AND STYLE OF FOREIGN RELATIONS

Standing Conferences and International Organization
Standing conferences have become increasingly large and the

weight which a small country like New Zealand can exert has become progressively less. The disposition in the past to attach very considerable weight to this form of diplomatic activity has therefore been weakened, and the bilateral connection through major alliances and major trading partners is correspondingly more important. Relations with the United States, Australia and Japan are pursued primarily through bilateral contacts, at the diplomatic and political level, as they are with Britain. The Commonwealth, with its standing consultative institutions, has therefore much declined in importance as it has increased in size. Perceiving herself as one of the outnumbered, outvoiced, older dominions in an association in which regional affinities and disparities are growing and whose whole future appears uncertain, New Zealand is little disposed to rely on Commonwealth institutions as instruments of her policy. Similar considerations apply to the United Nations. The United Nations Organization has undoubtedly declined in importance as an instrument of New Zealand foreign policy since the period of vigorous activity of the New Zealand delegation of 1945 led by the Labour Prime Minister, Mr Frazer, at San Francisco. Then Mr Frazer pressed for an unequivocal collective security guarantee, for the abolition of the rule of unanimity of the great powers on the Security Council, for extension of the competence of the General Assembly, for definition of trusteeship responsibilities, and for international protected status for UN officials. A body with real powers, capable of taking effective action in the interest of international security, in which a New Zealand voice would have equal formal weight to any other sovereign state would, it then seemed, obviously benefit a small country and enlarge its influence. The limited modifications of the Dumbarton Oaks proposals which ensued were, consequently, a disappointment. New Zealand thereafter continued to play its part, sending troops to Korea, a police contingent to Cyprus of UNFICYP (now withdrawn), and, though she had not supported UN resolutions opposed to the British, French, and Israeli action in Suez in 1956, offering troops (which were refused) to the UN force supervising withdrawal. There could be no disguising, however, that the United Nations Organization had become a forum for, and instrument of, the Cold War. Though New Zealand usually found itself able to support the United States, the organization itself became less and less a focus for her internationalist idealism. Then, as the United States and her allies found majorities more difficult to obtain with increased Afro-Asian membership, a sense of frustration ensued. Current attitudes are well summed up by the present permanent secretary of the Foreign Ministry, G. R. Laking,

I am hopeful that some lessons will have been learned from the fruitless efforts of the past decade – the denunciations, the striking of violent but ineffective attitudes, the subordination of deeds to words – and that those who command majorities in the General Assembly will see the value of seeking to marshal international opinion behind courses of action that if restrained, are reasonable.[23]

Permanent Missions
There are official New Zealand missions in thirty-eight countries. In Australia, Canada, India and the United States there are a number of consular posts in addition to the main mission. Some ambassadors, high commissioners, or trade commissioners are accredited to adjoining countries as a means of reducing the considerable financial burden of diplomatic representation for so small a country. A notable development in recent years is the establishment of increased representation in Western Europe. Though the Paris embassy was established in 1949, full resident posts of embassy status were only established in Bonn in 1966, The Hague, 1967, Brussels, 1967 and Rome, 1967. The most important and longest-established post overseas is London, to which an Agent-General was first appointed almost a century ago. Washington, Canberra and Ottawa are next in antiquity and importance, then the Asian and Pacific posts. In Europe, apart from the EEC posts, the presence of a Consulate General in Athens indicates the importance of lamb in the Greek diet! There are no Eastern European, Middle Eastern, Latin American or African diplomatic posts. This is because the pattern of posts and their size is a reflection of the prevailing conception of New Zealand's security and economic interests. There is a permanent mission to the United Nations. London and Washington are composite posts, and the London post is different from all others in having a representative of almost every department of government. In administrative terms these officers are part of the high commissioner's diplomatic staff, but

their functions are specialized and subject to close direct contact with their Wellington departments and they are the eyes and ears of their own department, reporting through the high commission only in respect of the general functions which are the concern of Foreign Affairs. Their technical specialized functions are carried out as a branch of the home department. In other embassies and high commissions their tasks are performed by officers of Foreign Affairs.

Generally speaking, the establishment of posts has been cautious. It has to be demonstrated to New Zealand ministers that the interests of New Zealand in the area are fairly diverse and weighty. Posts have not been opened as a mark of status. The Japanese post dates from the Peace Treaty and is a recognition of Japan's dominant position in the Pacific. Delhi followed. There is no representation in Pakistan. The establishment of an embassy in Indonesia marked the end of confrontation. A lack of interest in African affairs and a lack of response to African aspirations and resentments was acknowledged in an address by a member of the service to the Institute of International Affairs in 1966.[24] Continuity of rugby tends to have a higher priority than African sensitivity in relations between South Africa and New Zealand. In the United Nations a determinedly moderating stand on issues with racial overtones often places New Zealand among a minority opposing resolutions sponsored by the African states on Southern African questions.

The principal value of overseas representation for New Zealand is the maintenance of the continuous contact with local people and interests which facilitates the work of negotiating and conference teams from Wellington.[25]

Ad hoc *Missions*
The weight of New Zealand's interests are economic rather than political, though security interests also bulk large and are reflected in the disposition of New Zealand diplomatic resources. *Ad hoc* missions overseas, led by a minister, and/or a senior official of the department most concerned, are frequently used for complicated economic negotiations. The importance of the Common Market issue and the changes that are taking place generally in world trade have very much increased, for example, the burden of the Minister of Overseas Trade as negotiator of New Zealand's overseas relations and the focus of the working

relationship between the concerned departments. He will have with him on a visit to Europe, as a principal adviser, his own Permanent Under-Secretary or the Deputy Secretary of External Affairs, and will take others from both departments. His team is then completed by senior members of the very large London High Commission. He is briefed by both departments, and as chairman of the sub-committee of Cabinet he also gets advice from his ministerial colleagues on the European Economic Community.

Mr Marshall's shuttle travel between Europe and Wellington illustrates the importance now placed on bilateral negotiations and the relative disillusion with multilateral arrangements like GATT. As the National Development Conference of May 1969 noted, 'It has often been claimed that New Zealand gains little advantage from being a contracting party to the GATT, and the GATT itself has been accused of being more use to industrialised nations than to agricultural producers ... [restricting] the possibility of negotiating bilateral trading deals.'[26] New Zealand has complained in GATT about import restrictions on agricultural products which a number of countries apply contrary to GATT rules. The GATT Working Party on Dairy Products was established in November 1969 at New Zealand's initiative to reduce subsidies and price-cutting in the dairy trade. However, the principal barrier to progress in this field has been the EEC, which has not succeeded in producing a negotiating mandate. Bilateral negotiation mainly with Britain as guarantor of New Zealand's interests in the entry negotiations and directly with EEC countries is, therefore, regarded as being more useful.

An illustration, in a different context, of a typical New Zealand foreign policy initiative and its implementation shows a similar preference for bilateralism.

The New Zealand/Japanese Fishing Dispute[27]
Japanese trawling around New Zealand's coasts began in the late 1950s. It consisted of long-line tuna fishing between 70 and 250 miles offshore. There was little adverse reaction from the fishing industry or press. Between 1959 and 1963 Japanese vessels started trawling. As trawlers must operate in depths of less than 100 fathoms, these activities took place on New Zealand's continental shelf, at distances some ten to fifteen miles offshore. Japanese vessels were larger and more efficient,

and were operating in grounds hitherto used exclusively by New Zealand's fishing boats. This led to a direct conflict of fishing interests. During this period the Geneva Law of the Sea Conference (held in 1960) just failed by one vote to reach international agreement on giving each country, as of right, up to twelve miles for fishing limits. After failure of the conference, public debate and press comment in New Zealand focused on the possibility that, for lack of multilateral agreement, individual state claims might represent the only course open to a coastal state threatened with close-in foreign fishing. There were calls from sections of New Zealand's fishing industry for unilateral assertion of a twelve-mile exclusive fishing zone. Questions were asked in parliament about foreign fishermen. During this period, there was still some chance that international agreement might be reached on a twelve-mile exclusive fishing zone. During the period 1961 to 1963 Japanese activities increased. New forms of fishing – long-line fishing for snapper – began, and Japanese vessels moved even closer to New Zealand's coast. By 1963 it was clear that no international agreement was going to be reached on the question of exclusive fishing zones, and that states would have to claim exclusive fishing zones on a unilateral basis. The U.K. and Canada, among others, both announced their intentions to claim twelve miles exclusive fishery zones and, subsequently, enacted legislation to this effect.

1964 to 1965 was a period of intense Japanese long-line fishing around the New Zealand coast. There were numerous sightings of Japanese vessels. The experimental stage of Japanese fishing was over. It was transformed into a systematic and intensive exploitation of New Zealand's offshore waters. Greater surveillance of Japanese activities was embarked upon by the navy. There were numerous sightings of Japanese vessels reported 'poaching' inside New Zealand's territorial waters, i.e. inside the three-mile limit. Protests were made at governmental level with the Japanese. By now it was evident beyond doubt that New Zealand waters were becoming an established Japanese fishing ground. Japanese activities had become a major irritant to the New Zealand fishing industry, and there were numerous reports of incidents of line- and net-cutting involving New Zealand and Japanese fishermen. The New Zealand fishing industry was worried that stocks of snapper, in particular, would be depleted by indiscriminate fishing by foreigners, and there was worry that Japanese activities, if allowed to persist, might establish some sort of 'historic' or other acquired right to fish close in to the New Zealand coast.[28]

The stage was now set for the government to move towards the establishment of a nine-mile exclusive fishing zone outside the three-mile territorial limit (i.e. in reality, a twelve-mile exclusive fishing zone), and in 1965 parliament enacted the Territorial Sea and Fishing Zone Act. Full reasons for passage of the legislation (particularly the creation of an exclusive fishing zone beyond the territorial sea) were set out by the Prime Minister in the course of second reading debate. The Prime Minister made it quite clear that the act of taking the fishing zone had been in conformity with 'sufficient precedent'. (At that time some fifty or more states had exclusive fishing zones of twelve miles.) The Prime Minister implied that Japan had not established any customary or other right to continue fishing in the zone, and that that was why the legislation contained no provisions for 'phasing out' foreign fishing activities.

During the passage of legislation through parliament, the Japanese government had made no reaction. Immediately after the Act was passed in September 1965, however, Japanese representations led to lengthy talks between the two governments during which the Japanese sought modification of the legislation in order to take account of their interests. From the domestic political standpoint, the belated Japanese approach posed difficulties. For one thing, the Bill had been put through as an exclusionist measure aimed directly at the Japanese fishermen; for another, it had not been anticipated that, with a record of only one or two years of substantive fishing, the Japanese would seek any continuation of their activities – and it had been on the latter ground that no permissive provision to enable foreign fishing to continue for any length of time had been included in the Act. The talks ended without any agreement.

There followed a Japanese proposal that the two countries should jointly go to the International Court of Justice for a decision on the validity of New Zealand's action. Briefly, the Japanese position was its traditional one in matters such as this: that it did not recognize the right of a coastal state to assert exclusive jurisdiction over seas beyond the three-mile limit; that the validity of a unilateral extension of an exclusive fishing zone to twelve miles depended on prior agreement between the coastal state and any other state affected by that action; and that, in the case of New Zealand and Japan, the validity of New Zealand's action was conditional upon the recognition of Japan's 'acquired rights' to fish around the New Zealand coast. The New Zealand position was that there was a substantive body of state practice lending weight to the view that a coastal state was free to establish a twelve-mile fishing zone; and that, in so far as it might be required to recognize pre-existing rights of foreign fishermen, Japanese fishing activities were of too recent an origin to qualify for such recognition.

Japanese proposals were carefully examined, and the New Zealand government assembled expert legal advice both from within New Zealand and from overseas. The conclusion reached was that consideration of the legal issues confirmed and re-inforced the government's views about the international legal validity of its action in establishing the New Zealand exclusive fishing zone. Accordingly, in early 1967, the New Zealand Prime Minister announced that the government felt that it would not be fitting, in the circumstances, to agree to join with Japan in submitting the question to the International Court. Other factors that influenced New Zealand's decision were that a *joint* approach to the Court might have implied that New Zealand regarded the question as a moot one; the settlement of the terms of reference to the Court might have taken years of negotiation; and a court case would itself, on past experience, take two or three years before a decision was reached – and apart from the question of time there was the amount of money involved in any proceedings such as this (conceivably some millions of dollars).

However, the New Zealand government was concerned to dispose of the dispute. If it were prolonged it would risk injuring the friendly and beneficial trading relations which had been built up over the years between the two countries. For this reason, while maintaining its legal standpoint, New Zealand opened up with the Japanese government the possibility of an agreement being reached to enable their vessels to have a limited period of phase-out of fishing in the New Zealand fishing zone, providing it was in a satisfactory form embodying the conditions necessary to protect New Zealand's interests.

Subsequent events were rapid. Fisheries talks were held in Wellington in May and June 1967. Their general result was entirely satisfactory, since the delegations succeeded in devising a draft Agreement on Fisheries which both regarded as reasonable in its terms. The New Zealand/Japan Fisheries Agreement was a fairly notable achievement for New Zealand, as the coastal state involved, since the Japanese proved willing, in return for a moderate length of phase-out, to undertake definitely to withdraw entirely from the New Zealand fishing zone after the end of 1970, instead of demanding, as in other disputes, that her prior fishing efforts in such a zone be allowed to continue indefinitely. It was all the more noteworthy in view of the fact that only a month or so previously the Japanese had negotiated an agreement with the United States under which they were given rights to continue fishing in the American exclusive fishing zone for an indefinite period. In addition, in the interim period until the end of 1970, Japan accepted strict limitations on her fishing activities in the zone as to the number and type of ships, their method of fishing, and their area of operation. In broad effect, the agreement confined the Japanese phase-out activities to about the average level of operations obtained in recent years, to the outer six miles of the twelve-mile area, and to the coasts only of the North Island and of the northernmost part of the South Island of New Zealand. Another feature of the Agreement was the provision for concurrent jurisdiction in the policing of the Agreement. In practice, these jurisdictional provisions worked well during the period of the phasing-out of Japanese fishing activities.

In sum, the dispute showed New Zealand, as a small state, taking the initiative by unilateral action where her own interest was vital and that of the other party was not. New Zealand, further, declined to take the issue to the appropriate international organization, in this case the International Court of Justice, preferring to rely on the mutual interest which had been generated by a developing, negotiated relationship with the other country. New Zealand recognized that the overall trading position with Japan should not be harmed and was, therefore, ready to discuss the situation on a bilateral basis. The success achieved justified this choice of action, demonstrating that the bilateral relationship had become sufficiently important for both parties as to create favourable conditions for a settlement which would recognize the more vital of the interests at stake.

FREEDOM OF MANOEUVRE: LIMITATIONS AND STRENGTHS

Information Sources

The advantage of an alliance policy as opposed to non-alignment is that New Zealand is fortunate in having access to British, U.S. and Australian classified information. Even so, some of the efforts currently being made to extend the scope of trade may become inadequate unless supported by further permanent representation or information activity. Present coverage which is limited to the Pacific, Southeast Asia, Europe and the United States meets the requirements of existing trade. To date, as soon as needs have clearly emerged, there has been a readiness to meet them, as the recent development of representation to the EEC countries and to Southeast Asia shows. Too heavy a reliance on cost-effectiveness forecasts in the establishment of new posts, however, is a possible explanation for New Zealand's relative slowness, in comparison with Australia, in developing Southeast Asian outlets for her products.

Military Capacity and Internal Limitations on Defence Strategy

No particular defence policy can be satisfactorily rationalized for a small state like New Zealand. Given the low level of developed resources and manpower, it cannot support a defence industry of any size and variety, but must depend on foreign suppliers of equipment. Terrain, length of coastline, distribution of population and the supply problem are against a 'fortress' policy. On the other hand, to play a part in an alliance based on a modern conventional weapons system involves the difficulty that for a given effect a far greater proportionate social and economic effort is required than for a large state. For New Zealand, with its persistent balance-of-payments problem and shortage of labour, the danger of weakening the economy is a barrier against increasing the almost negligible contribution she makes to the alliance alternative she has chosen. The obligations she has assumed represent the estimated limit of her capacity in the mixed conditions of guarded peace and sustained limited war in the Pacific–Southeast Asian region.[29]

In January 1968 the British government announced that forces in Southeast Asia would be withdrawn by the end of 1971. Following subsequent meetings of the five Commonwealth governments concerned in the operation of the Anglo-Malaysian defence agreement of 1963 (the U.K., Australia, New Zealand, Malaysia and Singapore), New Zealand and Australia announced their decision to maintain forces in Malaysia at existing levels. For New Zealand the forces concerned were an infantry battalion, a frigate and an airforce transport squadron. The framework for collaboration has been developed subsequently in five-power talks. This is New Zealand's most explicit formal military obligation. The formal obligation under SEATO is for each signatory to 'act to meet the common danger in accordance with its constitutional processes'[30] in the event of a threat to peace in the area. SEATO exercises and involvement in the Vietnam war have added evidence of intention to this vague formula, and there is considerable pressure from the United States to maintain and increase the forces available.

Multilateralism in defence does not, in practice, seem to confer on small states the same bargaining position as a bilateral arrangement. SEATO is primarily a vehicle for legitimizing U.S. actions in the Pacific, the other member countries either accepting U.S. leadership or losing interest in the alliance. The small, local members of SEATO have clearly felt themselves obliged to adopt the first position; the European countries, Britain and France, the second. The smaller alliance ANZUS is, therefore, regarded as the indispensable element in security relations with the United States, providing protection and involving only a very general obligation to provide some of the military potential of the alliance.[31]

A memorandum of understanding was signed between Australia and New Zealand in September 1969 on co-operation in defence supplies, and a special section was subsequently created in the Department of Industries and Commerce to identify opportunities for defence supply to Australia and the United States which are within New Zealand's industrial capacity. Little saving on overseas exchange can be expected, however, to result from this understanding in the immediate future, and New Zealand's small defence establishment must continue to limit her freedom of manoeuvre. Total defence expenditure was NZ $86·34 million in 1968–69, or 6·3 per cent of government expenditure and 2 per cent of GNP. Total strength in 1969 of all services was 13,163 men. Ballot selective compulsory military service applies to 19-year-old males. It consists of a fourteen-week camp training plus three years' part-time training to a total of sixty days plus three years in the Reserve. In 1969, the navy comprised four frigates, a survey ship, a supply ship, two ocean minesweepers and twelve motor launches mainly engaged in fishery protection. The army comprises an infantry regiment and various functional corps. The airforce has seven operational squadrons. Defence liaison staffs are maintained in London, Canberra, Washington, Kuala Lumpur and Singapore, and New Zealand officers serve in the military planning office of SEATO in Bangkok. A co-operative logistics-support arrangement, agreed with the United States in May 1965, gives New Zealand forces the same priority as American forces in the supply of military equipment, and the United States is now the main source of military supplies, substantial credits having been arranged for their purchase.

Smallness and weakness have led New Zealand to seek security in alliances in which it can never be an equal partner. Reliance is placed primarily on the United States but, while Britain continues to maintain a political role and military presence in Southeast Asia, New Zealand attaches considerable importance to the Commonwealth commitment as one which adds to the security of Southeast Asia and gives New Zealand greater scope for an independent position. The despatch of a small force to Thailand in the crisis of 1962 and, subsequently, of a token force of combatant troops to Vietnam is more than matched by the Malaysian commitment. The dual alliance system not only offers slightly more room for manoeuvre but is more acceptable to public opinion. The despatch of troops to Vietnam raised violent differences of opinion. Malaysian involvement is generally accepted. However, supplementing the supports for the United States as guarantor and market, there is an overall strategic argument, influential in official, especially defence, circles, leading to approval of the pattern of United States activity in Vietnam and the rest of Southeast Asia. This is seen as the location from which a threat to New Zealand is most likely to come, and SEATO is New Zealand's 'first line of defence'.

Internal Political Situation

During the 1960s there was a surge of criticism of this strategic argument which eventually won the official support of the

Labour Party. The party fought the 1966 election committed publicly to bringing troops home and replacing them with a civilian contingent. Doubts were expressed about the continued relevance of SEATO. Membership of ANZUS was not questioned. The guarantee it provides was used rather as a stick with which to beat SEATO. The maintenance of the commitment in Malaysia was also strongly supported as creating a specific obligation and one more in keeping with Commonwealth membership. In the event, Labour lost the election and the leadership felt that its stand on this issue had lost it votes, including, in the opinion of the party leader, Mr Kirk, some traditional Catholic support. This, plus the fact that the United States has gone through its own crisis of confidence on the issue has reduced the partisan division which had developed and there is now little fire to the debate. On all other aspects of policy there is bipartisan support.

Economic Limitations
New Zealand's present economic structure imposes limitations on her ability to marry directly her security interests in the Pacific and South-east Asia with economic interests. Though Britain's negotiations for entry to the Common Market make it the more desirable that new markets be developed wherever possible, there seems little immediate chance that the Pacific and Southeast Asia will become a major trading area for New Zealand. Her industrial base remains small,[32] and the temperate agricultural products she exports are not in demand in the area. The possibilities of diversification of the economy to reduce dependence on the British market have been under continuous examination since 1960. Considerable importance is attached to stimulating exports of manufactured goods and to the encouragement of other earners of foreign exchange such as tourism and fishing. The National Development Conference predicted in 1969 that, in spite of expansion of production and exports in other sectors, agriculture would still be contributing 64 per cent of total exports in ten years' time. Dependence on the export of lamb and dairy products to the British market is still critical. The scope for diversification of agricultural production, given New Zealand's climate and topography, must be regarded as very limited, so the improvement of access to the American, European and Japanese markets for these products has become the vital concern of New Zealand foreign policy.

319

Table 2 *New Zealand Trade by Area 1960–1970*

Percentage of Total Imports

Area	1960	1961	Jan-June 1962	June[a] 1963	1964	1965	1966	1967	1968	1969	1970[b]
Sterling Area	60·85	58·46	55·86	55·99	55·63	60·30	54·93	54·15	55·89	52·59	50·18
Dollar Area	14·95	16·88	16·28	19·32	16·88	14·94	16·29	18·47	19·56	20·40	21·13
EFTA (exc. U.K.)	0·66	0·76	1·04	0·70	1·11	1·17	1·07	1·04	0·91	0·86	1·02
EEC	16·69	15·75	20·64	17·57	18·60	16·19	15·74	11·65	10·53	12·28	11·11
Other Countries	6·85	8·15	6·18	6·43	7·77	7·40	11·98	14·69	13·12	14·18	16·56

Percentage of Total Exports

Area	1960	1961	Jan-June 1962	June[a] 1963	1964	1965	1966	1967	1968	1969	1970[b]
Sterling Area	69·82	68·59	71·59	68·86	67·86	65·03	65·64	64·04	61·95	60·89	60·45
Dollar Area	14·40	14·19	12·81	13·52	13·94	15·80	15·87	17·28	16·20	16·44	17·63
EFTA (exc. U.K.)	2·38	2·46	2·02	2·34	3·53	3·14	2·51	2·70	2·99	2·95	2·39
EEC	6·95	8·03	7·07	6·60	6·56	6·39	6·61	7·38	7·08	8·03	7·47
Other Countries	6·45	6·72	6·51	8·68	8·11	9·64	9·37	8·60	11·79	11·69	12·06

Source: New Zealand Official Year Book 1971, p. 613.
Notes: (a) Year ended June, 1963. The figures for 1960 and 1961 are for calendar years and from 1963 onwards for June years.
(b) The figures for 1970 are provisional.

Even under present trading conditions, the worsening position of primary products in world trade has contributed to a slight reduction in the New Zealand standard of living, balance-of-payments deficits, running down of reserves, inflation, and in 1968, for the first time since the war, some unemployment. In responding to the British devaluation in 1967, New Zealand went further and reduced the dollar to parity with Australia, a devaluation of 25 per cent. These factors have made more acute the question of market access – European agricultural policy offers little prospect that the temporary concessions which may be made to New Zealand on British entry can be made permanent and trade expanded, except, possibly, and with strong promotion, the sales of lamb. Japan, as noted above, is determinedly developing, under heavy protection, its own dairy industry and in any case Japan's capacity to absorb the quantities of dairy produce and meat presently sold to Britain is very limited. The United States market is, therefore, receiving the most hopeful attention from New Zealand producers. At this point there does occur indirect contact between Pacific and Southeast Asian security interests and economic interest. One of the arguments used in support of New Zealand's military activity in her 'near north' is, in sum, that trade will follow the flag and that the reward for carrying American spears in Vietnam will be not only a degree of military protection but trade concessions in the American market. The United States response, however, has been a source of disappointment.[33]

External Limitations

In practice, New Zealand's alliance with the United States[34] has not seriously limited policy choice except in one respect. The Labour government of 1957–60 made it plain to the United States that it favoured recognition of Communist China and her admission to the United Nations, and it urged the United States to consider such a policy. The Prime Minister, Walter Nash, told the annual conference of the Labour party that the government had no intention of taking action unilaterally, out of step with the United States. Persuasion was best exercised as friend and loyal supporter. Though the continued exclusion of China from the United Nations and non-recognition by New Zealand has been strongly supported by the National party government which has held office since 1960, it may be assumed

L

321

Table 3 *Distribution of New Zealand Aid 1969–70*

Bilateral Assistance	NZ $(000
South Pacific	
Cook Islands	
Grants	2,079
Loans	180
Niue	
Grants	881
Loans	60
Tokelau Islands – Grants	197
Western Samoa	
Grants	250
Loans	150
Training Scheme – Cook, Niue, Tokelau Islands	105
Other South Pacific technical assistance	12
South Pacific airports (excluding Rarotonga)	131
General	28
	4,073
South and Southeast Asia	
Colombo Plan	3,646
SEATO Aid Fund	20
Ministry of Defence Contributions	
Road Construction Team, Thailand	110
Services Medical Team, Vietnam	115
	3,891
Commonwealth	
SCAAP	188
Commonwealth Education Scheme	105
Commonwealth Medical Scheme	39
Commonwealth Programme for Technical Co-operation	5
	337
Other	
Volunteer Service Abroad	65
Disaster Relief	2
	67
Total bilateral assistance	8,368
Multilateral Assistance	
Voluntary Programmes	
United Nations Development Programme	450

322

United Nations Children's Fund	120
United Nations High Commissioner for Refugees	20
United Nations Relief and Works Agency for Palestine Refugees	60
World Food Programme	224
South Pacific Commission	142
International Red Cross	6
Bank Subscriptions	
Convertible currency subscription to Asian Development Bank	1,007
Total multilateral assistance	2,029
Other Official Flows	
World Bank Bonds	4,465
Total other officials flows	4,465
Total aid	14,862

Source: New Zealand Official Yearbook 1971, pp. 42–3.

Note: The distribution of New Zealand government aid to overseas countries during the 1969–70 financial year is set out in the above table. The aid is shown as bilateral where the arrangements were concluded directly between the New Zealand government and the government of the recipient country or countries and multilateral where the aid was contributed to an international agency or fund. The table lists only government aid. It does not take into account the substantial aid given privately in cash and kind through CORSO and other private organizations.

that if the United States were to reverse its policy New Zealand would rapidly follow suit, and would also attempt to secure an immediate trading agreement.

United States pressure has been exerted on New Zealand policy-makers on a variety of other issues since the signing of the ANZUS treaty in 1952, but, apart from the exclusion of Britain from that pact, this pressure has not thwarted the New Zealand government in pursuit of any important interest, nor has it succeeded in its major objective which is to increase substantially the contribution of Australia and New Zealand to the total military strength of the alliance. Token military support of the United States action in Thailand in 1962 and the present small contribution to the Vietnam effort propitiate without

323

satisfying the United States. Other international groupings, apart from the United Nations, further rather than limit New Zealand's foreign policy effectiveness. As a Colombo Plan country, New Zealand makes her localized contribution to development aid under rules which enable donor countries to select those objectives of national plans of the developing countries which they prefer. Through the GATT, with increasing dissatisfaction, she pursues multi-lateral trade liberalization of agricultural products under rules which restrict trade contracts with Communist countries which rely on bilateral, virtually barter, agreements. Economic union with Australia was bruited in the sixties but there were fears that New Zealand would become an agricultural annexe of industrializing Australia, so the Australia-New Zealand free trade area agreement which came into force in January 1966, against United States objections it should be noticed, was limited in scope, though it provided for regular consultation and progressive improvement of trading conditions. It has led to some increase in trade with Australia.

The emergence of regional groupings in Southeast Asia and the Pacific, which might have involved New Zealand in obligations, has been hindered by Cold-War political divisions in the area. In June 1966, however, ASPAC (the Asian and Pacific Council) was inaugurated in Seoul with nine members: Australia, Japan, Malaysia, New Zealand, the Philippines, Taiwan, South Korea, Thailand and South Vietnam. Though somewhat vague in its objectives, which are 'to sponsor greater co-operation and solidarity among the free Asian and Pacific countries in their efforts to safeguard their national independence and integrity against any Communist aggression or infiltration', it has produced a forum for genuinely close consultation between New Zealand and important Asian countries, particularly Japan. Each country becomes a host to the organization for one year. The Philippines, South Vietnam, Taiwan and South Korea – countries with whom no resident mission is maintained – are thus embraced. The organization has no close parallel in political or military terms. Cultural and economic activities are taking tangible form, particularly in South Korea, but its principal significance at the moment is in the opportunity it creates for ministers to meet regularly for consultation and exchange of information. The closest parallel in this sense is with Commonwealth consultation.

More recently, in August 1967, another Asian economic, cultural and social grouping was inaugurated between Indonesia, Malaysia, Thailand, Singapore and the Philippines. Singapore and Indonesia are drawn in, thereby, to a pattern of overlapping regional co-operation, though they are unwilling to be associated directly with ASPAC. No formal co-ordination is possible but, since the two organizations run parallel, it seems possible that informal links will develop, and New Zealand has welcomed this development though she is not a member. Growing direct links between Indonesia and New Zealand were somewhat attenuated during the period of confrontation, but, since it ended, have been stepped up. The sense that friendly relations with Indonesia are a vital aspect of New Zealand security has led to considerable effort to broaden and make more complex the pattern of relations. However, the problem of size confronts New Zealand in its relationship with developing countries. Indonesia's interests in aid are enormous and New Zealand's capacity to meet them is very limited. This is comparable with the trade problem as an instrument of relations with the underdeveloped countries in the region. New Zealand's size limits the value of the trade and aid bargains it can offer (Table 3). To diversify markets and import sources (at least up to the point where increases in promotion, servicing and handling charges do not outweigh the intangible benefits of decreased dependence) is a priority of trade policy but one for which the Southeast Asian area offers little promise.

New Zealand is a signatory to the Antarctic Treaty of December 1969. She claims sovereignty over the large and important sector of Antarctica known as the Ross dependency and therefore attaches considerable importance to the sixteen nation Treaty as a guarantee of the security of her scientific, conservationist, and touristic activities in the area.[35]

CONCLUSIONS

New Zealand has played an active but dependent role in international affairs. Her economic relations are of vital importance and the direction of demand for her exports helps to explain the European and North American orientation of her policy since the war.

A small state cannot expect to take initiatives which will affect

THE OTHER POWERS

in any marked way the pattern of international politics. The choice in the post-war world, for such a state, has been between alignment and some form of non-alignment. For New Zealand, with the intimate, highly responsive form of parliamentary government which a small population has developed, the choice existed only in theory. There was no tradition of neutrality and there was an emotional, cultural, economic and political commit-ment to Britain, Europe and the United States which precluded the subtle ambiguities of non-alignment policy. The price of alliance has not been high, since it conforms with vital trading realities and because United States interest in Southeast Asia has enabled New Zealand to pay closer attention to the Pacific and Southeast Asia, particularly in the development of her own defence effort. It is at this regional level that there may exist some opportunity for effective intervention for a small state, and there has been growing interest in regional affairs since 1955 in New Zealand. Regional interest and bilateral exchange have taken the place of the attention paid in the inter-war years, and at the immediate end of the Second World War, to international organization and notions of collective security. However, New Zealand's effectiveness in a region of tropical developing countries is limited by the nature of its trade products and needs and by its capacity to offer aid.

In terms of operational efficiency, smallness has involved the disadvantage of the high proportionate cost of all forms of overseas representation. This disadvantage is offset to some degree by overlapping accreditation of ambassadors and effective use of the staff of the larger posts, particularly London, as members of negotiating teams to nearby countries. Another offsetting factor attributable to smallness, in a country which is culturally homogeneous and has high educational standards, is that co-ordination and communication problems in policy-making are at a minimum within New Zealand.

In sum, policy formation and execution is a collective activity undertaken in a spirit of British phlegmatic pragmatism, with little disposition towards dramatic, risk-taking gestures in sup-port of strongly-held political objectives.

NOTES AND REFERENCES

The basic official source for information on New Zealand is the annual

326

New Zealand Year Book which includes a section on external affairs. Invaluable too is *The New Zealand External Affairs Review*, now called *The New Zealand Foreign Affairs Review*. This includes long, informative and analytical articles, often of a high standard, reflecting viewpoints within the ministry and in most issues, the full texts of papers read to interested groups by foreign service officers, ministers and ambassadors. On trade and economic affairs as they affect foreign relations there are, in addition to the annual reports of the Department of Industries and Commerce and of the Ministry of Foreign Affairs, the occasional reports of the New Zealand Monetary and Economic Council. One of these, 'New Zealand and an Enlarged EEC', *Report*, no. 19 (Wellington, Government Printer, June, 1970), provides an excellent summary of the anticipated effects of British membership of the EEC on the New Zealand economy.

The information in this essay is based largely on interviews in New Zealand and in the New Zealand High Commission in London, and on official publications. However, T. C. Larkin (ed.), *New Zealand's External Relations* (N.Z.I.P.A., Wellington, 1962) is worth special mention in the unofficial category as it brings together in a symposium, sponsored by the New Zealand Institute of Public Administration, the views of ministers, parliamentarians, academics and officials, in a survey and evaluation of New Zealand foreign policy. The work is edited and introduced by a senior official of the ministry, and the specialist papers on which discussion is based are contributed by the diplomatic and treasury officers with primary responsibility. Thus, the paper on administration of foreign policy is contributed by the Permanent Head of the Prime Minister's Department and Secretary of External Affairs. The papers are both informative and broadly speculative.

For the historical background, demonstrating as it does the element of continuity in New Zealand policy since the colonial period, there is no one sufficient work. There are, however, studies which taken together provide adequate coverage. Angus Ross, *New Zealand Aspirations in the Pacific in the 19th Century* (Oxford University Press, London, 1964) and R. M. Burdon, *King Dick – a Biography of Richard John Seddon* (Whitcombe & Tombs, Wellington, 1955) give an account of the formative years for New Zealand foreign policy. New Zealand Institute of International Affairs, *Contemporary New Zealand: a Survey of Domestic and Foreign Policy* (N.Z.I.I.A., Dunedin, 1938), I. F. G. Milner, *New Zealand's Interests and Policies in the Far East* (Institute of Pacific Relations, New York, 1939) and F. L. W. Wood, *The New Zealand People at War* (War History Branch, Dept. of Internal Affairs, Wellington, 1958) carry the account beyond the turn of the century. Milner contains a good account of naval policy; Wood, whose historical introduction is very full, is particularly valuable because it was prepared with access to archives. R. A. Lochore, *From Europe to New Zealand* (A. H. & A. W. Reed in conjunction with the N.Z.I.I.A. and with the assistance of Dept. of Internal Affairs, Wellington, 1951) is a semi-official apologia for immigration policy. E. P. Chase, 'Peter Fraser at San Francisco', *Political Science* (Wellington), vol. 11, no. 1 (March, 1959) pp. 17–24; R. J. Harrison, 'ANZUS, SEATO and New Zealand', *Landfall* (N.Z.), vol. 12, no. 3 (September, 1958) pp. 256–66; K. Sinclair,

'New Zealand's Future Foreign Policy: A New Pacific Pact', *Political Science* (Wellington), vol. 18, no. 2 (September, 1966) pp. 68–77; and Trevor R. Reece, *Australia, New Zealand and the United States, a Survey of International Relations, 1941–1968* (Oxford University Press, London, 1969), cover recent developments. The most recent appreciation of the increasingly important question of New Zealand's relations with Southeast Asia, not referred to in this essay, is Keith Jackson's 'New Zealand and Southeast Asia', *Journal of Commonwealth Political Studies* vol. 9, no. 1 (1971) pp. 3–18.

Most of the works mentioned above contain bibliographies, and other specialized references are to be found below.

1. This approximation and the statistical approximations immediately following are derived from *The New Zealand Year Book, 1970* (Government Printer, Wellington, 1970) *passim*.
2. *Report of the Department of Industries and Commerce for the year ended 31 March 1970* (Government Printer, Wellington, 1970) p. 5.
3. Walter Lippmann, *United States Foreign Policy, Shield of the Republic* (Little, Brown and Co., Boston, 1943) pp. 61–5.
4. See Angus Ross, *New Zealand Aspirations in the Pacific in the Nineteenth Century* (Oxford University Press, London, 1964) pp. 41–2. This is the best detailed general history of New Zealand's Pacific policy to 1900.
5. For an account see R. M. Burden, *King Dick* (Whitcombe and Tombs, Wellington, 1955), pp. 223–32, and D. K. Fieldhouse, 'New Zealand, Fiji and the Colonial Office, 1900–1902', *Historical Studies: Australia and New Zealand*, vol. 8, no. 30 (May, 1958) pp. 113–30.
6. *New Zealand Parliamentary Papers*, 1901, A.1.
7. See F. L. W. Wood, *The New Zealand People at War: Political and External Affairs* (War History Branch, Dept. of Internal Affairs, Wellington, 1958) p. 329.
8. ibid., pp. 78–9.
9. See I. F. G. Milner, *New Zealand's Interests and Policies in the Far East* (Institute of Pacific Relations, New York, 1939) p. 5.
10. Quoted in Wood, op. cit., p. 15.
11. See symposium *Contemporary New Zealand: A Survey of Domestic and Foreign Policy* (New Zealand Institute of International Affairs, Wellington, 1938) p. 249.
12. Wood, op. cit., p. 47.
13. ibid., p. 69.
14. ibid., p. 189.
15. See pp. 319–21. For a detailed and contemporary analysis of external trade, see *New Zealand Year Book, 1969* (Government Printer, Wellington, 1969) pp. 607–78, and see *Industries and Commerce Report 1970*, cited above, pp. 27–66.
16. New Zealand Monetary and Economic Council, *Report No. 19, New Zealand and an Enlarged EEC* (Government Printer, Wellington, 1970) p. 16.
17. ibid., p. 31.

18. See also Keith Sinclair, 'New Zealand's Future Foreign Policy: A New Pacific Pact', *Political Science* (Wellington) vol. 18, no. 2 (September, 1966) pp. 68–9.
19. T. C. Larking (ed.), *New Zealand's External Relations* (Oxford University Press, London, 1962).
20. Sir Keith Holyoake, 'A Defence and Foreign Policy for New Zealand', *New Zealand External Affairs Review*, vol. 19, no. 3 (March, 1969) p. 3.
21. See 'Administration of New Zealand Foreign Policy', *New Zealand Foreign Affairs Review*, vol. 20, no. 4 (April, 1970) pp. 3–12.
22. See, for example, *New Zealand Parliamentary Debates* 366, 1970 (Government Printer, Wellington) cols. 999, 1082–93.
23. 'International Problems Confronting New Zealand in the 1970s', *New Zealand External Affairs Review* vol. 19, no. 8 (August, 1969) p. 16.
24. H. C. Templeton (Ministry of Foreign Affairs), 'New Zealand and Africa', *New Zealand External Affairs Review*, vol. 17, no. 1 (January, 1967) p. 7.
25. See C. Craw (Ministry of Foreign Affairs), 'The Work of a New Zealand Diplomat', *New Zealand Foreign Affairs Review*, vol. 20, no. 7 (July, 1970) pp. 3–16.
26. National Development Conference, *Report 13, Markets* (Government Printer, Wellington, May, 1969) p. 72.
27. For another case study see A. D. McIntosh, 'Administration of an Independent New Zealand Foreign Policy', in T. C. Larkin, op. cit., pp. 54–60.
28. See *New Zealand Parliamentary Debates*, 341, 1964, col. 3555.
29. It has been strongly and influentially argued that New Zealand's true regional potential lies in the much smaller South Pacific zone. See Frank Corner, 'New Zealand and the South Pacific' in Larkin (Ministry of Foreign Affairs), op. cit., pp. 130–52 and Keith Sinclair, 'New Zealand's Future Foreign Policy: A New Pacific Pact', *Political Science* (Wellington) vol. 18, no. 2 (September, 1966) pp. 68–77.
30. *South-East Asia Collective Defence Treaty*, Treaty Series 1955, no. 3 (Government Printer, Wellington, 1955) art. 4.
31. For detailed discussion see R. J. Harrison, 'ANZUS, SEATO and New Zealand', *Landfall*, no. 47 (September, 1958) pp. 256–66.
32. See Industries and Commerce report noted above, pp. 4–26.
33. *Annual Report of the Ministry of Foreign Affairs, 1969–70* (Wellington, Ministry of Foreign Affairs, 1970) p. 62.
34. For an evaluation see W. B. Harland (Ministry of Foreign Affairs), 'New Zealand's Relations with the United States of America', *New Zealand Foreign Affairs Review* vol. 20, no. 5 (May, 1970) pp. 3–16, and G. R. Laking, 'New Zealand/American Relations', *New Zealand Foreign Affairs Review* vol. 20, no. 8 (August, 1970) pp. 12–20. G. R. Laking, CMG, is Secretary of Foreign Affairs and Permanent Head, PM's Department.
35. See 'New Zealand's Interests in Antarctica', *New Zealand Foreign Affairs Review*, vol. 20, no. 2 (February, 1970) pp. 15–25.

Appendix

	Population Millions	Estimated GNP 1970 in Million U.S. Dollars
	Up to 1 million	
Fiji	519,000 (b)	199 (b)
Tonga	83,000 (b)	—
Western Samoa	140,000 (b)	—
Nauru	7,000 (b)	—
Mauritius	823,000 (b)	198 (b)
Barbados	323,000 (b)	111 (b)
Malta	319,000 (b)	183 (b)
Gibraltar	27,000 (b)	—
Iceland	202,191	416 (b)
Equatorial Guinea	290,000 (a)	70 (a)
Gabon	490,000	70
Gambia	360,000 (a)	200 (a)
Congo (Brazzaville)	1,000,000	175
Botswana	640,000 (b)	60 (b)
Lesotho	960,000 (a)	80 (a)
Swaziland	415,000 (a)	130 (a)
Guyana	742,000 (b)	215 (b)
Trinidad–Tobago	1,010,000	748 (b)
Bhutan	750,000 (b)	45 (b)
Sikkim	191,000 (b)	—
Maldive Islands	103,000	—
Kuwait	540,000 (b)	2,221 (b)
Bahrein	205,000	—
Muscat and Oman	565,000 (b)	—
Qatar	100,000 (b)	—
Cyprus	622,000 (b)	460 (b)
Luxembourg	342,000	910
San Marino	19,000 (b)	—
Liechtenstein	22,000 (b)	—
Andorra	19,000 (b)	—
Vatican City	1,000 (b)	—

	Population Millions	Estimated GNP 1970 in Million U.S. Dollars
	1–5 million	
Dahomey	2·700 (a)	200 (a)
Sierra Leone	2·550 (a)	335 (a)
Guinea	4·075	700
Ivory Coast	4·375	1,400
Mali	5·000	250 (a)
Liberia	1·160	245
Senegal	3·950	720
Niger	3·800 (a)	330 (a)
Mauritania	1·200 (a)	200 (a)
Togo	1·850 (a)	210 (a)
Upper Volta	5·330 (a)	250 (a)
Cameroun	5·700 (a)	860 (a)
Central African Republic (C.A.R.)	2·088 (a)	210 (a)
Chad	3·540 (a)	285 (a)
Rwanda	3·590 (a)	210 (a)
Burundi	3·525 (a)	160 (a)
Malawi	4·042	200
Rhodesia	5·425	1,440
Somalia	2·900	180
Zambia	4·250	1,580
Libya	2·000	4,000
Tunisia	5·050	1,240
Lebanon	2·775	1,560
Israel	3·040	5,400
Jordan	2·225	640
Yemen	5·000 (b)	—
South Yemen	1·220 (b)	—
Union of Arab Emirates	1·601	—
Dominican Republic	4·029 (b)	1,169 (b)
Jamaica	1·952	1,064 (b)
Haiti	4·671	423 (b)
El Salvador	3·390 (b)	945 (b)
Guatemala	5·014 (b)	1,645 (b)
Honduras	2·495 (b)	646 (b)
Nicaragua	1·541 (b)	728 (b)
Costa Rica	1·685 (b)	824 (b)
Panama	1·417 (b)	917 (b)
Ecuador	5·890 (b)	1,477 (b)
Bolivia	4·804 (b)	911 (b)
Paraguay	2·314 (b)	543 (b)
Uruguay	2·852 (b)	1,833 (b)
New Zealand	2·880	5,770
Laos	3·030	200
Singapore	2·100	1,820

	Population Millions	Estimated GNP 1970 in Million U.S. Dollars
	1–5 million	
Albania	2·190	900
Mongolia	1·315	630
Denmark	4·990	16,000
Norway	3·915	12,460
Finland	4·600	10,300
Republic of Ireland	2·921 (b)	3,415 (b)
	5–10 million	billion U.S. dollars
Chile	9·566 (b)	5·8 (b)
Venezuela	9·686	9·2
Cuba	8·074	—
Malagasy	7·200	0·8
Uganda	10·025	1·1
Ghana	9·050	2·0
Cambodia	7·000	0·9
Nepal	10·652	0·8
Saudi Arabia	7·400	4·1
Iraq	9·250	3·1
Syria	6·200	1·5
Greece	8·960	9·2
Bulgaria	8·555	8·9
Austria	7·445	14·3
Switzerland	6·375	20 5
Belgium	9·800	24 9
Sweden	8·125	31·2
Portugal	9·730	6·1
	10–15 million	
Netherlands	13·175	31·3
Czechoslovakia	14·700	30·3
Hungary	10·320	14·4
Algeria	14·150	4·4
Kenya	11·525	1·6
Tanzania	13·600	1·1
Ceylon	12·240 (b)	2·0 (b)
Malaysia	11·200	4·0
Taiway	13·957	3·96
N. Korea	13·975	2·8
	15–20 million	
South Africa	20·550	17·6
Afghanistan	17·600	—
Sudan	16·050	1·8
Morocco	16·000	3·3
South Vietnam	18·800	4·0
East Germany	17·150	34·0

	Population Millions	Estimated GNP 1970 in Billion U.S. Dollars
	20–30 million	
Canada	21·700	78·2
Colombia	20·463 (b)	7·4 (b)
Argentina	23·983 (b)	19·86 (b)
North Vietnam	22·675	6·1
Burma	28·175	3·2
Iran	29·500	10·9
Ethiopia	25·800	1·8
Congo (Kinshasa)	21·300	1·9
Rumania	20·400	21·4
Yugoslavia	20·800	11·8
	30–100 million	
West Pakistan	55·000	—
East Pakistan	65·000	—
South Korea	32·700	8·3
U.A.R. (Egypt)	34·150	6·4
Philippines	39·800	5·4
Thailand	35·000	6·1
Poland	33·200	42·5
Spain	33·600	32·3
Turkey	36·100	13·7
West Germany	60·000	185·0
Mexico	48·933	24·11
France	51·225	148·0
United Kingdom	56·000	121·0
Nigeria	62·000	9·1
Italy	54·000	93·2
Brazil	90·840	29·7
	Over 100 million	
Japan	104·600	195·0
Indonesia	114·500	11·6
U.S.A.	208·100	977·0
Soviet Union	245·700	490·0
India	557·000	49·0
China	760·000	90·0

Sources: The population and GNP figures are taken from *The Military Balance 1971–1972*, except those marked (a) which are taken from *The Armed Forces of African States*, Adelphi Papers, no. 67 (May, 1970), and (b) which are taken from the *United Nations Statistical Yearbook 1970*.

Note: The population and GNP figures for (a) and (b) are based on 1968–69. A comparative table (based on 1968) which includes population, and GNP, area is to be found in *The Europa Year Book*, vol. II (1970).

Index

94, 139, 261; builds Tanzania–
Zambia railway, 129; effect of
Sino-Soviet conflict, 230–1;
issue of UN membership, 263,
321–2; *see also under* Cuba and
Singapore
Clerides, G., 188–9
Cold War, 156, 220, 229, 237, 278,
304, 308, and relaxation of, 73,
237, 324
Colombo Plan, 255, 278–9, 324
Commonwealth, 128, 184, 189, 204,
252, 254–5, 261–2, 267, 279, 316–
19; advantages of membership,
147, 204, 277, 318; changed
nature of, 134, 276, 278, 308;
conferences, 147, 152 n. 27, 204,
264, 277
Confrontation, 266, 268, 310
Congo (Kinshasa), 18, 138, 146
Coomaraswamy, P., 259
Council of Copper Exporting
Countries, 138
Cuba: agrarian reform, 216; continuing problems of foreign
policy, 210; deterioration of
relations with United States,
233–4, 247 n. 10; differences with
Soviet Union, 224–5; diplomatic
isolation of, 241–2, 243–4, 249
n. 45; effect of economic difficulties on foreign policy, 223, 228,
231, 242; invasion of, 235–6, 248
n. 30; 'missile crisis', 227, 230,
237, 248 n. 27, 250 n. 64; policy
towards China, 229–33, 250 n. 56,
and Soviet Union, 220–9; pre-
Castro dependence on United
States, 213–15, 247 n. 8; reasons
for Latin American involvement,
236–7, 240–1; re-orientation of
foreign policy, 218–19; selective
support for guerrilla groups, 242,
and setbacks, 243–4
Cyprus, 158, 308; advantages of
Commonwealth membership for,
204; break-up of administration,
187; deterioration in relations
with Greece, 194, 208 n. 20;

dominance of Cyprus problem in
foreign policy, 191, and difficulties of management, 193–5; economic structure and weakness,
195–9; Greek Cypriot leadership,
188–9; importance of cultural
relations for, 204–5; legal role in
UN, 203–4, 208 n. 29; opposition
to Makarios, 191, 208 n. 20;
organization of foreign ministry
and service, 189–90; pre-independence history, 184–5; recognition of limited political influence, 187; replacement of
foreign minister, 208 n. 20;
sources of development assistance, 197–8; trade difficulties
with EEC, 199–201, and Eastern
bloc trade as safeguard, 201–2;
value of non-alignment for, 202–3
Czechoslovakia, 18, and Czech
crisis (1948), 44, (1968) 53, 145,
228, 239, 249 n. 42

Demographic balance, 21, 101, 104,
130–1, 184, 186–8, 238, 251 n. 70,
258, 262–3, 267
Denktash, R., 188
Denmark, 19, 31, 37, 52
Diplomatic representation, 49, 80–
2, 98, 128, 189, 242, 244, 259, 310,
and problems for small states, 20,
36–7, 128, 190, 241–4, 261
Dominican Republic, 241–2, 251
n. 80
Draper, T., 217
Dumbarton Oaks proposals, 308

East African Community, 138, 142
East Germany, 18, 129, 221
Economic vulnerability of small
states, 16, 19, 24–5, 124, 135, 137,
171–2, 196, 201, 210–13, 273,
275–6, 298–300
Ecuador, 24, 241–2
Egal, I., 142
Egypt, 18, 127, 166, 168–70, 175,
178–9

with Malawi, 143; compromise of principles 144, 149; dilemma over support for nationalist movements 140, 142; disillusioned with British policy on Rhodesia, 134, 144–5; dominance of UDI issue, 142; expatriate influence on, 123; financial and technical assistance, sources of, 129, 152 n. 14; foreign trade policy, 134–9; importance of non-alignment for, 130, 133; influence of domestic politics on foreign policy, 130–1; limitations on policies *vis-à-vis* Rhodesia and South Africa, 139–40, 142–3, 147; links with China, 134, 144; mediation in Kenya–Somalia border dispute, 142, 153 n. 33; pan-Africanism, 130, 132–3; reconciliation with Nigeria, 146; relations with Tanzania, 130, 144, 146–7; role in regional groupings, 145–8, 152 n. 27